THE FATHERS
OF THE CHURCH

A NEW TRANSLATION

VOLUME 53

THE FATHERS OF THE CHURCH

A NEW TRANSLATION

EDITORIAL BOARD

Hermigild Dressler, O.F.M.
Quincy College
Editorial Director

Robert P. Russell, O.S.A.
Villanova University

Thomas P. Halton
The Catholic University of America

Robert Sider
Dickinson College

Sister M. Josephine Brennan, I.H.M.
Marywood College

Richard Talaska
Editorial Assistant

FORMER EDITORIAL DIRECTORS

Ludwig Schopp, Roy J. Deferrari, Bernard M. Peebles

SAINT JEROME
DOGMATIC AND POLEMICAL WORKS

Translated by
JOHN N. HRITZU, Ph.D.

University of Notre Dame
Notre Dame, Indiana

THE CATHOLIC UNIVERSITY OF AMERICA PRESS
Washington, D.C.

NIHIL OBSTAT:

REVEREND HARRY A. ECHLE
Censor Librorum

IMPRIMATUR:

✠PATRICK A. O'BOYLE
Archbishop of Washington

March 26, 1965

The *nihil obstat* and *imprimatur* are official declarations that a book or pamphlet is free of doctrinal or moral error. No implication is contained therein that those who have granted the *nihil obstat* and *imprimatur* agree with the contents, opinions, or statements expressed.

Library of Congress Catalog Card No.: 65-20802

Copyright © 1965 by
THE CATHOLIC UNIVERSITY OF AMERICA PRESS, INC.
All rights reserved
Second Printing 1981
ISBN 978-0-8132-2632-3 (pbk.)

CONTENTS

GENERAL INTRODUCTION vii
ON THE PERPETUAL VIRGINITY OF THE
  BLESSED MARY AGAINST HELVIDIUS . . .   3
THE APOLOGY AGAINST THE BOOKS
  OF RUFINUS 47
THE DIALOGUE AGAINST THE PELAGIANS . . 223
INDICES 381

GENERAL INTRODUCTION

T. JEROME'S REPUTATION rests primarily on his achievements as a translator and as a scriptural exegete. The important service that he rendered to the Church in his doctrinal works is often overlooked or minimized by those who look for originality and independence of thought. St. Jerome was not a theologian in the strict sense of the word. He was no original thinker, and he never abandoned himself to personal meditation of dogma as St. Augustine did.[1] Although he kept strictly to what he found in tradition, the importance of his doctrinal authority is not thereby lessened. He entered into controversy against Helvidius, Jovinian, Vigilantius, the Origenists, and the Pelagians, and refuted their heretical teachings on grace, on asceticism, on the perpetual virginity of Mary, and on the veneration of saints and relics so eloquently and so soundly that these heresies never again seriously threatened the Church. In order to get a better understanding of these dogmatic-polemical treatises, and to see them in their proper perspective, it will be necessary to recall important details in the life of St. Jerome, and to discuss briefly the principal points in the history of these heretical controversies.

St. Jerome was born at Stridon, on the border of Pannonia and Dalmatia, about the year 347. The first part of his long life, from the year 347 to 379, was chiefly a period of formation and preparation. After spending twelve years of his early life at his native Stridon, he was sent to Rome in the year 359 to finish his literary studies. For the next eight years, from

---

1 Cf. F. Cayré, *Manual of Patrology and History of Theology* 1 (translated by H. Howitt; Belgium 1935) 587.

359 to 367, St. Jerome studied very diligently grammar, the humanities, rhetoric, and dialectics. He also took a passionate interest in the Greek and Latin classics, in the philosophers and poets, and, especially, in the satirists and comic poets. These studies, it seems, tended not to soften, but to exaggerate the temperament of St. Jerome who was by nature irascible and impulsive, and sensitive to criticism and contradictions.[2] The reading in the satirists and the comic poets developed in him a taste for caricature and a penchant for making damaging allusions. Moreover, the trials before the Roman tribunes, which he attended eagerly, and wherein the advocates indulged in mutual personal invective, further developed in him the art and science of polemics which he was to employ so effectively and skillfully in the controversies which were to engage his attention seriously.

From Rome, St. Jerome went to Trier, where he studied theology and yearned to become a monk. After a short stay at Trier, he went to Aquileia where he stayed and studied for seven years. Desiring to lead a more perfect life, St. Jerome withdrew from Aquileia in the year 374 to the desert of Chalcis, to the east of Antioch, where he became involved for the first time in a controversy with heretics. During the Sabellian heresy which was then agitating the Church of Antioch, he was accused by the Arians of the heresy of Sabellianism because he referred to the Holy Trinity as three persons, instead of three hypostases; and he was beset with demands for a confession of faith.[3] St. Jerome wrote a letter to Pope Damasus for his views as to which of the two formulas were the better.[4] This letter contains a precious witness to the Roman primacy. In it, as elsewhere,[5] St. Jerome stressed the fact that the

---

[2] Cf. J. Tixeront, *A Handbook of Patrology* (St. Louis 1920) 255.
[3] The followers of Sabellius maintained that the Divine Persons were not realities, but merely manifestations of the one and the same Person; cf. Cayré, *op. cit.*, 295.
[4] St. Jerome, *Epistola* 15, *ad Damasum*.
[5] St. Jerome, *Epistola* 63.2, *ad Theophilum; Epistola* 130.16, *ad Demetriadem*.

Church must always be regarded as the supreme rule and decisive standard of Christian faith, and that the Church gives the true sense of the Scriptures, and is representative of tradition. It was owing to this firm conviction on the part of St. Jerome that the years of his later life were consumed in endless conflicts with the enemies of the Church. St. Jerome never spared heretics, but always saw to it that the enemies of the Church were also his own enemies.[6] This encounter with the Sabellians was St. Jerome's first quarrel with an enemy of the Church. He gave notice early in his life that he would be a staunch protector of the doctrinal authority of the Church, and that he stood ready to attack any and all heresies that raised their head against the Catholic faith.

From the desert of Chalcis, St. Jerome returned to Antioch in the year 379. In the same year, he wrote his first controversial treatise against the schismatic Luciferians entitled the *Altercatio Luciferiani et orthodoxi*.[7] Lucifer, the bishop of Calaris in Sardinia, was one of the bitterest opponents of Arianism. When the council of Alexandria in the year 362 advocated mildness in the treatment of repentant Arians, Lucifer, considering this a betrayal of faith, withdrew from communion with the members of the synod. He refused to acknowledge as bishops those who had come over from Arianism, although he accepted the laymen who had been baptized by Arian bishops. This view led to the schismatic faction of the Luciferians. After the death of Lucifer, his followers continued to advocate the exclusion of former Arians from all church offices. Although St. Jerome had been ordained a priest by Paulinus, who had been consecrated a bishop by Lucifer, nevertheless, he had no sympathy with these views of Lucifer and the Luciferians. These views form the subject of the dialogue written by St. Jerome against this schismatic faction

---

6 St. Jerome, *Dialogus contra Pelagianos, Prologus* 2.
7 St. Jerome, *Altercatio Luciferiani et orthodoxi* PL 23.155-182. Others prefer to date this writing from Rome in the year 382; cf. Tixeront, *op. cit.*, 257.

seven years after the death of Lucifer. St. Jerome sets forth the reasonable requirements of the Church as regards the Arians who desired to reenter the Church; and he makes the fictitious adversary, the disciple of Lucifer, recognize the enormity of the punishments which the latter demanded against these repentants.

Leaving Antioch in the year 379, St. Jerome went to Constantinople, where for two years he was instructed by St. Gregory of Nazianzen in the science of biblical exegesis. While at Constantinople, he also met St. Gregory of Nyssa and other famous Greek theologians of the East; and he threw himself with unbounded enthusiasm into the study of the earlier Greek Fathers, especially Origen and Eusebius. At Constantinople, St. Jerome made his first attempt at translation,[8] and also tried his hands at exegesis.[9]

In the year 382, ecclesiastical business drew St. Jerome to Rome for a second visit, where a council was being held against the Meletian schism at Antioch. St. Jerome took part by invitation and remained at Rome at the request of Pope Damasus to help him with his ecclesiastical correspondence, and to write his answers to questions referred to him by the synods of the Eastern and Western churches.[10] St. Jerome's second visit to Rome was relatively short, but it was of great importance for his future career. It was here that he was to enter upon a project which was to fill twenty years of his life, namely, the revision and translation of Sacred Scripture; and it was also here that he was to become involved in the first of a long series of serious controversies against heretics which were to fill and disturb the last thirty years of his life. At the invitation of Pope Damasus, St. Jerome began the revision of

---

8 St. Jerome translated into Greek and Latin the Gospel according to the Hebrews, which the Jews of Beroea had sent him; cf. Cayré, *op. cit.*, 571, n. 5.
9 St. Jerome's *Epistola* 15, *ad Damasum*, written in the year 381, is an exposition of the vision of Isaia. It is his first known commentary.
10 St. Jerome, *Epistola* 123.10, *ad Geruchiam*.

the old Itala version of the New Testament and restored it to its original purity.

Because of his reputation as a scholar and as an ascetic, St. Jerome found congenial soil at Rome for the promotion of asceticism and the celibate and religious life. However, his ascetical propaganda and his outspoken criticism of the conduct of lukewarm Christians, and even relaxed clergy, was soon to involve him in a heated controversy over the celibate and married states of life; and, ultimately, over the doctrine of the perpetual virginity of Mary. An obscure individual by the name of Helvidius had brought forth a polemical pamphlet, in which he attacked the perpetual virginity of Mary.[11] St. Jerome was reluctant to enter the quarrel actively at the beginning; but, at the urgent request of his friends, he replied to Helvidius in the year 383 with his short treatise entitled *Liber adversus Helvidium de perpetua virginitate B. Mariae*,[12] in which he proved, chiefly by the Scriptures, the excellence of virginity and the perpetual virginity of Mary. After the death of Pope Damasus, opposition broke out angrily against St. Jerome, and complaints were brought against him to Siricius, the successor to Damasus. Although he was conscious of his innocence, St. Jerome decided to leave Rome, the Babylon, as he himself called it; and he left in the year 385 to seek a peaceful retreat in Palestine.[13]

After an extended trip in which he visited the Holy Places as a scholar and as a pilgrim, St. Jerome returned to Palestine, and settled down permanently in Bethlehem, where the last thirty years of his life were extraordinarily fruitful in literary labors, in spite of the many controversies which were to disturb this studious retirement. It was during this period that

---

11 For a detailed account of the circumstances of this controversy, cf. below, Introduction, pp. 3-9.
12 St. Jerome, *Liber adversus Helvidium de perpetua virginitate B. Mariae* PL 23.183-206.
13 St. Jerome described his feelings on the occasion of his leaving Rome in a letter written to Asella at the moment of his embarkation at Ostia *(Epistola 45, ad Asellam).*

he completed the translation of the Sacred Scriptures which was begun at Rome; and, at the same time, he brought out many commentaries on the Old and the New Testament, and translated many of the homilies of Origen. In the midst of the many controversies which engaged the attention of St. Jerome, one wonders how he found the time to produce so many scholarly works. We find the explanation in the words of Sulpicius Severus: 'He is constantly immerged in study, wholly plunged in his books, gives himself no rest either night or day, he is incessantly occupied in reading or writing.'[14]

In the year 393, St. Jerome was once again called upon to champion the cause of continence and the virginity of Mary. Jovinian,[15] an erstwhile monk, had published earlier at Rome a treatise in which he maintained the propositions, that all sins are equal, that it is impossible for man to sin after baptism, that the state of virginity in itself is no more meritorious than the married state, that all who have kept the grace of baptism will receive the same reward in heaven, and that Mary lost her virginity by a true parturition in the birth of our Lord.[16] These errors which were denounced to Pope Siricius by Pammachius, an intimate friend of St. Jerome, were condemned in a synod held at Rome in the year 390. The errors were far more serious than they seemed at first. The whole Christian system of morality was at stake; for Jovinian was preaching salvation by faith alone, and the uselessness of good works for salvation. Pammachius sent the books of Jovinian to St. Jerome who answered them with the third of his controversial treatises entitled *Adversus Jovinianum*.[17]

The greatest controversy in which St. Jerome was engaged was against Origenism, and it was to take up a large place in what has been referred to as the 'tribulations of St. Jerome.' In the later period of this controversy, he became seriously

---
14 Sulpicius Severus, *Dialogus* 1.9. PL 20.190.
15 Cf. St. Augustine, *De haeresibus* 82. PL 42.41-42.
16 Cf. J. Tixeront, *History of Dogmas* 2 (translated from the fifth French edition by H. L. B.; St. Louis 1923) 244.
17 St. Jerome, *Adversus Jovinianum* PL 23.211-338.

engaged in a quarrel over Origen with his very close friend and fellow monk, Rufinus of Aquileia. In the first phase of the controversy, from the year 393 to 397, St. Jerome was more involved with Bishop John of Jerusalem than he was with Rufinus, who sided with the bishop in the whole affair. Epiphanius, bishop of Salamis, had written a letter in the year 394 to Bishop John, clearing himself of the charges made against him and, at the same time, justifying the charge of Origenism against Bishop John.[18] At the request of one of his monks, Eusebius of Cremona, St. Jerome had made a free Latin translation of the letter in Greek, which turned up sixteen months later in the hands of Rufinus and Bishop John. St. Jerome was accused of falsification. St. Jerome wrote a long letter to his friend, Pammachius, known as his *Libellus de optimo genere interpretandi*.[19] Bishop John's reply to St. Jerome was a letter addressed to Theophilus, Patriarch of Alexandria, in which he gave a résumé of the whole affair and justified himself against the charge of Origenism. Encouraged by Pammachius, St. Jerome wrote a complete refutation of the apologetic letter of Bishop John in a letter known as the *Contra Johannem Hierosolymitanum*.[20] Theophilus intervened and effected a reconciliation between Rufinus and Bishop John and St. Jerome in the early part of the year 397 in the Church of the Resurrection in Jerusalem.

The controversy was reopened shortly thereafter, when, in the Spring of the year 397, at the request of a certain Macarius, Rufinus translated the *Periarchon* of Origen. Imprudently, Rufinus added a preface to his translation, in which he mentioned St. Jerome as his model. These documents were sent to St. Jerome by his friends, Pammachius and Oceanus. Disturbed by the translation and the contents of the preface affixed by Rufinus, St. Jerome made a literal translation of

---

18 Cf. *Epistola* 51 among the collection of St. Jerome's letters.
19 St. Jerome, *Epistola* 57, *ad Pammachium*. This letter is also known as *Libellus de optimo genere interpretandi*.
20 St. Jerome, *Contra Johannem Hierosolymitanum* PL 23.355-396.

the *Periarchon*, and sent it to Pammachius and Oceanus, along with a long letter in which he accused indirectly Rufinus, without mentioning his name, of falsification and heresy.[21] When Rufinus saw this letter a few years later, he became embittered, and answered it in the year 399 with his *Apologia* in two books,[22] in which he defended himself against the charge of heresy, and made damaging accusations against St. Jerome. The quarrel now became bitter and personal, and vindictive, and was never to be healed again. Without waiting to receive the actual text, St. Jerome set himself to refute it, together with the *Apologia* which Rufinus had sent to Anastasius to clear himself of the charges of Origenism.[23] St. Jerome's work, the *Apologiae adversus libros Rufini libri duo*,[24] written at the end of the year 401, and addressed to Pammachius and Marcella, is a sad result of the whole Origenistic controversy, and betrays a high degree of personal irritation.[25] Acceding to the wishes of Bishop Chromatius to make peace, Rufinus replied to St. Jerome with a private letter. St. Jerome refused to be pacified. Whatever may have been the contents of Rufinus' letter,[26] it was in the frame of mind occasioned by the letter that St. Jerome replied with his *Liber tertius vel ultima responsio adversus scripta Rufini*.[27] Rufinus dropped out of the controversy altogether. St. Jerome, however, continued to attack Rufinus by injurious epithets on various occasions even after his death.[28]

The controversy with Vigilantius forms a second episode in the general Origenistic controversy. During the controversy

---

21 St. Jerome, *Epistola 84, ad Pammachium et Oceanum*.
22 Rufinus, *Apologiae in sanctum Hieronymum libri duo* PL 21.541-624.
23 Rufinus, *Apologia ad Anastasium* PL 21.623-628.
24 St. Jerome, *Apologiae adversus libros Rufini libri duo* PL 23.397-456.
25 O. Bardenhewer, *Patrology* (translated from the second edition by Thomas J. Shahan; St. Louis 1908) 465.
26 This private letter written by Rufinus to St. Jerome is lost.
27 St. Jerome, *Liber tertius vel ultima responsio adversus scripta Rufini* PL 23.457-492.
28 Cf. Ferd. Cavallera, *Saint Jerome, sa vie et son oeuvre* 2 (Louvain-Paris 1922) 131-135, where he has collected the various references to Rufinus in St. Jerome's works and correspondence after the quarrel.

between St. Jerome and Bishop John of Jerusalem, Vigilantius, a priest of Italy and the friend of Paulinus of Nola, a good friend of St. Jerome, had come to Bethlehem to visit St. Jerome, carrying a letter of introduction from Paulinus of Nola.[29] On his return to the West, Vigilantius reported to Paulinus that St. Jerome was a confirmed Origenist. On hearing this, St. Jerome sent a letter to Vigilantius in 396 in the most severe tone, repudiating the charge of Origenism.[30] Five years later, Riparius, a priest of Aquitaine, wrote to St. Jerome that Vigilantius was preaching in southern Gaul against the veneration of the relics of saintly martyrs and the keeping of night vigils. St. Jerome refuted some of the errors of Vigilantius in his letter to Riparius,[31] and promised to reply with a complete refutation of Vigilantius if Riparius would send him the treatise of Vigilantius. Upon receiving this work, St. Jerome composed in one night in the year 407 his philippic *Contra Vigilantium*.[32] St. Jerome's work is an apology for the ecclesiastical cult of saints and relics, full of irony and invectives, and is one of the most violent of all of his controversial writings. It scored unquestionably a success upon his opponent.

The last great controversy in which St. Jerome became seriously involved was the Pelagian.[33] The basic principle of Pelagianism consists in the affirmation of the moral strength and self-sufficiency of man's free will. The Pelagians maintained that man, relying entirely on his own power, can always will and do the good; that there is no such thing as original sin; that baptism is not essentially necessary for salvation; and that sanctifying grace is not the necessary foundation of supernatural activity, but only a remedy for actual

---

29 Cf. St. Jerome, *Epistola* 58.13, *ad Paulinum*, written in the year 395, in which he speaks highly of Vigilantius.
30 St. Jerome, *Epistola* 61, *ad Vigilantium*.
31 St. Jerome, *Epistola* 109, *ad Riparium*.
32 St. Jerome, *Contra Vigilantium* PL 23.339-352.
33 For a detailed description of this controversy, cf. below, Introduction, pp. 223-229.

sins.³⁴ Pelagianism was popularized at Rome at the beginning of the fifth century by Pelagius and his chief disciple, Celestius. They preached their views in all earnestness, and made many converts to their belief in Rome, Carthage, and Palestine. In the year 414, St. Jerome had taken up a special stand against the Pelagians in a letter sent to Ctesiphon,³⁵ who had written to St. Jerome asking him for his opinion on the nefarious teachings of Pelagius on apathy and impeccability. Although Pelagius was active in Palestine preaching his heresy, and his tenets had been investigated at a council held at Jerusalem in the year 415, St. Jerome appeared to have taken no active part in the proceedings. It was only after his friends had urged him to answer Pelagius that he composed, in dialogue form, the three books of his *Dialogus contra Pelagianos*,³⁶ in which he refuted the principal propositions of Pelagius. This work is noteworthy for its demonstration of Catholic doctrine by means of the Scriptures. Although St. Jerome treated the subjects more calmly in this work than in his earlier doctrinal treatises, nevertheless, he showed no lack of his old vigor.

As a result of this work, St. Jerome incurred the hatred of the Oriental monks. A crowd of Pelagian monks revenged themselves on him, by pillaging and burning the buildings of his monasteries and slaying some of the inmates. St. Jerome, himself, managed to escape with his life. He had, at least, the consolation of seeing the new heresy condemned in the year 418, two years before he died at Bethlehem on September 30, 420.

It was inevitable that St. Jerome, who was a miracle of learning, who was preeminent in the biblical sciences, who was the pillar of the true faith, who possessed an unshakable devotion to tradition, who prided himself in his reputation for orthodoxy, and who insisted so strongly on the Roman Church as the supreme rule and definite norm of revealed truth,

---
34 Cf. Cayré, *op. cit.*, 391-392.
35 St. Jerome, *Epistola* 133, *ad Ctesiphontem*.
36 St. Jerome, *Dialogus contra Pelagianos* PL 23.495-590.

should never spare heretics and should be continually involved in any and all heresies which raised their heads against the Church. He may be justly accused of being immoderate and uncontrolled in the use of invective. For St. Jerome, questions of dogma and matters of polemic were in completely different spheres. In a controversy, he considered all manner of attack and defense legitimate.[37] No one can ever deny his role as the most energetic and indefatigable champion of the Catholic faith and tradition against heretics.

Three of the seven doctrinal treatises which St. Jerome wrote against heretics have been translated and fully discussed in this volume. They are the following: first, the *Liber adversus Helvidium de perpetua virginitate B. Mariae*;[38] second, the *Apologiae adversus libros Rufini libri duo*,[39] and the *Liber tertius vel ultima responsio adversus scripta Rufini*,[40] written shortly after the preceding work; and third, the *Dialogus contra Pelagianos*.[41] None of the doctrinal works written by St. Jerome is a dogmatic treatise in the strict sense of the word. They are all polemical and occasional books, in which he answered theological questions in defense of Christian doctrine and morality.[42]

The translation of these three doctrinal treatises is based on the edition of D. Vallarsi as reprinted in Migne. The citations from Scripture conform for the most part to Challoner's revision of the Rheims-Douay translation for the Old Testament except Genesis. For the New Testament and Genesis, the new translations under the auspices of the Confraternity of Christian Doctrine have been used.

---

37 In his letter to Pammachius, which, in effect, is an apology for his treatise written against Jovinian, St. Jerome states that the Church Fathers were sometimes compelled to say in their controversies with heretics, not what they thought, but what was needy; cf. St. Jerome, *Epistola* 48.13, *ad Pammachium*.
38 For the translation, cf. below, pp. 11ff.
39 For the translation, cf. below, pp. 59ff.
40 For the translation, cf. below, pp. 162ff.
41 For the translation, cf. below, pp. 230ff.
42 Unfortunately, the copy of David S. Wiesen's book, entitled *St. Jerome*

as a Satirist, a Study of Christian Thought and Letters (Ithaca, New York, 1964), reached me too late to allow me to study at any great length his excellent and comprehensive treatise of St. Jerome as a satirist. The typescript of my translation of the dogmatic and polemical works of St. Jerome was already in the hands of the printer. A careful reading of the book will convince the reader that the author has succeeded admirably in his undertaking of investigating exhaustively 'the origin, nature, and purpose of St. Jerome's satire with special regard for its relationship to the classical satire of the pagans (pref. viii).' From his study, Wiesen reached what I judged to be his two most important conclusions, namely, (1) that St. Jerome was the final chapter in the brilliant volume of ancient satire, and (2) that he was the most significant and most important of Christian satirists (cf. p. 264). In successive chapters, entitled 'O Tempora, O Mores (2),' 'The Church and the Clergy (3),' 'Women and Marriage (4),' 'Heretics, Jews, and Pagans (5),' and 'Personal Enemies (6),' Wiesen has accumulated sufficient examples from all categories of St. Jerome's writings to justify his first conclusion that St. Jerome deserves to be listed among the great Roman satirists. As for the second conclusion, it seems to me that St. Jerome's great significance and importance as a Christian satirist lies not so much in his native ability and talents to use satire so brilliantly in all categories of his writings as in his ability to employ satire as an effective instrument in his dogmatic-polemical treatises in defending and defining so eloquently and so successfully the traditional views and doctrines of the Church. Wiesen seems to hint at such a conclusion when he discusses briefly the satirical elements in St. Jerome's polemical works (cf. pp. 148-152; 177-179; 225-235), and in his final chapter (7), entitled "Retrospect and Conclusion," remarks that St. Jerome had both a program—Christian asceticism—and an instrument for putting this program into effect (cf. p. 270). I realize full well that the specific undertaking of Wiesen was to investigate the nature of St. Jerome's satire, not to attempt to evaluate the relationship between St. Jerome's skillful employment of satire and the resultant successful defense of the orthodox views of the Church against heretics. His hint, however, at St. Jerome's attempt to use satire to put his program of Christian asceticism into effect, seems to be a hint in the right direction. St. Jerome's program was wider, more inclusive than Christian asceticism. It embraced the entire body of views and doctrines of the Church. Consequently, his use and concept of satire was not determined by his own private views, but by the views of the Church. It was his honest and sincere belief that, when he attacked any individual and his heretical views, he was actually defending the Church. He felt that every type of defense and attack was legitimate in a controversy with a heretic of the Church. He had studied and absorbed the spirit and language and technique of the great classical satirists so thoroughly that satire became practically natural with him in any polemical work. Every form and type of satire in the classical tradition was used by him. It is difficult to distinguish an attack made by St. Jerome against an individual heretic from an attack on the whole heretic faction to which the individual belonged. When Rufinus expressed his resentment to St. Jerome over an attack against Origenism, this is the reply that St. Jerome gave him: 'Besides, if you assume that anything that is said against Origen and his followers has been said against you, are the letters, then of Theophilus, and Epiphanius, and of the other bishops which I translated at their bidding, also directed against you and meant as an attack on you (*Contra Ruf.* 1.12)?' Caution must be exercised at all times in attempting to judge or appraise the effectiveness or the appropriateness of any, example of personal satire and invective employed by St. Jerome against individual heretics who are the main targets of his polemics in his doctrinal works for the simple reason that some of the important works and letters of these heretics which have given rise to the controversy are either entirely lost or are extant only as fragments. The polemical treatise of Helvidius on marriage and virginity, as well as the reply of Carterius to this work, are both lost. We have to try to reconstruct these works from St. Jerome's own statements. The letter of Rufinus, written to St. Jerome near the end of their controversy over Origen, which occasioned the writing of the third book against Rufinus, is also lost. Only fragments remain of the important books of Pelagius which St. Jerome discusses and attacks in his *Dialogus contra Pelagianos.* It is safe to say in conclusion, I believe, that St. Jerome would not have been able to plead the cause of the Church so successfully in his dogmatic-polemical works, especially the *Contra Helvidium,* the *Contra Rufinum,* and the *Dialogus contra Pelagianos,* without his thorough knowledge and use of the classical satirical devices. It seems to me that another volume must be written to show how ably St. Jerome, the theologian, was assisted by St. Jerome, the satirist.

ON THE PERPETUAL VIRGINITY OF THE BLESSED MARY AGAINST HELVIDIUS

INTRODUCTION

HEN ST. JEROME arrived in Rome for his second visit in the year 382, his reputation as a scholar and ascetic and as the defender of the faith had preceded him. He had already won recognition for his translation of the homilies of Origen into Latin, for his biography of the monk, Paul, and for the composition of his *Chronicle*. As early as the year 370, he had organized a society of men at Aquileia who were interested in the ascetic life; and he himself had retired shortly after that, in the year 374, to the desert of Chalcis, east of Antioch, where he spent the next five years as a monk. The dogmatic controversies of this period profoundly agitated the Christians of Antioch and echoes reached even the depths of the desert of Chalcis. St. Jerome became involved in one of these controversies with the Arians, who had accused him of Sabellianism. A few years later at Antioch, in the year 379, he wrote his first controversial treatise against the Luciferians.

It was, therefore, with enthusiasm that scholars and ascetics and traditionalists received St. Jerome in Rome. New honors were bestowed on him at Rome. Pope Damasus appointed him as his secretary and chief counselor, and commissioned him to bring out an official text of the early version of the New Testament. So popular was St. Jerome with the people and with the Pope that it was rumored that he would succeed to the chair of Peter after the death of Damasus. St. Jerome found favorable soil at Rome for the preaching of asceticism. The promoters of the ascetic life and many Roman ladies who had been meeting in the palace of the saintly Marcella on Mount Aventine, where they convened to discourse on holy matters and read the Scriptures and sing psalms, found in St.

Jerome their champion and accepted him as their guide and counselor. St. Jerome's acceptance of their invitation and open espousal of the cause of the celibate and virgin life was soon to involve him in a serious controversy. Angry opposition was organized against him; for, in the expository letters[1] which he wrote for these ascetic women, St. Jerome reprehended the conduct of lukewarm laymen, as well as clerics. Because of the great favor that St. Jerome enjoyed with the Pope, his opponents did not dare to denounce him openly. Their opportunity came when Pope Damasus died and was succeeded by Pope Siricius.

The question of asceticism, and virginity and marriage, had been seriously discussed and debated at Rome previous to St. Jerome's arrival. In the year 380, a certain Carterius[2] had published at Rome a book on virginity and asceticism, drawing his main argument from his contention of Mary's absolute and perpetual virginity.[3] A certain Helvidius,[4] the leader of

---

1 Cf. especially, St. Jerome, *Epistola* 22, *ad Eustochium,* on the preservation of virginity.

2 Carterius was an obscure monk who lived at Rome at the time. Cf. Ferd. Cavallera, *Saint Jerome, sa vie et son oeuvre* 1 (Louvain and Paris 1922) 95. The work of Carterius is no longer extant.

3 The perpetual virginity of Mary is a solemnly defined dogma of the Catholic Church, expressed in the striking formula that Mary was a virgin *'ante partum, in partu, et post partum.'* For an excellent and thorough treatment of the subject, cf. Philip J. Donnelly, 'The Perpetual Virginity of the Mother of God,' in *Mariology* 2, ed. Juniper B. Carol (Milwaukee 1957). St. Matthew is an unassailable witness to the virginity of Mary *ante partum,* and his use of the prophecy of Isaia (7.14): 'Behold a virgin shall conceive, and bear a son, and his name shall be called Emmanuel,' implies, at least, the virgin birth. St. Luke not only teaches explicitly the virginal conception, but also furnishes elements on which to base the conclusions that Mary gave birth to Christ without the loss of her virginal integrity, and that she preserved her virginity throughout her life. The early Christian Fathers, St. Irenaeus, St. Justin, St. Ignatius, and St. Hippolytus, following the traditional apostolic teaching, affirmed explicitly Mary's absolute and perpetual virginity. For a more detailed discussion of the subject, cf. Donnelly, *op. cit.,* Section I, 'The Witness of Scriptures to the Virginity of Mary,' 229-264; and Section II, 'The Patristic Tradition concerning Mary's Virginity,' 264-296. During the fourth century, the question of Mary's perpetual virginity attracted special attention, and several sects arose which, though accepting Mary's virginity *ante partum,* nevertheless, denied her virginity *in partu* and *post partum.* We learn from

the adversaries of virginity and the monastic way of life, replied to Carterius with a book of his own, in which he sought to prove against Carterius that virginity was not superior to marriage, but rather perfectly equal in perfection and glory, and that Mary did not remain perpetually a virgin; for after the birth of Christ, she had relations with Joseph, and from this union there were born the children who are referred to in the Gospel as the brothers of the Lord. This book shocked Rome with its perverse views, and had such a disturbing effect even on the leading promoters of asceticism that it converted many of them to the erroneous views of Helvidius. The followers of St. Jerome and, in particular, the coterie of distinguished ladies who had found in St. Jerome a patron and a champion of their cause were deeply scandalized by these views and they earnestly begged St. Jerome to reply to Helvidius and refute his impious views. St. Jerome found many good reasons for holding his peace.[5] It was only after he fully realized the great scandal that had arisen among the brothers that he finally decided to answer Helvidius, and 'lay the axe at the root of the barren tree and deliver to the flames the tree

---

St. Epiphanius' *Panarion* (ch. 78), or, as it is usually entitled, *Haereses*, composed about 374-377, in which he surveyed all heresies with a refutation of each, that the Helvidians in the West, in Rome, and the Antidicomarianites in the East, in Africa, were preaching the erroneous views that Mary lost her virginity *post partum*, because she had relations with Joseph after the birth of Jesus, and bore children to him who were the brothers of the Lord referred to in the Gospels. Shortly after he became bishop of Milan, St. Ambrose published in the year 377 the fruits of his sermons and meditations on Mary in a small work entitled *De virginibus ad Marcellinam*, dedicated to his sister, in which he championed the cause of virginity, and proclaimed explicitly the absolute and perpetual virginity of Mary.

4 St. Jerome is our only contemporary source of information on Helvidius. He refers to him on many occasions in his *Liber adversus Helvidium de perpetua virginitate B. Mariae*, implying, among other things, that he was completely devoid of all theological and literary formation. According to Gennadius, a priest of Marseilles, who composed his *De viris illustribus* between 467-480, Helvidius was a disciple of the Arian bishop, Auxentius, and an imitator of the pagan senator and defender of idolatry, Symmachus (ch. 32). The work of Helvidius is no longer extant.

5 Cf. below, ch. 1.

with its unfruitful leaves, so that he who had never learned to speak might at length learn to hold his tongue.'[6] St. Jerome's reply to Helvidius was a short treatise of twenty-four chapters,[7] but it was sufficiently long to permit him to 'tear his adversary to pieces.'[8] Helvidius had directed his principal attack against the virginity of Mary *post partum,* citing the testimonies of Matthew[9] and Luke,[10] and the authority of Tertullian and Victorinus of Pettau, to prove his view that, after the birth of Jesus, Mary had relations with Joseph, and that she gave birth to the children who were the brothers and sisters of the Lord.[11] St. Jerome rejected and dismissed the authority of Tertullian with the curt remark that he was not a man of the Church.[12] Tertullian, to be sure, had never denied the virginal conception and birth of Christ; but once launched into his polemics against the Gnostics, he was unsparing in advocating the birth of Christ as entirely normal, and in describing Mary as the mother of several children after Christ.[13] As regards the authority of Victorinus of Pettau, St. Jerome contended that Helvidius had badly interpreted the bishop; and that Victorinus understood by the expression, 'brothers of the Lord,' not blood brothers, but relatives.[14]

St. Jerome vigorously maintained the traditional teaching on the perpetual virginity of Our Lady. It was in his unshakable devotion to tradition that St. Jerome found his strength when attacking heresy, and he was at his best in this domain.[15] Using the very same scriptural testimonies, St.

---

6 Cf. below, ch. 1.
7 In the text of Migne, there are twenty-two chapters, but the numbering is faulty. Chapters seven and eight are repeated. Cf. below, ch. 7a, n. 40; ch. 8a, n. 43.
8 Donnelly, *op. cit.,* 283.
9 Cf. Matt. 1.18-25.
10 Cf. Luke 2.7.
11 Cf. below, ch. 13, n. 66.
12 Cf. below, ch. 17.
13 Cf. below, ch. 17, n. 102.
14 Cf. below, ch. 17, n. 103.
15 Cf. F. Cayré, *Manual of Patrology and History of Theology* 1 (translated by H. Howitt; Belgium 1935) 588.

Jerome soundly and eloquently repelled the attack of Helvidius against Mary's virginity *post partum*. Helvidius argued that the expressions 'before they came together'[16] and 'he did not know her till she brought forth her child'[17] refer to sexual relations. Making much of the meaning of the conjunctions 'until' and 'before,' he contended that, in scriptural usage, these conjunctions prejudicated what would actually take place; and, therefore, when Matthew said that Mary was found to be with child 'before they came together,' and that Joseph 'did not know her until she brought forth her child,' he implied that they did come together and that Joseph did know Mary after the birth of her child.

St. Jerome did not deny that the phrase, 'to come together,' could be interpreted in the sense of copulation, but he showed from many scriptural references that the conjunction 'before' does not imply that Mary and Joseph actually came together. 'It does not follow,' he says in his *Commentary on Matthew*, 'that they came together afterwards, but Scripture shows what did not take place.'[18] To prove his point, St. Jerome replied with an example in kind,[19] and completely confounded his adversary: 'As if the sentence could not stand, if one were to say: "Before I dined, I sailed to Africa," unless he should dine at the harbor eventually. Or if we were to say this: "Before the Apostle Paul went to Spain, he was cast into prison," or, to be sure, this: "Before Helvidius did penance for his sins, he was overtaken by death," Paul would have to go at once to Spain after his imprisonment, or Helvidius would have to do penance for his sins immediately after his death; when Scripture says: "And who shall confess to thee in Hell?"'[20]

The favorite argument of the adversaries of the perpetual virginity of Mary is derived from the scriptural references to

---
16 Matt. 1.18.
17 Matt. 1.25.
18 St. Jerome, *Commentarius in evangelium Matthaei* PL 26.25.
19 Cf. below, ch. 14.
20 Ps. 6.6.

the brothers of the Lord. Helvidius used the testimonies of all four Evangelists,[21] the Acts of the Apostles,[22] and St. Paul[23] to prove that the brothers of the Lord were brothers in the literal sense of the word, that is, sons of the same father and mother. In scriptural usage, the Hebrew word for brother had a very extensive meaning. It was used to designate, not only real brothers, but also half-brothers and cousins, and varying and even remote degrees of relationship.[24] In two eloquently composed chapters (14-15), St. Jerome proved by citing scriptural references that the word brother meant, not only brother by birth, but also by kinship, by race, and by affection. It was in the sense of kinship that the scriptural references were to be understood. St. Jerome's answer to this question of the brothers of the Lord has become traditional in the bosom of the Church.[25]

Helvidius made use of the text from Luke: 'and she brought forth her firstborn son,'[26] to prove that Mary had other children *post partum*. He contended that a firstborn child was one who had subsequent brothers, just as an only child was one that was the only child born of his parents. St. Jerome replied that there was no justification in concluding from the expression 'firstborn' that Mary had other children. 'It is the custom of Scripture,' he remarks in his *Commentary on Matthew*, 'to designate with the title of "firstborn," not only one who has subsequent brothers, but one who is born first.'[27] 'Every only child is a firstborn child,' says St. Jerome, 'but not every firstborn is an only child.'[28] After citing several examples from Scripture, St. Jerome concluded his remarks on this

---

[21] Cf. Matt. 13.55; Mark 3.12; 6.3; Luke 8.20; John 2.12; 7.3-5.
[22] Cf. Acts 1.14.
[23] Cf. Gal. 1.19; 1 Cor. 9.5.
[24] Cf. Donnelly, *op. cit.*, 246.
[25] Cf. P. de Labriolle, *History and Literature of Christianity from Tertullian to Boethius* (translated from the French by Herbert Wilson; London 1924) 351.
[26] Luke 2.7.
[27] St. Jerome, *Commentarius in evangelium Matthaei* PL 26.26.
[28] Cf. below, ch. 10.

subject by stating that the firstborn, according to the words of God, was: 'All that openeth the womb.'[29]

Helvidius defended in his book the thesis that marriage was not inferior to virginity, and that it was equally glorious, since it was a state that was natural and was willed by God. St. Jerome, who had always defended and championed the cause of virginity with vigor and eloquence, devoted two chapters (20-21) to a comparison of virginity and marriage; and, although he did not mean to disparage marriage, declaring that virginity itself was the flower of marriage (ch. 19), nevertheless, he was convinced of the superiority of virginity over marriage, citing in proof of his contention the many references of praise regarding virginity found in the New Testament. As a final argument in favor of virginity, he contrasted the moral and religious advantages of virginity with the difficulties and cares entailed by marriage (chs. 20-21).

This brief, but piquant, treatise against Helvidius, written in the latter part of the year 383, is a classic in Catholic theology, and it is the first treatise by a Latin specially devoted to Mariology. St. Jerome not only gained back whatever ground had been lost to Helvidius, but he also succeeded so well in implanting the doctrine of Mary's virginity *in partu* and *post partum* that it was never again seriously doubted in Roman circles.[30]

---

29 Exod. 34.19.
30 For an appraisal of the merit of St. Jerome's *Liber adversus Helvidium de perpetua virginitate B. Mariae,* cf. de Labriolle, *op. cit.,* 350-351; Cavallera, *op. cit.,* 99-100; Donnelly, *op. cit.,* 282-283.

SELECT BIBLIOGRAPHY

Text and Translation:

Fremantle, W. H. 'The Perpetual Virginity of Blessed Mary,' in *A Select Library of Nicene and Post-Nicene Fathers of the Christian Church*, second series, vol. 6 (New York 1912) 334-346.

Migne, J. P. *Patrologiae Latinae cursus completus* (Paris 1846) 23.183-206.

Secondary Writings:

Cavallera, Ferd. *Saint Jerome, sa vie et son oeuvre* 1 (Louvain-Paris 1922).

Cayré, F. *Manual of Patrology and History of Theology* 1 (translated by H. Howitt; Belgium 1935).

Donnelly, Philip J., S.J. 'The Perpetual Virginity of the Mother of God,' in *Mariology* 2, ed. Juniper B. Carol, O.F.M. (Milwaukee 1957) 228-296.

Labriolle, Pierre de. *History and Literature of Christianity from Tertullian to Boethius* (translated from the French by Herbert Wilson; London 1924).

ON THE PERPETUAL VIRGINITY OF THE BLESSED MARY AGAINST HELVIDIUS

I WAS ASKED RECENTLY by my brothers to reply to the treatise written by a certain Helvidius,[1] but I delayed doing so; not because I would have encountered any difficulty in defending the truth and refuting a rough boor, who had scarcely taken the first steps in letters, but because I did not want to give him the honor of a refutation by answering him. Added to this was the fact that a turbulent individual, who thinks of himself as the only example in the whole world of a layman and a cleric (who, in the words of a certain individual,[2] mistakes garrulity for eloquence and believes that it is the duty of a man of good conscience to speak ill of all men), would appropriate the materials of this disputation, and would proceed to utter more serious blasphemies, and would proclaim to the whole world views as if coming from a highly authoritative source; and unable to lacerate me with the truth, he would lash me with reproaches. All of these reasons seemed very just to me for holding my peace. But since these motives have at length yielded to a more just reason for intervening because my brothers have become seriously disturbed and scandalized by his ravings, the axe of the Gospel must now be laid at the roots of the barren tree[3] and the tree must be delivered to the flames with its unfruitful leaves, so that he who has never learned to speak might learn at length to hold his tongue.

---

1 For an account of Helvidius, cf. above, Introduction, pp. 3-9.
2 St. Jerome is referring here to Tertullian. This reference is almost a verbatim quotation of Tertullian's description of the Gnostic Hermogenes; cf. Tertullian, *Adversus Hermogenem* 1.
3 Cf. Matt. 3.10.

(2) Therefore, we must invoke the Holy Spirit to defend through our lips and his understanding the virginity of the Blessed Mary. We must call upon the Lord Jesus to preserve free of all suspicion of copulation the inn of that sacred womb wherein He dwelled for ten months. We must also invoke God the Father, Himself, to prove that the mother of His Son, who was a mother before she was wed, remained a virgin after she brought forth her son. We do not have to rely on the outbursts of rhetorical eloquence; we do not need to employ the sophistic schemes of the dialecticians; we have no need for the subtleties of Aristotle. We need only to quote the actual words of the Scriptures; let him be refuted by the very testimonies that he used against us, so that he might come to realize that he could have read what was written down, but he could not understand what has been confirmed by piety.

(3) *Helvidius.* This was his first quotation: 'Matthew says: "The birth of Christ was as follows: When Mary, his mother, had been betrothed to Joseph, before they came together, she was found to be with child by the Holy Spirit. But Joseph, her husband, being a just man, and not wishing to expose her to reproach, was minded to put her away. But while he thought on these things, behold, an angel of God appeared to him in a dream saying: 'Do not be afraid, Joseph, son of David, to take to thee Mary thy wife, for that which is begotten in her is of the Holy Spirit.' " '4 'Notice,' he says, 'that the word used is "betrothed" and not "entrusted," as you say,5 and she was betrothed, to be sure, for no other reason except to be given in marriage eventually. For the Evangelist would not have said, "Before they came together," of people who did not intend to come together. For no one says, "Before he dined," of a person who does not intend to dine. Furthermore, she was called by the angel a wife and one who was

---

4 Matt. 1.18-20.
5 This is a reference to Carterius who had precipitated the controversy in an essay in which he defended the perpetual virginity of Mary. St. Jerome is quoting Helvidius' reply to this work; cf. above, Introduction pp. 4ff.

united in marriage. Let us now listen to what Scripture says: "Joseph, arising from sleep," he says, "did as the angel of the Lord had commanded him, and he took his wife unto him. And he did not know her till she brought forth her son." [6]

(4) *Jerome. What the preposition ante signifies. Why Mary conceived as a betrothed virgin.*

Let us examine his statements individually and, tracing the development of his impiety from its source, step by step, let us point out the contradictions in his statements. He admits that she was betrothed, and he would have her, who, he admitted, was betrothed, be forthwith a wife. Furthermore, he says that she whom he calls a wife was betrothed for no other reason except to be eventually married; and lest we make little account of his statement he says: 'Thus, she was betrothed, and not entrusted, that is to say, she was not yet a wife, she was not yet united by bonds of matrimony.' However, as regards this statement of his: 'For the Evangelist would not have said of them: "Before they came together," if they did not intend to come together because no one says of a person: "Before he dined, if he does not intend to dine," ' I do not know whether to take it seriously or lightly. Shall I convince him of impudence or accuse him of ignorance? Just as if the sentence could not hold, if someone were to say: 'Before I dined, I sailed to Africa,' unless he should dine at the harbor eventually. Or, if we were to say: 'Before Paul the Apostle went to Spain, he was cast into prison,' or, to be sure, this: 'Before Helvidius did penance for his sins, he was overtaken by death,' Paul would have to go at once to Spain after his imprisonment, or Helvidius would have to do penance for his sins immediately after his death; when Scripture says: 'And who shall confess to thee in Hell?'[7] Rather, it should be understood that the preposition 'before,' although it often indicates a result, nevertheless, sometimes simply reveals an action that was previously planned. Hence, the action that was planned does

---
6 Matt. 1.24, 25.
7 Ps. 6.6.

not necessarily take place, when something else intervenes to prevent the action that was planned from taking place. Therefore, when the Evangelist says: 'Before they came together,' he is indicating that the time of the marriage was very close at hand, and conditions were such that she who previously had been betrothed would begin to be a wife. As if he had said: Before they joined in kisses and embraces, before they consummated the marriage, she was found to be with child. However, she was found in this condition by none other than Joseph, who now noticed the teeming womb of his betrothed with anxious glances and with the privilege of one who was at this time practically a husband. But it does not follow, as we have shown in the examples cited above, that he came together with Mary after she brought forth her son, with whom he suppressed the desire of sexual relations when she conceived in her womb. Moreover, the words that are spoken to Joseph in a dream: 'Do not be afraid to take Mary to thee as thy wife,'[8] and again: 'Joseph, arising from sleep, did as the angel had commanded him, and took his wife unto him,'[9] should not disturb anybody, as if she ceased to be betrothed because she was called a wife, when we realize that it is the custom of Sacred Scripture to give the title of wife to those who are betrothed. Just as it is confirmed by the following testimonies from Deuteronomy: 'If anyone,' he says, 'find a damsel that is betrothed in a field and taking hold of her lie with her, he shall die; for he hath humbled his neighbor's wife.'[10] And in another place: 'If a man has espoused a damsel, and someone find her in the city and lie with her, thou shalt bring them both out to the gate of that city and they shall be stoned and they shall die; the damsel because she cried not out, being in the city; the man because he hath humbled his neighbor's wife; and thou shalt take away the evil from the

---

8 Matt. 1.20.
9 Matt. 1.24.
10 Cf. Deut. 22.24, 25.

midst of thee.'¹¹ And also in another place: 'What man is there that hath espoused a wife and not taken her? Let him go and return to his house, lest he die in war and another man take her.'¹² But if anybody has feelings of scruples because a virgin conceived when she was betrothed rather than without a betrothed, or (as Scripture calls him) a husband, let him know it was done for three reasons: first, that the origin of Mary¹³ might also be revealed through the lineage of Joseph, to whom she was related; second, that she might not be stoned as an adulteress according to the law of Moses; third, that, in her flight to Egypt, she might have the solacing comfort of a guardian rather than of a husband. For at that time who would have believed the Virgin that she had conceived of the Holy Spirit; that the angel Gabriel had visited her; that he had announced to her the will of God? On the contrary, would they not have rather voted unanimously to condemn her as an adulteress, as they did in the case of Susanna, when today, with the whole world now believing, the Jews contend that in the passage where Isaia says: 'Behold a virgin shall conceive and bear a son,'¹⁴ the word written in the Hebrew was *juvencula*, not *virgo*, that is, *AALMA*, not *BETHULA?* We shall discuss this matter at greater length with them elsewhere.¹⁵ Finally, everybody, with the exception

---

11 Deut. 22.23, 24.
12 Deut. 20.7.
13 St. Jerome discusses in detail in his *Commentarius in evangelium Matthaei* (PL 26.24) this whole question of Mary's conceiving as a betrothed virgin. According to the law of Moses (Num. 36.6-8), all men were obliged to marry wives of their own tribe and kindred, and all women, husbands of the same tribe. Mary was betrothed to Joseph to show that she was of the same tribe as Joseph in order to satisfy this law of Moses. It was not the custom of Scripture to give the genealogy of women.
14 Isa. 7.14.
15 St. Jerome discusses fully the meaning of *aalma* and *bethula* in his *Liber Hebraicarum quaestionum* (PL 23.973-974), and in his *Commentarius in Isaiam prophetam* (PL 24.107-110). *Bethula* and *aalma* both mean virgin in Hebrew; but *aalma*, which is an ambiguous term in Hebrew, means not only *adulescentia* or *virgo*, but also *abscondita virgo*, that is, a virgin who is kept from the sight of men and is guarded carefully by her parents. It never means in Hebrew a married

of Joseph, Elizabeth, and Mary herself, and a few others at most, if we can assume that others were informed of this fact by them, considered Jesus to be the son of Joseph; to such a degree that even the evangelists, quoting the view of the people (and this is the true function of history), called him the father of the Savior, as in the following passage: 'He'— (Simeon, to be sure)—'came by inspiration of the Spirit to the temple. And when his parents brought in the child Jesus, to do for him according to the custom of Law.'[16] And in another place: 'And his father and mother were marvelling at the things spoken concerning him.'[17] And again: 'His parents were wont to go every year to Jerusalem at the Feast of the Passover.'[18] And again: 'After they had fulfilled the days, when they were returning, the boy Jesus remained in Jerusalem, and his parents did not know it.'[19] Listen to what even Mary herself, who had replied to Gabriel, saying: 'How can this be, for I know not man?'[20] says of Joseph: 'Son, why hast thou done so to us? Behold, in sorrow thy father and I have been seeking thee.'[21] This is not said in the manner of the Jews, as many maintain; this is not an expression of mockery. The Evangelists call Joseph father; Mary acknowledges him as father, not because Joseph was truly the father of the Savior (as I have indicated above), but rather because he was regarded as His father by all, in order to protect the reputation of Mary. Before he was admonished by the angel in these words: 'Do not be afraid, Joseph, the son of David, to take to thee Mary thy wife, for that which is begotten in her is of the Holy

---

woman. St. Jerome concludes: 'Let the Jews, therefore, show me that *aalma* is used anywhere in Scriptures, where it means merely *adulescentia* and not *virgo*, and we will concede that in Isaia *aalma* means not a *virgo adulescentia*, but an *adulescentia* already married.' (Cf. St. Jerome, *Liber Hebraicarum quaestionum* PL 23.974.) According to St. Jerome, it would be nothing wondrous or miraculous for a young girl to conceive and bring forth a child.

16 Luke 2.27.
17 Luke 2.33.
18 Luke 2.41.
19 Luke 2.43.
20 Luke 1.34.
21 Luke 2.48.

Spirit,'[22] he minded to put her away privately. He was so confident that the child that had been conceived was not his own. But we have already given adequate consideration to the question as to why Joseph was called the father of the Lord, and why Mary was called a wife, inasmuch as we have intended this to serve more as an introduction than as a reply to the question. Included briefly in this discussion is also the question as to why some individuals are referred to as the brothers of the Lord.

(5) *Helvidius*. However, since there is a special section reserved for a discussion of the latter question, and my discourse is hurrying on to the consideration of other matters, we must now take up for consideration the meaning of the following words of Scripture: 'So Joseph, arising from sleep, did as the angel of the Lord had commanded him, and took unto him his wife. And he did not know her till she brought forth her son. And he called his name Jesus.'[23] In the first place, my opponent labors tediously, but in vain, to make the verb 'to know' refer to sexual relations rather than to factual knowledge; as if anyone ever denied this fact, and any intelligent person could ever have imagined those silly assertions that he had refuted. In the second place, he seeks to prove that the adverb 'until' or 'up to' designates a definite time, and that when that time has been realized an event, which up until that prescribed time did not take place, takes place, as in the present passage: 'And he did not know her, until she brought forth her son.' It is apparent, he says, that she was known after she brought forth her child, and that the birth of her child merely delayed sexual relations. And to prove this point, he collects many examples from Scripture, brandishing his sword in the dark like the *andabatae*[24] and inflicting wounds

---
22 Matt. 1.20.
23 Matt. 1.24, 25.
24 *Andabatae* were gladiators who wore helmets without any aperture for the eyes, so that they were obliged to fight blindfolded, and this excited the mirth of the spectators; cf. Cicero, *Epistulae ad familiares* 7.10.2.

on the members of his own body by rattling his tongue.

(6) *Jerome.* In answer to all this, we say briefly that in Sacred Scripture the phrases 'to know' and 'until' have a double meaning. And, to be sure, as regards the expression 'to know,' he was the very person who asserted that it must denote sexual relations. No one doubts that it often refers to factual knowledge, as in the following passage: 'the boy Jesus remained in Jerusalem, and his parents did not know it.'[25] Now it must be pointed out that just as he accepted the custom of Scripture in the one instance, so also he should yield to the authority of that same Scripture as far as the conjunction 'until' is concerned, which is often used to indicate a definite time (as he himself asserted), and often an indefinite time, as in the following passage where God addresses some individuals in the Prophets: 'I am, I am, and I am till you grow old.'[26] Will God cease to be after they grow old? And in the Gospel, the Savior says to His apostles: 'Behold, I am with you all days, even unto the consummation of the world.'[27] Will the Lord, therefore, leave His disciples after the consummation of the world and, when they shall judge the twelve tribes of Israel on twelve thrones, will they be deprived of the company of the Lord? The Apostle Paul also writes, saying: 'Christ as first-fruits, then they who are Christ's, who have believed, at his coming. Then comes the end, when he delivers the kingdom to God the Father, when he does away with sovereignty, authority and power. For he must reign, until "he has put all of his enemies under his feet." . . . for "he has put all things under his feet." '[28] Granted, that this was said of a man; we do not deny that it was said of Him who bore the cross, who is commanded afterwards to sit on the right. What does he mean when he says: 'For he must reign, until "he has put all his enemies under his feet" '? Will the Lord rule only until

---

25 Luke 2.43.
26 Cf. Isa. 46.4.
27 Matt. 28.20.
28 1 Cor. 15.23-26.

His enemies begin to be under His feet? And will He cease to rule after they are under His feet? When, to be sure, He shall begin to rule more precisely then and only then, when His enemies begin to be under His feet? David, also, says in his fourth gradual Canticle: 'Just as the eyes of the handmaid are upon the hands of her mistress, so are our eyes unto the Lord, our God, till He have pity on us.'[29] Will the prophet, therefore, have his eyes upon the Lord only until he obtain mercy, and after he has obtained it, will he turn his eyes to earth? He says in another place: 'My eyes have fainted after thy salvation and for the word of thy justice.'[30] I could collect innumerable examples to exemplify this point, and bury completely under an avalanche of testimonies the impudence of this calumniator; but I shall add just a few more, and let the reader find similar examples for himself.

(7) The word of God says in Genesis: 'And they gave Jacob the strange gods that they had in their possession and the earrings which were in their ears. And Jacob buried them under the turpentine tree in the city of Sichem and he lost them to this day.'[31] And, also, in the concluding chapter of Deuteronomy: 'And Moses, the servant of God, died in the land of Moab by the commandment of the Lord and they buried him in Geth over against the home of Phegor, and no man hath known of his sepulchre until this present day.'[32] The phrase 'this day' must certainly be regarded as referring to the time when the narrative itself was composed; I have no objections whether you want to call Moses the author of the Pentateuch, or Esdras the reviser of the same work. Now the question is whether or not the phrase, 'until this present day,' refers to the period when the books were published or composed. Let him, therefore, prove that either the strange idols that had been hidden under the turpentine tree have been

---
29 Ps. 122.2.
30 Ps. 118.123.
31 Gen. 35.4.
32 Deut. 34.5, 6 (Septuagint).

found, or the sepulchre of Moses has been discovered, because he is unyielding in his assertion that after the time of 'until' and 'up to' has been realized, an event, which did not take place, as long as the time of 'until' and 'up to' was being realized, takes place. Nay rather, let him observe carefully the idiom of Sacred Scripture, and come to realize, as we do, this fact, the ignorance of which was the source of his embarrassment, that those facts are recorded, about which there could be some contention, if they were not written down, while the rest is left to our own understanding. For, if the sepulchre of Moses could not be found when times were still recent, and people who had seen him in the flesh were still alive, the possibility of its discovery, after the lapse of so many centuries, was much less remote. Accordingly, it is clear, also, in the case of Joseph that the Evangelist indicated a fact over which there could have arisen scandal, namely, that she was not known by her husband until her delivery, so that we might much more clearly realize that she was not known after her delivery by her husband, who kept himself from her at the very time when he still could have had doubts about the dream.

(8) To conclude, I ask you this question: Why did Joseph keep himself from her until the day of her delivery? He will reply, to be sure, because he heard the angel say: 'For that which is begotten in her is of the Holy Spirit.'[33] And to this we add the words, and he certainly had heard them: 'Do not be afraid Joseph, son of David, to take Mary to thee as thy wife.'[34] He had been admonished not to leave his wife; he had been admonished not to consider her an adulteress. Did he also sever relations with his wife, when, to be sure, he had been very strongly admonished not to sever relations? And did a just man, he says, dare to think of sexual relations with his wife after hearing that the Son of God was present in her womb? Fine! Did he, therefore, who had put so much trust in

---
33 Matt. 1.20.
34 *Ibid.*

a dream that he did not dare touch his wife, dare to do so after he had learned from the lips of the shepherds that the angel of the Lord had come from heaven and had said to them: 'Do not be afraid, for behold, I bring you good news of great joy which shall be to all people; for today in the house of David a Savior has been born to you, who is Christ the Lord';[35] and that they had sung with him the praises of the heavenly host: 'Glory to God in the highest, and on earth peace among men of good will';[36] who had seen Simeon, a just man, embrace the infant and proclaim: 'Now thou dost dismiss thy servant, O Lord, according to thy word, in peace; because my eyes have seen thy salvation';[37] who had seen Anna, the prophetess, the wise men, the star, Herod, and the angels; did he, I say, who had seen such wonders, dare to touch the temple of God, the sanctuary of the Holy Spirit, the mother of his Lord? And, to be sure: 'Mary kept in mind all these things, pondering them in her heart.'[38] And lest you be impudent enough to deny that Joseph had any knowledge of these things, Luke says: 'And his father and mother marvelled at the things told them concerning him.'[39] You might argue in your strange and impudent manner that these things have been falsified in the Greek codices, things which have not only been left intact in the volumes of practically all commentators of Greece, but even taken over by some of the Latins exactly as they exist in the Greek. Nor is it necessary to discuss at this time the question of the variety of the copies, since every document of both the Old and the New Testament has been translated into Latin from that source. It must be granted that the waters of a fountain flow much more purely than those of a stream.

(7a) [40] *Helvidius.* 'In my opinion,' you say, 'these arguments

---
35 Luke 2.10, 11.
36 Luke 2.13, 14.
37 Luke 2.29-31.
38 Luke 2.19, 51.
39 Luke 2.33.
40 The numbering of the chapters at this point is faulty. This should be chapter 9. I have allowed it to stand as chapter 7a.

are nugatory and superfluous, and the disputation is more fanciful than real. Could Scripture not have said: "And he took unto him his wife and he did not dare to touch her anymore,"[41] as it said of Thamar and Juda? Was Matthew at a loss for words with which he could express what he meant to be understood? "He did not know her," he says, "until she brought forth her son."[42] Therefore, after she brought forth her son, he did know her with whom he had delayed having sexual relations till her delivery.'

(8a) [43] *Jerome.* If you are so eager to argue this point, without further ado, you shall be convinced in your own mind of your error. Let no time intervene between delivery and sexual relations. Do not say: 'A woman who has conceived and borne a son, shall be unclean seven days, according to the days of her separation and purification. And on the eighth day, the infant shall be circumcised. But she shall remain three and thirty days in the blood of her purification. She shall touch no holy thing';[44] and the rest. Let Joseph assail her forthwith, and let him hear immediately the words spoken by Jeremia: 'They are become to me as amorous horses towards mares; everyone neighed after his neighbor's wife.'[45] Otherwise, how will the following sentence be able to stand: 'He did not know her, until she brought forth her son,' if he waits till after the time of her purification, if his sexual desire which has been kept in check for such a long period of time is again delayed for forty days? Let a woman lately delivered be defiled in blood; let midwives take up the whimpering infant; let the husband hold in embrace an exhausted wife. Let the marriage begin in this manner lest the Evangelist turn out to be a deceiver. But far be it from us to have to entertain such a thought about the mother of our Savior and of a just man! There was no mid-

---

41 Cf. Gen. 38.26.
42 Matt. 1.25.
43 The numbering of the chapters at this point is faulty. This should be chapter 10. I have allowed it to stand as chapter 8a.
44 Lev. 12.2-4.
45 Jer. 5.8.

wife present; there were no women attendants present to wait on her and to care for her. She herself wrapped the infant in swaddling clothes; she herself was both mother and midwife. 'And she laid him in a manger,' he says, 'because there was no room for them in the inn.'[46] These words refute the nonsense of the Apocrypha,[47] as long as Mary herself wrapped the infant in swaddling clothes; and they keep Helvidius from satisfying his desire, as long as there was no room in the inn for the marriage.

(9) *Helvidius.* However, since we have already said more than enough in reply to the texts that he had proposed, namely, 'before they came together,' and 'he did not know her till she brought forth her son,' we must turn our attention to the third question, so that the order of our reply might proceed according to the order of his disputation. For he thinks that Mary bore other children, too; and from the words that are written: 'And Joseph also went to the town of David, to register with Mary his wife who was with child. And it came to pass while they were there that the days for her to be delivered were fulfilled. And she brought forth her firstborn son',[48] he seeks to prove that no child can be called firstborn but one who also has brothers; just as he is called an only child who is the only child born to his parents.

(10) *Jerome.* However, this is our definition: Every only child is a firstborn child; but not every firstborn is an only child. A firstborn child is not only one after whom other children are also born, but also one before whom no other child is born. 'All that openeth the womb,' says the Lord to Aaron, 'of all flesh that are offered to the Lord, of men and beasts, shall belong to thee; only the firstborn of men shall be

---

46 Luke 2.7.
47 This is a reference to the Apocryphal book entitled *De sancta Maria et obstrice,* listed as non-canonical in the decree of Gelasius (PL 59.13). According to the *Protoevangelium Jacobi,* or the *Infancy Gospel of James* (ch. 18-20), Joseph secured a midwife in the district of Bethlehem before Mary gave birth to her child.
48 Luke 2.4-7.

redeemed with a price and the firstborn of beasts that are unclean.'[49] The word of God defined what was meant by a 'firstborn.' 'All,' it says, 'that openeth the womb.' Otherwise, if no child is a firstborn child but only one who subsequently has brothers, the firstborn are not due the priests until others are also born, lest, perchance, a child be an only child and not the firstborn child, in the event that no other child shall be born subsequently. 'And the redemption of it,' he says, 'shall be after one month for the price of five sicles of silver. A sicle by the weight of the sanctuary hath twenty obols. Only the first line of cows, and of sheep and of goats thou shalt not redeem, because they are holy.'[50] The word of God obliges me to vow to God all that opens the womb, if it be of animals that are clean; and to redeem it, if of animals that are unclean, paying the price to the priest. I could answer and say: Why do you limit me to the short period of one month? Why do you call him the firstborn who, I do not know, will subsequently have brothers or not? Wait until a second child is born. I owe nothing to the priest unless that child will also be born, through whom he, who was born first, will begin to be the firstborn child. Will not the very words, themselves, tell me, and convict me of folly, that the child who opens the womb was called firstborn, and not the child who also has brothers? Finally, I ask you whether or not John, who, it is agreed, is an only child, was also a firstborn child? Was he completely subject according to the law in all respects to that law or not? There can be no argument about this fact. Scripture, to be sure, speaks thus of the Savior: 'And when the days of her purification were fulfilled according to the law of Moses, they took him up to Jerusalem to present him to the Lord—as it is written in the law of the Lord: "Every male that openeth the womb shall be called holy to the Lord"—and to offer a sacrifice according to what is said in the law of the

---
49 Num. 18.15; cf. also, Exod. 34.19.
50 Num. 18.16, 17.

Lord, "a pair of turtle-doves or two young pigeons." '⁵¹ If this law applies only to children who are the firstborn, and if subsequent children make a child the firstborn, the child who had no knowledge of subsequent children should not have been subject to the law of the firstborn. But since even that child is subject to the law of the firstborn who subsequently has no other brothers, the conclusion follows that he is called the firstborn child who opens the womb and who has no brother born before him, and not the child who subsequently has a brother born after him. Moses writes in Exodus: 'And it came to pass at midnight, and the Lord slew every firstborn in the land of Egypt, from the firstborn of Pharao who sat on his throne, unto the firstborn of the captive woman that was in prison, and the firstborn of all the cattle.'⁵² Tell me: Were they, who were slain at that time by the executioner, the firstborn or also the only born? Therefore, if only those children are called firstborn who have brothers, then, those who were the only born were delivered from the execution. But if those who were the only born children were executed, it was contrary to the edict for the only born to die also together with the firstborn. You will either spare those who were the only born from the punishment, and you will become the object of ridicule; or, if you will admit that they were killed, then we will establish our point, in spite of your reluctance, that the only born children were also called the firstborn.

(11) *The final proposition of Helvidius.* The final proposition that he set up (although he hoped to prove this same thesis when discussing the question of the firstborn) was that of the reference to the brothers of the Lord in the Gospels, as in the following passage: 'Behold, thy mother and thy brethren are standing outside, waiting to speak to thee.'⁵³ And in another place: 'After this he went down to Capharnaum, he and his mother and his brethren.'⁵⁴ And in the following pas-

---
51 Luke 2.22-24.
52 Exod. 12.29.
53 Luke 8.20.
54 John 2.12.

sage: 'His brethren therefore said to him, "Leave here and go into Judea that thy disciples also may see the works that thou dost; for no one does a thing in secret if he wants to be publicly known. If thou dost these things, manifest thyself to the world." '[55] And John adds the following verse: 'For not even his brethren believed in him at that time.'[56] Similarly, Mark and Matthew say: 'And he began to teach them in their synagogues in his own country, so that they were astonished, and said: "How did this man come by this wisdom and these miracles? Is not this the carpenter's son? Is not his mother called Mary, and his brethren James and Joseph and Simon and Jude? And his sisters, are they not all with us?" '[57] Luke, also, speaks thus in the Acts of the Apostles: 'All these with one mind continued steadfastly in prayer with the women and Mary, the mother of Jesus, and with his brethren.'[58] The Apostle Paul is in agreement with the very truth of the account, using the same words: 'And I went up in consequence of a revelation, and I saw no one except Peter and James, the brother of the Lord.'[59] And again in another place: 'Have we not a right to eat and to drink? Have we not a right to take about with us our wives, as do the other apostles, and the brethren of the Lord, and Cephas?'[60] And he protected himself very cleverly against the possibility that somebody, perchance, might not accept the testimony of the Jews, who have even published the names of His brethren, by asserting that they were deceived by the same error in respect to the question of the brothers into which they fell in respect to the question of the father, and declared: 'These same names are mentioned by the Evangelists in another place and the brothers of the Lord and the sons of Mary are the same persons. Matthew says: "And there were also many women there"— (undoubtedly

---

55 John 7.3, 4.
56 John 7.5.
57 Matt. 13.54-56; Mark 6.1-3.
58 Acts 1.14.
59 Gal. 2.2; 1.19.
60 1 Cor. 9.4, 5.

before the cross of the Lord) —"looking on from a distance, who had followed Jesus from Galilee, ministering to him Among them were Mary Magdalene, Mary the mother of James and Joseph, and the mother of the sons of Zebedee."[61] Similarly, Mark says: "And some women were also there, looking on from a distance. Among them were Mary Magdalene, Mary the mother of James the Less and of Joseph, and Salome."[62] And a little later on in the passage he says: "Besides many other women who had come with him to Jerusalem."[63] Luke, also, says: "Now there was Mary Magdalene and Joanna and Mary, the mother of James, and other women with them." '[64]

(12) *Jerome.* We have quoted these texts in full, lest he rail at us and exclaim that the things that promoted his cause were passed over in silence by us, and that his view was overthrown, not by the testimonies of Scripture, but rather by deceitful argumentation. 'Observe,' he says, 'James and Joseph, the sons of Mary, are the same individuals whom the Jews called brothers. Observe that Mary is the mother of James the Less and of Joseph. This is, however, James the Less as distinguished from James the Greater, who was the son of Zebedee, just as Mark, also, quotes in another place: "But Mary Magdalene and Mary, the mother of James and Joseph, saw where he was laid: and when the Sabbath was past, they bought spices and came to the tomb." '[65] And, to be sure, he says: 'How horrible and impious a thought it would be to think of Mary in such a way as to say that, when the other women were concerned about the burial of Jesus, His mother was absent; or to suppose that she was some other obscure Mary, especially when the Gospel of John bears witness to the fact that she was present there, when our Lord from the cross

---

61 Matt. 27.55, 56.
62 Mark 15.40.
63 Mark 15.41.
64 Luke 24.10.
65 Cf. Mark 15.47; 16.1, 2.

entrusted her, now a widow, to the care of John as his mother. Or are the Evangelists themselves mistaken and are they deceiving us in calling Mary the mother of those whom the Jews said were the brothers of Jesus?'

(13) O blind madness, and a crazed mind bent on its own destruction! You say that the Mother of the Lord was present at His cross, that she was entrusted to the care of John, His disciple, because she was a widow and was alone, as if, according to you, she did not have four sons and a host of daughters[66] whose companionship she might have enjoyed? You also call her a widow, a fact that Scripture does not mention. And while you quote all the testimonies of the Evangelists, you find only the words of John unacceptable. You say, in passing, that she was present at the cross of the Lord, lest it appear that you passed over this fact on purpose; and yet you make no mention of the women who were with her. I should excuse you if you did not know any better, if I did not see that you kept silent on purpose. Listen to what John says: 'Now there were standing by the cross of Jesus his mother and his mother's sister, Mary of Cleophas, and Mary Magdalene.'[67] No one questions the fact that there were two apostles who were called James: James, the son of Zebedee, and James, the son of Alpheus. Do you think that that rather obscure James the Less, whom Scripture calls the son of Mary, but never the son of Mary, the mother of the Lord, is an apostle or not? If he is an apostle, he will be the son of Alpheus and a believer in Jesus; and he will not be one of those brothers, of whom it is written: 'For not even his brethren believed in him at that

---

66 In order to explain the reference to the brothers of the Lord, Helvidius published the heretical view that Mary and Joseph had four sons and a host of daughters after the birth of Jesus, quoting as his reference the text of Matthew (13.55, 56). Others, however, and among them was St. Epiphanius, relying on the testimonies of the Apocryphal writings, admitted that Joseph had children by a previous marriage, and that these were the brothers of the Lord. The *Protoevangelium Jacobi* mentions the two sons of Joseph who accompanied him and Mary to Bethlehem and were present at the birth of Jesus (ch. 17-18).
67 John 19.25.

time.'[68] If he is not an apostle, but some obscure third James,[69] how will he be regarded as a brother of the Lord, and for what reason will a third person be called the less to distinguish him from the greater, when the terms 'the Less' and 'the Greater' normally show a distinction, not among three persons, but rather between two? And how is the brother of the Lord an apostle, when Paul says: 'Then after three years I went to Jerusalem to see Peter, and I remained with him fifteen days. But I saw none of the other apostles, except James, the brother of the Lord'?[70] And in the same Epistle: 'And when they recognized the grace that was given to me, Peter and James and John, who were considered the pillars.'[71] However, lest you think that this James is the son of Zebedee, read the Acts of the Apostles.[72] He had by now been put to death by Herod. The conclusion remains that the Mary, who is designated as the mother of James the Less, was the wife of Alpheus and the sister of Mary, the mother of the Lord, whom John surnames Mary of Cleophas,[73] giving her this title either after her father or some relationship of her family, or for some other reason. But if she seems to you to be one person in one place and then another in another place, because elsewhere she is called Mary, the mother of James the Less, and here, Mary of Cleophas, you should know that it is the custom of Scripture to call the one and the same person by different names. Raguet, the son-in-law of Moses, is also called Jethro. Jerobaal is suddenly read as Gedeon, without any reason given in advance for the change in his name. Ozian, the king of Juda, is, in turn, called Azarias. Mount Tabor is called

---

68 John 7.5.
69 For information regarding James the Less, the son of Alpheus, and James the Greater, the son of Zebedee, and the 'third James,' cf. St. Jerome's *Commentarius in epistolam ad Galatas* PL 26.354-356.
70 Gal. 1.18, 19.
71 Gal. 2.9.
72 Cf. Acts 12.2.
73 According to Hegesippus, Cleophas was the brother of Joseph; hence, Mary, the wife of Cleophas, was the Blessed Virgin's sister-in-law, and her children were paternal cousins of our Savior.

Itabyrium. Again, the Phoenicians surname Hermon Sanior, and Amorraeus surnames him Sanir. The same district is referred to by three names, Nageb, Theman, Derom. Read Ezechiel. Peter is called both Simon and Cephas. Judas is called Zelotes; in another Gospel, Thaddeus. And the reader will be able to collect for himself from all the volumes of Scripture many other examples that illustrate the point of these examples just cited.

(14) What we are now trying to show is how the sons of Mary, the aunt of the Lord, who previously did not believe in Him, but subsequently did believe, can be called the brothers of the Lord. It is quite possible that, while one of them believed immediately, the others did not believe for a long time, and that she was the mother of James and Joseph, that is to say, Mary of Cleophas, the wife of Alpheus, and that she was called Mary, the mother of James the Less. If she were the mother of the Lord, John would have preferred to call her His mother, as he does on every occasion, and would not have wanted her to be regarded as the mother of someone else, by calling her the mother of other individuals. However, I am not going to prolong the argument, and take up for consideration the question whether Mary of Cleophas was one person and Mary, the mother of James and Joseph, another, as long as we agree that Mary, the mother of James and Joseph, is not the same person as the mother of the Lord. Why, then, you say, were those who were not brothers called the brothers of the Lord? Without further ado, you will be shown that individuals are given the title of brothers in Sacred Scripture for four reasons, namely, birth, race, kinship, and affection. Esau, Jacob, the twelve Patriarchs, Andrew and Peter, James and John are called brothers by reason of birth. Individuals are called brothers by reason of race, the way that all Jews call themselves brothers, as in Deuteronomy: 'However, if thou buy thy worker who is a Hebrew man or Hebrew woman, he shall serve thee six years; in the seventh year thou shalt

let him go free from thee.'[74] And in the same book: 'Thou shalt set as king over thee him whom the Lord thy God shall choose, him who is of the number of thy brethren. Thou mayest not set over thee a man of another nation, for he is not thy brother.'[75] And again: 'If thou seest thy brother's ox or his sheep go astray in the way, thou shalt not pass them by; but thou shalt return and bring them back to thy brother. But if thy brother is not nigh, or thou know him not, thou shalt gather them together in thy house and they shall be with thee until thy brother seek them and thou return them to him.'[76] And the Apostle Paul says: 'For I could wish to be anathema myself from Christ for the sake of my brethren, who are my kinsmen according to the flesh; who are Israelites.'[77] Those individuals, to be sure, are called brothers by reason of kinship, who are of the same family, that is to say, *patriá*, which the Latins term *paternitas*,[78] when a large number of descendants is derived from a single stock of a family, as in Genesis: 'Abram therefore said to Lot, "Let there be no quarrel between me and thee, between my herdsmen and thy herdsmen; for we are all brethren." '[79] And in the following: 'And Lot chose to himself the country about the Jordan, and he departed from the east; and they were separated one brother from the other.'[80] Lot is certainly not the brother of Abraham, but the son of his brother, Aaron. Thara, to be sure, begot Abraham, and Nachor and Aaron; and Aaron begot Lot. And again in Genesis: 'Abram, however, was seventy-five years old

---

74 Cf. Deut. 15.12; Exod. 21.2; Jer. 34.14.
75 Deut. 17.15.
76 Deut. 22.1, 2.
77 Rom. 9.3, 4.
78 St. Jerome discusses in detail the meaning of *paternitas* in his *Commentarius in epistolam ad Ephesios* (PL 26.518-521). Paternitas is termed in Greek, *patriá*, and in Hebrew, *mi-phahrath*, that is, *cognatio* or *familia*, a group of persons claiming the same descent or race. We read in Numbers (1.2): 'Take the sum of all the congregation of the children of Israel by their families and houses.' The term 'families' is translated as *paternitates*.
79 Gen. 13.8.
80 Gen. 13.11.

when he left Haran. And Abram took Sarai his wife and Lot his brother's son.'[81] But if you still doubt that the son of a brother is called a brother, take this illustration: 'However, when Abram had heard that his brother Lot was taken captive, he numbered of the servants born in his house, three hundred and eighteen.'[82] And after describing the slaughter that took place during the attack at night, he added: 'And he took all the cavalry of the Sodomites and brought back Lot his brother.'[83] These examples should suffice to prove my assertions. But to keep you from quibbling and wiggling free like some slippery eel, you must be bound fast by the chains of testimonies, lest you complain and hiss at me in contempt, and say that you were defeated rather by tortuous arguments than by the truth of Scripture. When Jacob, the son of Isaac and Rebecca, had gone to Mesopotamia, because he feared the threats of his brother, he went and rolled away the stone from the mouth of the well, and watered the sheep of Laban, the brother of his mother.[84] 'And Jacob kissed Rachel and lifting up his voice, wept; and he told her that he was her father's brother and the son of Rebecca.'[85] Notice that he, who is the son of a sister, is also called brother, in the same way as specified above. And again: 'Laban, however, said to Jacob: "Because thou art my brother, thou shalt not serve me without wages. Tell me, what are thy wages?"'[86] And so he spent twenty years in that place, and, while he was returning to his own country, accompanied by his children and wives, without the knowledge of his father-in-law, he was overtaken by Laban on Mount Galaad. And after Laban had searched for the idols that Rachel had hidden, and he could not find them in the packs, Jacob replied and said to Laban: 'For what fault of mine and for what offense on my part hast thou pursued

---

81 Gen. 12.4, 5.
82 Gen. 14.14.
83 Cf. Gen. 14.16.
84 Cf. Gen. 28, 29.
85 Gen. 29.11, 12.
86 Gen. 29.15.

me, and searched all my vessels? What hast thou found of all thy substance? Lay it here before my brethren and thy brethren and let them judge between us two.'[87] Answer me: Who are those brothers of Jacob and Laban who were at that time present in person? Esau, the brother of Jacob, was certainly absent, and Laban, the son of Bathuel, had no brothers, save one sister, Rebecca.

(15) There are countless examples of this kind inserted in the Sacred Books. But, to avoid making a long story of it, I shall take up for consideration the last of the subdivisions of brothers, that of calling individuals brothers by reason of affection. Affection is divided into two kinds, the spiritual and the common. It is spiritual, because all of us Christians are called brothers, as in the following passage: 'Behold, how good and how pleasant it is for brethren to dwell together in unity.'[88] And the Savior says in another Psalm: 'I will declare thy name to my brethren.'[89] And in another passage: 'Go, tell my brethren.'[90] It is common, to be sure, because all of us, being born of one father, are bound together by a common brotherhood. 'Tell those,' He says, 'who hate you: "You are our brothers." '[91] And the apostle writes to the Corinthians: 'One who is called a brother, if he is immoral, or covetous, or an idolator, or evil-tongued, or a drunkard, or greedy; with such a one not even to take food,'[92] and other passages similar to these. Now I ask you: For what reason do you think are the individuals in the Gospel called brothers of the Lord? Is it birth? But Scripture does not say this; for it calls them neither the sons of Mary nor sons of Joseph. Is it race? But it is absurd that a few of the Jews were called brothers, when all who were Jews there according to this definition could have been called brothers. Is it affection, which is a human

---
87 Gen. 31.36, 37.
88 Ps. 132.1.
89 Ps. 21.23.
90 John 20.17.
91 Cf. Isa. 66.5.
92 1 Cor. 5.11.

right and is spiritual? But if it is for this reason, who were more truly brothers than the apostles, whom He taught privately and whom he called mothers and brothers? Or if all men are brothers because they are human beings, it was foolish to make the following announcement, referring to specific individuals: 'Behold, your brothers are looking for you,'[93] since all men, generally speaking, are brothers according to this proposition. It remains, therefore, for you to believe, according to the foregoing exposition, that they were called brothers by reason of kinship, not of affection, or racial prerogative, or birth. Just as Lot was called the brother of Abraham, just as Jacob was called the brother of Laban, even as the daughters of Salphaed also number Clerus among their brothers, even as Abraham regarded Sara, his wife, as his sister. For he says: 'She is truly my sister, by my father, not by my mother,'[94] that is to say, she is the daughter of a brother, not of a sister. Otherwise, it would seem as if Abraham, a just man, had taken for his wife the daughter of his own father; whereas Scripture does not mention such a custom among men of old in order to protect the sanctity of their reputation, but prefers rather to hint at such a custom than to make an explicit declaration; and God subsequently forbids it by law under pain of punishment and utters the threat: 'If any man will take his sister by father or by mother and shall see her shame and she herself see his shame, it is an abomination; and they shall perish from the midst of their people. He has uncovered the shame of his sister, he shall receive his sin.'[95]

(16) O thou most ignorant of men, you have not read those testimonies and, disregarding the whole field of Scripture, you have brought disgrace upon the Virgin with your madness, like the character[96] spoken of in fables, who set fire to the temple of Diana, because he was unknown among the peo-

---
93 Cf. Mark 3.32.
94 Gen. 20.12.
95 Lev. 18.9, 29.
96 Cf. Valerius Maximus, *Facta et dicta memorabilia* 8.13.

ple and he could not think of anything good to do that might make him famous. And since no one had made known the sacrilege, it is said that, on his own accord, he went before the public and loudly exclaimed that he had caused the fire. And when the Ephesian magistrates asked him the reason for wanting to commit such a crime he replied: 'that I might become known to all by doing something evil, since I could not achieve renown by doing anything good.' And, to be sure, that is a story told in Greek history. You, however, have set fire to the temple of the Lord's body, you have defiled the sanctuary of the Holy Spirit, from which you would have issue four brothers and a host of sisters. Finally, joining voices with the Jews, you say: 'Is not this the carpenter's son? Is not his mother called Mary, and his brethren James and Joseph and Simon and Jude? And his sisters, are they not all with us?'[97] The word 'all' is not used except when speaking of a crowd. Who, I ask you, knew you before you uttered this blasphemy? Who thought you were worth three pence? You have gained your goal; you have become famed through your crime. I, myself, who am writing against you, do not know whether you are black or white, as they say, although I live in the same city with you. I overlook the faults of your language, with which your whole book is replete. I pass over in silence that ridiculous introduction: *'O tempora, O mores!'* I am not looking for eloquence, which you demanded in the case of brother Carterius,[98] although you yourself did not have it. I am not demanding, I say, elegance of tongue; I am looking for purity of heart. For in the eyes of Christians it is a gross impropriety and a crime either to say or do anything that is base. I am coming to the end of my discourse, and I am confronting you with a horned question; and I shall consider the question with you, as if I had said nothing about it previously: they were called brothers of the Lord in the same way in which Joseph was called father. 'In sorrow,' she says, 'thy father and I have

---
97 Matt. 13.55; Mark 6.3.
98 Cf. above, Introduction, pp. 4ff.

been seeking thee.'⁹⁹ It is the mother who is saying this, not the Jews. And the Evangelist himself says: 'And his father and mother were marvelling at the things spoken concerning him,'¹⁰⁰ and passages similar to these which we have already quoted, in which they are referred to as parents. And lest, perchance, you use the argument of the variety of the copies, because you have very foolishly convinced yourself that the Greek codices have been falsified, I turn to the Gospel of John, in which he writes very clearly: 'Philip found Nathanael, and said to him, "We have found him of whom Moses in the Law and the Prophets wrote, Jesus the son of Joseph of Nazareth." '¹⁰¹ I am sure that this passage is contained in your copy. Answer me: In what way is Jesus, who, it is agreed, was born of the Holy Spirit, the son of Joseph? Was Joseph truly His father? However dull you may be, you will not dare to say that he was, will you? Or was he regarded as His father? They should also be regarded as His brothers in the same way that he was regarded as His father.

(17) But since my discourse has now passed safely beyond the dangerous crags and the rough spots, I must spread sails and rush into his epilogues where he, who considers himself a sciolist, cites Tertullian as his witness, and quotes the words of Victorinus, the bishop of Pettau. Regarding Tertullian,¹⁰² I say nothing more than that he was not a man of the Church. Regarding Victorinus,¹⁰³ however, I repeat the statement that

---

99 Luke 2.48.
100 Luke 2.33.
101 John 1.45.
102 In the *De carne Christi*, Tertullian attacked the Gnostics, and established against Docetism that the body of Christ was real. To give more force to this doctrine, he went so far as to deny the virginity of Mary, not *ante partum*, of course, but *in partu*. He denied her virginity *post partum* for other reasons. Cf. F. Cayré *Manual of Patrology and History of Theology* 1 (translated by H. Howitt; Belgium 1935) 237-238. Concerning Christ's birth, cf. *Adversus Marcionem* 3.11; 4.21; *De carne Christi* 7; *De virginibus velandis* 5; *De monogamia* 8; *De pudicitia* 6. Tertullian manifested not the slightest awareness that his denials of the perpetual virginity of Mary contradicted any ecclesiastical tradition, at least, known to him.
103 Of the works attributed to Victorinus, bishop of Pettau, by St. Jerome

I also made regarding the Evangelists, that he called them brothers of the Lord, not the sons of Mary, brothers, however, in the sense in which we explained above, of kinship, not of birth. But we are wasting time on trifles and, disregarding the fountain of truth, we are pursuing the streams of opinions. Could I not compile for you a whole list of the ancient writers,[104] Ignatius, Polycarp, Irenaeus, Justin the Martyr, and many other apostolic and eloquent men, who composed volumes, replete with wisdom, against Ebion, and Theodotus of Byzantium, and Valentinus,[105] all of whom held these same views? If you had read these volumes some time in the past, you would be a wiser man. But I believe that it is better to reply briefly to each of these topics separately than to enlarge this volume by discussing them at great length.

(18) I now attack the section where you wished to appear eloquent by comparing virginity and marriage. We found the proverb, 'We see a camel dancing,' amusing and relevant in your case. You say: 'Are virgins better than Abraham, Isaac,

---

in his *De viris illustribus* (74), one only remains, the *Commentarius in apocalypsim Joannis*. In the *De viris illustribus*, St. Jerome does not make mention of any commentary written by Victorinus on Matthew. But St. Jerome's list of the works of Victorinus is not complete; for he adds at the end of his notice the remark that Victorinus wrote *'et multa alia.'* In the preface to his own *Commentarius in evangelium Matthaei*, St. Jerome mentions Victorinus as one of the many composers of commentaries on Matthew (PL 26.20).

104 The perpetual virginity of Mary was explicitly affirmed in the early Church by St. Irenaeus, St. Ignatius, and St. Justin. Cf. above, Introduction, p. 4, n.3. The *Adversus haereses* of St. Irenaeus, which was the source for St. Epiphanius' great work against the heretics, was the principal authority for the study of Gnosticism. In this work, St. Irenaeus attacked the Valentinians and killed Gnosticism. Cf. F. Cayré, *op. cit.*, 146.

105 These men were disciples of Gnosticism, the most influential of the primitive heresies. Theodotus, a disciple of the Oriental school of Valentinus, is referred to by St. Irenaeus as the father of the Gnostic heresy (*Contra haereses* 1.11.1). The Ebionites are listed as number 10 in St. Augustine's *De haeresibus*, the Valentinians, number 11, and the Theodotions, number 33. The Ebionites, who derived their name from the Jewish word meaning 'the poor,' saw in Jesus the son of Joseph, and denied His birth of the blessed Mary and the Holy Ghost. They maintained, furthermore, that Mary lost her virginity before the birth of Jesus through the natural process of generation.

'and Jacob, who had wives? Are not babies fashioned daily in wombs by the hands of God, that we should have reason to blush at the thought that Mary was wed after she brought forth her son? But if such a thought seems degrading to them, it remains that they do not believe that even God was born through the organs of a virgin. For according to their view, it is more degrading that God was born through the lower organs of a virgin, than that a virgin was married to her husband after she brought forth her son.' Add,[106] also, if you like, the other humiliations of nature, a womb teeming for nine months, nauseation, the birth of the child, blood, swaddling clothes. Let the infant himself be described for you, wrapped in the usual webbing of membranes. Include the rough crib, the wailing of the infant, the circumcision of the eighth day, the period of purification, to prove that He was unclean. We are not ashamed, we are not left speechless. The more humiliating the things that He suffered for me, the greater the debt that I owe Him. And when you have disclosed all of these details, you will mention nothing that is more degrading than the cross; we confess it, in this we believe, and in this we triumph over our enemies.

(19) But just as we do not deny these statements which have been written down, so also, by the same token, we do deny those things which have not been written down. We believe that God was born of a virgin, because we have read such a statement. We do not believe that Mary married after she brought forth her son, because we have not read such a statement. We are not saying this in order to condemn marriage; virginity itself, to be sure, is the fruit of marriage; but because it is not right for us to make rash judgments about holy men. For if we base our judgment on probability, we can argue that Joseph had many wives, because Abraham had many wives, because Jacob had many wives; and that the brothers of the

---

106 This description of the birth of Christ is taken from Tertullian's *De carne Christi*, in which he established against Docetism that the body of Christ was real flesh (ch. 5).

Lord were born of these wives, as many imagine is the case, based not so much on a pious as on a brazen rashness. You say that Mary did not remain a virgin; as for me, I claim more emphatically that Joseph himself was also a virgin through Mary, so that a virgin son might be born of a virgin wedlock. For if fornication ill befits a holy man, and it is not written down that he had a second wife, but was the guardian rather than the husband of Mary whom he supposedly possessed as his own, the conclusion follows that he, who was deemed worthy to be called the father of the Lord, remained a virgin with Mary.

(20) And since I intend to make a few comments on a comparison of marriage and virginity, I ask my readers not to think that I have disparaged marriage in praising virginity, and that I have discriminated between the holy men of the Old and New Testament, that is to say, between those who had wives and those who had completely renounced the embraces of women; for those who lived in the days of old were subject to one pronouncement in keeping with the conditions of the times, while we, after the passage of many centuries, are subject to another pronouncement. As long as the following law remained in force: 'Increase and multiply and fill the earth,'[107] and: 'Cursed be the sterile woman that bringeth not forth seed in Israel,'[108] they all married and were given in marriage and, leaving behind father and mother, they became one flesh. However, when that voice exclaimed: 'The time is short: it remains, that those who have wives be as if they had none';[109] 'for clinging to the Lord we are made one spirit with him';[110] and why? 'For he who is unmarried is concerned about the things of the Lord, how he may please God. Whereas he who is married is concerned about the things of the world, how he may please his wife; and he is divided. And the un-

---
107 Gen. 1.28.
108 Cf. Exod. 23.26.
109 1 Cor. 7.29.
110 1 Cor. 6.17.

married woman, and the virgin,[111] thinks about the things of the Lord, that she may be holy in body and in spirit. Whereas she who is married thinks about the things of the world, how she may please her husband';[112] why do you rail at me, why do you oppose me? These are the words of the Chosen Vessel who says: 'Divided is the unmarried woman and virgin.' Notice how fortunately even the designation of sex has been omitted. A virgin is now not called an unmarried woman. 'She who is not married thinks about the things of the Lord, that she may be holy in body and spirit.' This is the definition of a virgin: one who is holy in body and spirit; for it would avail a virgin nothing to have flesh if she were married in spirit. 'For she who is married thinks about the things of the world, how she may please her husband.' Do you think that it is one and the same thing to spend days and nights in prayer and fastings, and to paint the face in anticipation of the arrival of a husband, to break step, to feign flattery? The former makes herself appear more ugly, and she obscures a natural good by debasing it. The latter paints herself for the mirror, and, in her attempt to improve her natural beauty, she insults the artist. Add to this the prattling of infants, the noisy clamoring of the whole household, the clinging of children to her neck,

---

111 There are variant readings for this text. The reading that St. Jerome follows here is found in many Latin copies, but it is not according to the Vulgate or the apostolic truth. The Vulgate version, which St. Jerome quotes in his *Adversus Jovinianum* 1.13, reads as follows: 'Whereas he who is married is concerned about the things of the world, how he may please his wife; *and he is divided. And the unmarried woman, and the virgin. . . .*' The reading adopted by St. Jerome in this work is as follows: 'Whereas he who is married is concerned about the things of the world, how he may please his wife. *And divided is the unmarried woman and virgin. . . .*' In explaining this text in his *Adversus Jovinianum*, St. Jerome admits using this version which is not according to the Vulgate, but adds that it has its merits when used properly, to make a distinction between an 'unwed woman,' and a 'virgin.' This same reading occurs in St. Jerome's letter to Eustochium (22.21). Tertullian, in his *De velandis virginibus* (ch. 4), quotes this same reading to show that, when Scripture wants to make a distinction between a virgin and a non-virgin, it used the words *virgo* and *mulier*.

112 1 Cor. 7.32-34.

the computing of expenses, the preparing of budgets. Then, there is the pounding of meats by a busy band of cooks; there is the chattering of a crowd of women weavers. In the meantime, she is told that her husband has arrived with friends. Like a swallow, she flies over the entire interior of the house, to see if the couch is properly arranged, if the floors have been swept, if the drinking bowls have been set in order, if the dinner has been prepared. Tell me, I ask you, where is there any opportunity to think of God in the midst of all this? And are such homes happy homes? Moreover, with kettle drums resounding, flutes blaring, lyres shrieking, cymbals clashing, what kind of fear of God prevails amidst such a commotion? The parasite exults in insults; exposed victims of lust enter in, and women, practically naked, dressed in flimsy clothes, are exposed to the gaze of immodest eyes. The wretched wife either expresses a delight with this sort of entertainment and she is ruined; or she expresses disgust and her husband is provoked to wrangling. Discord, the seed-plot of divorce, is the result. Or if you find a home where such conditions do not exist—and such a case is a rarity—would not the very management of the home, however, the education of the children, the tending to the needs of the husband, the disciplining of the young servants, distract a person from thoughts of God? 'It has ceased to be with Sara,' says Scripture, 'after the manner of women,'[113] and thereupon it is said to Abraham: 'In all that Sara says to thee, hearken to her voice.'[114] She who is no longer subject to the anxieties and pain of childbirth, she who has ceased to be a married woman with the cessation of the function of the menstrual blood, is freed from the curse of God. Nor is she placed under the power of her husband, but, on the contrary, her husband is made subject to her, and he is commanded by the word of God: 'In all that Sara says to thee, hearken to her voice.' And then they begin to have time for prayer; for as long as they

---

113 Gen. 18.11.
114 Gen. 21.12.

discharge the obligations of marriage, they pass up the opportunities of prayer.

(21) We do not deny that widows, we do not deny that married women turn out to be holy women; but we say that those women turn out to be holy who have ceased to be married women, who imitate the chastity of virgins within the very intimacy of marriage. It was to this fact that the apostle briefly referred, with Christ speaking within him: 'The unmarried woman thinks about the things of God, how she may please God; but the married woman thinks about the things of the world, how she may please her husband,' leaving us free to comprehend the full meaning of the matter. Moreover, he is not forcing or casting a snare on anyone, but is promoting rather what is proper; for he would want all to be like himself. And although he has no command of the Lord concerning virginity, because this is beyond the power of men; and, in a certain sense, it would be highly presumptuous to force men to act contrary to nature and to say to them in other words: 'I want you to be like angels'; whence even the reward of a virgin is greater, since she takes for naught what is not a sin to do; nevertheless, he says to those who remain steadfast: 'Yet I give an opinion, as one having obtained mercy from the Lord to be trustworthy. I think, then, that this is good on account of the present distress, that it is good for man to remain as he is.'[115] What is this distress? 'Woe to those who are with child, or have infants at the breast on that day.'[116] A forest grows up so that it may subsequently be cut down. A field is sown with seeds so that it may be harvested. The world is already filled; the earth is too small for us. Every day we are cut off by wars, we are carried off by diseases, we are swallowed up by shipwrecks; and do we, nonetheless, argue over boundaries? In this group are those who follow the Lamb,[117] who have not soiled their garments; for they have re-

---
115 1 Cor. 7.25, 26.
116 Matt. 24.19; Mark 13.17.
117 Cf. Apoc. 14.4.

mained virgins. Note the significance of the term 'soiled.' I do not dare to explain its meaning, lest Helvidius make some disparaging remarks. However, as far as your statement is concerned that some virgins are shopkeepers, I say to you, over and above this, that there are among them even adulteresses; and to amaze you even more, there are clerics who are innkeepers and monks who are debauchees. But who would not readily understand that a shopkeeper cannot be a virgin, or a debauchee a monk, or an innkeeper a cleric? Is virginity to be blamed, if it is the dissembler of virginity who is at fault? But, to pass over the other persons and to get back to the virgin, I certainly do not know whether she who is engaged in the shopkeeping business remains a virgin in body, but I do know that she does not remain a virgin in spirit.

(22) We have played the rhetorician and have sported a bit in the manner of declaimers. You, Helvidius, have forced me to do this, who think that virgins and married women are equally glorious, at a time when the Gospel is already in full splendor. And because I realize that you, overcome by the truth, will resort to making disparaging remarks of my life and to slandering (for little women also are wont to act in this fashion, who, when bested, wish their lords ill in the corner), I say to you in advance that your taunts will redound to my glory, since you will lacerate me with the same lips with which you have disparaged Mary; and the servant of the Lord and His Mother will experience in equal measure your currish eloquence.

THE APOLOGY AGAINST THE BOOKS OF RUFINUS

INTRODUCTION

 YEAR AFTER ST. JEROME had written his treatise against Helvidius at Rome, Pope Damasus died and was succeeded by Pope Siricius, who was less intimate with St. Jerome. While Pope Damasus was still alive, the opposition against St. Jerome and his ascetic propaganda remained within bounds. After the election of Pope Siricius, it broke out angrily and St. Jerome felt constrained to leave Rome in the year 385 and seek peace in Palestine. Peaceful and fruitful in literary labors though the years were that he spent at Bethlehem, nevertheless, they were seriously disturbed by no less than five doctrinal controversies. The most serious of these controversies, and the one which caused him the greatest tribulation, was the quarrel over the great Alexandrian master, Origen,[1] and his works, and, in particular, his *Periarchon*.[2] This quarrel, which, strictly speaking, was not of

---

[1] Opinions vary regarding St. Jerome and Rufinus in this controversy. For a thorough and excellent discussion of the origins of the quarrel, cf. Ferd. Cavallera, *Saint Jerome, sa vie et son oeuvre* 1 (Louvain-Paris 1922) 193-195.

[2] Origen's most important theological work is the *Periarchon*, which has survived in the Latin translation of Rufinus. St. Jerome made a literal translation of the work after Rufinus, but only about twenty-seven short fragments have survived of this work. The *Periarchon*, a sort of *Summa theologica*, is divided into four books and deals with the fundamental principles of theology. Book one deals with the three Divine Persons, with created spirits, and with the question of the animation of stars. Book two treats of the material world and of man, of the human soul, and of Origen's eschatological doctrine. Book three discusses the foundations of morality, the free will, the struggle with the devil, the world and the flesh, and with the final victory of good over evil. Book four is wholly concerned with Scripture and with Origen's exegetical method. The two most important doctrines which are discussed by St. Jerome and Rufinus in their quarrel are Origen's theology and eschatology. Cf. F. Cayré, *Manual of Patrology and History of Theology* 1 (Belgium 1935) 198-199.

their own making, involved two very close friends and ascetics, St. Jerome and Rufinus, and led to their final estrangement amid such shocking and scandalous conditions that it caused St. Augustine to cry out in anguish: 'Is there any friend one will not now dread, when this that we bewail has raised its head between Jerome and Rufinus, once so closely knit in genius and friendship?'[3]

Rufinus and St. Jerome had spent the greater part of their youth together, as students in Rome and as ascetics in Aquileia, bound by the noblest of friendships. Both of them were ardent admirers and faithful disciples of Origen in their youth, and had shared the enthusiasm of nearly all of their Eastern contemporaries for Origen. The principal source of the contention which was to come between them was their attitude towards Origen and his works. Rufinus, who was a fervent disciple of Origen and had learned to appreciate his works while living in Egypt, never wavered in his loyalty and attitude toward Origen. St. Jerome, on the other hand, who had become acquainted with the writings of Origen while residing in Constantinople, and had translated many of his homilies,[4] prior to the outbreak of the Origenistic controversy, began to waver in his allegiance to Origen, under the influence of Epiphanius, bishop of Salamis in Cyprus, and allowed himself to be counted among the adversaries of Origen. When he was accused of wavering in his allegiance to Origen, St. Jerome replied in the letter written to Pammachius during the Origenistic controversy that he had praised and admired 'the commentator, but not the theologian, the man of intellect, but not the unbeliever, the philosopher, but not the apostle.'[5] St. Jerome had recognized Origen's literary service to the Church,

---

3 St. Augustine, *Epistola* 73.6.
4 About the year 380, St. Jerome translated at Constantinople nine of Origen's homilies on Isaia, fourteen on Jeremia, thirty-nine homilies on St. Luke. St. Jerome praised Origen every time that he had an occasion to speak of him, even in his *De viris illustribus* written in the year 393.
5 St. Jerome, *Epistola* 84.2, *ad Pammachium*.

but had cautioned that his doctrinal views were to be read with extreme caution, and that his heretical views were to be impugned.

A trifling and obscure incident, which in itself was of no immediate consequence, preceded the open break between Rufinus and St. Jerome. In the beginning of the year 393, a monk by the name of Atarbius accused Rufinus and St. Jerome of favoring Origenism. He approached them in their respective monasteries and demanded of them a formal rejection of Origenism. St. Jerome, apparently under the influence of Epiphanius, offered Atarbius a formal abjuration of the errors attributed to Origen. Rufinus, on the other hand, would not even see the monk. Atarbius, thereupon, linked Rufinus with the supporters of Origen. That might have been the end of the incident. But Epiphanius and Bishop John of Jerusalem were responsible for continuing the quarrel over Origen. The former was the most ardent and most convinced adversary of Origen at the end of the fourth century. For him Origenism and its devotees were to become an obsession.[6] In contrast to the position taken by Epiphanius, Bishop John claimed the right to continue using the works of Origen for spiritual benefit and theological riches.[7] This was also the stand taken by Theophilus, the powerful bishop of Alexandria. A letter sent by Epiphanius to Bishop John regarding their views on Origen was to aggravate the situation. A Latin version of this letter, which St. Jerome had transcribed for Eusebius of Cremona on

---

6 St. Epiphanius, who became bishop of Salamis in Cyprus in the year 369, was the most ardent and the most convinced adversary of Origenism at the end of the fourth century. He assigned himself the task of ruining Origen and Origenism in Catholic opinion. He carried on his fight for nearly thirty years, and he never ceased to combat Origen's writings, condemning, in particular, his Trinitarian errors. He prided himself on being the 'hammer of heretics.' His chief work is the *Panarion*, usually cited under the title of *Haereses*. This work, which was composed about 374-377, was a compendium of eighty heresies with a refutation of each, and was intended to serve as a guide for the safekeeping of orthodoxy. A whole section was devoted to Origen.
7 Cf. Francis X. Murphy, C.SS.R., *Rufinus of Aquileia, His Life and Works* (Washington 1945) 68.

the margin of a Greek copy of the original, turned up sixteen months later in the hands of Rufinus and Bishop John. St. Jerome was charged with having given a false interpretation of the letter. Pammachius, one of St. Jerome's friends, wrote to him for an explanation. St. Jerome's reply in a long letter, written in the year 395, is known as the *Libellus de optimo genere interpretandi*.[8]

The quarrel, which had begun so obscurely, appeared to be getting out of hand. Bishop John wrote a letter to Theophilus and asked him to settle the whole matter. In his letter, Bishop John gave a résumé of the whole affair, and he justified himself against the charge of Origenism. Fearing the possible effect of this letter at Rome, which Pammachius regarded as an apology, he warned St. Jerome to answer the letter of Bishop John. Between the years 396-399, St. Jerome composed his *Contra Johannem Hierosolymitanum*,[9] in which he refuted the long letter of Bishop John. Theophilus was stirred into action by these two works and he put together a Festal Letter in the interest of peace. The reconciliation between Rufinus and St. Jerome, when it came a little later in the early part of the year 397 in the Church of the Resurrection in Jerusalem, was wholehearted. But it was to mark the close only of the first phase of the quarrel over Origen between Rufinus and St. Jerome. Rufinus departed for the West and was accompanied part of the way by St. Jerome.

Shortly after arriving at Rome in the Spring of 397, Rufinus undertook the translation of the writings of Origen, an

---

[8] In this long letter to Pammachius (*Epistola* 57, ad *Pammachium*), St. Jerome recounts the circumstances which led to its composition, and repudiates the charge of having falsified the letter of St. Epiphanius to Bishop John. He defends his method of translating sense for sense, and not word for word, by appealing to the practice of the classical (ch. 5), and the ecclesiastical (ch. 6), and the New Testament writers (chs. 7-10). Eusebius was interested in the thought, not in a word for word translation. St. Jerome had marked on the margin of the letter the contents of the several chapters. St. Jerome singles out one instance of the charge of falsification of the original, where he translated the phrase 'honorable sir' as 'dear friend' (ch. 2).

[9] St. Jerome, *Contra Johannem Hierosolymitanum* PL 23.355-396.

endeavor which was to reopen the Origenistic controversy. Rufinus was met on his arrival in Rome by a scholar named Macarius,[10] who was engaged at the time on a work against fate. In his dream, he had seen a ship approaching the harbor of Rome, which, when it docked, contained the answers to his problems on the providence of God. When he was informed of the arrival of Rufinus, he went to see him immediately and begged him to give him the opinion of Origen on this matter. Rufinus told him that the martyr, Pamphilus, had touched upon these problems in his *Apologia* for the works of Origen. At the request of Macarius, Rufinus translated the first book of the *Apologia* of Pamphilus,[11] adding by way of supplement a small treatise of his own, entitled *The Falsification of the Books of Origen*, in which he defended the works of Origen against the tamperings by heretics. Rufinus, furthermore, had added a preface to the translation, in which he was careful to give an exposition of his own belief. With his curiosity and interest now aroused, Macarius begged Rufinus to translate for him the *Periarchon* of Origen. Rufinus finished the translation of the first two books of the *Periarchon* during Lent of the year 399, and then embarked on the second two after Lent.

In the preface[12] prefixed to the translation of the first two books of the *Periarchon*, Rufinus first justified his own position, and then praised St. Jerome as the very eloquent translator of the homilies of Origen. He further declared that, inasmuch as other occupations prevented St. Jerome from fulfilling his promise made in the preface to his translation of the two homilies of Origen on the Canticle of Canticles of translating the rest of the homilies and many other works of Origen, his own work was a continuation of that of St. Jerome. He said that he was imitating St. Jerome, not in the power of

---
10 Rufinus describes his experience with Macarius in his *Apologia* 1.11.
11 For a discussion of the *Apologia* of Pamphilus, cf. below, p. 68, n. 18.
12 This preface of Rufinus is included as letter 80 among the letters of St. Jerome.

his eloquence, to be sure, but in his rules and methods. This reference to St. Jerome was to give rise to the second phase of the controversy between Rufinus and St. Jerome.

The monk, Eusebius of Cremona, arrived in Rome at the time that Rufinus was finishing the rough draft of the translation of the *Periarchon*. He managed to secure a copy of the translation and passed it on to Pammachius, and Marcella, and other friends of St. Jerome. Having misjudged the intent of the preface prefixed to the translation, and interpreting the declarations made therein as a sly and hypocritical attempt by Rufinus to compromise St. Jerome, Pammachius and Oceanus sent a letter[13] to St. Jerome, along with Rufinus' translation of the *Periarchon,* and requested him to answer Rufinus. In the meantime, they denounced the new work of Rufinus and organized a campaign against him throughout Italy. Alarmed by this opposition organized against him, Rufinus left Rome for Aquileia in the early part of the year 399.

When St. Jerome received the rough draft of Rufinus' translation of the *Periarchon* sent to him by Pammachius and Oceanus, he noticed that Rufinus had paid particular attention to the statements concerning the Trinity, but had passed over some matters lightly; that he had modified or even suppressed certain passages of questionable orthodoxy; and that he had inserted in their places passages taken from other works of Origen. St. Jerome did not doubt the sincerity of the remarks made about him and his work by Rufinus in the preface, but, being persuaded by his friends, he decided to make a literal translation of the *Periarchon* in order to reveal the inaccuracies of Rufinus. There was bound to be a vast difference between the two translations, for each had approached the work from a different viewpoint. Rufinus was interested solely in the apologetic value of the work. In order to explain and justify his position, St. Jerome wrote in answer

---

13 Cf. *Epistola* 83, ad *Hieronymum* in the collection of St. Jerome's letters.

to the preface of Rufinus a brief letter,[14] which was calm and moderate and conciliatory. As a companion letter, St. Jerome composed a long letter addressed to Pammachius and Oceanus,[15] which, though calm and objective, was, nevertheless, querulous and bitter in tone, and intended for a general audience. In it, St. Jerome justified his attitude towards Origen and minimized his early enthusiasm for him. He admired Origen in the same way that Cyprian admired Tertullian, but did not in any way adopt his errors. He accused Rufinus, without mentioning his name, of heresy, lying, and perjury. Although there was no Origenist sect, as such, at the time, it was imprudent on the part of Rufinus to have continued to spread Origen's work, and to have brought St. Jerome into his own undertakings. St. Jerome was too strictly orthodox to let the errors of Origen and Rufinus go by without comment. It was this strict orthodoxy on the part of St. Jerome that caused him to assume such a violent and bitter attitude throughout the controversy.[16]

St. Jerome sent his literal translation of the *Periarchon*, together with these two letters, to his friends. They, however, took it upon themselves to withhold the explanatory letter addressed to Rufinus, and they made public only the long letter of justification that St. Jerome meant for a general audience. In this letter, St. Jerome did not mention anyone by name. It was a general attack against the propagators of Origenism; but taken by itself, it was easily susceptible of being an attack on Rufinus and his recent translation of the *Periarchon*. And unhappily, it was interpreted in that way by Rufinus when the letter was given to him many months later. At the same time, Marcella[17] circulated a manuscript contain-

---

14 St. Jerome, *Epistola* 81, *ad Rufinum*.
15 St. Jerome, *Epistola* 84, *ad Pammachium et Oceanum*.
16 Cf. F. Cayré, *Manual of Patrology and History of Theology* 1 (Belgium 1935) 563.
17 Cf. St. Jerome, *Epistola* 127.9-10, *ad Principiam*. This letter addressed to Principia, the greatest friend of Marcella, is in reality a memoir of Marcella. After describing her history, character, and favorite

ing excerpts from St. Jerome's and Rufinus' translations of the *Periarchon*, for the purpose of demonstrating Rufinus' faulty translation. Copies were made of this document and scattered at Rome and in the various towns and villages, as well as in the monasteries throughout Italy.[18] The controversy was reopened, and the break between Rufinus and St. Jerome was soon to become complete and, henceforth, irreparable.

While Rufinus was living in Aquileia, whither he had gone from Rome in the year 399, certain conditions arose that were to involve him once again in the Origenistic controversy. Pope Siricius had died, and he was replaced by Anastasius who proved to be more amenable to the anti-Origen forces then functioning in Rome. Under the new Pope, the friends of St. Jerome renewed their agitation against Rufinus. The false impression given the Pope by the complaints of the friends of St. Jerome was strengthened by a letter which Anastasius received at this time from Theophilus of Alexandria, in which the bishop of Alexandria outlined the results of a council held at Alexandria where Origenism was categorically condemned. The Pope issued a condemnation of the propositions contained in Theophilus' document. In consequence of these circumstances, Rufinus felt it necessary to explain his position and to defend himself before the Pope himself. Towards the end of the year 400, he composed his *Apologia ad Anastasium*.[19] In his *Apologia*, Rufinus renewed his profession of faith in everything just as the Church teaches it; in the Trinity, the incarnation and the redemption, the resurrection of the body, and in the final judgment. As for the origin of the soul, he knows of three opinions: creationism, traducianism, and the theory of preexistence, but he refrains from expressing any definite view on the matter.

It is problematical whether Rufinus would have written

---
studies, St. Jerome recounts her eminent services in the cause of orthodoxy at a time when, through the efforts of Rufinus, it seemed likely that Origenism would prevail at Rome.
18 Cf. Murphy, *op. cit.*, 127.
19 Rufinus, *Apologia ad Anastasium* PL 21.623-628.

his *Apology* in answer to St. Jerome and the anti-Origenistic critics, If the friendly letter that St. Jerome had written to Rufinus had been delivered promptly to him by his friend. But when Apronianus showed Rufinus the letter that St. Jerome had written in the Spring of 399 to Pammachius in reply to Rufinus' translation of the *Periarchon*, Rufinus felt hurt and angered, and resolved to clear himself once and for all. Just when the *Apology* was begun by Rufinus is not known; but the work itself, composed of two books,[20] was not finished until well on in the year 401. It was addressed and dedicated to his friend Apronianus at Rome, and was intended as a reply to St. Jerome's letter to Pammachius.

In the first book of the *Apology*, Rufinus made a profession of his Christian standing and faith, especially on the points raised by the Origenistic controversy. He declared that his method of translation was the same which St. Jerome himself had used. Where he found passages in Origen's writings that were contradictory to the orthodox opinion expressed elsewhere, he restored the orthodox statements which he believed were originally there. He turned on St. Jerome by showing that in his *Commentary on the Ephesians* he had adopted the same opinions that he was now condemning as heretical, such as the fall of souls from a previous state into the prison house of the bodies, and the universal restoration of spiritual beings. In the second book of the *Apology*, he took a wider view of St. Jerome's writings, showing how he had ridiculed various classes of Christians in some of his writings, how he had praised Origen indiscriminately, how he had defamed men like Ambrose, and how he had boasted of having taken as teachers Origenists, and heretics, and Jews.

The work was not negligible. In the history of polemical literature, Rufinus' *Apologia* is an outstanding production.[21] St. Jerome tried to answer the *Apologia*, together with the *Apologia ad Anastasium*, which had been added as a supple-

---
20 Rufinus, *Apologiae in sanctum Hieronymum libri duo* PL 21.541-624.
21 Murphy, *op. cit.*, 140.

ment, even before he received a copy of the whole of the *Apologia*. His friends did manage to get hold of enough of it to supply St. Jerome with leading ideas for a reply. His brother, Paulinian, had been able to secure certain sections of the work before returning from Italy. St. Jerome wrote his reply to the *Apology* of Rufinus at the end of the year 401.[22] The two books, which were dedicated and addressed to Pammachius and Marcella, were undoubtedly the most important writing of the whole controversy.[23] The first two paragraphs of the first book are indicative of the impassioned mood in which St. Jerome set out to write his *Apologia*. In the first book, he justifies his literal translation of the *Periarchon* which was undertaken to show what the *Periarchon* really was, in view of the ambiguous version of Rufinus. He declared that the *Apology* of Origen, which was translated by Rufinus as the work of Pamphilus, was really written by Eusebius. He defended his method of translation in his *Commentary on the Ephesians*, and ridiculed the idea of perjury in a dream. St. Jerome must have felt that the influence of the *Apology to Anastasius* was considerable, since he devoted a good part of the second book of his *Apology* in discussing it. He then defended his translation of the Old Testament, showing that he had done nothing condemnatory of the Septuagint translators, whose version he had translated into Latin and used in familiar expositions.

Rufinus received the two books of St. Jerome's *Apology* through the good graces of a merchant from the East who had stopped at Aquileia for several days' trade. He allowed Rufinus

---

22 When St. Jerome started to write his *Apologia* in answer to Rufinus, he had the following documents before him: (1) Rufinus' translation of the *Apologia* of Pamphilus for Origen, together with the preface prefixed to it; (2) Rufinus' treatise on the *Falsification of the Books of Origen;* (3) the translation of the *Periarchon* and Rufinus' two prefaces to it; (4) Rufinus' *Apologia ad Anastasium;* (5) the letter of Pope Anastasius to John of Jerusalem; and (6) the letters of Marcella and Pammachius regarding the *Apologia* of Rufinus.
23 Cf. Cayré, *op. cit.*, 575.

but two days for a reply.²⁴ Bishop Chromatius made attempts to bring peace between the two former friends, advising them to settle the matter through private correspondence. Rufinus was wise enough to heed the advice, and he sent a letter to St. Jerome, along with a copy of his own *Apology* which St. Jerome had answered without seeing it. In the letter, Rufinus warned St. Jerome to put an end to his attacks; otherwise, he threatened to expose some of the former deeds which St. Jerome had confided to him, or, at least, to bring him before the court on a charge of defamation and calumny. This letter of Rufinus must have been very strong and menacing in tone, judging from the few references that St. Jerome quoted from it in his *Apology*.²⁵ St. Jerome disregarded the advice of Bishop Chromatius and came back with the third book of his *Apologia* in the year 402, entitled *Liber tertius vel ultima responsio adversus scripta Rufini*.²⁶ In this book, St. Jerome took up the old charges of perjury, of lying, of heresy, and of falsification. The tone was extremely bitter and vitriolic, filled with insinuations and charges of the most violent nature. 'Never was his talent as a controversialist employed with such animation and eloquence as in this work.'²⁷

As far as Rufinus was concerned, this reply of St. Jerome closed the controversy. St. Jerome, on the other hand, did not relent, and continued to attack Rufinus on various occasions, even after his death.²⁸ St. Augustine himself tried to make peace between them, but his advice went unheeded.²⁹

---

24 Cf. St. Jerome, *Liber tertius vel ultima responsio adversus scripta Rufini* 3.10. St. Jerome indicates that this information was supplied him by Rufinus in a private letter in which he answered his *Apologia*.
25 This letter of Rufinus has not survived. We learn of its contents from St. Jerome who quotes it in his *Apologia*. Cf. Cavallera, *op. cit.*, 280, n. 3, for an attempt to reconstruct this letter.
26 St. Jerome, *Liber tertius vel ultima responsio adversus scripta Rufini* PL 23.457-492.
27 Cayré, *op. cit.*, 576.
28 Cf. St. Jerome, *Epistola* 125.18, *ad Rusticum*, where he refers to Rufinus as the 'grunter' and describes his method of instruction.
29 Cf. St. Augustine, *Epistola* 73.6-10.

It is, certainly, the friends of St. Jerome who organized campaigns in Italy and Rome against Rufinus and Origen, rather than either Rufinus or St. Jerome, who must bear in great measure the responsibility of this miserable controversy which lasted twelve years and astounded the faithful and sickened many of the saints.[30]

SELECT BIBLIOGRAPHY

Text and Translation:

    Fremantle, W. H. 'Jerome's Apology for Himself against the Books of Rufinus,' in *A Select Library of Nicene and Post-Nicene Fathers of the Christian Church*, second series, vol. 3 (New York 1906) 482-541.

    Migne, J. P. *Patrologiae Latinae cursus completus* (Paris 1846) 23.397-492.

Secondary Writings:

    Bardenhewer, O. *Patrology* (translated from the second edition by Thomas J. Shahan; St. Louis 1908).

    Cavallera, Ferd. *Saint Jerome, sa vie et son oeuvre* 1 (Louvain-Paris 1922).

    Cayré, F. *Manual of Patrology and History of Theology* 1 (translated by H. Howitt; Belgium 1935).

    Muller, Liguori G., O.F.M. *The De Haeresibus of Saint Augustine* (Washington, 1956).

    Murphy, Francis X., C.SS.R. *Rufinus of Aquileia, His Life and Works* (Washington 1945).

    Tixeront, J. *History of Dogmas* 2 (translated from the fifth French edition by H. L. B.; St. Louis 1923).

---

30 Cf. Cayré, *op. cit.*, 576.

THE APOLOGY AGAINST THE BOOKS OF RUFINUS

Book One

HAVE LEARNED both from your letters[1] and from those of many others that objections are being raised in the school of Tyrannius,[2] 'by the tongue of my dogs from the enemies by himself,'[3] against my translation of the books of the *Periarchon* into Latin. What singular impudence! They accuse the physician because he has exposed the poison, so that they, to be sure, might protect their own dispenser in drugs, not because of the merit of his innocence, but rather because of their complicity in his crime: as if the mere numbers of sinners would minimize the blame, and the accusation were concerned with personalities and not with facts. Books are being written against me; they are passed out to everyone for reading; and yet they are not published, so that as a result the hearts of the simple people are disturbed and I am deprived of the opportunity of replying in my own behalf. This is, indeed, a novel kind of malice, to bring charges that you are afraid to make public; to write stories that you intend to keep secret. If the things that he is writing are true, why was he afraid to publish them? If they are false, why did he write them? Long ago as boys we read: 'I deem it intemperance to

---

1 St. Jerome had before him the letters of Marcella and Pammachius when he started to write his *Apologia* which he dedicated to them.
2 The cognomen of Rufinus was Tyrannius, taken from the name of his fatherland, which in ancient times was called Tyranius or Toranius. Some have felt that this was an obvious pun on Rufinus' cognomen, and was deliberately introduced in view of Acts 19.9, where St. Paul is spoken of as holding 'daily discussions in the school of one Tyrannius.'
3 Cf. Ps. 67.24.

write anything that you intend to keep secret.'[4] I ask: What is the cause of their grievance? Why are they burning with hatred? Why are they so raving mad? Is it because I have refuted false praises? Is it because I have refused to be praised by deceitful lips? Is it because I have detected the wiles of an enemy, parading under the name of a friend? In the preface,[5] I am referred to as brother and colleague, and my crimes are very openly exposed for having myself written works in which I praised and extolled Origen to the skies. He says it was with good intentions that he did this. Why is it that now, as my enemy, he objects to the very same things that he praised then as my friend? He intended to use me as his model, as it were, in his own translation and gain approval for his own work from our own little treatises. To have mentioned but once the fact that I had written would have been sufficient. Why did he have to repeat the remark over and over, and mention it repeatedly, and quote the very words themselves, as if no one would believe him and his praises? Praise that is pure and simple is not so highly concerned about its acceptance on the part of the listeners. Why was he afraid that the people would not believe his praises in my behalf without the testimony of my very own words? You see, we are very well acquainted with his cleverness and we, too, have often sported in school in these tricks of deceitful praises. The man in whom there is detected artful malice cannot plead simplicity as an excuse. To have erred once, or, at most, twice, might be considered accidental. But why does he err so cleverly and so often, and weave this error into every remark in such a way that I find it impossible to deny what he praises? It would have been the mark of a prudent man and of a friend, after the reconciliation of differences, to have avoided even the slightest indications of suspicions lest it appear that he had done with deliberation what he had done through accident. Whence, also, Cicero says in commenting on his reasons for

---

4 Cicero, *Academica* 1.
5 Rufinus, *Prologus in libros Periarchon Origenis presbyteri* PG 11.111.

defending Gabinius: 'I have always been of the opinion that all friendships must be guarded very religiously and very faithfully, and in particular those friendships that have been restored to good standing after a falling out. For any failure to do one's duty, while friendship is intact, is excused on the grounds of imprudence, or (to use a stronger term) of negligence. But anything offensive committed after friendship has been conciliated is no longer reckoned as negligence, but rather as a violation, nor is it ordinarily imputed to impudence, but rather to perfidy.' Flaccus Horace, also, says in his letter addressed to Florus: 'Friendship that is badly conciliated brings people together to no avail and breaks up.'[6]

(2) *Hilary, the translator of Origen, and Ambrose, and Victorinus. The three books of Rufinus.*

What does it profit me now that he swears on oath that he made a mistake innocently? You see, I am being taunted with his praises, and the compliments of a very innocent friend, that are neither pure nor innocent, are a source of reproach to me. If it was approval that he was seeking for his work, by trying to point out the authors that he was imitating, he had at hand Hilary, the Confessor, who translated almost 40,000 verses of Origen on Job and the Psalms. He had at hand Ambrose, whose books are practically all filled with his words; and Victorinus, the martyr, who proves his innocence by the fact that he lays snares for nobody. He makes no mention of any of these authors; and passing over individuals who are pillars, so to speak, of the Church, he pursues me, who am but a flea and an insignificant nobody, through alleys and streets. Unless perchance, he swears on oath, with that same innocence with which he unwittingly brought charges against his friend, that he had no knowledge of these men. And who would believe it possible for a man who is so learned and who has so much knowledge of the ancient authors, especially the Greeks, that he has practically forgotten his native writers, while pursuing

---

6 Horace, *Epistles* 1.3.32.

the foreigners, to be ignorant of the writers of very recent times and the Latins? From all this, it is apparent that it is not so important that I was praised by him as it is that those men were not accused by him; so that, whether his praises are genuine praises (as he tries to convince the foolish), or accusations (as I know they are, judging from the pain that I suffer from the wound), I enjoy neither the glory in the praising of equals nor comfort in the censuring of equals.

(3) I have your letter in which you write that I have been accused, and in which you urge me to reply to my accuser, lest it be assumed, if I hold my tongue, that I acknowledge the charge. I have replied, to be sure, to this letter; and, although I was hurt, I respected the rights of friendship in such a way that I defended myself without making charges against my accuser; and stated that the charge that one of my friends had brought against me at Rome had been uttered by many of my enemies throughout the whole world, so that it would not appear that I was replying to an individual, but rather to the charges. It would be a different case if I were obliged to hold my peace, even though accused, out of respect for the rights of friendship, and, while having my face besmirched and, if I may so describe it, spattered with the foul filth of heresy, not even to wash it with the water of honesty, lest it be thought that he had done me harm. But such a behavior is neither befitting a man nor expected from any man, to attack a friend openly and expose his crimes under the guise of praises; and not even to allow him the freedom to prove that he is Catholic, and to reply that his praising of a heretic, with which he is being taunted, arose, not from any agreement with his heresy, but rather from an admiration of his genius. He had decided, or as he himself would want it to appear, he was compelled to translate into Latin what he did not want to. Why was it necessary for him to get me involved in the whole controversy who was living in seclusion and separated from him by so many oceans and distant lands, and expose me to the envy of many individuals, with the

result that he did more harm to me by his praises than good to himself by following me as his example? Now, too, because I have refuted my praises and, doing an about face, I have shown that I was not the person that my good friend said I was in his praises, they say that he is raving mad and has composed three books[7] against me with all of the charm of the Attic style, condemning the very same things that he had praised before, and taunting me with nefarious doctrines in my translation of Origen; although he had said of me in the preface in which he praised me: 'I shall observe the methods and rules of my predecessors, and in particular of that distinguished man, whom I have mentioned above, who, after translating into Latin more than seventy of the treatises of Origen, which he called homilies, and also a considerable number of his commentaries written on the apostle, in which a goodly number of stumbling blocks is found in the Greek, so smoothed and corrected them all in his translation that the reader will find nothing in them contrary to our faith. We are, therefore, following his example to the best of our ability, if not with the power of his eloquence, yet, at least, with the rules and methods.'[8]

(4) *The Roman faith is the faith of the Catholics.*
These are certainly his own words, he cannot deny them. The very elegance itself of the style and the artful arrangement of words and, what is more important than these considerations, the Christian simplicity reveal the character of their author. It would be another matter if Eusebius had distorted these works and he, who is the accuser of Origen and a disciple of mine, had testified that in the one and the same work he and I held either the wrong or the right views. But he, who is now my enemy, cannot call me a heretic, whom he declared a short while ago not to be at variance with his own faith. And at the same time, I also ask him to explain the

---
7 The three books referred to here are the two books of the *Apologia* of Rufinus and his *Apologia ad Anastasium.*
8 Rufinus, *Prologus in libros Periarchon Origenis presbyteri* PG 11.112.

meaning of his cautious and ambiguous remark: 'The reader will find nothing in them contrary to our faith.' What does he mean by 'our faith'? Is it the faith that distinguishes the Roman Church? Or is it the faith that is contained in the works of Origen? If he replies that it is the Roman faith, then we, who have translated none of the errors of Origen, are Catholic. But if he replies it is the blasphemies of Origen, then he means his faith; and, while imputing to me the charge of inconstancy, he proves that he is a heretic. If my praiser is correct in his belief, by this very confession of his, he accepts me as an associate; if he is wrong, he proves that the only reason why he praised me before was that he assumed that I was party to his error. But I shall endeavor to answer those books that are whispering in out-of-the way places and attacking me with deceitful charges when they have been published and have left their dark hiding places and come out into the open and they get into our hands, either through the efforts of my brothers, or the rashness of my rivals. Books, to be sure, which their own author was afraid to publish, and which he decreed were to be read only by his associates, should not present too much of a problem. At that time, I shall either acknowledge the charges, or refute them, or cast back at the accuser the charges with which I have been taunted; and I shall prove that the reason for my silence up to now was modesty, not a guilty conscience.

(5) *The author defends himself.*

I wanted, in the meantime, to clear myself in the silent judgment of the reader, and to refute this very serious charge in the eyes of my friends, lest it appear that I, who did not hurl any charges at all against my persecutor, even though I had been wounded, but tended strictly to my own wounds, had struck the first blow. I beseech the reader not to prejudge any personalities, but to impute the blame to him who was responsible for the maligning. It was not enough for him to have wounded me; but he composed by the light of the lamp three elaborate books against me, whom he considered to be some speechless individual who would keep perpetual silence, and has constructed from my volumes a sort of Marcion's *Antitheses*.⁹ Our soul yearns to know immediately his doctrine and our unlooked for folly. Perhaps he has learned something within a short period of time that he should impart to us; and a sudden burst of eloquence will reveal information that no one ever thought he had. 'Thus may that Father make him a god: thus may great Jesus. Let him begin the fight.'¹⁰ Though he brandish the shafts of his charges and hurl them at us with all his might, we trust in the Lord Savior, for His truth shall protect us with its shield, and we shall be able to sing with the Psalmist: 'The arrows of children are their wounds.'¹¹ And: 'If armies in camp stand against me, my heart shall not fear: if a battle should rise up against me, in this will I be confident.'¹² But we shall discuss this matter at another time. But, for the present, let us return to the point where we started.

(6) *Why he translated Origen's Periarchon. Didymus, the defender of Origen.*

His followers, 'wearied with their lot, take out the corn of Ceres,'¹³ and taunt me with my Latin translation of the books of Origen's *Periarchon*, which are harmful and contrary to the faith of the Church. My reply to them is brief and succinct: Your letter, brother Pammachius, and those of your friends

---

9 Marcion, a Gnostic of the second century, excogitated a doctrinal system based upon the irreconcilability of justice and grace, the Law and the Gospel, and Judaism and Christianity. He gave his disciples a new sacred scriptures. To justify his recension of the Bible, he composed a work known as *Antitheses*, in which he arranged in parallel columns sentences of the Old and New Testament, and from their pretended antilogies concluded that the two component parts of the Bible of the Church were irreconcilable. Cf. O. Bardenhewer, *Patrology* (translated from the second edition by Thomas J. Shahan; St. Louis 1908) 79-80.
10 This verse is altered from Vergil, *Aeneid* 10.875. In Vergil it reads as follows: 'Thus may that Father make him a god: thus may great Apollo. Let him begin the fight.'
11 Ps. 63.8.
12 Ps. 26.3.
13 Vergil, *Aeneid* 1.177-178.

have forced me to do it, in which you declared that someone else had put out a fraudulent translation of these books and that many things had been interpolated and many things had been either added or changed. And, lest I put little trust in your letters, you sent me samples of that same translation, together with the preface in which I was praised. Upon reading and comparing them with the Greek, I noticed immediately that the impious views expressed by Origen about the Father, the Son, and the Holy Spirit, and others that could not be tolerated by the Roman ears, had been changed by the translator and a more gentle construction put on them. But as far as the other doctrines are concerned, the fall of the angels, the casting down of the souls, his illusions of the resurrection, the world or the spaces between the worlds of Epicurus,[14] the restoration of all things to a state of equality, and other doctrines much worse than these, which it would take too long to enumerate, I noticed that he translated them exactly as he found them in the Greek, or quoted them in an exaggerated and more forceful form taken from the commentaries of Didymus,[15] a very open defender of Origen; so that anyone who had read his Catholic view on the Trinity might not be on his guard against his heretical views on other matters.

(7) Someone else, perhaps, who was not his intimate friend, might say: 'Either change completely what is evil, or publish completely what you believe is good. If you delete everything that is harmful, for the benefit of the innocent people, and you do not wish to translate into a foreign language things which, you allege, have been added by heretics, tell them what is harmful. But if you observe fidelity to truth in your translation, why do you change some things and keep others in-

---

14 The spaces between the worlds, in which, according to Epicurus, the gods reside.
15 Didymus, the Blind, wrote many dogmatic and apologetical works. Among these is a work devoted to the exposition and defense of Origen's *Periarchon*. His most important work is his treatise *On the Trinity* in three books in which he was undoubtedly orthodox in his views. Only fragments remain of his commentaries.

tact? And yet you have openly confessed in that same preface that you have amended what was distorted and have allowed to stand what was best. Consequently, you will be held responsible for anything that is proven heretical in the things that you have translated, not according to the freedom of a translator, but rather according to the authority of an author. And you will be accused of a manifest crime, that your sole purpose in wanting to smear the edge of the cup of poison with honey was to conceal with this deceptive sweetness a very deadly venom.' These are the remarks that an enemy might make, and others much harsher. And he might drag you before the ecclesiastical court, not as the translator of an evil work, but as its defender. But since I was content with my own defense, I translated in the books of the *Periarchon* simply what was contained in the Greek, not that the reader might believe what I had translated, but that he might not believe what you had previously translated. The usefulness of my translation was twofold: It brought to light a heretical author, and proved that the translator was not truthful. And, lest it be assumed by anybody that I was in agreement with the views that I had translated, I defended the need for my translation with a preface,[16] and pointed out to the reader the things that he was not to believe. The first translation contains praise for the author; the second, reproof. The former urges the reader to believe; the latter induces him not to believe. In the one, it is even assumed against my will that I am his praiser; in the other, I am so far from being the praiser of the man whom I am translating that I am forced to accuse the praiser himself. The task that was undertaken was the same, but the purpose was not the same. In fact, the one and the same path led to entirely different ends. He removed things that were not there, claiming that they had been discussed by the same author in other places. But unless he can reveal the very places from whence he says that he transferred

---

16 Only a few fragments remain of St. Jerome's translation of the *Periarchon* of Origen.

them, he will not be able to prove his assertion. It was my desire to change nothing from the truth. For my sole purpose in translating was to expose the evils that I had translated. Do you classify me as a translator? I was an exposer; I exposed a heretic in order to defend the Church against the charge of heresy. The treatise prefaced to this work tells clearly why I had earlier praised Origen in certain matters. For the present, I am simply explaining the reason for my translation. And since it was undertaken in the name of piety, I must not be charged with impiety for exposing as impious a thing that was handed down to the churches as something pious.

(8) *Eusebius, the standard bearer of the Arian faction.*

I had translated into Latin seventy of Origen's books, as my good friend charges, and many of his commentaries.[17] My work has never been questioned; it has never thrown Rome into a turmoil. Why was it necessary for you to make available to Roman ears a work that is repugnant even to Greece, and is condemned by the whole world? Although I translated so many volumes for so many years, I have never become a source of scandal to anyone. But you, who before now were unknown, have become famed for your impudence in your very first and only work. The preface itself informs us that you also translated the book of Pamphilus, the martyr, in defense of Origen. You are doing your utmost to prevent the Church from condemning a man whose faith is confirmed by a martyr. Eusebius, the bishop of Caesarea, the erstwhile standard bearer of the Arian faction, wrote in defense of Origen (as I have already mentioned above) a very copious and elaborate work in six books.[18] And he adduced many testimonies to prove that, according to his standard, Origen was

---

17 Cf. above, Introduction, p. 48, n. 4.
18 Eusebius, the student, became a very close friend of Pamphilus, his teacher, the head of the School of Caesarea. During the persecution of Diocletian-Galerius, Pamphilus was imprisoned. While in prison, he wrote, with the help of his friend, Eusebius, an *Apology* for Origen in five books, to which, after the martyr's death, Eusebius added a sixth. Only the first of the six books has been preserved, and that in the version of Rufinus. St. Jerome claimed that Eusebius, the Arian, was

Catholic, that is to say, an Arian, according to our standard. You translated the first of these books under the name of the martyr. And do I wonder if you insist that I, an insignificant and unimportant individual, am the praiser of Origen, when you insult a martyr? Changing a few of the testimonies regarding the Son of God and the Holy Spirit, which you knew would displease the Romans, you allowed the rest of them to stand down to the very end. You followed the same procedure in regard to the *Apologia*, falsely ascribed to Pamphilus, that you did in the translation of Origen's *Periarchon*. If this is Pamphilus' book, which one of the six books of Eusebius will be his first book? In the very volume that you falsely claim to be the work of Pamphilus, mention is made of succeeding books. In the second book, as well as in the others, Eusebius says that he had already mentioned the same things in book one and that there was no need to repeat them. If the whole work is the production of Pamphilus, why do you not translate the rest of the books? If it is the production of someone else, why do you change the name? You are silent; the facts speak for themselves. The answer, to be sure, is that those who would find the chief of the Arians detestable would believe a martyr.

(9) *Pamphilus, the martyr, wrote nothing at all.*

What shall I say, my very dear friend, was your motive? That you could assign the name of a martyr to the book of a heretic, and could convert the ignorant into defenders of Origen by using the authority of a witness of Christ? In view of your great learning which wins for you renown and such great praise as an outstanding Suggrapheus in the East that all of the members of your faction hail you as their Coryphaeus, I cannot imagine that you were ignorant of the Suntagma[19] of Eusebius and that you did not know that Pamphilus composed no works at all. For Eusebius himself, who was an ad-

---
the true author of the work, although years before he had already rightfully assigned the books to Pamphilus.
19 No work of Eusebius appears to have had such a title.

mirer and a praiser and a friend of Pamphilus, composed three very eloquent books containing the life of Pamphilus. In the third book of this volume, after praising highly his other virtues and extolling to the skies his humility, he also added the following remark: 'Who among the learned was not a friend of Pamphilus? If he saw anyone who lacked the necessities of life he gave generously according to his ability. He was also ever ready to distribute copies of Sacred Scriptures not only for reading, but even for private keeping. Not only to men, but even to the women whom he found to be interested in reading them. Thus he prepared many copies, so that he might present them as gifts, when the occasion arose, to those who wanted them. And he himself composed no work at all of his own, with the exception of letters that he chanced to write to his friends. He so humbled himself because of his humility. But he read the treatises of the ancient writers very diligently, and spent his time in constant meditation upon them.'[20]

(10) *Theophilus and Anastasius declared Origen a heretic.*

A defender of Origen and an admirer of Pamphilus states that Pamphilus wrote nothing at all, and published no work of his own. And he makes this statement at a time when Pamphilus had already won the crown of martyrdom, lest you use the excuse that Pamphilus composed this work after Eusebius had published his books. What will you do? The consciences of very many people have been wounded by the book that you published under the name of the martyr. As far as they are concerned, the authority of the bishops concerning the condemnation of Origen is of little avail, who, in their opinion, was praised by the martyr. What good will the letters of Bishop Theophilus[21] do, what good will the letters of

---

20 The biography of Pamphilus in three books, written by his disciple and friend, Eusebius, has perished. Only references to it and some quotations, such as the one given here by St. Jerome, are known.
21 Marcella, one of St. Jerome's close friends, had approached Pope Anastasius, pointing out to him the Origenistic propaganda of Rufinus'

Anastasius do, which pursue the heretic throughout the world, when your book, published under the name of Pamphilus, contradicts their letters, and the testimony of a martyr is opposed to the name of a bishop? Follow the same procedure also in regard to this falsely ascribed book that you followed in the case of the books of the *Periarchon*. Heed the advice of a friend; do not feel sorry for your composition; either say that it is not your production, or that it was distorted by the priest, Eusebius.[22] How will they be able to prove that the translation is yours? Your style is not exposed. Your eloquence is not so outstanding that no one can imitate you. Or, if the case comes to the proof, and the testimonies of many witnesses effect a condemnation of your impudence, you should certainly sing your palinode in the manner of Stesichorus.[23] It is better that you repent of your deed than that the martyr remain under false accusation, and that those who have been deceived continue in error. Nor should you be ashamed of a change of view. Your prestige and fame are not so outstanding that you should feel ashamed of having committed an error. Imitate me, whom you love so much, without whom you can neither live nor die; and openly proclaim with me the very things that I myself, who was praised by you, said in my own defense.

Latin translation of the *Periarchon* of Origen. The false impression thus given the Pontiff was strengthened by a letter which Anastasius received from Theophilus of Alexandria at this time. In the early part of the year 400, a council was held at Alexandria, in which Origenism was categorically condemned. Theophilus, then, sent a letter detailing these proceedings to the Pope. The latter issued a condemnation of the propositions contained in Theophilus' document, and communicated his decisions to Simplician, bishop of Milan, inviting him and his colleagues in upper Italy to associate themselves with the Pope in disavowing Origenism. Cf. Francis X. Murphy, C.SS.R., *Rufinus of Aquileia, His Life and Works* (Washington 1945) 127-129.

22 Eusebius of Cremona was accused by Rufinus of stealing and publishing the rough draft of his translation of the *Periarchon*.

23 The expression, 'sing a palinode,' is a pedantic allusion to the story of Stesichorus, who, having written a poem in condemnation of Helen, was struck blind, until he was allowed to recover his eyesight after he had written a complete recantation of his former calumnies.

(11) *Eusebius taunted the martyr, Methodius. The translation of the works of Eusebius by Jerome.*

Eusebius, the bishop of Caesarea, whom I mentioned a moment ago, taunts Bishop Methodius[24] in the sixth book of his *Apologia for Origen* with the very same charge with which you taunt me in connection with your praising of me, and says: 'How did Methodius, who said this and that about the doctrines of Origen, now have the audacity to write against Origen?' This is not the proper occasion to speak in defense of the martyr, for one should not discuss every topic on every occasion. For the present, it should suffice to call attention to the fact that the Arian taunts a very outstanding and eloquent martyr with the very same thing that you praise in me, when a friend, and condemn, when offended. You have an opportunity at the present moment, if you wish, to heap calumny upon my head for also disparaging Eusebius at the present time whom I praised before. The name of Eusebius is different, to be sure; but the calumny that is associated with the name of Origen is the one and the same. I praised Eusebius for his *Ecclesiastical History*, his *Chronicle*, his *Topography of the Holy Land;* and I translated these same works[25] into Latin and made them accessible to men of my tongue. And am I an Arian simply because Eusebius, who composed these books, is an Arian? If you are bold enough to call me a heretic, remember the preface to the *Periarchon*, in which you declared that I was of your faith. At the same time, I ask you to listen patiently to your former friend as he remonstrates with you. You quarrel with others; you either give or receive insult. Those whom you accuse and by whom you are accused are of your order. Whether rightly or wrongly is something for you to decide. I myself frown upon bringing charges against a brother, even when they are true, nor do I reprehend others,

---

24 St. Methodius, bishop of Olympus, had taken a firm stand against Origenist allegorism.
25 St. Jerome did not translate into Latin the *Ecclesiastical History* of Eusebius, but only the *Canon of the Times*, which is the second part of the *Chronicle* or *Universal History* of Eusebius.

but I tell them what I myself would not do. What sin have I committed against you, separated as I am from you by so many distant seas and lands? What wrong have I done? Did I wrong you because I said that I was not an Origenist? Is my defense your condemnation? If you are not an Origenist, or never have been an Origenist, I believe your solemn affirmation by oath. If you were an Origenist, I welcome back a penitent. Why do you complain if I am what you say you are? Is it because I dared to translate the books of the *Periarchon* after you, and my translation is considered as a reproof to your work? What could I do? Your laudation, that is to say, my condemnation, was sent to me. You praised me so strongly and so lavishly that, if I had acquiesced in your praises, everyone would have considered me a heretic. Mark what the closing line of the letter sent to me from Rome says: 'Allay the suspicions of the people and refute your accuser, lest it appear that you concur if you take no notice of it.'[26] Listen to what I wrote after I was put under such an obligation and I decided to translate those same books: 'My friends have placed me in such a predicament (I did not say "my friend," lest it appear that I was accusing you), that if I hold my peace, I shall be judged guilty of the charges; if I reply, I shall be judged an enemy. Both conditions are hard, but I shall choose the one that is the easier to bear. Dissension can be repaired, but blasphemy deserves no pardon.'[27] Do you see that this grave burden was placed on my shoulders against my will and over my protests, and that I steeled myself against the dissension that would ensue from such an undertaking by the plea of necessity? If you had translated the books of the *Periarchon* and had made no mention of my name, you would be justified in complaining that my purpose in bringing out my translation after yours was to reprehend you. But under the present circumstances, there is no justification to your complaint that

---

26 Cf. *Epistola Pammachii et Oceani* 83, *ad Hieronymum*, in the collection of St. Jerome's letters.
27 St. Jerome, *Epistola* 84.11, *ad Pammachium et Oceanum*.

I replied to you regarding a work for which I stand accused because of your praises. For what you call praise is interpreted by everyone as an accusation. Understand the nature of the charge you brought against me, and then you will not be offended by my reply. Granted, that you wrote with good intentions and that you, who are innocent and a very faithful friend, out of whose mouth no lie ever proceeded, wounded me unwittingly. What is that to me who was struck? Should I not attend to my wound, simply because you inflicted the wound with good intentions? I have been pierced and I lie prostrate; the wound throbs in my heart; my limbs which were pure and white before have been defiled with blood, and you say to me: 'Do not administer to your wound, lest it appear that I have wounded you.' And yet the translation itself is more of a condemnation of Origen than of you. For you amended what, in your opinion, had been added by heretics. I translated what all Greece proclaims was written by him. It is neither for you nor for me to decide which of us was the more correct in his views. Let the writings of both of us be subject to the critical review of the reader. The letter[28] in which I justified myself is directed solely against heretics and my accusers. How does it concern you, who are Catholic and my praiser, if I am very severe against heretics, as you say, and bring out into the open their schemings? Express joy over my invectives, lest it be assumed that you are a heretic if you feel hurt. When anything is written against faults, anonymously, he who becomes angry becomes his own accuser. It would have been the part of a prudent man, even if he felt hurt, to have concealed his feelings, and to have dispelled the gloom of heart by an appearance of serenity.

---

28 Together with his translation of the *Periarchon* of Origen, St. Jerome sent two letters to his friends, the one destined for Rufinus, the other addressed to Oceanus and Pammachius, but meant for a general audience. There was considerable difference between the tone and purpose of the two letters. St. Jerome's friends withheld the explanatory note to Rufinus, and publicized the other letter by itself. St. Jerome is here referring to this public letter.

(12) *The letter of Theophilus and Epiphanius and the Imperial rescripts against Origen.*
Besides, if you assume that anything that is said against Origen and his followers has been said against you, are the letters, then, of Theophilus,[29] and Epiphanius, and of the other bishops which I recently translated at their bidding, also directed against you and meant as an attack on you? Were the Imperial rescripts, which ordered the Origenists to be banished from Alexandria and Egypt, also dictated at my suggestion? Was it on my advice that the Pontiff of Rome detested them with an intense hate? Was it the work of my pen that the whole world, after the publication of your translation, burned with hate against Origen, whom they used to read previously without prejudice? If my influence is so powerful, I am surprised that you do not tremble before me. I, who kept within due bounds in my public letter[30] and was very careful not to have you think that I had said anything against you, immediately wrote you a brief letter,[31] expostulating over your praises. Since you were not at Rome, my friends refused to send it to you, because they said that you and your associates were making remarks about my conversion, unbecoming the name of Christian. I have attached a copy of this letter to this volume, so that you might see for yourself the great restraint that I exercised in controlling my profound grief, all in the name of necessity.

(13) *Jerome's Jewish instructor. Gregory of Nazianzen, Jerome's master. Huillus, the Jew. The anonymous Psalms.*
I hear, moreover, that you are criticizing certain parts of

---
29 Theophilus was embarked on a ruthless campaign against every semblance of Origenism in the East. He was ably assisted by Epiphanius. St. Jerome gave his approval to this activity, placing himself at the service of the cause, and acting as intermediary with the West, particularly, by translating a number of Theophilus' letters and synodal acts into Latin and sending them to Rome. These letters, which St. Jerome translated, are incorporated in his letters 90-94.
30 St. Jerome, *Epistola 84, ad Pammachium et Oceanum.*
31 St. Jerome, *Epistola 81, ad Rufinum.*

my letter after the manner of a philosopher, and, wrinkling your forehead and raising your eyebrows, you mock me in the manner of the witty Plautus, because I said that Barrabas the Jew[32] was my instructor. It is not surprising if you have written Barrabas instead of Baranina, where there is some similarity in the names, since you take so much liberty in changing names that you have made a Pamphilus out of an Eusebius, and a martyr out of a heretic. One must avoid such a man, and I, in particular, must be on my guard, lest in a moment's notice you refer to me as Sardanapalus instead of Jerome. Pay attention, then, O pillar of wisdom and the model of the severity of a Cato. I did not say that he was my master; but I wanted to verify my study of Sacred Scripture to prove that I had read Origen just as I had heard it also from the Jew. And I did not have to learn Hebrew from you. Have I done you wrong because I followed Apollinaris and Didymus[33] as my model instead of you? Could I not have mentioned in that letter Gregory,[34] a very eloquent man? Who among the Latins is his equal? I glory and exult in him as my master. But I quoted only those individuals who had come under censure to bear witness to the fact that I had read Origen in like manner, not for the truth of his faith, but rather for the excellence of his learning. Origen himself, and Clement and Eusebius, and a host of others, whenever they discuss things from Scripture and wish to prove what they say, usually write as follows: 'A Hebrew told me this'; and: 'I heard it from a Hebrew'; and: 'This is the view of the Hebrews.' Even Origen, to be sure, mentions the Patriarch Huillus, who was his contemporary, and he concludes the thirtieth commentary on

---

32 In order to perfect his knowledge of Hebrew, St. Jerome took lessons in Hebrew at Bethlehem from a Jew named Baranina. From time to time, he consulted other Jewish scholars. Cf. St. Jerome, *Epistola* 84.3, *ad Pammachium et Oceanum*.
33 Cf. St. Jerome, *Epistola* 84.3, *ad Pammachium et Oceanum*, for his comments on Apollinaris and Didymus as his teachers.
34 Attracted by the reputation of St. Gregory of Nazianzen, St. Jerome went to Constantinople in the year 379 and for two years took advantage of the teaching of this unrivaled master.

Isaia (where at the end he explains the following verse: 'Woe to thee, city of Ariel, which David took'[35]) with the commentary of Huillus, saying that his earlier view was quite different, and confessing that he was taught the more correct view by Huillus. He follows the opinion of Huillus and believes that the same Moses is, likewise, the author of the eighty-ninth Psalm, which is entitled 'A prayer of Moses the man of God,' as well as of the other eleven Psalms that have no titles. He does not deem it below his dignity to insert the views of the Hebrews on certain passages when translating Hebrew Scripture.

(14) *Origen is condemned.*

They say that upon reading recently the letters of Pope Theophilus, in which he exposed the errors of Origen, he stopped up his ears and condemned with a loud voice, in the presence of all, the author of so great an evil; and he said that up until that moment he had no idea that he had written such a nefarious work. I do not doubt it nor do I say what someone else, perhaps, might say, that it was impossible for him not to know what he himself translated and the *Apologia* for which, written by a heretic, he had published under the name of a martyr, for whom he himself had composed an *Apology* in a special volume of his own.[36] I say one thing to him that he cannot gainsay. If it is allowed, in his case, that he did not know what he translated, why should it not be allowed in my case that I did not know the books of the *Periarchon* which I had not read before; and that I had read only those homilies which I translated, which, according to his own testimony, contained nothing that was evil? But if contrary to his view, he now condemns me for things for which he had praised me before, he will be completely caught in an embarrassing situation. For he either praised me, if I were a heretic, because he shared the same views with me, or

---
35 Isa. 29.1.
36 Rufinus, *Epilogus in Apologeticum S. Pamphili martyris ad Macarium seu Liber de adulteratione librorum Origenis* PG 17.615-632.

he brings futile charges against me now, because of his enmity, whom he praised before as orthodox. But, perhaps, he kept quiet about my errors at that time because he was a friend, and he is now exposing to view what he had concealed before because he is angry with me.

(15) *He defends his Commentary on the Epistle to the Ephesians.*

Although inconstancy is not worthy of trust, and openly professed enmity raises suspicions of deceit, nevertheless, I shall make bold to come to grips with him in my desire to find out what I had written that was heretical, so that I may either do penance like him and affirm on oath that I was ignorant of the evils of Origen, and that it is now for the first time that I have learned of his impiety from Pope Theophilus; or that I may certainly prove that I was, to be sure, correct in my views, but that he, according to his usual wont, was slow to comprehend. For it is impossible that I should have said both what was good and what was evil in the same books to the Ephesians,[37] which I hear he is reprehending; and that both the sweet and the bitter should have proceeded from the same source in such a way that I, who condemned throughout the whole work those who believe that souls were created from angels, should suddenly have forgotten myself and defended what I had previously condemned. He cannot taunt me with stupidity, whom in his own works he praised as being very eloquent and learned. Besides, foolish verbosity must be considered as characteristic of one who is a prattler and a babbler rather than of one who is eloquent. I have no knowledge of the particular charges that he is making against my books, for it is only the rumor of his charges that has reached me and not his writings. And in the words of the apostle, it is foolish to beat the air with the fists. But, until I receive something

---

37 In the second book of his *Apologia*, Rufinus quotes passages from the *Commentary on the Ephesians* of St. Jerome, showing that at every turn St. Jerome either encourages others, or he himself advances opinions which he now calls up for condemnation. Hence, St. Jerome is still a follower of Origen at heart.

definite, I shall reply to what is indefinite. As an old man, I shall teach my rival the lesson that I learned as a boy, that there are many styles of compositions, and that not only do the ideas vary, but even the phraseology of Scripture, depending upon the nature of the subject matter.

(16) *The function of commentators. Donatus, the teacher of Jerome.*

Chrysippus and Antipater occupy themselves with the intricate and the thorny. Demosthenes and Aeschines thunder at each other in turn. Lysias and Isocrates flow along smoothly and sweetly. Each and every one of them is singularly different, yet each is perfect in his own style. Read the *Ad Herennium* of Cicero; read his *Rhetorica*. Or, since he declares that these works have left his hand in an unfinished and imperfect form, read the three volumes of his *De Oratore*, in which he introduces the most eloquent orators of his day, Crassus and Antonius, engaged in debate; and the fourth volume, the *Orator*, which he wrote, when already an old man, to Brutus. And you will come to know that History, Orations, Dialogues, Letters, Commentaries are composed in different styles. In my *Commentary to the Ephesians*, I followed as my models, to be sure, Origen and Didymus and Apollinaris (who hold doctrines that are certainly contradictory) in such a way that I did not lose sight of the truth of my faith. What is the function of commentators? They expound the statements of someone else; they express in simple language views that have been expressed in an obscure manner; they quote the opinions of many individuals and they say: 'Some interpret this passage in this sense, others, in another sense'; they attempt to support their own understanding and interpretation with these testimonies in this fashion, so that the prudent reader, after reading the different interpretations and studying which of these many views are to be accepted and which rejected, will judge for himself which is the more correct; and, like the expert banker, will reject the falsely minted coin. Will the person, who has quoted the interpretations of many individuals in a work that he is expounding, be held responsible for the different interpretations and contradictory views? I suppose that as a boy you read the commentaries of Asper on Vergil and Sallust, of Volcatius on the Orations of Cicero, of Victorinus on his Dialogues and on the Comedies of Terence, as well as those of Donatus, my teacher, on Vergil, and of others on other writers, such as Plautus, to be sure, Lucretius, Flaccus, Persius, and Lucan. Condemn their commentators for not adopting one interpretation, and for quoting either what they themselves or others believed on the same point.

(17) *The faults of Rufinus' language.*

I pass over the Greeks, whom you boast you know (although, while you were concerned with foreigners, you have practically forgotten your own native tongue), lest I appear to be 'teaching the expert,' as the old proverb goes, and 'carrying coals to New Castle.' But I am surprised that you, the Aristarchus[38] of our day, do not know matters that young boys know. And yet you, who are occupied with the matter of views and are quick to heap insults upon my head, have disregarded the precepts of the grammarians and rhetoricians, and you show little concern to close the figures of hyperbaton after the transportation of words, and to avoid the harsh combination of consonants, and to shun a hiatus. It would be ridiculous to single out a few wounds on a body that is completely distorted and mangled. I am not singling out any one detail for reprehension; let him single out one item that is flawless. He could not have known that famous saying of Socrates: 'I know that I do not know.' 'One ignorant of a ship is afraid to steer a ship; none dares to give a physic to the sick, unless he who hath studied it; doctors undertake what is the province of doctors; mechanics practice mechanical trades; we write poems everywhere, unlearned and learned.'[39] Unless, per-

---

[38] Aristarchus, the celebrated grammarian of Samothrace, flourished in the year 156 B.C. He was a pupil of Aristophanes, and founded at Alexandria a grammatical and critical school. Aristarchus was the greatest critic of antiquity.
[39] Horace, *Epistles* 2.1.114-117.

chance, he will swear on oath that he has not studied literature (and this we very readily believe in his case without an oath), or he will take refuge with the apostle who confesses: 'And even though I be rude in speech, yet I am not so in knowledge.'[40] Although the latter was versed in Hebrew letters, and took instructions at the feet of Gamaliel, whom he is not ashamed to call his master, when he had already attained the dignity of an apostle, nevertheless, he showed a contempt for Greek eloquence, or, at any rate, he kept it a secret, because of his humility, so that his preaching lay not in the persuasiveness of his words, but rather in the power of his signs. He who was rich in his own resources spurned those of others. And yet, Festus never would have made the remark before the tribunal to one who was ignorant and who stumbled in every sentence like you: 'Paul, thou art mad; and thy great learning is driving thee to madness.'[41] You who mumble in Latin, and creep along at a snail's pace rather than proceed in dignified fashion, should either write in Greek so that you might appear to people, ignorant of the Greek language, to be versed in a foreign tongue; or, if you attempt the Latin, you should first become a student of a grammarian, and you should withdraw your hand from the rod, and, as an old student, should study the art of speaking along with little children. A man may be a Croesus or a Darius, but learning does not attend a money bag. It is the companion of sweat and toil; it is the traveling companion of fasting, not of feasting, of continence, not of luxury. Demosthenes is said to have consumed more oil than wine, and that he excelled all artists by constantly studying at night. He took a dog in order to learn to pronounce the letter *rho;* you condemn me because I learned Hebrew from a man. This is the reason why some people remain illiterate literates, because they refuse to learn what they do not know. Nor do they heed the advice of Horace: 'Why do I in my perversity choose to be ignorant

---
40 2 Cor. 11.6.
41 Acts 26.24.

rather than to learn.'[42] Wisdom, which we read under the name of Solomon, also says: 'For wisdom will not enter into a malicious soul, nor dwell in a body subject to sins. For the holy spirit of discipline will flee from the deceitful, and will withdraw itself from thoughts that are without understanding.'[43] It would be quite a different matter if people were content with vulgar reading, and despised the tastes of the learned; and turned a deaf ear to that famous saying in which impudent ignorance is branded: 'Was it not your wont, O ignorant fellow, to undo the wretched song on the street corners with a screeching reed pipe?' As if the crowd of curly-haired boys[44] did not sing snatches of Milesian tales composed in the schools, and the *Testament and Last Will of the Pig* of the Bessi[45] did not split the sides of the people with loud laughter, and such nonsense were not the common fare at the banquets of buffoons. Every day in the public streets a sham diviner wacks the buttocks of fools, and with a twisted scorpion shatters the teeth of those who carp at him. And are we surprised if the books of the ill-informed find a reader?

(18) They are indignant because I wrote that the Origenists were banded together by the orgies of lies. I mentioned the book where I read this statement written down, that is to say, the sixth book of the *Stromata*[46] of Origen where he compares

---

42 Horace, *De arte poetica* 127-128.
43 Wisd. 1.4, 5.
44 Cf. Persius, *Satires* 1.29-30.
45 The Bessi, a people of Thrace dwelling in a district known as Bessica, were probably a troupe of traveling actors, who put on at Rome the *Testament and Last Will of a Little Pig*. This little satirical piece purports to be the will of a little pig who is about to be killed by the cook, and who formally bequeathes the parts of his body to his friends and relatives. St. Jerome states that it was repeated by boys at school exhibitions as an amusing bit of fun. Cf. St. Jerome, *Commentariorum in Isaiam prophetam liber* 12 PL 24.409-410.
46 At Alexandria about the year 230, Origen wrote his ten books of *Stromata* or *Miscellanies*, on the aim and content of which the few fragments throw no clear light. St. Jerome tells us that Origen imitated Clement of Alexandria who composed eight books of *Miscellanies;* and that Origen compared the opinions held respectively by Christians and by philosophers, and confirmed all the dogmas of our religion by quotations from Plato and Aristotle, and from Numenius and Cornutus. Cf. St. Jerome, *Epistola* 70.4, *ad Magnum*.

of his father by means of an artful lie. Thus it is clear that, unless we use a lie in such a way that we derive some great benefit for ourselves from it, we must be judged as enemies of Him who says: "I am the truth." '⁵¹ These are statements written by Origen, we cannot deny them. He wrote them in the books which he addressed to those who were perfect and who were his disciples. And he teaches that masters may employ the lie, but that the disciples must have nothing to do with it. Therefore, he proves that he who is an excellent liar, and who fabricates without any sense of shame against his brothers whatever comes into his mind, is the best master.

(19) *He defends his explanation of the second Psalm. The word kiss used for adoration among the Hebrews.*

They say that he also criticizes me for using in the commentaries to my translation of the second Psalm the phrase 'worship the son' in place of what we read in the Latin as 'learn discipline,' and what is written in the Hebrew volume as *Nescu Bar;* and again for apparently forgetting the earlier interpretation in my translation of the entire *Psalterium* into Latin,⁵² and for using the phrase 'worship purely,' a phrase which, as it is certainly apparent to everyone, is a contradiction. And we must, indeed, excuse an individual who even makes occasional slips in the Latin for being ignorant of the truth of the Hebrew language. *Nescu,* to translate it literally, means 'kiss,' that is to say, *deosculamini.* And because I did

---

51 John 14.6.
52 St. Jerome composed at an early date commentaries on all the Psalms, which were scholia supplementary to Origen's Psalm-scholia. At the request of Pope Damasus, he revised the translation of the Psalter according to the version of the Septuagint. This revised edition was known as the *Psalterium Romanum* and was henceforth used in the Roman liturgy. Later on, independently of this version, St. Jerome made another translation at the request of Paula and Eustochium. This was not an emendation, but a fresh translation of the Greek of the Septuagint into Latin. In this translation, he used obeli to show what was over and above that of the Septuagint and was not found in the Hebrew; and asterisks to mark what he had put in anew, in accordance with the Hebrew truth. St. Jerome made a third translation of the Psalms directly from the Hebrew into Latin word for word.

our doctrine with the views of Plato and speaks as follows: 'Plato says in the third book of the *Republic:* "We must surely prize truth most highly. For if we were right in what we were saying, that falsehood is in every deed unbecoming and useless to god, but to men useful at times as a remedy and as a form of medicine, it is obvious that such a license must be assigned to physicians and laymen should have nothing to do with it." "Obviously," he replies. "The rulers, then, of cities may, if anybody, fitly lie at times, either against enemies or for the benefit of the state and the citizens; others, who do not know the technique of lying, should have nothing to do with it." '[47] These are the words of Origen: 'And we, therefore, being mindful of the precept: "Speak truth each one with his neighbor,"[48] should not ask: Who is my neighbor? but rather we should consider well the cautiously worded remark of the philosopher: "Falsehood is in every deed unbecoming and useless to god, but to men useful on occasions," and realize that it is never to be assumed that God tells a lie on any occasion, even in the name of dispensation. But if the interest of the hearer demands it, He employs ambiguous words, and speaks His intentions through enigmas, so that He also preserves the dignity of truth, and He utters in a guarded and veiled manner a statement that otherwise might prove harmful if it were expressed publicly and openly. But a person who is obliged by necessity to lie must exercise extreme caution to use the lie as a remedy or as a form of medicine on occasions so as to preserve moderation in its use, lest he overstep its limits as Judith did against Holofernes, whom she overcame with her clever simulation of words.[49] He should imitate Esther who mitigated the decree of Artaxerxes by concealing the true identity of her race for a long while.[50] And in particular Jacob, the Patriarch, who, as we read, obtained the blessings

---

47 Plato, *Republic* 3.389B.
48 Eph. 4.25.
49 Cf. Judith 13.
50 Cf. Esth. 15.

not want to translate the word in a pedantic fashion, I chose rather to adapt its meaning and used the phrase 'worship.' Since people are wont to kiss their hand and bow their head in an act of veneration (an act that the blessed Job says he never performed before elements and idols, saying: 'If I beheld the sun when it shined, and the moon walking in brightness and my heart in secret hath rejoiced, and I have kissed my hand with my mouth, which is a very great iniquity, and a denial against the most high God') ;[53] and since the Hebrews in the idiom of their language use the phrase 'kiss' for 'adoration,' I translated it according to the meaning given it by the very people who coined the word. The word *Bar* has various meanings in their language. For it means son, as for example: Barjona, son of a dove, and Bartholomaeus, son of Tholomaeus, and Barthimaeus, and Barhiesu and Barrabas; it also means 'wheat' and 'a sheaf of corn' and 'elect' and 'pure.' Therefore, what sin did I commit if I translated an ambiguous word according to various interpretations, and I, who had used the phrase 'worship the son' in the commentaries where one is free to discuss, used the phrase 'worship purely' or 'electively' in the text itself, lest I appear to be forcing the translation and afford the Jews an opportunity of calumniating me? Both Aquila and Symmachus translated it that way. Therefore, what harm does it do the faith of the Church if the reader is shown the many ways in which a single phrase may be interpreted among the Hebrews?

(20) *The errors of Origen.*

Your Origen is allowed to discuss the transmigration of souls, to introduce countless worlds, to clothe rational creatures first with one body and then with another, and to say that Christ suffered many times, and will suffer many more times so that what once was beneficial will be taken to be always beneficial. Even you yourself assume so much authority that with a lie you create a martyr out of a heretic, and forgeries

---
53 Job 31.26-28.

of heretics out of the books of Origen. Shall I not be allowed to discuss words, and impart to the Latins in a volume of commentaries what I learned from the Hebrews? For were it not for the fact that it would take up too much time, and might be taken as boasting, I would without further ado show you how profitable it is to frequent the home of a master, and to learn art from artists; and you would realize the great mass of ambiguous names and words that exists among the Hebrews. It was this situation that provided the opportunity for a variety of interpretations; for each individual chooses what he thinks is the most plausible from a number of uncertain interpretations. But why refer you to foreign volumes? Read Aristotle and Alexander's[54] exposition of the volumes of Aristotle. And from your reading of their works, you will come to realize the presence of a great mass of ambiguous words; so that you will finally put an end to this reprehending of your friend regarding matters that you, to be sure, have never learned even in your dreams.

(21) *The Commentary on the Ephesians.*

But since my brother, Paulinian,[55] has told me that several sections of my *Commentary on the Ephesians* have been reprehended by him, some of which he has committed to memory, and showed me the very sections themselves, I must no longer dodge the issue. And I ask the reader to be indulgent, in the name of necessity, if I take up some time in proposing and refuting the charges. For I am not bringing charges against someone else, but am simply endeavoring to defend myself, and to refute the charge of heresy that has been leveled

---

54 Alexander of Aphrodisias in Caria flourished about the year 200 A.D. and is known as Expounder for his exposition of the commentaries of Aristotle.
55 St. Jerome was greatly disturbed by what he heard about Rufinus' *Apologia* against him. He tried to answer the work, even before he got his hands on it. His Roman partisans managed to get hold of enough of it to supply him with leading ideas for a reply. Besides, his brother, Paulinian, who had returned from Palestine about this time, had been able to commit to memory certain sections of the *Apologia* of Rufinus.

against me. Origen wrote three books on the Epistle of Paul to the Ephesians.⁵⁶ Both Didymus and Apollinaris composed special works of their own.⁵⁷ I shall append what I wrote in the preface of the same work regarding my method of either translating or imitating these men: 'I also inform you in the preface that you may know that Origen wrote three volumes on this Epistle whom we have even followed in part; and that Apollinaris and Didymus, as well, have published certain commentaries on it. We have selected passages from them, although only a few; and we have added or deleted several passages as we saw fit to do; so that the careful reader will recognize from the very beginning this work as being either mine or someone else's.'⁵⁸ Therefore, if I shall not be able to prove that any fault that can be pointed out in my commentary on this Epistle exists in those Greek volumes from which I said it was translated into Latin, I shall acknowledge the fault, and I shall be held responsible for anything which will not be imputed to someone else. Nevertheless, lest it appear that I am again raising captious objections, and am using this artifice as an excuse, and I do not have the courage to stand up to him, I shall quote the very testimonies which are involved in the charge.

(22) *The duty of the commentator. The time of the composition of the Commentary on the Epistle to the Ephesians.*

At the very beginning of the volume, in my interpretation of the testimony of Paul, in which he says: 'Even as he chose us in him before the foundation of the world, that we should be holy and without blemish in his sight,'⁵⁹ I said that these words do not refer, as Origen holds, to the election of those

---

56 Only a few fragments remain from Origen's commentary on the Epistle of Paul to the Ephesians. A Latin fragment is preserved in St. Jerome's *Apologia adversus Rufinum* 1.28.
57 Didymus' immense exegetical work is almost entirely lost. Apollinaris was primarily an exegete and, according to St. Jerome, he wrote countless volumes on Scripture (*De viris illustribus* 104).
58 St. Jerome, *Prologus Commentarii in epistolam ad Ephesios* PL 26.442.
59 Eph. 1.4.

who have existed previously, but rather to the foreknowledge of God. Finally, I said: 'His statement, moreover, that we have been chosen before the foundation of the world, that we should be holy and without blemish in his sight, that is, in the sight of God, is a reference to the foreknowledge of God, for whom all things that shall take place have already taken place, and to whom all things are known before they come to pass. Just as Paul himself was also predestined in the womb of his mother and Jeremia was sanctified in the womb and chosen, and strengthened, and sent forth to the nations as a prophet, as a prefiguration of Christ.'[60] There is certainly no crime in this interpretation. While Origen holds the opposite view, we have adopted that of the Church. And, since it is the duty of the commentator to quote the views of many individuals, and I had promised to do so in the preface, I also presented the interpretation of Origen, without, in any way, casting aspersion on his name, and said: 'But another individual, who tries to prove that God is just on the grounds that He chooses each of the elect, not on the basis of the prejudgment of His knowledge, but rather on the merit alone of the elect, says that there existed, prior to the existence of visible creatures, of heaven, earth, seas, and everything that exists in them, other invisible creatures, and among them also souls which were cast down, for certain reasons known only to God, into this vale of tears, this place of our sojourning and affliction, wherein the saint was placed and prayed that he might return to his former abode, saying: "Woe is me, that my sojourning is prolonged! I have dwelled with the inhabitants of Cedar; my soul hath been long a sojourner."[61] And the apostle: "Unhappy man that I am! Who will deliver me from the body of this death?"[62] And: "Desiring to depart and to be with Christ, a lot by far the better."[63] And in

---

60 St. Jerome, *Commentarius in epistolam ad Ephesios* 1.1.4 (PL 26.446).
61 Ps. 119.5, 6.
62 Rom. 7.24.
63 Phil. 1.23.

another place: "Before I was humbled I offended,"[64] and other passages similar to these which would take too long to write down.'[65] Mark what I said: 'But another individual who tries to prove that God is just.' 'He tries to prove,' I said, not, 'he proved.' But if you are scandalized because I described in brief manner Origen's very lengthy discourse, and made known to the reader his view; and if you assume that I am a secret follower of his because I left out nothing that was stated by him, I am afraid that I did it only to avoid your accusations, lest you say that I kept silent about the things that were spoken by him in convincing fashion, and that his arguments are more cogent in the Greek. Therefore, I quoted everything, although in a rather brief fashion, that I found in the Greek, so that his disciples would have nothing new to din into the ears of the Latins. For it is easier for us to condemn things that are known to us than things that are suddenly thrust upon us. But listen to what I said at the end of the chapter, after presenting his interpretation: 'For the apostle did not say: "He chose us before the foundation of the world, since we were holy and without blemish," but rather: "He chose us that we should be holy and without blemish," that is to say, that we who were not holy and without blemish before should subsequently be such. This can be said also of sinners who have changed for the better, and the following utterance will stand good: "In thy sight no man living shall be justified,"[66] that is to say, during the whole course of his life, during the entire period that he has existed in this world. Such an interpretation also gainsays the individual who says that before the creation of the world souls were chosen because they were holy and free of every blemish of sins. For Paul and those like him were not chosen (as we just mentioned a moment ago) because they were holy and without blemish; rather, they were chosen and predestined that they

---
64 Ps. 118.67.
65 St. Jerome, *Comm. in ep. ad Eph.* 1.1.4 (PL 26.447).
66 Ps. 142.2.

might become holy and without blemish in their future life through their own efforts and virtues.'[67] And is anyone bold enough to accuse me of the heresy of Origen after expressing such a view? It is almost eighteen years since I dictated those books, at a time when the name of Origen was highly respected throughout the world, and when the Latin ears had not yet heard of his work, the *Periarchon*. And yet I proclaimed my own faith, and made clear the things which did not meet with my approval. Consequently, even if my enemy could have pointed out anything heretical in other matters, I would have been considered guilty not so much of the perverse doctrines, which I have often condemned in this and in other works, as of a careless mistake.

(23) *The faith of the Church.*

The second passage, which my brother showed me and which was reprehended by him, I shall quote briefly because it is very petty, and brings calumny clearly down upon his own head. After quoting various interpretations on the testimony, where Paul says: 'Setting him at his right hand in heaven above every name that is named, not only in this world, but also in that which is to come,'[68] I came to the duties of the ministers of God, and after speaking of Principalities and Powers, and Virtues, and Dominations, I also added the following remark: 'It is necessary that they have subjects who might fear them and serve them and who might be fortified by their strength. These distributions of duties will exist, not only in the present world, but in the world to come as well, so that anyone might be promoted or demoted through the various advancements and offices, through ascensions and descensions, and be subject first to one and then to another Power, Virtue, Principality, and Domination.'[69] And, after citing the example of an earthly king and giving a detailed description of his palace, which I used as an illustration of the various duties

---

67 St. Jerome, *Comm. in ep. ad Eph.* 1.1.4 (PL 26.448)
68 Eph. 1.20, 21.
69 St. Jerome, *Comm. in ep. ad Eph.* 1.1.20-21 (PL 26.461).

of the ministers of God, I added the following: 'And do we suppose that God, the Lord of Lords, and King of Kings is content with only a simple ministry of attendants?'[70] And just as only he who is chief of angels is called an archangel, so also only those are referred to as Principalities, and Powers, and Dominations who have some subjects, inferior to them in rank. But if he assumes that I am a follower of Origen simply because in my exposition I mentioned the phrases 'advancements and honors,' 'ascensions and descensions,' 'increasings and diminishings,' he should be made to know that there is a vast difference between saying that devils and men are created from angels and Seraphim and Cherubim, a view that is affirmed by Origen, and saying that the angels themselves have various duties allotted to themselves—a view that is not opposed to that of the Church. But even as among men there are various orders, distinguished by the work itself, since the bishop, priest, and every ecclesiastical order have their own rank, and they, nevertheless, all remain human beings; so also among angels there are different merits, and they all, nevertheless, retain their angelic dignity. Men are not created from angels, nor are men changed back again into angels.

(24) *He did not quote the name of the interpreters for reasons of modesty.*

The third passage is reprehended because I quoted a threefold interpretation for the words of the apostle: 'That he might show in the ages to come the overflowing riches of his grace in kindness towards us in Christ Jesus.'[71] The first was my own interpretation; the second, the opposite view of Origen; the third, the simple explanation of Apollinaris. If I failed to quote their names, excuse me in the name of modesty. It would not have been fitting for me to criticize those whom I was imitating in part, and whose views I was translating into Latin. 'But,' I said, 'the diligent reader will immediately ask

---
70 *Ibid.* (PL 26.462).
71 Eph. 2.7.

and say . . .'⁷² And, again, I said at the end: 'But another individual puts the following construction on his statement: "That he might show in the ages to come the overflowing riches of his grace." '⁷³ 'I see,' you will say, 'you have set forth the views of Origen in the person of a diligent reader.' I admit my mistake; I should not have said 'diligent,' but rather 'blasphemous.' Had I done so, and had I known that you would follow up such nonsense with some sort of dire prophecy, I might have even avoided the charges of calumny. It is a serious crime, if I said that Origen was a diligent reader, when I had translated seventy of his books,⁷⁴ and had extolled him to the skies with praises for which I was compelled to reply two years ago with a brief treatise⁷⁵ to those praises of yours against me. In those praises, you charge that I said that Origen was a master of the churches; and you feel that I should be greatly alarmed, if, as my enemy, you accuse me of having said that he was a diligent reader. We are wont to refer to miserly merchants, and frugal servants, and disagreeable pedagogues, and very clever thieves as diligent. And in the Gospel, the unjust steward is said to have acted prudently in some ways;⁷⁶ and: 'The children of this world are more prudent than the children of the light';⁷⁷ and: 'The serpent was more subtle than any of the beasts which the Lord had made on earth.'⁷⁸

(25) *The meaning of the phrase 'body of death.'*

The fourth passage that he reprehends is found in the be-

---

72 St. Jerome, *Comm. in ep. ad Eph.* 1.2.7 (PL 26.469).
73 *Ibid.* (PL 26.469).
74 St. Jerome translated nine homilies of Origen on Isaia, fourteen on Jeremia, fourteen on Ezechiel, two on the Canticle of Canticles, and thirty-nine on St. Luke.
75 Together with his literal translation of the *Periarchon* of Origen, St. Jerome sent two letters to his friends, one addressed to Rufinus, and the other addressed to Pammachius and Oceanus, which was an objective, justificatory piece for his stand on Origen. It is this latter letter, to which St. Jerome is here referring. Cf. St. Jerome, *Epistola 84, ad Pammachium et Oceanum.*
76 Cf. Luke 16.3.
77 Luke 16.3.
78 Gen. 3.1.

ginning of book two, where I quoted the following testimony of Paul: 'For this reason, I, Paul, the prisoner of Christ Jesus for the sake of you, the Gentiles.'[79] And, inasmuch as the passage is self-evident, I shall quote just that section of the exposition that is subject to the calumny: 'It can be concluded even from his martyrdom that Paul was a prisoner of Christ Jesus for the sake of the Gentiles; for while he was imprisoned at Rome, he sent this letter at the time that he wrote letters, as we have shown in another place, to Philemon, to the Colossians, and to the Philippians. Or, to be sure, since we have read in very many places that this body of ours is called the prison of the soul, where it is detained, so to speak, in an enclosed cell, we say, therefore, that Paul is bound by the chains of his body, and does not return and reside with Christ, so that through him may be fulfilled the perfect preaching to the Gentiles; although some introduce another meaning for this passage, that Paul, who was predestined and sanctified in his mother's womb for the preaching to the Gentiles before he was born, received subsequently the chains of the flesh.'[80] And I quoted three interpretations of this passage, as I did above: in the first, my own view; in the second, the assertions of Origen; and in the third, the views of Apollinaris who opposed the doctrine of the latter. Read the Greek commentaries. And unless you find it so, I shall acknowledge the charge brought against me. What sin am I guilty of in this passage? Is it, perhaps, the sin to which I replied a moment ago, that I did not mention by name those by whom these statements were made? It would be superfluous in the case of each and every testimony of the apostle to quote the names of those whose works I had mentioned in the preface I was going to translate. And yet to call the soul a prisoner of the body until it returns to Christ, and, in the glory of the resurrection, exchanges this corrupt and mortal body for incorruption and immortality, is by no means an absurd interpretation. Whence,

---

79 Eph. 3.2.
80 St. Jerome, *Comm. in ep. ad Eph.* 2.3.2 (PL 26.477-478).

also, the apostle says: 'Unhappy man that I am! Who will deliver me from the body of this death?'[81] And he uses the term, 'the body of death,' because it is subject to vices and sickness, and disorders and death, until it rises in glory with Christ, and what was once fragile clay is purified in the fire of the Holy Spirit into a very solid rock, changing its glory, not its nature.

(26) The fifth passage is a very important one, where, in my exposition of the following testimony of the apostle: 'From him the whole body (being closely joined and knit together through every joint of the system according to the functioning in due measure of each single part) derives its increase to the building up of itself in love,'[82] I summarized in a brief passage Origen's very lengthy interpretation that repeats the same ideas in different words, but I did not omit any of his examples and assertions. And when I reached the conclusion, I appended the following: 'Therefore, in the restoration also of all things, when Christ Jesus, the true physician, will come to heal the body of the whole Church, which is now dispersed and rent asunder, each and every one shall receive his proper place according to the due measure of his faith and his recognition of the Son of God (we say "recognition" of Him because he formerly knew Him and afterwards ceased to know Him) and he shall begin to be what he had been; but not in such a way that all shall be placed in the same condition, that is to say, that all shall be changed back into angels, according to the view of one of the heresies; but rather that each single part shall be perfect, according to its due measure and function. For example, the fugitive angel shall begin to be what he was created; and man, who had been expelled from paradise, shall be restored again to the cultivation of paradise,'[83] and the rest.

---

81 Rom. 7.24.
82 Eph. 4.16.
83 St. Jerome, *Comm. in ep. ad. Eph.* 2.4.16 (PL. 26.503).

(27) *The two heresies.*

I am surprised that a man of your great intelligence did not understand the art of my exposition. For when I say: 'but not in such a way that all shall be placed in the same condition, that is to say, that all shall be changed back into angels, according to the view of one of the heresies,' I am making it clear that the matter that I am discussing is heretical, and that one heresy is opposed to the other heresy. Therefore, what are the two heresies? The one is that which states that all rational creatures are changed back into angels; the other, that which asserts that in the restoration of the world each and every thing shall be in the same state in which it was created. For example, devils will become again angels, because devils are created from angels, and souls of human beings will be changed back into the state in which they were created, not into angels, but into the state in which they were created by God, so that both the just and the sinners will be made equal. Finally, that you might know that I was not expounding my own views, but rather comparing the two heresies with one another, both of which I had read in the Greek, I concluded my discussion with the following remark: 'As I have remarked above, all of this sounds a bit confusing to us for the simple reason that it is expressed metaphorically in the Greek. And whenever any metaphor is translated literally from one language into another, the meanings and the new shoots of words are choked off, so to speak, by various brambles and briers.'[84] Unless you find these very statements in the Greek, you may reckon as my own any statement that has been made.

(28) The sixth, which is also the last objection (if, indeed, my brother has not forgotten any along the way), which they say he raises against me is that, in my interpretation of the following passage of the apostle, where he says: 'He who loves his own wife, loves himself. For no one ever hated his own

---

84 *Ibid.* (PL 26.503-504).

flesh: on the contrary he nourishes and cherishes it, as Christ also does the Church,'[85] after I gave a simple explanation, I introduced the question of Origen, in whose person I made the following statement without mentioning his name: 'The objection might be raised against me that the view expressed by the Apostle is not true when he said: "No one ever hates his own flesh," since people who are plagued with jaundice, and consumption and cancer, and dropsy, prefer death to life, and they hate their own bodies" ';[86] and I added at the same time my own personal views: 'These words, to be sure, are to be taken more properly in a figurative sense.'[87] When I use the term 'figurative,' I mean that the statement is not literally true, but is shrouded in a mist of allegory. But let us quote the very exact words that appear in the third book of Origen: 'We may say that the soul loves and nourishes the flesh that shall see the salvation of God and cherishes it, schooling it with disciplines, feeding it with the heavenly bread, and bathing it in the blood of Christ, so that refreshed and refined it can follow its husband with unfettered step and not be burdened and weighed down by any weakness. Like Christ, nourishing and cherishing the Church, and saying to Jerusalem: "How often would I have gathered thy children together, as a hen gathers her young under her wings, but thou wouldst not,"[88] the souls also in beautiful fashion nourish their own bodies, so that this corruptible body may put on incorruption, and, supported by the lightness of wings, it may rise more readily into the air. Therefore, let us husbands cherish our wives, and let our souls cherish their bodies, so that wives may be turned into husbands and bodies into souls, and that there may be no distinction between the sexes; but just as among angels there is neither male nor female, so let

---

85 Eph. 5.29.
86 St. Jerome, *Comm. in ep. ad Eph.* 3.5.29 (PL 26.533).
87 *Ibid.* (PL 26.533-534).
88 Matt. 23.37.

us also, who shall be as angels, begin right now to be what has been promised we shall be in heaven.'[89]

(29) Regarding the simple interpretation, which seemed to me to be logical for this testimony, I expressed myself as follows, saying: 'As far as the simple interpretation is concerned, in view of the precept of the holy love between man and wife, we are commanded right now to nourish and cherish our wives, to furnish them, to be sure, with food, and clothing, and whatever necessities of life they may need.'[90] This is my own view. Everything else that follows thereafter, and can be brought forward as an objection against me, I have made clear must be understood as said not in my own name, but in the name of those who disagree with me. Although my reply is brief and concise, and, in the light of what I have stated above, even a twisting of the meaning from what is an actual case to one that does not exist, since it is obscured by the mist of allegory, nevertheless, I shall view the matter more closely, and try to discover what it is in this argument that displeases you. Perhaps it is the remark I made that souls should cherish their bodies, as husbands their wives, so that this corruptible body may put on incorruption and, supported by the lightness of wings, it may rise more readily into the air. When I say: 'That this corruptible body may put on incorruption,' I am not changing the nature of bodies, but rather increasing their glory. Likewise, as to what follows: 'That supported by the lightness of wings, it may rise more readily into the air,' he who takes on wings, that is to say, immortality, that he may fly more lightly to heaven, does not lose his former state. But you will say: 'The following remark disturbs me: "Therefore, let us husbands cherish our wives, and let our souls cherish their bodies, so that wives may be turned into husbands and bodies into souls, and that there may be no distinction between sexes; but just as among angels there is

---

89 This is the only Latin fragment which has survived of Origen's commentary on the Epistle to the Ephesians.
90 St. Jerome, *Comm. in ep. ad Eph.* 3.5.29 (PL 26.533).

neither male nor female, so let us also, who shall be as angels, begin to be right now on earth what has been promised we shall be in heaven." ' The remark: 'Let us begin to be right now what has been promised we shall be in heaven,' would have rightly disturbed you had I not said it after making the previous statement. When I say: 'Let us begin to be here on earth,' I am not doing away with the nature of the sexes; but I am doing away with lust and copulation between husband and wife, as the apostle says: 'The time is short; it remains that those who have wives be as if they had none.'[91] When the Lord was asked in the Gospel of which of the seven brothers the woman would be the wife at the resurrection, He replied: 'You err because you know neither the Scriptures nor the power of God. For at the resurrection they will neither marry nor be given in marriage, but will be as angels of God in heaven.'[92] And as a matter of fact, when chastity is observed between husband and wife, the state is such that there begins to be neither male nor female, but, while still living in the body, they are being changed into angels, among whom there is neither male nor female. This view is also stated by the same apostle at another place: 'For all of you who have been baptized in Christ, have put on Christ. There is neither Jew nor Greek; there is neither slave nor freeman; there is neither male nor female. For you are all one in Christ Jesus.'[93]

(30) *The false accusations of Rufinus. Rufinus had learned Greek without a master. He had translated Gregory of Nazianzen.*

But, since my argument has worked its way clear of the rough and craggy places, and I have refuted with complete frankness the charge of heresy hurled against me, I shall pass on to other items included in his charge, with which he tries to malign me. The first of these is that I am a maligner, a slanderer of all men; and that I am forever railing at my pred-

---
91 1 Cor. 7.29.
92 Matt. 22.29, 30.
93 Gal. 3.27, 28.

AGAINST RUFINUS 99

ecessors. Let him name just one individual whose reputation I have besmirched in my works, or whom I have hurt with fictive praise, according to his practice. But if I speak against the malicious, and wound with the sharp point of my pen Luscius Lavinius or Asinius Pollio[94] of the clan of the Cornelii, if I cast aside from me one who is envious and spiteful of heart, and direct all my shafts at one simpleton, why does he portion out to many others his own wounds? Why does he make it clear by his very impatience in answering that he is the one who is being assailed? He taunts me with perjury and implicity in sacrilege, because in the book[95] in which I spoke instructions to a virgin of Christ, I made a promise[96] in my dream before the tribunal of the judge that I would never again interest myself in secular literature, and that I have, nevertheless, on occasions recalled the learning that I had condemned. He is without question that Sallustian Calpurnius[97] who instigated the orator, Magnus, to propose to me an insignificant question which I satisfied in a brief treatise. But, at the present time, I must reply to the pressing charge of the sacrilege and perjury of my dream. I said that, hence-

---

94 Luscius Lavinius was a Roman playwright, was a rival and bitter critic of Terence, and was often referred to by Terence in his plays as *malivolus vetus poeta*. (Cf. Terence, *Heaut.* 22; *Andria* 7). Asinius Pollio was a stern critic of Cicero. St. Jerome often compared Rufinus to these critics. Rufinus boasted that he was a descendant of the great Cornelian family.
95 This is a reference to St. Jerome's letter to Eustochium, in which he advised her how she should guard her virginity. Cf. St. Jerome, *Epistola* 22, *ad Eustochium*.
96 This is a reference to the famous dream of St. Jerome, in which he was charged with being a Ciceronian, and not a Christian, because of his great admiration for Cicero and his works. In his dream, he was brought before the tribunal of the judge, where he made a solemn promise never to read secular literature again. Rufinus taunted St. Jerome very frequently with this dream and his promise. Cf. St. Jerome, *Epistola* 22.30, *ad Eustochium*.
97 Magnus, a celebrated Roman orator, had been urged by Rufinus to write to St. Jerome to explain his reason for quoting passages from secular literature in his writings. In making answer to Magnus, St. Jerome referred to Rufinus under the title of Calpurnius. A Calpurnius is mentioned by Sallust who betrayed the republic by his infamous avarice during the Jugurthian war. Cf. St. Jerome, *Epistola* 70.6, *ad Magnum*.

forth, I would not read secular literature; it was a promise for the future, not the deleting of past recollection. 'How can you remember,' you will ask, 'what you have not read for such a long time?' Again, if I defend myself with some quotation from the ancient books, and say: 'So strong is habit in tender years,'[98] I become liable to the charge while I deny it, and, while I produce testimony in my defense, I am convicted by the very testimony by which I defend myself. I should, perhaps, at this point compose a lengthy composition on an experience that each and every one of us is conscious of. Who of us does not remember his childhood? To make a very serious individual like you laugh, so that you might finally imitate Crassus, who, according to Lucilius,[99] laughed but once in his lifetime, I recall very definitely how I ran through the apartments of our servants, how I spent my holidays playing games, and how I was caught and dragged from the lap of my grandmother to a raging Orbilius.[100] And to increase your amazement, I often see myself in my dream, who am now a greying and balding old man, as a young man with curly hair and dressed in a toga, delivering a declamation before my teacher of rhetoric. On awaking, I congratulate myself on escaping this ordeal of speechmaking. Believe me, childhood recalls many things very clearly. If you had studied letters, the jar of your little genius would still have the odor of that with which it was once imbued. No amount of water can wash off the purple dye of wools. Even donkeys and brute animals remember the inns the second time, even on a long trip. Are you amazed if I have not forgotten Latin literature when you yourself learned Greek without a master? The elements of logic have taught me the seven moods of syllogisms; they have

---

98 Vergil, *Georgics* 2.272.
99 Cicero, quoting Lucilius, states that M. Crassus, who was praetor in 105 B.C. and was the grandfather of the triumvir, laughed only once in the course of his whole life, and was known as Agelastus, the non-laugher. Cf. Cicero, *Tusculan Disputations* 3.15.31.
100 Orbilius was the famous pedagogue, recorded by Horace (*Epistles* 2.1.71), who passed into a general name for boys' tutors.

AGAINST RUFINUS 101

taught me the meaning of the term *axīoma* which we can translate in our language as *pronuntiatum;* how a sentence cannot be composed without a noun and a verb; the series of sorites,[101] the subtleties of the false syllogism, and the tricks of sophisms. I can swear on oath that I have never read any of these matters after I had once left school. Therefore, I would have to drink deep of the waters of Lethe, according to the stories of the poets, lest I be accused of knowing what I have learned. But then, tell me, why did you, who taunt me with little learning and who consider yourself something of a critic and a Rabbi, make bold to write anything, and to translate Gregory,[102] that very eloquent man, with equal splendor of eloquence? What is the source of that abundance of words, that flash of phrases, that variety of translations in a man like you who had barely tasted oratory with the tip of your tongue in your youth? I am either wrong, or else you continue to read Cicero in secret. And are you so eloquent, and do you hurl at me the charge of reading him, so that you alone, among the exegetes of the Church, may glory in a flow of eloquence? Although it is true that you give the impression of imitating more the philosophers, the subtleties of Cleanthes, and the sophistries of Chrysippus,[103] not in art, of which you are ignorant, but rather in the greatness of intellect. And since the Stoics lay claim to logic, and you reckon as of little

---

101 Sorites was an abridged series of syllogisms in a series of propositions so arranged that the predicate of the first is the subject of the second, and so on, the conclusion uniting the subject of the first proposition with the predicate of the last.
102 Shortly after settling in Aquileia, Rufinus embarked upon his translation work once again. Among his first efforts were two sets of homilies belonging to the Cappadocians, St. Basil and St. Gregory of Nazianzen, whom he seemed quite anxious to introduce to the West. He translated nine sermons of St. Gregory. St. Jerome seems to witness by his remark to the competence of Rufinus' translation of St. Gregory.
103 Cleanthes was a Stoic philosopher of Assos in Asia Minor. He was Zeno's disciple for nineteen years, and in the year 263 B.C. succeeded him as head of the Stoic school. Chrysippus was a disciple of Cleanthes. His discourses abounded more in curious subtleties and nice distinctions than in solid arguments.

value the nonsense of this science, in this respect, you are an Epicurean; for you are not interested in the style, but in the content of your remarks. Therefore, what is it to you if someone else does not understand what you want to say, since your remarks are addressed, not to all the people, but to your own friends? Finally, although at times I do not understand the meaning of your remarks, even though I have reread your writings, and I feel that I am reading Heraclitus,[104] nevertheless, I do not complain about it, nor am I displeased over my slowness to comprehend; for I am experiencing the same difficulty in reading your works that you are in writing them.

(31) *He defends his dream. The popularity of the Holy Places and meeting of peoples from all over the world. Why Rufinus vilified Jerome.*

This is what I would say if I had made the promise, to be sure, while wide awake. But now he resorts to a novel type of impudence, and taunts me with a dream. I wish that the reputation of this place, and the gathering of saints from all over the world would allow me to read the Sacred Scriptures! So little opportunity do I have for external considerations. But an individual who taunts with a dream should heed the words of the prophet that we are not to put trust in dreams, because adultery in a dream does not lead me to hell, nor does the crown of martyrdom raise me up to heaven. How often have I seen myself in a dream dead and placed in a tomb! How often have I seen myself flying over lands, and sailing through the air, and crossing over mountains and seas! Therefore, let him convince me that I am not alive, or that I have wings at my sides, because my mind has often deluded me by flights of the imagination. How many people who are rich in their dreams are suddenly paupers upon opening their eyes! People drink oceans of water in their thirst, and they awake with burning and parched throats. You expect me to keep

---

104 Heraclitus is known among the ancients as the obscure philosopher. His style was so careless that the syntactical relations of the words were often hard to perceive and his thoughts obscure.

a promise made in a dream; I shall confront you with a more frank and specific question: Have you kept all of the promises that you made in baptism? Which one of us fulfilled all that is expected of him in the name of the monk? See to it lest you see the mote in my eyes through the beam in yours. I speak with reluctance, and my grief forces my unwilling tongue to speak. The stories that you make up about a man in his waking hours are not enough for you, unless you can also taunt him with his dreams. You are so curious about my activities that you make whatever I have said or done in my dreams a topic of discussion. I pass over the discredit that you have brought to your promise with these remarks that you make against me, and the disgrace that you brought upon all Christians by your words and your deeds. I tell you this one thing, and I shall remind you of it by repeating it over and over again. You are going after a wild horned-beast, and, were I not mindful of these words of the apostle: 'The evil tongued will not possess the kingdom of God,'[105] and: 'You who bite one another, will be consumed by one another,'[106] you would without further ado realize the great discord that has come out of concord[107] into the world. What does it profit you to heap insults upon my head in the presence of both friends and strangers alike? Are we accused of being sinners on earth because we are not Origenists, and we know that we have not sinned in heaven? And were we reconciled so that I would not be allowed to speak against heretics for fear that you might assume that I had assailed you if I described them? As long as I did not decline your praises, you adopted me as your master, you called me brother and colleague, and admitted that I was Catholic in every respect. After I disavowed your praises, and judged myself unworthy of the praises of such a great man, you immediately change your tune and reprehend

---

105 1 Cor. 6.10.
106 Gal. 5.15.
107 An attempt is apparently made here by St. Jerome to make a pun on the word concord. The name of Rufinus' home town was Concordia.

everything that you had praised before, uttering both the sweet and the bitter from the same lips. Do you see why I am silent, why I do not furnish words to a raging heart, and why I say with the psalmist: 'Set a watch O Lord, before my mouth, and the door round about my lips. Incline not my heart to evil words.'[108] And in another place: 'When the sinner stood against me, I was dumb, and was humbled and kept silence from good things.'[109] And again: 'I am become as a man that heareth not; and that hath no reproofs in his mouth.'[110] But the Lord, my avenger, shall reply to you in my behalf, who says through the prophet: 'Vengeance is mine; I will repay, says the Lord.'[111] And in another place: 'Sitting thou didst speak against thy brother and didst lay a scandal against thy mother's son; these things hast thou done, and I was silent. Thou thoughtest unjustly, that I shall be like to thee: but I will reprove thee and set before thy face,'[112] so that you may come to realize that the things that you falsely reprove in others have been condemned in you.

(32) *Chrysogonus, the follower of Rufinus.*

I hear, moreover, that Chrysogonus,[113] one of his followers, taunts me for having said that all sins are forgiven in baptism, and that a husband of two wives dies and a new man arises in Christ; and that there is a goodly number of priests in the churches who fall in that category. I shall reply to him briefly. They have in their possession the little treatise[114] which they

---

108 Ps. 140.3. 4.
109 Ps. 38.2, 3.
110 Ps. 37.15.
111 Rom. 12.19.
112 Ps. 49.20, 21.
113 Beyond the fact that he was a monk and a friend of Rufinus, nothing more is known of Chrysogonus. Cf. St. Jerome, *Epistola* 9, *ad Chrysogonum.*
114 The treatise referred to here is St. Jerome's letter to Oceanus, in which he defended Carterius, bishop of Spain, against the charges of bigamy. The bishop had a wife before his baptism, and remarried after the death of his first wife. Oceanus argued that he was to be condemned as a bigamist. St. Jerome regarded his first marriage as part of the old life which is washed away by baptism. Cf. Jerome, *Epistola* 69, *ad Oceanum.*

are censuring. Let him answer this letter; let him refute it with arguments of his own, and confute my writings with writings of his own. Why does he weigh out hollow words by knitting his brow, and turning up and wrinkling his nose, and feigning holiness among the ignoble crowd with an air of simulated austerity? Let him hear me proclaim again, that the old Adam dies completely in the laver of baptism, and a new Adam arises with Christ in baptism; that the man of clay dies, and the super-celestial man is born. We say this not because we ourselves are concerned with this question, thanks to the mercy of Christ, but we replied to our brethren who asked us to express our own views, without biasing in any way the mind of anyone as to what view he should adopt, or subverting in any way the decree of someone else with this view of ours.[115] We who are living a secluded life in cells do not solicit the episcopacy, nor do we condemn humility, and proceed to bribe the papacy with gold; nor do we desire to strangle, with our rebellious attitude, the Pontiff chosen by God; nor do we prove that we are heretics by favoring heretics. We neither have money nor do we desire to have it: 'Having food and sufficient clothing, with these we are content,'[116] continually singing the hymn of him who shall ascend the mountain of the Lord: 'He that hath not put out his money to usury, nor taken bribes against the innocent; he that doeth these things shall not be moved forever.'[117] Therefore, he who does not do these things has already perished forever.

---

115 The decree here referred to is either that of Pope Siricius or that of Innocent. Pope Siricius addressed a decretal letter to Himerius of Terragona, in which he answered fifteen questions put to Damasus by this bishop concerning various matters of ecclesiastical discipline. One of these matters concerned marriage. Pope Innocent laid down special measures for the sacrament of order. He maintained that successive bigamy applied even to those whose marriage had been contracted and ended by the death of the other party before baptism. Cf. F. Cayré *Manual of Patrology and History of Theology* 1 (translated by H. Howitt; Belgium 1935) 516-517. St. Jerome maintained the contrary opinion. Cf. St. Jerome, *Epistola* 69, *ad Oceanum*.
116 1 Tim. 6.8.
117 Ps. 14.5.

Book Two

(1) *He wishes to defend himself, not to accuse others.*

Thus far, I have made answer about the charges, or rather in defense of myself against the charges which my erstwhile sly praiser has heaped upon my head, and which his disciples keep constantly alleging against me. I have answered and have restrained my grief, not as I should have, but as I was able to do. It was my intention, to be sure, not so much to attack others as to defend myself. I shall take up his *Apologia*,[1] in which he seeks to clear himself before the saintly Anastasius, bishop of the city of Rome, and again heaps slanders upon me in order to defend himself. And he shows so much love for me that, being caught in a whirlpool and being dragged down to the bottom, he takes firm grip of my feet, in particular, hoping either to be saved or to perish together with me.

(2) *The Apology of Rufinus. Close friends and blood relatives are referred to in the vernacular as parents.*

He says that he is answering, first of all, the rumors[2] that are besmirching at Rome the faith of a man who has been approved most outstanding in respect to his faith, as well as his love of God. He would have come in person, except for the fact that, having just returned to his parents after thirty years,[3] he did not want to desert them whom he had but so

---

1 On the twenty-sixth of November, 399, Pope Siricius, a friend of Rufinus, died. He was replaced by Anastasius who at once proved more amenable to the anti-Origen forces then functioning in Rome. The friends of St. Jerome had denounced Rufinus and his translation of Origen to the new Pope. In consequence of these factors, Rufinus felt it necessary to explain his own position and defend himself before the Pope himself. Towards the end of the year 400, he composed his *Apologia ad Anastasium* PL 21.623-628.

2 Rufinus, *Apol. ad Anast.* 1 PL 21.623.

3 Rufinus had left Aquileia in the year 371 for Alexandria and the desert and returned towards the close of the year 400.

recently come to visit, lest he be thought to be inhuman or cruel; and, being well worn out by the hardships of such a long trip, he was too weak to undergo the hardships a second time. In view of the fact that he did not come in person, he sent a literary stick against his barkers which the Pope might wield in his right hand, and drive off the dogs that are raging against him. If he has been approved before the whole world in respect to his faith and love of God, and, in particular, before the Pope himself, to whom he is writing, how do you account for the fact that he is being attacked and censured at Rome, and the rumor is growing that his worth has been assailed? Moreover, what sort of humility is it for a man to assert that he has been approved for his faith and his love of God, when the apostles themselves pray: 'Lord, increase our faith,'[4] and they hear it said to them: 'If you have faith even like a mustard seed';[5] and it is said to Peter himself: 'O thou of little faith, why didst thou doubt?'[6] What shall I say of charity, which is greater than both faith and hope, which Paul himself prays for rather than assumes to himself, without which the crown of rewards cannot be won, even in martyrdom, by the spilling of blood and the delivering of the body to the flames? He arrogates to himself both of these virtues in such a way that he still finds barkers barking at him, who will not stop their barking unless repelled by the staff of an illustrious Pontiff. It is, indeed, ridiculous for a man who has neither father nor mother to boast that he is returning to his parents after thirty years; and to long to see in his old age his parents when they are dead, whom he left in his youth when they were alive. Unless, perchance, in the vernacular of the people and of the camp, he is referring to his close friends and associates as parents; and because he does not want to desert them lest he be thought to be inhuman and cruel, he has left his fatherland and now lives at Aquileia. His highly approved

---

4 Luke 17.5.
5 Luke 17.8.
6 Matt. 14.31.

faith is on trial at Rome and, lying indolent and a bit wearied here after thirty years, he cannot make the very easy trip over the Flaminian Way in a two-wheeled chariot; and so he alleges as his excuse the weariness of a long trip, as if he had been running continuously for thirty years, or after residing for two years at Aquileia, he has been completely worn out by the trials of the past trip.

(3) *The words of Rufinus.*

Let us examine the rest of the statements, and quote the very words of his letter: 'Therefore, although our faith was approved at the time of the persecution of heretics, when we were living in the Church of Alexandria, by imprisonments and exiles which we suffered for the faith.'[7] I am surprised that he did not add: 'I was a prisoner for Jesus Christ,' and, 'I was liberated from the jaws of the lion,' and 'I fought against wild beasts at Alexandria,' and 'I have run my course, I have kept the faith, there remains for me the crown of justice.' What exiles, what imprisonments is he referring to? I blush at this very manifest lie, as if imprisonments and exiles are imposed without the decrees of judges. However, I would like to be informed of the imprisonments and the provinces where he affirms he endured exiles. He can easily mention, I am sure, just one of the many imprisonments and the countless number of exiles. Let him relate to us the acts of his confession that have escaped our notice till now, so that we may also recite his deeds, together with the other martyrs of Alexandria, and he can say against his barkers: 'Henceforth let no man give me trouble, for I bear the marks of the Lord Jesus in my body.'[8]

(4) *The question of the soul of Christ.*

'Nevertheless, if there is anyone now who wants either to test our faith, or hear and learn what it is, let him know that this is our belief concerning the Trinity,'[9] and the rest. Above,

---

[7] Rufinus, *Apol. ad Anast.* 2 PL 21.624.
[8] Gal. 6.17.
[9] Rufinus, *Apol. ad Anast.* 2 PL 21.624.

you offer the Pope a staff against your dogs, with which he may arm himself and proceed to defend you. Now you seem to be wavering, and you say: 'If there is anyone who wants to test our faith.' You are again hesitating since the barkings of many people have reached your own ears. I am not discussing for the moment your eloquence, which you both despise and condemn. I shall reply only to your views. You are being asked one question and you answer an entirely different question. You have already fought your fight against the teachings of Arius at Alexandria by imprisonments and exiles, not with words, but with blood. At the present time, calumny is being brought down upon your head over the heresy of Origen. Do not look to applying medicine to wounds that are already healed. You say that the Trinity is one Godhead. With the whole world already confessing its belief in this doctrine, I suppose that even the devils would confess that the Son of God was born of the Virgin Mary, and that He assumed the flesh of human nature and a soul. If I question you on a more specific point, you will call me contentious. If you say that the Son of God assumed the flesh of human nature and a soul, I ask you to answer the following without any rancor: 'Did the soul that Jesus[10] assumed have existence before He was born of Mary? Or was it created simultaneously with the body in a state of virginal origin which was born of the Holy Spirit? Or was it created and sent down from heaven, when the body was already formed in the womb?' I would like to know which one of these three views is your view. If it existed before He was born of Mary, then it was not yet the soul of Jesus, and

---

10 The Greek theology of the fourth century engaged in battle with heresy on an essential point of Christian dogma, the genuine and full divinity of the Word, and, therefore, Jesus. Arius held that there was but one God. He alone is unbegotten, eternal, without beginning, and truly God. He created first a superior being, which we call the Word. The Word is, then, truly created. He is not of the substance of God, but exists by the will of God. Lucian had already taught that the Word assumed a body without a soul. This was also the teaching of Arius. Cf. J. Tixeront, *History of Dogmas* 2 (translated from the fifth French edition by H. L. B.; St. Louis 1923) 27.

it was active in some way, and, for the merits of its virtues, it was subsequently made His soul. If He received His soul through insemination, then the condition of human souls, which we acknowledge to be eternal, and those of brute animals that disintegrate with the body is one and the same. But if the soul is created and sent down at the same time that the body is formed, make a simple admission of this fact and relieve us of scruples.

(5) You answer none of these questions; but, engrossed in other matters, you abuse our simplicity and, by your deceptions and ostentatious display of words, you allow us no opportunity to stick to the question. 'But then,' you will say, 'was not the question concerned with the resurrection of the flesh, and the punishments of the devil?' I admit that it was. Therefore, give me a brief and simple answer. I am not concerned with your statement that the same flesh will rise again in which we now live, without the cutting off of any limb, and without the severing of any part of the body; for these are your own words. But my question is whether you hold the view which Origen denies, that bodies will arise possessing the same sex that they had when they died, and that Mary will rise again as Mary and John as John; or whether there will be a mingling and a mixing of sexes, and there will be neither male nor female, but a combination of both or neither? And whether the bodies themselves will remain forever incorruptible and immortal, and, as you so cleverly proclaim after the apostle, spiritual; and not only the bodies, but the flesh and blood that is infused throughout and poured into the veins and the bones, the very flesh that Thomas touched? Or whether they will dissolve, to be sure, into nothingness, and disintegrate into the four elements of which they were composed? These are the questions that you should have answered either in the affirmative or negative, instead of mentioning the views that Origen admits in a deceitful manner, as if to deceive the foolish and the children, 'without the cutting off of any limb, and without the severing of any part of the body.' We

were afraid, I suppose, that we would rise again without noses and ears, and there would be established in the heavenly Jerusalem a city of eunuchs with genitals cut off and severed.

(6) However, he tempers his views about the devil in this fashion: 'We also say that there will be a judgment, in which judgment each and every man will receive the due rewards of the body, according to that what he has done, whether good or evil. But if men will receive due rewards for their deeds, how much more will the devil who exists as the cause of sin of all men? We hold the view that is written of him in the Gospel that both the devil himself and all his angels, together with those who do his work, that is to say, who slander their brothers, shall possess in equal portion with him the inheritance of eternal fire. Therefore, if anyone denies that the devil is subject to eternal fires, let him share a portion of the eternal fire with him, so that he may come to experience what he has denied.'[11] Let us repeat each statement separately. 'We say,' he says, 'that there will be a judgment, in which judgment,' and the rest. I had intended to say nothing about the faults of his diction; but since his disciples admire the eloquence of their master, I shall touch upon a few of them briefly. He had stated that there would be a judgment; but, being a careful individual, he was afraid to use the simple phrase 'in which,' and wrote 'in which judgment,' for fear that, if he had not repeated a second time the word 'judgment,' we might have forgotten the preceding statement, and might have supposed it was 'ass' instead of 'judgment.' The expression that follows: 'those who slander their brothers, shall possess the inheritance of eternal fire,' is also an example of the same kind of embellishment. For who has ever heard of 'possessing fires,' and of enjoying punishments? It seems to me that he, being a Greek, wanted to explain himself, and in place of the word *klēronomēsousin,* which is the expression used in Greek, and which in our language can be expressed as *haereditabant,* he used the rather elegant and ornate expression of

[11] Rufinus, *Apol. ad Anast.* 5 PL 21.625-626.

haereditate potientur. His entire discourse is replete with such trivialities and inaccuracies of expressions. But to get back to his views.

(7) *He ridicules the words of Rufinus. Eternal fire according to Origen.*

The devil who exists as the cause of sin of all men is struck a serious blow, if, like man, he shall render an account of his deeds, and shall possess the inheritance of eternal fire together with his angels. For such a condition would render it impossible for the devil to possess eternal fires that he had longed to possess for so long a time, if human beings were subjected to this torture. And it seems to me that on this point you are reviling the devil, and accusing him with false charges as the slanderer of all men. For you say: 'he who exists as the cause of sin of all men.' And since you impute sins to him, you free men of guilt, and take away the freedom of the will, whereas the Savior says: 'Out of our heart come evil thoughts, murders, adulteries, immorality, thefts, false witnesses, blasphemies.'[12] And again we read of Judas in the Gospel: 'And after the morsel, Satan entered into him';[13] for he had sinned before the morsel of his own will, and was not moved to repentance either through humility or through the mercy of the Savior. Whence the apostle says: 'Whom I have delivered up to Satan that they may learn not to blaspheme.'[14] And in another place: 'I have delivered such a one over to Satan for the destruction of the flesh, that the spirit may be saved.'[15] He has delivered over to Satan as to the executioner for punishment those who, before they were delivered over, had blasphemed of their own will. And David says: 'From my secret sins cleanse me, O Lord: and from those of others spare thy servant';[16] referring briefly both to the error of his own will, and to the incentives of vices. We also read in

---
12 Matt. 15.19.
13 John 13.37.
14 1 Tim. 1.20.
15 1 Cor. 5.5.
16 Ps. 18.13, 14.

Ecclesiastes: 'If the spirit of him that hath power, ascend upon thy heart, leave not thy place.'[17] From this, it is clearly evident that we have committed a sin if we surrender our place to him who ascends upon us, and if we have not cast down headlong the enemy ascending upon the walls. However, it seems to me that when you call down upon the heads of your brothers, that is to say, upon your slanderers, eternal fires with the devil, you are not so much dashing your brothers to the ground as you are elevating the devil, since he is to be punished in the same fires as Christians. But, I presume, you are well aware that the phrase 'eternal fires,' according to the usual interpretation of Origen, means the consciousness, to be sure, of sins, and a deep sense of sorrow that burns the very inners of the heart, of which Isaia also speaks: 'Their worm shall not die, and their fire shall not be quenched.'[18] And it is written to Babylon: 'You have coals of fire, you will sit upon them: these shall be your help.'[19] And in the Psalm the penitent hears it said to him: 'What shall be given to thee, or what shall be added to thee, to a deceitful tongue? The sharp arrows of the mighty, with coals that lay waste,'[20] so that the arrows of the commandments of God, of which the prophet speaks in another place: 'I am turned in my anguish, whilst the thorn is fastened,'[21] might wound and pierce a deceitful tongue, and create therein a wilderness of sins. The following testimony, in which the Lord says: 'I have come to cast fire upon the earth and what will I but that it be kindled,'[22] is also interpreted in the following sense: 'It is my desire that all men do penance for their sins and that they burn out their sins in the fire of the Holy Spirit. For I am he of whom it is written: "God is a consuming fire." '[23] Therefore, it is nothing

---

17 Eccles. 10.4.
18 Isa. 66.24.
19 Isa. 47.14 (Septuagint).
20 Ps. 119.3, 4.
21 Ps. 31.4.
22 Luke 12.49.
23 Deut. 4.24.

complimentary to say this of the devil, since it has also been prepared for all men. You should rather have said (in order to avoid any reference to the salvation of the devil): 'Thou art brought to nothing, and thou shalt never be any more,'[24] and the following words spoken in the person of the Lord to Job concerning the devil: 'Behold his hope shall fail him, and in the sight of all he shall be cast down.'[25] 'I will not stir him up, like one that is cruel: for who can resist my countenance? Who hath given me before that I should repay him? All things that are under heaven are mine. I will not spare him, nor his mighty words, and framed to make supplication.'[26] Such statements can be excused on the grounds that they were spoken by a simple man, so to speak; and although they do not deceive the learned, they can assume the appearance of innocence to the uninformed.

(8) The following statement regarding the state of souls cannot be excused on any grounds whatsoever: 'I also hear that a controversy has been stirred up regarding the question of the soul. You be the judge whether the wrangling over this question should be heard or dismissed. But if I am asked my personal view, I admit that I have read different views on this question in the works of very many of the exegetes. I have read some who say that souls are also diffused in the same manner as bodies through insemination of the human seed, and they confirmed this view by any argument that they could bring forward. This, I suppose, was the view among the Latins of Tertullian[27] or of Lactantius, and perhaps also of some others. Others assert that God creates souls daily and infuses them in bodies that have been formed in the womb. Still others, that God made souls once and for all, that is to say, at the time when He created all things out of nothing, and now He disposes by His own judgment that they be born in

---

24 Ezech. 28.19 (Septuagint).
25 Job 40.28 (a literal translation of the Vulgate).
26 Job 41.1-3 (a literal translation of the Vulgate).
27 Tertullian, in his *De anima*, deals with the origin of souls (chs. 23-41).

bodies. This is the view of Origen and of some others among the Greeks. But as for myself, although I have read these individual views, I say, with God as my witness, that, up to the present moment, I hold no certain or definite view on this question. But I leave it to God to know what is the truth, or to whomsoever He Himself will deem it worthy to reveal. But I do not deny that I have read these individual views, and I confess that I still do not know for certain anything but what the Church clearly teaches, that God is the creator of both souls and bodies.'[28]

(9) Before taking up for discussion these views, I shall examine the strange phraseology of this Theophrastus: 'I hear,' he says, 'that a controversy has been stirred up regarding the question of the soul. You be the judge whether the wrangling over this question should be heard or dismissed.' If a controversy has been stirred up at Rome regarding the status of the soul, what does he mean by the term 'wrangling' or 'complaints' on a question that is left to the judgment of the bishops to decide whether it should be heard or not? Unless, perhaps, he assumes that the term 'question' and 'wrangling' are synonymous, because he finds such a figure in the commentaries of Caper.[29] Next, he states: 'I have read some who say that souls are also diffused in the same way as bodies through insemination of the human seed, and they confirmed this view by any arguments that they could bring forward.' I ask: Whence this license in the use of figures of speech, whence this confusion of tenses and moods? 'I have read some who say'; 'they confirmed by any arguments that they could bring forward'? And in the following sentences: 'Others assert that God creates souls daily and infuses them in bodies that have been formed in the womb. Still others, that God made souls once and for all, that is to say, at the time when He

---
28 Rufinus, *Apol. ad Anast.* 6 PL 21.626.
29 Flavius Caper was a Roman grammarian who flourished under Trajan. Of him, we have two small treatises on orthography and doubtful words.

created all things out of nothing, and now He disposes by His own judgment that they be born in the bodies.' This is, indeed, a very beautiful arrangement. 'Others,' he says, 'make this or that assertion; still others, that God made the souls once and for all, that is to say, at the time that He created all things out of nothing, and now He disposes by His own judgment that they be born in the bodies.' His manner of speaking is so affected and confused that I have more difficulty reprehending his statements than he in writing them. His concluding remark was as follows: 'But as for myself, although I have read these individual views,' and, with the sentence still dangling, he added, as if he were introducing some new statement: 'Yet as for myself, I do not deny that I have read these individual views, and I confess that I still do not know.'

(10) *The mystery of the Trinity unknown to the men of old.*

O the unfortunate souls that are pierced with such lances of errors! I suppose that when souls fell to earth from heaven and were clothed in crass bodies, according to the erroneous view of Origen, they did not suffer as much as they do now, buffeted on all sides by these words and views, not to mention the vulgar view, according to which souls are said to be infused through the insemination of the human seed. I know that it is not customary among Christians to reprehend faults of speech; but I wanted to show from a few examples what gross impudence it is to teach something that you do not know, and to write what you have no knowledge of; so that we may also look for the same kind of wisdom in the matter of views. He sends a letter, that is to say, a very stout staff, with which the Bishop of Rome might arm himself; and he says that he does not know why objections are being raised relative to the very question that is causing the dogs to bark. If he does not know the reason why calumny is being heaped upon his head, why is it necessary for him to send an *Apology* which is not a defense of himself, but rather a confession of his ignorance? Such action does not allay the suspicions of men, but rather sows them. He quotes three views of the state of souls, and he concludes by saying, 'I do not deny that I have read the individual views, and I confess that I still do not know.' You would imagine him to be an Arcesilaus[30] or a Carneades,[31] who proclaim that all things are uncertain, although he even surpasses them in being cautious. For inasmuch as they could not brook the ill-will of all the other philosophers, for taking truth out of life, they invented the doctrine of probability, in order to temper the ignorance of things with the assertion of probability. He, on the other hand, says he is uncertain and does not know which one of these three views is the truth. If this was the reply he intended to give, what logical reason impelled him to make so great a Pontiff a witness of his ignorance? Beyond question, this is that weariness that he gave as his excuse, that he could not come to Rome because he was completely worn out by a thirty-year trip. We are ignorant of these and other important matters, and yet we do not try to find witnesses of our ignorance. He speaks boldly of the Father, and the Son, and the Holy Spirit, and of the Nativity of the Lord, the Savior, over which Isaia exclaims: 'Who shall declare his generation?'[32] and he proudly arrogates to himself knowledge of a mystery, unknown to all past gen-

---

30 Arcesilaus, the philosopher, was born at Pitane in the year 316 B.C. He became the founder of what was termed the Middle Academy. His love for quibbling has been referred to as the source of his scepticism. Upon the death of Crantor, the school in the Academy was transferred to Arcesilaus. The latter did not commit his opinions to writing. His opinions can be derived only from the works of his opponents, of whom Chrysippus was the most eminent. According to these statements the results of his opinions would be a perfect scepticism, expressed in the formula that he knew nothing, not even that which Socrates had ever maintained that he knew, his own ignorance. Cf. Cicero, *Academica* 1.12.
31 Carneades, a philosopher of Cyrene in Africa, was the founder of a sect called the Third or New Academy. It was the doctrine of the New Academy that the sense, the understanding, and the imagination frequently deceive us, and, therefore, cannot be infallible judges of truth; but that, from the impression which we perceive to be produced on the mind by means of the senses, we infer appearances of truth or probabilities.
32 Isa. 53.8.

erations. And there is one fact that he does not know, the ignorance of which causes all men to be scandalized. He knows how the Virgin gave birth to God, but he does not know how he himself was born. He admits that God is the creator of souls and bodies, whether the souls existed before bodies, whether they are born from the same beginnings as the bodies, whether they are infused in bodies that have already been formed and fashioned in the womb. We know that God is the author of all things. The question at issue at the moment is not whether God or someone else created souls, but he says that he does not know which of the three views that he has quoted is the true one. See to it, lest someone immediately raise the objection that the only reason why you confess an ignorance of these three views is that you may avoid the necessity of condemning one of them; and that you are sparing Tertullian and Lactantius so that you may not strangle Origen along with them. If my memory serves me well, unless I am mistaken, I cannot recall having read in Lactantius where he refers to the soul as *suspeiroméne*. But you who write that you have read this statement, mention the book in which you have read it, lest it appear that, just as you calumniated me while I was asleep, so also you have calumniated him who is now dead. But, in this matter, you also proceed slowly and cautiously. For you say: 'This, I suppose, was the view among the Latins of Tertullian, or of Lactantius, and perhaps also of some others.' Not only are you uncertain of the state of souls, but you even express mere suppositions as to the views of the authors. And yet there is some difference. For as far as souls are concerned, you openly declare that you are in ignorance, and you make a confession of your ignorance; but as far as the authors are concerned, you say that you know them, but your knowledge is more suppositive than presumptive. It is only with regard to Origen that you have no doubts. For you say: 'This is the view of Origen.' I shall ask you: Is his view good or evil? 'I do not know,' you say. Why, then, do you send me couriers and messengers so frequently just to let me know what you do not know? And lest, perchance, I distrust your confession of ignorance, and think that it is all a clever scheme on your part to keep silent about what you know, you swear, with God as your witness, that, up to the present moment, you have no definite or certain view on this question, and that you leave it to God to know what is the truth, and to whomsoever He will deem it worthy to reveal. Was there no one in your opinion worthy enough, throughout so many centuries, to whom God would have made some revelations on this question? Was no patriarch, no prophet, no apostle, no martyr worthy? Were such mysteries not even made manifest to you when you were detained in imprisonments and exiles? The Lord says in the Gospel: 'Father, I have manifested thy name to men.'[33] He who manifested the Father kept silent about the state of souls. And do you wonder if scandals arise against you among the brethren, when you swear on oath that you do not know what the churches of Christ admit that they do know?

(11) After this exposition of his faith, or should I say, after this confession of his ignorance, he passes to another matter and seeks to clear himself for having translated the books of the *Periarchon* into Latin. And these are the exact words that he uses: 'Since I hear that even objections have been raised against me because I translated certain works of Origen from Greek into Latin at the urgent request of my brothers, I am sure that everybody knows that the only reason why these translations are being reprehended is envy. If, indeed, there is anything in the author that displeases, why should it be hurled back at the translator? I was asked to translate for the Latins the exact original of the Greek. I simply applied Latin words to the Greek ideas. Therefore, if there is any merit in these views, the merit is not mine; by the same token, if there is any fault in them, the fault is not mine.'[34] 'I hear,' he says, 'that objections have been raised.' How clever of

---
33 John 17.6.
34 Rufinus, *Apol. ad Anast.* 7 PL 21.626.

him to refer to an accusation made against him as objections! 'Because I translated certain works of Origen from Greek into Latin at the urgent request of my brothers.' What are those 'certain works'? Have they no titles? Are you silent? The books of the accusers mention them by name. 'I am sure,' he says, 'that everybody knows that the only reason that these translations are reprehended is envy.' Envy of what? Are they envious of your eloquence? Or have you accomplished something that no man has ever been able to accomplish? You know, I have also translated many books of Origen. And no one but you either envies me or slanders me. 'If, indeed,' he says, 'there is anything in the author that displeases, why should it be hurled back at the translator? I was asked to translate for the Latins the exact original of the Greek. I simply applied Latin words to the Greek views. Therefore, if there is any merit in these views, the merit is not mine; by the same token, if there is any fault in them, the fault is not mine.' And do you wonder if men think evil of you, when you say of manifest blasphemies: 'If there is anything in the author that displeases'? They are displeased with everything that is stated in those books; and you are the only one who entertains doubts and complains that the things that you praised in the preface to your translation are hurled back at the translator. You had been asked to translate into Latin the exact original of the Greek. Would that you had done what you pretend you had been asked to do! You would now not be subject to any envy. If you had kept faithful to the translation, there would not have been any need for me to nullify a false translation with a true one. Your own conscience knows what you have added, what you have deleted, what you have changed, one way or the other, as you saw fit. And do you have the courage after all this to say that both the good and the evil should be imputed not to you, but to the author? And, although you are overwrought with envy, you still modify your words, and, like one treading tiptoed on grains of corn, you say: 'If there is any merit in these views, if there is any fault in them.' You do not dare to defend your translation, and yet you do not want to condemn it. Of these two alternatives, choose the one you like; a choice is offered you. If your translation is good, praise it. If it is bad, condemn it. But he justifies himself, and subjoins another dodge. For he says: 'Why I even added something, as I indicated in my preface; so that I deleted several things, to the best of my ability; but only the things that came under suspicion, because it appeared to me that these things were not stated in that way by Origen, but were inserted by others, because I had read statements expressed in a Catholic way on the very same matters in other places of the same author.'[35] The following are strange examples of eloquence, colored with Attic elegance: 'Why I even,' and 'things that came under suspicion.' I am surprised that he had the courage to dispatch such verbal monstrosities to Rome. You would imagine that his tongue, with its impediments and tied in inextricable knots, could hardly utter a human sound. But to get back to the point at issue.

(11a) *The blasphemies of Origen.*

Who gave you this license to cut many passages from your translation? You had been asked to translate the Greek into Latin, not to amend it; to produce the words of another, not to compose your own. The fact that you cut so many passages is, itself, an admission on your part that you did not do what you were asked to do. And yet, would that you had cut out what was bad, and had not put in so many things of your own to defend what was bad! I shall cite one of these instances so that the rest may also be recognized from this one. In the first book of the *Periarchon,* where Origen uttered with sacrilegious tongue the blasphemy that the Son does not see the Father, you even give the reasons, as if spoken in the name of the person who wrote it, and expound the commentary of Didymus,[36] in which he seeks to defend the error of the other person with wasted efforts, to prove that Origen, to be sure,

---
35 *Ibid.* 626-627.
36 Didymus' immense exegetical work is almost entirely lost.

has spoken correctly; but we simple men and gentle lambs of Ennius[37] cannot understand either his wisdom or yours, his translator. That preface of yours that you mention, and in which you adorn me with so much praise, proves you guilty of a very bad translation. For you say that you cut many things from the Greek, although you keep silent about the things that you added. Were the things that you cut good or evil? Evil, of course. Were the things that you kept good or evil? Good, of course. For you could not have translated what was evil. Therefore, you cut what was evil and left what was good? Undoubtedly. But practically everything that you translated is proven to be evil. Therefore, whatever I will prove to be evil in your translation, will be imputed to you, who translated it as being something good. It is quite a different matter, if you, being guilty of the same crime, expel some from the senate, like an unjust censor, and retain others in the senate house. But you say: 'I could not change everything; but I felt that I should cut only what I thought had been added by heretics.' Fine! If you cut what you thought had been added by heretics, then what you left is to be imputed to him whom you translated. Tell me whether these things are good or evil? You could not have translated what was evil. For you cut once and for all what had been added by heretics. Unless, perchance, you should have cut the evils of the heretics, and translated into Latin the errors of Origen intact. Tell me, then: Why did you translate into Latin the evils of Origen? Was it to expose him as the author of evil, or to praise him? If you are exposing him, why do you praise him in the preface? If you praise him, you are proven to be a heretic. It remains that you translated what seemed good. If all of these things are proven to be evil, then, both the translator and the author will be guilty of one and the same crime,

---

37 Ennianus, or Ennius, the celebrated poet, lived on the Aventine Hill, and he found his contentment in the strictest frugality and the services of a little handmaid. Or else he knew how to domesticate wild animals. Hence, the name of the gentle, domesticated lambs of Ennianus.

and the following judgment will be fulfilled: 'You saw a thief and you ran with him, with adulterers thou hast been a partaker.'[38] There is no need to confuse a clear-cut issue by argumentations. As for the rest, let him tell me whence he began to suspect that these things had been added by heretics. 'Because,' he says, 'I had read views expressed in a Catholic fashion on the same matters in other places of the same author.'

(12) *The heretical teachings of Origen.*

Let us consider his first position, in order to reach logically his second position. Among the many evil doctrines of Origen, I consider the following especially heretical: that the Son of God is a creature; that the Holy Spirit is a minister; that there are innumerable worlds which succeed one another throughout eternal centuries; that angels have been changed into souls of men; that the soul of the Savior existed before He was born of Mary; that this is the very soul 'which, though it was by nature God, did not consider being equal to God a thing to be clung to, but emptied itself, taking the nature of a slave';[39] the resurrection of our bodies will be of such a nature that they shall not have the same members, because, with the cessation of the functions of the members, the bodies themselves shall be rendered useless; and the bodies themselves, being tenuous and spiritual, shall gradually fade away and dissipate into thin air and even into nothingness; that in the restitution of all things, when the time of the principal forgiveness shall arrive, the Cherubim and Seraphim, the Thrones, Principalities, Dominations, Virtues, Powers, Archangels, Angels, the devil, the demons, and all of the human souls of Christians, as well as of Jews, Gentiles, and Pagans, shall have the one and the same state and equality; and when they have attained this form and measure of equality, and a new army of people, returning from exile in the world, will reveal rational creatures stripped of every taint of bodily

---
38 Ps. 49.18.
39 Phil. 2.6, 7.

corruption, then, again, another world shall arise from another beginning, and other bodies, in which souls that fall from heaven shall be clothed; so that we must be apprehensive lest we who are now males may subsequently be born females; and that she who is a virgin today may then, perhaps, be a common prostitute. These are the doctrines that I point out to be heretical in the books of Origen; you, on the other hand, show me a work of his in which you have read doctrines that contradict these.

(13) *The six thousand books of Origen.*

Now, do not say: 'the views that I had read expressed in a Catholic way on the same matters in other places of the same author,' lest you refer me to his six thousand books, which you charge the holy Pope Epiphanius[40] has read. But name the passages themselves. Nor will the citation be enough for me, unless you quote the very statements word for word. Origen is no fool and I know it; he cannot make contradictory statements. Therefore, the final conclusion that follows from all this reasoning is that the statements that you cut were not those of the heretics, but of Origen, and that you translated his evil statements because you felt that they were good; and both the evil and the good must be imputed to you who approved his writings in your preface.

(14) *Hilary and Ambrose, translators of Origen. The letter of Anastasius to John of Jerusalem.*

He continues in the same *Apology:* 'I am neither a defender nor an advocate of Origen. Nor am I the first translator. Others before me have engaged in this same work. I, too, finally undertook this work at the urgent request of the brothers. If an order is issued not to engage in a work, the order is customarily observed in the future. If those who engaged in the work before the order was issued are guilty,

---

40 St. Jerome's charge that Rufinus had invented the attribution of Epiphanius of six thousand books of Origen is wrong. Rufinus may have misunderstood the meaning of Epiphanius' remarks, but the number is furnished by that bishop. Cf. Ferd. Cavallera, *Saint Jerome, sa vie et son oeuvre* 2 (Louvain-Paris 1922) 100.

the guilt should commence with the first ones.'⁴¹ He has finally spewed out the words he wanted to say, and all the fury of his heart has erupted into a malicious accusation against us. When he translates the books of the *Periarchon*, he says that he is following me as his model; when he is accused for having engaged in such a work, he cites my example; he cannot live without me either when he is secure or when he is exposed to danger. Therefore, let him hear what he pretends he does not know. No one taunts you with your translation of Origen, otherwise, Hilary and Ambrose will be considered guilty of this crime; but because you approved the heretical doctrines that you translated by praising them in your preface. I myself, whom you are accusing, have translated seventy of his homilies and many of his commentaries, in such a way that I removed what was evil while translating what was good, and clearly pointed out to the reader what he should avoid in the books of the *Periarchon*, showing up the falsity of your translation. Do you wish to translate Origen into Latin? You have many of his homilies and his commentaries in which some topic pertaining to morals is expounded, and obscure passages of Scripture are explained. These are the works that you should translate. These are the works that you should distribute to those who are making demands of you. Why does your first effort begin in infamy? Why do you, while considering a translation of heretical doctrines, send ahead in defense of these doctrines a book supposedly that of a martyr,⁴² and force upon the ears of the Roman a work, the translation of which frightened the whole world? Or if the purpose of your translation is to prove him a heretic, you should certainly change nothing from the Greek, and you should confirm this fact in your preface, as Pope Anastasius expressed so very

---

41 Rufinus, *Apol. ad Anast.* 7 PL 21.627-628.
42 Before Rufinus translated the *Periarchon* of Origen for Macarius, he first translated the first book of the *Apologia* of Pamphilus, adding, by way of supplement, a small treatise of his own on *The Falsification of the Books of Origen*, in which he put forth the theory that the works of Origen had been tampered with and falsified by heretics.

wisely in his own words in a letter[43] which he wrote to Bishop John against you, acquiting me for complying, and condemning you for refusing to comply. And lest, perchance, you also deny this fact, I have appended a copy of the letter, so that, if you are unwilling to take the advice of a friend, you may heed the condemnation of the Bishop.

(15) *Rufinus is proven to be a defender of Origen. Eusebius, the chief of the Arians. Rufinus' preface to the Apologia of Pamphilus for Origen.*

You say that you are neither a defender nor an advocate of Origen. I shall without further ado produce for you your own book of which you speak as follows in that notorious preface to your famous work:[44] 'We have explained more fully the cause of this diversity in the *Apology*, which Pamphilus wrote for his own books, in a small treatise[45] that we added by way of supplement, in which we made it clear by evident proofs, as I think, that his books had been falsified in many places by heretics and malicious individuals and, in particular, the books that you are now asking me to translate, that is, the *Periarchon*.'[46] Were you not satisfied with the *Apologia* of Eusebius for Origen, or, to be sure, the *Apologia* of Pamphilus, as you prefer to call it, unless you, being wiser and more learned, so to speak, could add to the statements that you felt were understated by them? It would take too much time if I were to insert your whole book into this volume, and were to reply to all the heads that you have proposed, one by

---

43 In the year 401, Pope Anastasius received a letter from John of Jerusalem, consulting him about Rufinus. In making answer, the Pope confirmed the condemnation of Origen and all his works and declared that he desired to know nothing of Rufinus. The Pope would approve of Rufinus if, in his translation, he sought to bring to light the harmfulness of Origen. Otherwise, he was definitely opposed to such an enterprise and he condemned it absolutely. Cf. Francis X. Murphy, C.SS.R., *Rufinus of Aquileia, His Life and Works* (Washington 1945) 136.

44 Cf. *Origenis Periarchon libri quatuor interprete Rufino Aquileiensi presbytero* PG 11.111-414.

45 Rufinus, *Epilogus in Apologeticum S. Pamphili martyris ad Macarium seu Liber de adulteratione librorum Origenis* PG 17.615-632.

46 Rufinus, *Prologus in libros Periarchon Origenis presbyteri* PG 11.113.

one, pointing out in them the faults of speech, the assertions of lies, and the very illogical connection of words. Hence, to avoid the unpleasantries of a long, drawn out discourse and to reduce my remarks, I shall reply only to his views. As soon as he set sail from the harbor, he drove his ship against the rock. For in referring to the *Apologia* of the martyr, Pamphilus (which I have proven to be that of Eusebius, the chief of the Arians), of which he had said: 'We have translated it in the Latin language to the best of our ability, or as the occassion demanded,'[47] he stated: 'My dear Macarius, thou man of desires,[48] I want to advise you of this fact, that you may know that the rule of faith, to be sure, that we set forth above from his books is such that it should be both embraced and observed. For it is clearly proven that the view expressed in all of these books is Catholic.'[49] Although he cut many things from the book of Eusebius, and tried to change in good part the views regarding the Son and the Holy Spirit, nevertheless, many stumbling blocks are found in it, and very manifest blasphemies, declaring as Catholic views that he will not be able to deny are his very own. Eusebius says in this work, or rather Pamphilus (as you would have it), that the Son is the minister of the Father; that the Holy Spirit is not of the same substance as the Father and the Son; that the souls of men fell from heaven; and that, inasmuch as we have been changed from angels, angels and demons and human beings shall all be equal in the restoration of all things; and many other doctrines so impious and wicked that even to repeat them would be a crime. What will the advocate of Origen, the translator of Pamphilus, do? If there is so much blasphemy in the things which he has corrected, how much sacrilege is contained in the things which, as he pretends, have been falsified by heretics? His alleged reason for this opinion is that neither a fool nor a mad man could have said things that

---

47 Rufinus, *Liber de adulteratione librorum Origenis* PG 17.615.
48 This phrase is taken from Dan. 10.11.
49 Rufinus, *De adulter. libror. Orig.* PG 17.615.

were contradictory. And lest, perchance, we suppose that he wrote different things on different occasions, and occasionally pronounced views that were contradictory, he added: 'What do we do when there is found inserted in the very same places, and, if I may so say, in practically the next head, a sentence containing a contradictory view? Could he have been so forgetful of himself in the same volume of the same book and at times, as we have said, in the very next head? For example, that he, who previously had said that nowhere was it found in the entire volume of Scripture where the Holy Spirit was referred to as having been made or created, would immediately add that the Holy Spirit was created along with the other creatures? Or again, that he who said that the Father and the Son were of the same nature, termed *homooùsios* in Greek, could have stated in the very next heading that He, whom he had but a moment ago declared to have been born of the same nature as God the Father, was of a different nature and was created?'[50]

(16) *Eusebius and Didymus agree with the doctrines of Origen.*

These are his words, he cannot deny them. Do not say: 'For example, that he who previously had said,' but name the book itself, where he had previously expressed the correct, and subsequently the wrong view; where, after writing that the Holy Spirit and the Son were of the same substance as God the Father, he asserted in the very next sentence that they were creatures. Do you not know that I have all of the works of Origen? That I have read very many of them? 'To the mob with your trappings! I know you within and on the skin.'[51] Eusebius, a very learned man (I called him 'very learned,' not 'Catholic,' lest, according to your usual manner, you heap calumny on my head for this remark, too), accomplished nothing more or less with his six volumes than to show that Origen was of his own faith, that is, a follower of the Arian

---
50 *Ibid.* 616-619.
51 Persius, *Satires* 3.30.

perfidy. He quotes many examples, and consistently substantiates this fact. Therefore, in what dream of an Alexandrian prison was it revealed to you that you should concoct the story that the things that he admits to be true were falsified? But he, perchance, being an Arian, took advantage of these 'additions by heretics' to justify his own error, lest he be thought to be the only one who held the wrong views against the Church. What answer will you give in defense of Didymus,[52] who certainly was Catholic in his views of the Trinity, and whose book on the Holy Spirit even I translated[53] into Latin. He certainly could not have agreed with the things that were added by heretics in the works of Origen; and he dictated brief commentaries[54] on the very books of the *Periarchon* which you translated; in these he did not deny that the things that were written by Origen were written by him. But we simple human beings cannot understand his remarks, and he tries to make us see the sense in which they should be taken in good part. So much on the Son and the Holy Spirit. But as far as the other doctrines are concerned, both Eusebius and Didymus assent to the views of Origen very clearly, and they defend as pious and Catholic the statements that all the churches condemn.

(17) *Rufinus on the falsification of the books of Origen.*

But let us consider the arguments by which he seeks to prove that the writings of Origen have been corrupted by

---

52 Didymus' work *On the Trinity* takes up in three books a much firmer attitude against those who deny the divinity of the Holy Spirit. He takes for granted the divinity of the Father, and goes on to establish the divinity of the Son and the Holy Spirit, finally answering the objections of the Arians and, particularly, the Macedonians. Cf. F. Cayré, *Manual of Patrology and History of Theology* 1 (translated by H. Howitt; Belgium 1935) 403.

53 Didymus was primarily a theologian of the Trinity. The short treatise *On the Holy Spirit*, in sixty-three very brief chapters, is one of the best of its kind in Christian antiquity. Cf. O. Bardenhewer, *Patrology* (translated from the second edition by Thomas J. Shahan; St. Louis 1908) 308. We have only the Latin translation of St. Jerome.

54 Didymus wrote many dogmatic, polemic, and apologetic works, among which was a work devoted to the exposition and defense of Origen's *Periarchon*. His immense exegetical work is almost entirely lost.

heretics. 'Clement,'[55] he says, 'the disciple of the apostles, who was bishop of the Church of Rome and a martyr, after the apostles, published books, entitled *Anagnōrismós*, that is, *Recognitio*. In these, although there is set forth in very many places in the person of the Apostle Peter a doctrine that is certainly Catholic, yet, there is inserted in some places the doctrine of Eunomius[56] in such a way that it would seem exactly as if Eunomius himself were disputing, asserting that the Son of God was created out of no existing matter.'[57] And after making many statements too numerous to mention, he says: 'Why, I ask you, should it be assumed from all this that the apostolic man wrote heretical statements? Or should it rather be assumed that malicious individuals, in order to defend their own doctrines, inserted under the name of saintly men, in hopes that they might be more readily accepted, views which the former obviously could never be believed either to have held or expressed?'[58] He writes that Clement,[59] a priest of the Church of Alexandria, a Catholic man, also says in his books at times that the Son of God was created; and that Dionysius,[60] the bishop of Alexandria, a very learned man, in

---

55 Certain writings have been attributed to St. Clement of Rome, among which is the *Recognitiones* of Clement. The ten books of this work are no longer extant in the original Greek, but only in a Latin version made by Rufinus, and in a Syriac revision. The work relates the story of the life of St. Clement: his problems in youth with questions of human destiny; his conversion by St. Peter; his discovery of his lost family. The chief scope, however, of the work was not the story of the life of St. Clement, but rather the recommendation of certain teachings of St. Peter that are interwoven with the narrative. Cf. Bardenhewer, *op. cit.*, 82.
56 Eunomius of Cappadocia brought Arianism to its logical conclusion. He taught that God alone was unbegotten and not produced. The Son is begotten, created by God; but in His physical being He is in no way like the Father.
57 Rufinus, *De adulter. libror. Orig.* PG 17.620-621.
58 *Ibid.* 621.
59 Photius, who was acquainted with the *Outlines of Clement*, stated that Clement reduced the Son to a mere creature. This work was a series of notes in eight books on selected passages of the Old and New Testament. Only fragments of these are now extant. Cf. Cayré, *op. cit.*, 180.
60 Eusebius mentions this work of Dionysius against Sabellius. Sabellius

the four books in which he disputes against Sabellius, slips into the Arian doctrine. And with these examples, he seeks not to prove that the ecclesiastical and Catholic men held the wrong views, but that their writings were corrupted by heretics, and he concludes at the end by saying: 'So also in the case of Origen, in whose works the same kind of discrepancy is found, as in the works of those whom we mentioned above, we should not be satisfied to hold the same view of him that is held and entertained about the Catholic men who have already been prejudged, lest a like defense suffice for a like cause.'[61] If it is granted that whatever is found to be harmful in books has been corrupted by others, nothing will be ascribed to those in whose name it is said, but will be imputed to those by whom it is said to have been corrupted. And yet it will not be imputed even to those whose names are not certain; and so it will come that nothing will be ascribed to anybody, while everything is ascribed to everybody. In the face of such a disorderly type of defense, it will be impossible to accuse Marcion or Manichaeus or Arius or Eunomius; for whatever we charge has been said impiously by them, their disciples will reply that it was not published by their masters in that form, but was distorted by their enemies. According to this logic, even this very book of yours will not be yours, but, perchance, mine. And my own book which I am defending against the charges made by you, if you find fault with anything in it, will not be imputed to me, but to you who are finding fault with it. And since you refer back everything to heretics, what will you as-

---

had taught a form of Modalism, according to which the Trinity was not a real, but a modal relation of one Person to the world. There were three forms of appearance and activity assumed by the One Personal God in the role of Creator, Redeemer, and Sanctifier. Cf. Liguori G. Muller, O.F.M., *The De Haeresibus of Saint Augustine* (Washington 1956) 155. In order to emphasize very plainly the personal distinction between the Father and the Son, in his controversy with the Sabellians, Dionysius had made use of expressions and similes that implied a distinction in substance, and reduced the Son to the rank of creature. Cf. Bardenhewer, *op. cit.*, 155.

61 Rufinus, *De adulter. libror. Orig.* PG 17.622.

sign to the churchmen, to whom you leave nothing as their own? 'And why is it,' you will say, 'that there are many things in their books that are faulty?' If I reply that I do not know the sources of these errors, I will not be forthwith judging them to be heretics. For it is quite possible that the writers either simply erred, or expressed a different view, or that their writings were gradually corrupted by inexperienced transcribers. Or, to be sure, before Arius, a sort of noonday demon, was born at Alexandria, people expressed themselves in certain matters in an innocent and less cautious manner, and made statements that could not avoid the slanders of perverse men. Charges are being heaped upon Origen and, instead of defending him, you accuse others; instead of refuting the charge, you look for a group of men guilty of the crime. If you were asked to name Origen's associates in his heresy, you would be justified in producing such matters. But the question put to you at this time is: whether the things that are found written in the books of Origen are good or evil. You are silent, and, instead, you mention other matters. 'This is what Clement says'; 'Dionysius is found guilty of this error'; 'Pope Athanasius defends the error of Dionysius as follows'; 'the writings of the apostles have been falsified in the same way'; just as now the charge of heresy is being heaped upon your head by others, and you keep silent in your own behalf and make declarations about me. I make no charges against anybody, being content with having answered solely in my own behalf. I am not what you charge I am. If you are what they accuse you of being, see to it yourself. My acquittal will not prove me innocent nor will your arraignment prove you guilty.

(18) *The letter of Origen to his friends in Alexandria. The first part of the letter.*

After having first introduced the subject of the falsification by heretics of the apostles, and of the two Clements, and of Dionysius, he comes to Origen and speaks as follows: 'We have proven this fact from his own words and writings in which he deplores and complains about such a situation. For what he suffered from either the falsifications of the words or the forged editions of his books, while still living in the flesh, while still feeling and seeing, is clearly revealed in the letter[62] which he writes to some of his close friends in Alexandria.'[63] And he promptly appends a copy of the letter; and he who imputes to heretics the falsification of the writings of Origen, himself begins with a falsification; for he does not translate the exact original of the Greek, nor does he reveal to the Latins what he himself states in his own letter. And, although in the whole letter he assails Demetrius, the bishop of Alexandria, and inveighs against the bishops and clerics of the whole world, and he says that he was excommunicated in a deceitful manner by the churches; and that he does not care to render like for like in reviling lest, to be sure, he appear to be a reproachful individual, who is so careful not to revile anyone that he does not dare revile even the devil; whence he even afforded an opportunity to Candidus,[64] a follower of the Valentinian doctrine, to heap calumny on his head for saying that the devil was of a nature that was to be saved; nevertheless, concealing the real theme of the letter, he invents statements in defense of Origen which the latter does not make. For this reason, I have translated a small portion of the letter a bit beyond the first part, and placed it alongside of his fraudulent translation, composed of short sentences and clauses, so that the reader might see for himself his purpose for passing over in silence the first part of the letter. Consequently, after arguing against the priests of the Church in general, by whom he had been judged unworthy of com-

---

62 In Rufinus' *Epilogus in Apologeticum S. Pamphili martyris*, this letter is entitled *De adulteratione vel corruptione librorum suorum ex libro epistolarum Origenis quarto.* (*Epistulae scriptae ad quosdam charos suos Alexandriam*) PG 17.624-626.
63 Rufinus, *De adulter. libror. Orig.* PG 17.622-623.
64 Origen himself tells us of a discussion with the Valentinian Candidus, probably at Athens about 240, on the origin of the Son from the Father, and on the possibility of the devil's conversion. Cf. below, ch. 19.

munion with the Church, he stated the following: 'What need is there to speak of the very threatening words which the prophets used so often against the pastors, and the elders, and the priests, and leaders of nations, and the accusations that they made against them? You can search them out for yourself from Sacred Scripture without my help, and it will become clearly evident to you that this, perchance, is the age of which it is said: "Believe not in friends and trust not in princes";[65] and that the prophecy is now being fulfilled: "The leaders of my people have not known me; they are foolish and senseless children. They are wise to do evils, but to do good they have no knowledge."[66] We should rather pity such people than hate them, and should rather pray for them than revile them. For we were created to bless and not to revile. Whence, also, Michael, when he was arguing with the devil over the body of Moses, did not dare to bring an accusation of blasphemy against him even for such a serious offense, but said: "May the Lord rebuke thee."[67] Even in Zacharia, we read something similar to this. "The Lord rebuke thee, O Satan, and the Lord that chose Jerusalem rebuke thee."[68] And so we also pray that those who refuse to be rebuked by their friends with humility may be rebuked by the Lord. But when Michael says: "May the Lord rebuke thee, O Satan," and likewise Zacharia, let him see to it whether God will rebuke him or not. And if He rebukes him, let him see to the manner himself in which He will rebuke him.'[69] And after many a remark which would take too long to write down, he adds: 'It is our view that not only will those be cast from the kingdom of heaven who have committed grievous sins, as for example, fornicators and adulterers, and homosexuals, and thieves, but those as well who have committed less serious sins, according to what is written: "Neither the drunkards nor the evil-tongued will possess the

---
65 Mich. 7.5.
66 Jer. 4.22.
67 Jude 9.
68 Zach. 3.2.
69 This portion of the letter is supplied by St. Jerome.

kingdom of God";[70] and that there is just as much a limit to God's goodness as there is to His sternness. Whence we seek to do everything with due reflection, even in the matter of drinking of wine, and moderation of speech, so that we dare not revile a single soul. And yet, although we guard against reviling anybody on account of our fear of God, recalling to mind the words: "He did not venture to bring against him an accusation of blasphemy,"[71] that are spoken of Michael in his argument with the devil; and in another place: "These men disregard authority, deride majesty,"[72] certain individuals, who delight in arguments, ascribe blasphemy to us and to our doctrine, and they should see to this charge themselves, lest they hear it said to them: "Neither the drunkard nor the evil-tongued will possess the kingdom of God"; although they say that the father of evil and of destruction of those who shall be cast from the kingdom of God can be saved, a statement which not even a demented individual can make.'[73] He translated, to be sure, the rest of that same letter in place of the part we have translated at the end of Origen's words: 'And yet, although we guard against reviling anybody on account of our fear of God,' and the rest; and, cutting the first sections in this fraudulent fashion, on which the later sections depend, he began his translation of the letter as if the first section opened with this statement, and he said: 'Certain individuals, who delight in bringing charges against their friends, ascribe to us and to our doctrine the charge of blasphemy, which they have never heard from us; they should see to this charge themselves, since they refuse to heed the command that states that, "the evil-tongued will not possess the kingdom of heaven"; for they say that I assert that the father of evil and of destruction of those who shall be cast from the kingdom of God, that is to say, the devil, is to be saved, a statement that

---

70 1 Cor. 6.10.
71 Jude 9.
72 Jude 8.
73 This portion of the letter is supplied by St. Jerome.

not even a mentally deranged or manifestly insane person can make.'[74]

(19) *Origen's dialogue with Candidus. Novatianus' book on the Trinity.*

Compare the words of Origen that I have translated above, literally, with those that were not turned, but overturned, by him, and you will clearly recognize the great discrepancy that exists between them, not only of words, but even of meanings. I hope that you do not find this rather detailed translation boring. For I translated everything in order to make clear his purpose in keeping silent about the first section. There is extant among the Greeks the dialogue between Origen and Candidus, the defender of the Valentinian heresy, in which I admit I beheld two *andabatae*[75] locked in combat. Candidus says that the Son is of the substance of the Father, erring in his use of the term *probolē*, that is, *prolatio*.[76] Origen, on the contrary, following the view of Arius and Eunomius, opposes the view that He was either begotten or born, lest God the Father be divided into parts; but says that He came into being as a sublime and the most excellent of creatures by the will of the Father just like the other creatures. Then, they come to the second question. Candidus asserts that the devil is of a nature that is very wicked and one that can never be saved. Origen replies correctly against this assertion that he is not of a substance that is doomed to destruction, but that he fell of his own will and can be saved. Candidus interprets this view as calumny, as if Origen said that the nature of the devil was to be saved. And the latter refutes this false charge of the former. And we know that it is in this dialogue

---

74 Rufinus, *De adulter. libror. Orig.* PG 17.624-625.
75 *Andabatae* were gladiators who wore helmets without any aperture for the eyes, so that they were obliged to fight blindfolded, and thus excited the mirth of the spectators. Cf. Cicero, *Epistulae ad familiares* 7.10.
76 *Probolē* or *prolatio* are terms that imply generation, and hence, in the teachings of the Arians, must be rejected absolutely because they imply parts, or a body, and that is impossible; for by definition God is unbegotten. God cannot communicate His being.

alone that a heretical falsity is condemned by Origen, and in none of the other books that were never questioned. Otherwise, if everything that is heretical will not be ascribed to Origen, but to heretics, and practically all of his volumes are replete with these errors, nothing will be imputed to Origen, but to those whose names we do not know. He is not content with reviling the Greeks and the ancients, about whom he can freely concoct any story that he wants to because they lived in former ages and in distant lands. He comes to the Latins and cites, first of all, the case of Hilary the Confessor because his book[77] was falsified by heretics after the synod at Ariminium. And, consequently, when the question was put to him in the council of the bishops, he requested that the book be produced from his own home, a heretical version of which was placed in his own library without his knowledge; and when the book was produced and was judged heretical by all of them, the author of the book was excommunicated and left the assembly of the council. He imagines that he exerts such great influence that when he tells this dream to his friends, no one will venture to contradict this story that he concocts against the Confessor. Tell me, I ask you: In what city was the synod held by which he was excommunicated? Give the names of the bishops; produce the results of the votes of the subscriptions, whether split or unanimous.[78] Who were the consuls of that year? Who was the emperor who ordered the convening of the synod? Were the bishops of Gaul alone present or were the bishops of Italy and Spain also present? At any rate, tell me the reason for the convening

---

77 The book referred to here is the *De synodis* of Hilary. The second part of the work is dogmatic. Sometime later, Hilary was accused of heresy before the bishops assembled in council. He referred to this book for a substantiation of his faith, only to find in the book that was produced from his own library the very errors of which he was accused.

78 The consuls were Jovian and Varronianus, or possibly Valentinian and Valens; the emperor was Valentinian; the place, Milan; the bishops were presumably those of Cisalpine Gaul; and the cause was the heresy of Auxentius. Cf. Murphy, *op. cit.*, 87, n. 30.

of the synod. You mention none of these matters; but in order to defend Origen, you charge that a very eloquent man, and the clarion voice of the Latin language against the Arians, was excommunicated by a synod. But this calumny against a confessor must be tolerated to the best of our ability. He passes to the celebrated martyr, Cyprian, and says that Tertullian's book, entitled *De Trinitate,* is read under his name at Constantinople by the heretics of the Macedonian sect. In making this charge, he utters a double lie; for it is neither Tertullian's book, nor is it ascribed to Cyprian; but it is the book of Novatian,[79] and his name is also inscribed in the title. The peculiarity of style reveals the author's manner of expression.

(20) *The tale about Jerome.*

And I suppose it is a waste of time to confute manifest absurdities, when I am taunted with my own story, coming without question out of the synod;[80] and I am assailed under the name of a certain friend of Damasus, Pope of Rome, to whom he assigned the task of dictating the ecclesiastical letters. The trick of the Apollinarists was made known because they falsified the book of Athanasius, in which occurred the phrase *Dominicus homo.*[81] They had borrowed this book to read, and falsified it in such a way that they rewrote over the erasure the words that they had erased, so that it would appear, to be sure, that the phrase had not been falsified by them, but had been added by me. I ask you, my dearest friend, to dismiss

---

[79] Novatian is the author of the work *De trinitate.* It was later held to be either the work of Tertullian or Cyprian. In the sixteenth century, the *De trinitate* was published under the name of Tertullian, but the correct attribution was made shortly afterwards. Cf. Cayré, *op. cit.,* 250.

[80] This was the Ecumenical Council which was held at Rome in the year 382 under Pope Damasus. St. Jerome was present by invitation.

[81] St. Jerome was charged with composing a formula for Pope Damasus which the Apollinarists were to sign. There he made use of the expression *Dominicus homo.* The heretics protested against the phrase as a novelty. St. Jerome justified it by quoting ancient authors, and in particular St. Athanasius. Recent research has identified the work of St. Athanasius, in which he used the expression *kuriakòs ànthrōpos.* Cf. Murphy, *op. cit.,* 89, n. 37.

such nonsense from ecclesiastical treatises, where we are inquiring into the truth of doctrines, and where we are making examination of the authority of our elders on the matter of the salvation of our souls, and to stop considering tales that belong to dinners and banquets as proof of the truth. For it is possible that, even if you heard the truth from me, someone else who is ignorant of the circumstances may say that it was concocted by you, and fashioned in elegant style as a sort of mime of Philistion or a strophe of Lentulus and Marullus.[82]

(21) *The complaint about Saint Epiphanius.*

O the limits to which impudence will not go once it is given free rein! After telling the story of the excommunication of Hilary, of Cyprian's falsely ascribed book of heresy, of the erasure of Athanasius, and the simultaneous writing in of the phrase over the erasure, while I was asleep, he finally vent his rage against Pope Epiphanius; and in his *Apology for Origen*[83] reveals the pain felt in his heart because the Pope condemned him as a heretic in the letter[84] which he had written to Bishop John, and consoles himself with these words: 'Nay more the hidden truth must be made manifest at this point. For it is impossible for any man to exercise such an unreasonable judgment as not to express the same opinion on the same case. However, the instigators of the slandering brought against him are they who either are wont to argue at greater length in the Church or even write books, and who take everything that they either say or write from Origen. Therefore, lest many people recognize their thefts, which, without question, would never have been considered reproachful if they had not been ungrateful towards their master, they prohibit all the simple people from reading his works. Finally, a certain individual[85] amongst them, who supposes that he

---

82 Cf. Marius Mercator, *Liber subnotationum in verba Juliani* PL 48.126-127, where he mentions these three men together: '*Unus tu, unus Philistion, unus Latinorum Lentulus, unus tibi Marullus comparandus.*'
83 Rufinus, *Liber de adulteratione librorum Origenis* PG 17.615-632.
84 This letter appears in the collection of St. Jerome's letters as *Epistola* 51, *S. Epiphanii ad Joannem Hierosolymorum* PL 22.517-527.
85 i.e., Epiphanius.

has an obligation to speak ill of Origen, just as he has of preaching the Gospel, to every nation and in every tongue, has admitted at a very large gathering of the brethren that he had read six thousand of his books.[86] If he read these books (as he himself is wont to say) for the purpose of acquiring knowledge of his evils, ten books, or certainly twenty, or at most thirty books, would have been sufficient to gain this knowledge. But to read six thousand books can no longer be considered a desire to acquire knowledge, but rather a dedication of practically a whole lifetime to his teachings and studies. Therefore, how can we have any real respect for him who reprehends individuals who have read just a few of his works for the sake of private information (without in any way doing harm to their rule of faith or impairing their piety)?'[87]

(22) *Epiphanius knew five languages.*

Who are those individuals who are wont to argue at greater length in the Church, and who write books, and who take everything they say and write from Origen; and who prohibit the simple people from reading his books, because they do not want their thefts recognized, and are ungrateful towards their master? You should mention these men by name and mark them out. Therefore, should the blessed Bishops Anastasius and Theophilus, and Venerius and Chromatius,[88] and every synod of the Catholics of the East and the West, who denounced him to the people as a heretic with one voice because they were also one in spirit, be judged pilferers of his books; and when they preach in the churches, do they not mention the mysteries of the Scriptures, but rather the thefts of Origen? Are you not content with making disparaging remarks promiscuously against everyone, unless you direct in a special way the lance of your pen against a blessed and outstanding priest

---

86 Cf. above, p. 124, n. 40.
87 Rufinus, *De adulter. libror. Orig.* PG 17.630-632.
88 Anastasius was bishop of Rome, Theophilus of Alexandria, Venerius of Milan, and Chromatius of Aquileia.

of the Church? Who is that person who imagines that he has an obligation of speaking ill of Origen, as he has of preaching the Gospel to every nation and in every tongue, and who has admitted at a very large gathering of the brethren that he had read six thousand of his books? Were you also present at this gathering and meeting of the brethren, when he complains in his letter that nefarious doctrines had been published by you in defense of the heresy of Origen? Must he be charged with a crime for knowing Greek, Syrian, Hebrew, Egyptian, and, in part measure, also Latin? Therefore, are both the apostles and the apostolic men, who spoke various languages, considered guilty; and will you, who are bilingual yourself, ridicule me who am trilingual? But as far as those six thousand books are concerned which, you allege, were read by him, who will either believe that you are telling the truth, or that he could have told a lie? For if Origen had written six thousand books, it could have been quite possible for a highly learned individual, and one schooled in sacred Letters from his infancy, to have read the works of another man out of curiosity, and for the sake of gaining information. But how could the latter have read what the former, to be sure, did not write? Count the titles of his books that are contained in the third book of Eusebius, in which he wrote the biography of Pamphilus, and you will not find a third of that number, not to mention six thousand. We have the letter of the above-mentioned Pontiff, in which he replies to this slander of yours while you were still in the East, and confutes this very manifest lie frankly and candidly.

(23) *He had intended to write against the Apologia of Pamphilus. The book De viris illustribus addressed to Dexter. He translated the homilies of Origen in his youth.*

After making such outlandish statements, you dare to state in the *Apologia* that you are neither a defender nor an advocate of Origen, in whose defense Pamphilus and Eusebius did not seem to you to have said enough. I shall endeavor to reply to these volumes on another occasion (if the Lord will afford me an opportunity during this life). For the present time, it should suffice to have opposed solely your assertions, and to have briefly informed the reader of the fact that I saw that book which was circulated under the name of Pamphilus written for the first time in your own manuscript; and that, inasmuch as I was not concerned with any heretical statements made therein, I had always assumed that the work of Pamphilus and Eusebius were separate volumes. But when the matter was subsequently brought up for investigation, I decided to answer their writings, and, for that reason, I read the views held by each one regarding Origen; and I clearly perceived that the first of the six books of Eusebius was the very one that was published by you as the single volume under the name of Pamphilus, in the Greek as well as in the Latin, in which you had changed in the right measure those views regarding the Son and the Holy Spirit which betrayed manifest blasphemy. Whence, also, about ten years ago, when my good friend, Dexter,[89] who was in charge of the praetorian guard, asked me to prepare for him a list of the authors of our religion, I listed among the exegetes this book that was published by Pamphilus, for I assumed that the information given out by you and your disciples was true. But when Eusebius himself states that Pamphilus wrote nothing, with the exception of brief letters to his personal friends, and when the first of his six books contains the same views, expressed in the same words as those that have been concocted by you under the name of Pamphilus, it is obvious that the reason why you wanted to circulate this book was to introduce heresy in the person of the martyr. And since you have distorted many things from the very book which you pretend is the work

---

[89] St. Jerome's work on Christian writers, his *De viris illustribus*, was composed at Bethlehem in the year 392 at the suggestion of the praetorian guard, Dexter. It professes to be a brief account of all those ecclesiastical writers who have written on the Sacred Scriptures, from the Crucifixion to the fourteenth year of the reign of Theodosius (392).

AGAINST RUFINUS 143

of Pamphilus, and there is one version in the Greek and a different one in the Latin, you should not impute your fraud to my error. For I believed that the book was the work of the person indicated in the title, just as the *Periarchon*, and many other works of Origen and of very many exegetes of Greece, which I either did not read before now and am now forced to read, since the question of heresy has been raised, in order to know what to avoid and what to approve. Whence, also, in my youth, I translated in compliance with simple requests only those homilies of his addressed to the people, which did not contain such serious stumbling blocks, without influencing anyone to accept, through the views which were approved, those which are manifestly heretical. (To make a long story short), just as I am making it known that I received my book from those who transcribed it from your own copy, so also, in like manner, you should certainly reveal the source from whence you received your copy; so that he who will not be able to produce someone else as the author of the book will himself be proven guilty of a falsification. 'The good man from his good treasure brings forth good things';[90] and a tree of excellent seed is also known by the sweetness of its fruits.

(24) *The letter falsely ascribed to Jerome.*

Brother Eusebius writes that he found among the African bishops, who had convened at the imperial residence on ecclesiastical matters, a letter supposedly written in my name, in which I did penance and solemnly declared that I was induced in my youth by the Hebrews to translate into Latin the Hebrew books, in which there is no truth. I was amazed to hear this story. And because, 'on the word of two or three witnesses every word is confirmed,'[91] and one witness, not even Cato, is believed, letters written by many of my friends in the City informed me of this incident, in which they asked about the truth of the story, and they sadly revealed the name of the individual by whom this letter had been circulated. What

90 Matt. 12.35.
91 2 Cor. 13.1.

else would he not dare to do who circulated such a story? It is well that evil does not match its connivings with its power. Innocence would have perished from the earth, if power went hand in hand with villainy and calumny succeeded in fulfilling all its desires. In spite of his great eloquence, it was impossible for him to imitate my style and my manner of writing, such as they are; but in the midst of his tricks and his impersonation of another person in whose character he had falsely arrayed himself, he clearly betrayed his own identity. It is the same man, therefore, who had concocted in my name this letter of penance because I had translated evilly the Hebrew volumes, who is said to make the charge that my reason for translating Sacred Scripture was to condemn the Septuagint, so that I stand accused whether the things that I have translated are false or true, as long as I admit that I have erred in the new undertaking, or as long as the new edition is considered a condemnation of the old. I wonder why he did not say in the same letter that I was a homicide, an adulterer, sacrilegious, and a parricide, and any foul name that the mind can think of in its silent meditation. I should thank him that he reproached me with only the charge of error or falsity, when there was such a multitude of charges. Did I say anything against the Septuagint translators, whose work I revised[92] very carefully many years ago, and gave to the students of my own language, and expound daily in the convent of my brethren; whose Psalms I constantly sing and meditate upon? Was I so foolish as to wish to forget in my old age what I learned in my youth? All of my treatises are interwoven with their testimonies. My commentaries on

---

92 Once at Bethlehem, St. Jerome began the revision of the Latin text of the Old Testament, in accordance with the Hexaplar text of the Septuagint. He began with the Psalms, and emended the Itala text in exact conformity with the Hexaplar text of the Septuagint. In the same way, St. Jerome also revised most of the other books of the Old Testament, making use in his manuscript of the critical signs of Origen. The greater part of these revised texts have unfortunately disappeared. Cf. O. Bardenhewer, *Patrology* (translated from the second edition by Thomas J. Shahan; St. Louis 1908) 459-460.

the twelve prophets[93] are an explanation of both my version and that of the Septuagint. O the labors of men which are always uncertain! O the pursuits of mortal beings which, at times, achieve the opposite goals! By this endeavor I felt I merited well of my Latin brethren, and had stirred the minds of our brethren to learning; for even the Greeks[94] do not despise a work translated from the Latin after such great translators. Now it is the source of my condemnation and is adding fuel to my sick heart. And what is there safe for man, if innocence is considered reproachful? While the householder was asleep, an enemy oversowed weeds.[95] 'The boar out of the wood hath laid the vine waste; and a singular beast hath devoured it.'[96] I hold my peace, and a letter that is not mine speaks against me. I am ignorant of the charge, and I acknowledge the charge throughout the whole world. 'Woe is me, my mother! Why hast thou borne me, a man to be condemned and judged by all the earth?'[97]

(25) *From the Preface to Genesis.*

All of the prefaces to the Old Testament, examples of which I have appended in part, are testimonies to this very fact. It would be superfluous on my part to write the statements that were made in the prefaces otherwise than they were written there. Therefore, I shall begin with Genesis, the preface to which is as follows: 'I have received the desired

---

93 The great series of commentaries, to which St. Jerome gave special care, is devoted to the prophets. The first set of commentaries was on the twelve minor prophets. This is the work referred to here. St. Jerome began in the year 392 with Nahum, Michea, Sophonia, Ahheus, and Habacuc. He treated Jona and Abdia in the year 396; and brought the series to an end with Zacharia, Malachia, Osee, Joel, and Amos. Cf. F. Cayré, *Manual of Patrology and History of Theology* 1 (translated by H. Howitt; Belgium 1935) 583.
94 After finishing his great work of revision of the Latin text of the Old Testament, St. Jerome decided to translate the entire Old Testament from the the original Hebrew. The Psalms was one of the first books translated. St. Jerome mentions a certain Sophronius in his *De viris illustribus* (134), who translated many of his works into Greek including the Psalter.
95 Cf. Matt. 13.25.
96 Ps. 79.14.
97 Jer. 15.10 (Septuagint).

letters of my dear friend, Desiderius, who got his name, as Daniel did, from his ability to foretell to a certain degree future events, begging me to translate the Pentateuch from the Hebrew into Latin, and make it available to the ears of our brothers. This, to be sure, is a dangerous undertaking, and one that is subject to the barkings of my detractors, who assert that my purpose in composing a new version in place of the old one is to reprehend the Septuagint translators. They apply the same test to talent that they apply to wine; although I have very often affirmed that I was offering to the best of my ability in the tabernacle of God what I could, and that the wealth of one man was not disgraced by the poverty of another. I was prompted to undertake this venture by the zeal of Origen,[98] who blended the translation of Theodotion with the ancient version, marking the entire work with an asterisk and obelisk, that is, with a star and a lance; thus, either rendering more clear the passages that before had been less clear, or cutting and rejecting every passage that was superfluous, and especially those that were promulgated on the authority of the evangelists and apostles. Among these, we read many passages from the Old Testament that are not found in our copies, such as the following: "I called my son out of Egypt";[99] and: "For he shall be called a Nazarene";[100] and: "They shall look upon him whom they have pierced";[101] and: "From within him there shall flow rivers of living water";[102] and: "Eye has not seen nor ear heard, nor has it entered into the heart of man, what things God has prepared

---

[98] The Hexapla of Origen contained five different texts of the Old Testament arranged in six parallel columns: the Hebrew text in Hebrew letters, the Hebrew text in Greek letters, and the four Greek versions of Aquila, Symmachus, the Septuagint, and Theodotion. The text of the Septuagint was marked with obeli and asterisks to indicate the words wanting in the Hebrew or the words wanting, but present in another Hebrew version. Apart from the Septuagint, very little of the Hexapla remains. Cf. Cayré, *op. cit.*, 196.
[99] Matt. 2.15.
[100] Matt. 2.23.
[101] John 19.37.
[102] John 7.38.

for those who love him";[103] and many others that lack a special context. Therefore, let me ask them where these passages are written down; and since they might not be able to tell me, we shall produce them from the Hebrew books. The first testimony is in Osee, the second in Isaia, the third in Zacharia, the fourth in Proverbs, the fifth also in Isaia. Since many individuals do not have this information, they accept the nonsensical views of the Apocrypha and prefer the Spanish lullabies to the canonical books.[104] It is not within my province to explain the causes of this error. The Jews say that it was all a part of a clever scheme to keep Ptolemy,[105] who was a worshiper of the one God, from detecting the existence of a double divinity also among the Jews; but that the most important reason for such a scheme was the fact that the king appeared to be leaning towards the teachings of Plato. Finally, wherever Scripture made any sacred pronouncement about the Father, and the Son, and the Holy Spirit, they either interpreted the statement in a different sense, or kept silent about it all together, so that they satisfied the king without revealing the secrets of their faith. And I do not know who was the first author to invent the lies about the seventy cells of Alex-

---

103 1 Cor. 2.9.
104 St. Jerome tells us in his *Commentariorum in Isaiam prophetam liber* 17, cap. 64 (PL 24.622-623) that certain silly women in Spain, and specially in Lusitania, had been deceived into accepting as truth the marvels of Basilides and Balsaneus' treasury. He states further that Irenaeus, in explaining the origin of many heresies, pointed out that the Gnostics deceived many noble women of the parts of Gaul around the Rhone, and afterwards those of Spain, framing a system partly of myths, partly of immorality, and calling their folly by the name of philosophy.
105 Ptolemy, commonly known as the son of Lagus, but the reputed son of Philip of Macedon, reigned over Egypt from 323-285 B.C. He was a great patron of learning, and, according to traditions current among the Fathers of the Church, wishing to adorn his library at Alexandria with the writings of all nations, requested the Jews of Jerusalem to furnish him with a Greek version of their Scriptures. Thus originated the Septuagint. The Jews withheld some of the secrets of their faith, especially the prophecies referring to Christ, lest the king, who was a monotheist, believe that the Jews were believers in two deities. Cf. St. Jerome's preface to his *Liber Hebraicarum quaestionum in Genesim* PL 23.937.

andria, in which they were divided, and wrote the same things, since Aristaeus, a champion of the same Ptolemy, and Josephus,[106] many years later, made no mention of such an incident, but write that they were all gathered together in one apartment and consulted and did not prophesy. For it is one thing to be a prophet, quite another matter to be a translator. In the one case, the spirit foretells what is to come; in the other, learning and abundance of words translate what is known. Unless, perchance, it must be assumed that Cicero was inspired by the spirit of rhetoric when he translated Xenophon's *Oeconomicus,* and Plato's *Protagoras,* and Demosthenes' *Speech in Defense of Ctesiphon;* so that the Holy Spirit composed from the same books one set of testimonies through the Septuagint translators, and another one through the apostles; so that what the former passed over in silence, the latter pretended that it was written down. What then? Are we condemning the ancients? Absolutely not! But after the efforts of our predecessors, we are laboring in the house of the Lord to the best of our ability. They translated before the coming of Christ, and what they did not know, they expressed in doubtful terms. What we write after His Passion and Resurrection is not so much prophecy as it is history. For things that are heard are narrated in one style, things that are seen in quite another style. What we understand better, we also express better. Therefore, listen, my dear rival, and pay attention, my dear detractor. I am not condemning, I am not reprehending the Septuagint translators, but I am preferring the apostles to all of them with confidence. Christ speaks to me through the lips of those who, I read, have been set above the prophets in spiritual gifts; in this respect, the translators occupy practically the lowest level. Why do you torture yourself with envy? Why do you stir up the minds of the ignorant against me? If you think that I am in error anywhere in my translation, ask the Hebrews; consult the

---

106 Cf. Josephus, *Antiquities* 12.2.

masters of the various cities. What they have said about Christ in their copies, your copies do not have. It were quite another matter, if they proved that the testimonies had been subsequently used by the apostles against them, and the Latin copies were more correct than the Greek, and the Greek more correct than the Hebrew.'[107]

(26) *From the Preface to the Books of Kings.*

Also in the books of Samuel and Malachim,[108] which we refer to as the books of the four Kingdoms, after giving a catalogue of the books of Sacred Scripture, I made the following remarks: 'Such being the case, my dear reader, I beg you not to consider my work as a condemnation of the ancients. In the tabernacle of God, each and every man offers what he can. Some offer gold, and silver, and precious stones; others offer cotton stuff, purple garment, scarlet cloth, and hyacinth. We do well if we offer skins and goats' hairs. And yet the apostle judges our lowlier gifts as the more necessary.[109] Whence, also, that entire beauty of the tabernacle, and the distinction of the Church, present and future, throughout all its adornments, is covered with skins and goats' hairs, and the cheaper gifts protect against the heat of the sun and damage from rain storms.'[110] Notice how puffed up I am with pride against the Septuagint translators that I admit that they offered gold, and precious stones, and the purple robe in the tabernacle of God, and I, goats' skins and hairs?

---

107 St. Jerome, *Praefatio in Pentateuchum* PL 28.147-152. (St. Jerome refers to this as *Prologus in Genesim* in his *Apologia* 2.24.)
108 In his *Praefatio in libros Samuel et Malachim* (PL 28.553), which serves as an exposition of all the translations from Hebrew, St. Jerome says, in giving a cataloguing of the books, that the first and second books of Kings were called Samuel, and the third and fourth books were called Malachim, that is, Kings. It is far better to call the books Kings, than Kingdoms, because the author does not describe the kingdoms of many nations, but that of a single people, the people of Israel.
109 Cf. 1 Cor. 12.22.
110 St. Jerome, *Praefatio in libros Samuel et Malachim* PL 28.557.

(27) *From the Preface to the Paralipomenon. The corrupted version of the Septuagint translators.*

I shall also cite another testimony, lest you say that I was compelled by the necessity of circumstances to change my views. In the book of Times, that is the Paralipomenon, which in Hebrew is referred to as *Dabre Jamin,* I wrote the following in the preface addressed to the saintly Pope Chromatius: 'If the version of the Septuagint translators had remained pure and in the state in which it was translated by them into Greek, it would have been superfluous on your part, my dear Chromatius, the most saintly and most learned of bishops, to induce me to translate for you into Latin the Hebrew volumes. For it would have been right for us to approve by our silence what the ears of men had once heard, and what had strengthened the faith of the budding Church. But now, when copies are being circulated that differ according to different regions of the world, and that true and ancient translation has been falsified and corrupted, you put your trust in my ability either to decide which one of the many versions is the true one, or to compose a new work out of the old one, and overreach, as the saying goes, the jeering Jews. Alexandria and Egypt laud Hesychius as the author of their Septuagint. Constantinople, all the way to Antioch, approves the copies of Lucian, the martyr. The provinces that lie between them read the Palestinian copies, which Eusebius and Pamphilius had worked out from Origen and published. And the whole world is in contention with itself over this triple variety. Origen, to be sure, not only composed copies of the four versions,[111] marking each word according to the region, so that one which disagreed with the rest which were in agreement would immediately be detected; but what is a greater presumption on his part, he blended the edition of Theodotion with the Septua-

---

111 Origen prepared a work known as the Tetrapla, a collation of the four principal Greek versions of the Old Testament, namely, that of Aquila, Symmachus, the Septuagint, and Theodotion. This was in addition to his famous Hexapla. Cf. above, p. 146, n. 98.

gint edition, marking, to be sure, with asterisks the things that had been missing, and with obelisks the things which seemed to have been added superfluously. Therefore, if others had the right not to keep what they had once accepted, and, if after the story of the seventy cells which is circulated in public without any authority, they opened individual cells, and, if passages which the Seventy were ignorant of are read in the churches, why should my Latin brethren not accept me, who kept intact the old version and composed a new edition in such a way that I established my work by citing the authorities of the Hebrews and (what is more important) those of the apostles? I composed recently the book *De optimo genere interpretandi*,[112] in which I pointed out that the following passages taken from the Gospel are found in the books of the Hebrews: 'I called my Son out of Egypt';[113] and: 'For he shall be called a Nazarene';[114] and: 'And they shall look upon him whom they have pierced';[115] and the following passage of the apostle: 'Eye has not seen nor ear heard, nor has it entered into the heart of man what things God has prepared for those who love him';[116] and others similar to these. The apostle and the evangelists certainly had knowledge of the Septuagint translators. And whence is the source of their statements which are not found in the Septuagint? Christ, our Lord, the author of both Scriptures, says in the Gospel according to John: 'He who believes in me, as the Scripture says, "from within him there shall flow rivers of living water."' [117] What the Savior declares was written down was certainly written down. Where is it written down? The Septuagint does not have it, and the Church does not recognize the Apocrypha. Therefore, we must go back to the book of the Hebrews, which

---

112 For the circumstances accompanying the composition of this work, which is also known as *Epistola* 57, *ad Pammachium*, cf. above, Introduction, p. 50, n. 8.
113 Matt. 2.15. This is quoted from Josue 11.1.
114 Matt. 2.23. This is quoted from Isa. 11.1.
115 John 19.37. This is quoted from Zach. 12.10.
116 1 Cor. 2.9. This is quoted from Isa. 64.4.
117 John 7.38. This is quoted from Prov. 18.4.

is the source of the statements quoted by the Lord, as well as the examples cited by the disciples. I say this with all due respect to the ancients, and am replying only to my detractors who bite back at me with dog teeth. They attack me in public, but read me in secluded corners; and they are, at the same time, both my accusers and my defenders, since they approve in others what they reprove in me; as if virtue and vice resided not in the facts, but changed with the author. But I recall that I once corrected the edition of the Septuagint translators from the Greek and made it accessible to our brethren. I should not be judged an enemy of those whom I always expounded in the convent of my brothers. My sole purpose in my recent translation of the *Dabre Janim*, that is, the Words of the Days, was to put in more proper order the inextricable entanglements and mass of names, which were a jumbled mess due to the faults of scribes, and the labyrinth of views; and to arrange the work in lines of verse, which I might sing to myself and to my brothers, in the manner of Hismenia,[118] if others turn a deaf ear.'[119]

(28) *From the Preface to Esdras.*

I also said the same things in my preface to Esdras and, after making many observations, I added the following statement: 'The remark that I am going to make is very honest. I published what is not found in the Greek, or what is found in a form different from that of my version. Why do they tear the translator to pieces? Let them ask the Hebrews; and let them either credit or discredit my translation on the basis of their authority. It is a different matter, to be sure, if they close their eyes to what is said, and seek to revile me, and refuse to imitate the zeal and good will of the Greeks, who read carefully the Septuagint translators, when the Gospel of Christ is already flourishing, as well as the Jewish and Ebionite trans-

---

[118] Hismenia was a disciple of the song master, Antigenides. His singing did not meet the approval of the public, and his tutor suggested to him: 'Sing your songs to me and to the muses.'
[119] St. Jerome, *Praefatio in librum Paralipomenon* PL 28.1323-1328.

lators of the old law, Aquila, to be sure, and Symmachus and Theodotion, and have dedicated to the churches through the efforts of Origen the *Hexapla;* how much more grateful should my Latin brethren be, when they see arrogant Greece borrow something from them! For, in the first place, it is an undertaking involving great expense and infinite labor to secure all of the copies. Moreover, those who possess copies and have no knowledge of the Hebrew language will make more mistakes, since they do not know which one of the many versions is the more accurate one. Such was the experience of even a very learned individual[120] among the Greeks, who abandoned at times the sense of Scripture, and adopted the error of any translator without distinction. But I, who have at least a little knowledge of the Hebrew language, and am not, nevertheless, deficient to any degree in the Latin language, can judge the views of others more accurately, and express in my own language views that I myself understand.'[121]

(29) *From the Preface to Job.*

I shall pass on to the book of Job[122] which I had translated in Latin many years ago in accordance with the edition of the Septuagint translators, which Origen had marked with obeli and asterisks. When I had translated it a second time, according to the Hebrew itself, I made the following remark: 'In the case of all of the books of Sacred Scripture, I am forced to answer the slanders of my adversaries, who charge that my translation is a rebuke to the Septuagint translators;

---

120 i.e., Apollinaris of Laodicea.
121 St. Jerome, *Praefatio in Ezram* PL 28.1404-1406.
122 Once St. Jerome was settled at Bethlehem, he started the revision of the books of the Old Testament in accordance with the Hexaplar text of Origin. The greater part of these revised texts disappeared. Only his text of Job, which he completed shortly after the revision of the Psalter, has reached us. He had scarcely finished this work of revision when he undertook the translation of the entire Old Testament from the original Hebrew. He translated about the year 390 the four books of Kings, then the book of Job, afterwards the Prophets, and at the same time the Psalms. A tedious spell of sickness interrupted his labors. He began again towards the end of the year 393. Cf. above, p. 144, n. 92.

as if among the Greeks, Aquila, Symmachus, and Theodotion had not also translated word for word, and thought for thought, or had not composed a kind of translation that was a blend and a slightly modified version of both types; and Origen had not marked all of the books of the Old Testament with obeli and asterisks, which he inserted in the ancient translation, either those which he added on his own or borrowed from Theodotion, indicating that what he had supplied was missing. Therefore, let my detractors learn either to accept in its entirety what they had accepted in part only, or erase my translation together with their asterisks. For it is impossible for them not to admit that the same individuals, who, as they have clearly seen, have omitted many things, also erred in some matters; especially in Job, which will be mutilated, for the most part, if you cut the things that have been added and marked with asterisks. So much for the Greeks. But among the Latins, there were almost seven or eight hundred verses missing, previous to the translation that I recently composed marked with asterisks and obeli, so that the book in its abridged, and mutilated, and greatly damaged form represented to the reading public a disgraceful copy of the original.'[123] And, after making many observations that I pass over in the interest of brevity, I added this remark in conclusion: 'Let my dogs, therefore, hear that the reason why I undertook this volume was not to reprove the ancient translation, but rather to render more clear by my translation the things that are obscure in it, or had been omitted, or, to be sure, had been corrupted through the fault of scribes; for we have learned the Hebrew language after a fashion, and were conversant with Latin, practically from our cradle days, in the company of teachers, grammarians, and rhetoricians, and philosophers. But if among the Greeks, after publication of the Septuagint version, at a time when the Gospel of Christ is already flourishing, Aquila, the Jew, and Symmachus, and

---

[123] St. Jerome, *Praefatio in librum Job* PL 28.1079-1080.

Theodotion, the Judaizing heretics, are welcomed, who have concealed many of the mysteries of the Savior in their deceitful translation, and, in spite of it all, the *Hexapla* occupies a place in the churches and is expounded by the church men, how much greater the reason why I, a Christian, the son of Christian parents, and who carry the sign of the cross on my forehead, and whose sole concern was to recover what had been omitted, to correct what had been falsified, and to reveal the mysteries of the Church in simple truthful language, should not be rebuked either by the fastidious or the reproachful readers?'[124]

(30) *From the Preface to the Psalter.*

After I translated for the second time the Psalter according to the Hebrew, which, to be sure, had been corrected very carefully and with much labor some time ago by me, according to the Septuagint translators, and was well received by Rome, I also strengthened it with a preface and made the following remark in one section of the preface: 'Therefore, since you[125] had quoted certain testimonies from the Psalms in defending the Lord Savior in a recent argument with a Hebrew, and he, wishing to mock you, asserted in the case of practically each and every passage that the reading of the testimonies in the Hebrew was not the same as the one you produced from the Septuagint translators against him, you begged me most earnestly to translate a new edition in Latin in addition to those of Aquila, Symmachus, and Theodotion. For you said that you were quite confused by the variety of translations, and that you were content with either my translation or my judgment because of the love to which you feel yourself drawn. And thus being influenced by you, to whom I must not deny even what I cannot do, I exposed myself once again to the barkings of my detractors; and I preferred that you find my ability than my good will wanting in our friend-

---
124 *Ibid.* 1082-1083.
125 i.e., Sophronius, to whom St. Jerome had dedicated his translation of the Psalms.

ship. I can say with assurance and with confidence, and I can cite many witnesses to this volume of mine, that, to the best of my knowledge, I have changed nothing from the Hebrew truth. Therefore, if my edition is at variance in any place with the ancients, ask any Hebrew you like, and you will clearly understand that I am being maliciously assailed by my rivals, who would rather be thought despisers than hearers of what is excellent. Men are very malicious; for why is it that, while they are constantly searching for new pleasures, and their thirst cannot be quenched by the waters of the seas that are close at hand, they are satisfied with the old flavor, only in the matter of the study of Scripture. I do not say this because I am assailing my predecessors, or because I am speaking ill in any way of those whose translation I corrected very carefully some time ago and made available to the people of my language, but because it is one thing to read the Psalms in the churches of Christ of the believers, and quite another matter to reply to the Jews who caluminate every word.'[126]

(31) *From the Preface to the Books of Solomon.*

I also translated from the Hebrew the books of Solomon, which I had translated a long time ago into Latin according to the Septuagint, and added obeli and asterisks; and I dedicated it to the saintly bishops, Chromatius and Heliodorus, and added the following remark at the end of my preface: 'If the edition of the Septuagint translators is more pleasing to anybody, he can avail himself of the edition which we corrected a long time ago. For our purpose in composing a new edition is not to destroy the old.'[127]

(32) *From the Preface to Isaia.*

I shall also consider Isaia, and add a portion of its preface relative to the Septuagint translation. Since I had stated that he was more of an evangelist than a prophet, because he de-

---

[126] St. Jerome, *Praefatio in librum Psalmorum juxta Hebraicam veritatem* PL 28.1124-1126.
[127] St. Jerome, *Praefatio in libros Salomonis* PL 28.1243-1244.

scribed all of the mysteries of the Church of Christ so vividly that you would assume he was not prophesying about the future, but rather was composing a history of past events, I also added the following remark: 'Hence, I assume that the Septuagint translators at that time did not want to reveal openly to the pagans the mysteries of their faith, lest they cast sacred things to the dogs, and cast pearls to the swine. When you[128] read this edition of mine, you will recognize the things that were concealed. I am fully aware that it is a tremendous task to understand the prophets, and that no one can readily pass judgment upon a translation unless he has first understood what he has read. I also realize that I am exposing myself to the attacks of very many individuals who, being spurred on by envy, despise what they themselves cannot understand. Therefore, I am putting my hand into the fire with full knowledge and with my eyes wide open. And, nonetheless, I make this one request of my fastidious readers: just as the Greeks read along with the Septuagint translators, Aquila, and Symmachus, and Theodotion, either because of their zeal for personal information, or that they might better understand the Septuagint, through a comparison of these editions, they, too, in like manner, should deem it an honor to have at least one translator in addition to the earlier ones. Let them first read, and despise later, lest it seem that they condemn what they do not know, not after due deliberation, but rather through a preconceived hatred.'[129]

(33) *On Daniel.*

Concerning Daniel, however, I shall reply briefly that I did not deny that he was a prophet, for I admitted in the beginning of my preface that he was a prophet; but I wanted to disclose the views of the Hebrews, and the arguments with which they sought to prove their views; and to inform the reader that the churches of Christ read this prophet according

---

128 Paula and Eustochium, to whom St. Jerome dedicated his translation of Isaia.
129 St. Jerome, *Praefatio in librum Isaiae* PL 28.772-773.

to Theodotion, and not according to the Septuagint translators. If I said that their version of this book was far from the truth, and that it was rightly condemned by the judgment of the churches of Christ, I am not to be blamed for making this statement, but rather they who read the version. There are four available editions: that of Aquila, of Symmachus, of the Septuagint, and of Theodotion. The churches read Daniel according to Theodotion. What sin have I committed if I followed the judgment of the churches? But he who brings charges against me for relating the objections that the Hebrews are wont to raise against the story of Susanna, the Song of the Three Children, and the story of Bel and the Dragon,[130] which are not found in the Hebrew volume, proves that he is just a foolish sycophant. For I was not relating my own personal views, but rather the remarks that they are wont to make against us. If I did not reply to their views in my preface, in the interest of brevity, lest it seem that I was composing not a preface, but a book, I believe I added promptly the remark, for I said: 'This is not the time to discuss such matters.'[131] Otherwise, he will also be able to bring charges against me because I asserted that Porphyry had spoken at length against this prophet, and I introduced as witnesses to this fact, Methodius, Eusebius, and Apollinaris,[132] who answered his nonsense in many thousand verses,

---

[130] The story of Bel and the Dragon (Dan. 3), and of Susanna (Dan. 14), and the Song of the Three Children (Dan. 13) were placed in the beginning of the book of Daniel in all the ancient Greek and Latin Bibles, till St. Jerome in his translation detached them thence, because he did not find them in the Hebrew. But both the one and the other are received by the Catholic Church, and were from the very beginning a part of the Catholic Bible. Cf. the letter of Africanus to Origen *(Africani de historia Susannae epistola ad Origenem* PG 11.41-48) about the story of Susanna and Origen's reply *(Origenis epistola ad Africanum* PG 11.47-86). The Song of the Three Children is found in the Apocrypha.

[131] St. Jerome, *Praefatio in Danielem prophetam* PL 28.1294.

[132] Porphyry, the chief pupil of Plotinus, the Neo-Platonist, was one of the defenders of the old faith against Christianity. He composed *Against the Christians* in fifteen books, which was answered by many of the Fathers of the Church. St. Methodius, bishop of Olympus, composed up to ten thousand verses against him; and Eusebius of

and I did not write against the books of Porphyry in my preface. Let him who agrees with such nonsense, and refuses to accept the truth of the Hebrew Scripture, hear me proclaim freely: 'No one, to be sure, is compelled to read what he does not want to. I wrote for those who asked me, not for the fastidious; for the grateful, not for the envious; for the studious, not for the listless. And yet I wonder why he reads Theodotion, the heretic and Judaizer, and despises the translation of any Christian sinner without distinction.'

(34) I ask you, my very dear friend, who are so curious that you even know my dreams, and bring charges against everything that I wrote for so many years without fear of future rebuke, to tell me how it happens that you have no knowledge of the prefaces of the books against which you are bringing charges? The prefaces themselves have replied to this future reviling in a sort of prophetic way, fulfilling the proverb: 'The antidote before the poison.' What harm does my translation do the churches? You bought off, I know, at great cost, the Jewish translators of Aquila, and Symmachus, and Theodotion, and of the fifth and sixth editions. Your Origen, and (lest, perchance, you complain that you have been touched keenly by this fictive praise) our Origen (I call him ours for the excellence of his genius, not for the truth of his doctrines) explains and expounds in all of his books the translations of the Jews and the Septuagint translators. Both Eusebius and Didymus do the same thing. I pass over Apollinaris, who sought with good intentions, to be sure, but not with knowledge, to weave together patches from the translations of all of these men into one garment, so to speak, and to compose a consequence of Scripture, guided not by the rule of truth, but rather by his own judgment. The apostolic men use the Hebrew Scripture. It is clear that the apostles themselves

---

Caesarea, and Apollinaris of Laodicea wrote twenty-five and thirty volumes, respectively, against Porphyry. Cf. St. Jerome, *Epistola* 70.3, *ad Magnum*. Twenty of the books of Eusebius were known to St. Jerome. Cf. *De viris illustribus* 81.

and the evangelists did likewise. The Lord and Savior, whenever He refers to ancient Scripture, quotes examples from the Hebrew volumes, such as the following: 'He who believes in me, as the Scripture says, "From within him there shall flow rivers of living water." '[133] And on the cross itself: 'Eli, Eli, lema sabacthani,'[134] which means: 'My God, my God, why hast thou forsaken me?'[135] not, as it is quoted in the Septuagint: 'O God, my God, look upon me: Why has thou forsaken me?'[136] and many other passages similar to these. We do not say this because we wish to rebuke the Septuagint translators, but because the authority of the apostles and of Christ is greater; and wherever the Septuagint translators are not at variance with the Hebrew, there the apostles took their examples from their translation; but where they differ, they quoted in Greek what they had learned from the Hebrews. Therefore, just as I am pointing it out that there are many quotations in the New Testament taken from the ancient books which are not found in the Septuagint, and am showing that they were written in Hebrew, in like manner, my accuser should also point out any passage in the New Testament taken from the Septuagint translators which is not found in the Hebrew, and the argument is settled.

(35) *The conclusion of the work.*

From all of this, it is clear that the edition of the Septuagint translators, which has been established by the antiquity of its readers, is useful to the churches, since the Gentiles heard of the coming of Christ before He came; and that the other translators are not to be reproved because they translated not their own, but sacred volumes; and that my good friend should accept from a friend and a Christian an edition that he has sought to transcribe from the Hebrews at great cost to himself. I have exceeded the limits of a letter; and

---

133 John 7.38.
134 Matt. 27.46.
135 Matt. 27.48; Mark 15.34.
136 Ps. 21.1.

I, who had already attacked a nefarious heresy with my pen, have been forced to reply in my own defense, while I await the three volumes of my friend,[137] and worry about the mass of charges; except that it is easier to be on guard against an avowed enemy than to resist an enemy hiding under the name of a friend.

---

[137] The three volumes of Rufinus referred to here are his *Apologia ad Anastasium* and his *Apologiae in sanctum Hieronymum libri duo*.

Book Three

THE FINAL REPLY OF ST. JEROME AGAINST THE WRITINGS OF RUFINUS.

(1) *He replies to the books of Invectives which he received from Rufinus himself.*

After reading the letter[1] of your wisdom in which you inveigh against me, and in which you now provoke your friend, once praised by you and called a true colleague and brother, to reply to your books, and you terrify with charges, I have come to realize that the words of Solomon have been fulfilled in you: 'In the mouth of a fool is the rod of pride,'[2] and: 'A fool receiveth not the words of prudence: unless thou say those words which are in his heart.'[3] And Isaia says: 'The fool will speak foolish things, and his heart will work iniquity, to practice hypocrisy and to speak to the Lord deceitfully.'[4] For why was it necessary to send the volumes of charges, and bring slanders out into the open, if you frighten and threaten me with death in the concluding sections of your letter, lest I dare to reply to your charges or, should I say, to your praises? You praise, to be sure, and condemn the same things; and there

---

1 Rufinus received the *Apologia* of St. Jerome, written in answer to his own *Apologia*, from a merchant from the East who had stopped at Aquileia for several days' trade. Chromatius, Rufinus' bishop, fearing that the controversy was getting out of hand, intervened, and advised both parties concerned to make an end to the quarrel. Rufinus, heeding the advice, wrote St. Jerome an informal letter and sent it along with the two books of his *Apologia*. It is to this letter to which St. Jerome is here referring. The letter has not survived.
2 Prov. 14.3.
3 Prov. 18.2.
4 Isa. 32.6.

proceed from the same source both the sweet and the bitter. Wherefore, I beseech you to first practice the respect and modesty that you demand of me; and you, who level the charge of lying against someone else, should stop lying yourself. I am not causing anybody to be scandalized, nor am I, in the meanwhile, your accuser. For I am not concerned with the penalty that you deserve, but rather with the course of action that is right for me to pursue; and I am apprehensive of the words of the Savior, who says: 'Whoever causes one of these little ones who believe in me to sin, it were better for him to have a great millstone hung around his neck, and to be drowned in the depths of the sea';[5] and: 'Woe to the world because of scandals! For it must needs be that scandals come, but woe to the man through whom scandal does come.'[6] I, too, could have heaped up false charges against you, and could have said that I either heard or saw things that nobody had observed, so that impudence might be reckoned by the ignorant as truth, and madness as constancy. But far be it from me to follow your example and do the very things myself that I reprehend in you. Let him utter foul statements who can commit foul deeds. 'The evil man from the evil treasure of his heart brings forth that which is evil. For out of the abundance of the heart the mouth speaks.'[7] Meanwhile, you should consider it your good fortune that your erstwhile friend, who now stands accused, has no desire to reproach you with base charges. And I say this, not because I am apprehensive of the shafts of your accusation, but because I would rather be accused than accuse, and suffer injury than inflict it, fully aware of the command laid down by the apostle: 'Do not avenge yourselves, beloved, but give place to the wrath, for it is written: "Vengeance is mine; I will repay, says the Lord." But if thy enemy is hungry, give him food; if he is thirsty, give him drink; for by so doing

---

5 Matt. 18.6.
6 Matt. 18.7.
7 Luke 6.45.

thou wilt heap coals upon his head.'[8] For he who avenges himself is not worthy of the vengeance of the Lord.

(2) *The apostles disagreed without impairing their friendships.*

And, yet, before I answer your letter, I would like to reason earnestly with you, the elder among the monks, a good priest, an imitator of Christ: Can you kill your brother whom you are guilty of murdering if you merely hate him? Is this the lesson you learned from the Savior, that you should also turn the other cheek to him who strikes you on the one cheek? He Himself gave this reply to the man who struck Him: 'If I have spoken ill, bear witness to the evil; but if well, why dost thou strike me?'[9] You threaten me with death, which even snakes can inflict. Death is the common lot of all men, murder, of villains. Furthermore, shall I be immortal, unless you kill me? In fact, I am grateful to you for making a virtue out of a necessity. Did not even the apostles disagree among themselves without impairing their friendships? Paul and Barnabas[10] quarreled with each other over John, surnamed Mark, and a parting of ways separated those whom the Gospel of Christ united. Did not this same Paul withstand Caiphas to his face,[11] because he did not walk uprightly according to the Gospel? And yet he calls him his precursor, and the pillar of the Church,[12] and confers with him on the preaching of the Gospel, lest he run or had run in vain. Do not even children disagree with their parents over religion, and wives with husbands without doing violence to their piety? If you hold the same view as I, why do you hate me? If you hold a different view, why do you want to kill me? Must he who disagrees with you be killed? I call upon Jesus, who shall judge both this letter of mine and yours, to be witness of my conscience, that I wanted to hold

---

8 Rom. 12.19, 20.
9 John 18.23.
10 Cf. Acts 15.39.
11 Cf. Gal. 2.11.
12 Cf. Gal. 2.9.

my peace on the advice of saintly Pope Chromatius,[13] and put an end to this feud, and overcome evil with good; but because you threaten me with death unless I hold my peace, I am forced to reply, lest it appear that I am admitting the charge by holding my peace, and you interpret my gentleness as the sign of a bad conscience.

(3) *The words of the letter of Rufinus.*

Such, indeed, is the dilemma that you present, fashioned not according to the art of logic, of which you are ignorant, but in the workshop and in the minds of your hangmen. If I hold my peace, I shall be considered guilty of the charge; if I reply, I shall be considered guilty of slander. Therefore, you keep me from answering and, at the same time, force me to answer. Under the circumstances, I shall act judiciously in both cases; I shall refute the charges and, at the same time, refrain from inflicting any harm. For who would not be apprehensive of an individual who is prepared to kill? For I shall discuss the main points of your proposition, leaving the rest for those very learned books of yours which I confuted, even before I had read them. You say[14] that you sent your accusation against me only to those individuals who had been injured by my words, and not to a multitude of people; for Christians should not speak for the sake of ostentation, but rather for the sake of edification. And what is the source, I ask you, from whence the report of your books has reached me? Who circulated them at Rome, who in Italy, who throughout the island of Dalmatia? If the books were lying hid in your own library, and in those of your friends, how did the charges made against me come to my attention? And do you dare to say that you are a Christian and that you are not speaking for the sake of vain display, but rather for the sake of edification, when in your old age you concoct stories about another old man which a cutthroat would

---

13 Cf. above, n.1.
14 For an attempted reconstruction of this private letter of Rufinus, cf. Francis X. Murphy, C.SS.R., *Rufinus of Aquileia, His Life and Works* (Washington 1945) 153, n.62.

not tell about a thief, a harlot about a courtesan, a buffoon about a clown; when you bring forth mountains of charges against me, and have been sharpening for a long time daggers which you might plunge into my throat? Did your Ceres and *Anabasii*[15] scurry throughout all of the different provinces simply to read my praises, and to recite your panegyric on street corners, and at public gatherings, and in the shops and factories of little women? This is what you mean by holy modesty; this is what you mean by Christian edification; you are so decent, so modest, that people coming in crowds from the West tell me about your slandering in such vivid and consistent fashion that I was forced to reply, not to your writings, which I had not read as yet, but to your views, and withstand with the shield of truth the shafts of falsehood sent flying throughout the whole world.

(4) *A monk servant of Rufinus pilfered the letter of Epiphanius.*

Your letter continues in this fashion: 'Do not bribe my scribe with a large sum of money, as your friends did in the case of my scrolls of the *Periarchon*,[16] which were not yet corrected, and were not yet put in final shape, so that they might be able to falsify more readily scrolls that nobody had in his possession, or a few at the very most. Accept with my compliments this copy sent to you, which you sought to procure at great cost.' Are you not ashamed of such an introduction? Would I bribe your scribe with money? Who wields so much power and influence that he would dare to contend in wealth

---

15 It has been suggested that these appropriate titles were coined for the followers of Rufinus from the proper names of Ceres and *Anabasioi*. The Roman Ceres is the Greek goddess, Demeter, who roamed for nine days over the whole earth in search of her daughter, Persephone, who had been carried off by Hades. *Anabasii* was a term applied to individuals who made speed by mounting chariots and horses.
16 Rufinus had accused Eusebius of Cremona of stealing the rough draft of his translation of the *Periarchon* of Origen. Pammachius and Oceanus refer to the copy as an unfinished manuscript; cf. *Epistola* 83, *ad Hieronymum*.

with Croesus and Darius,[17] that he would not dread to encounter Demaratus and Crassus?[18] Have you grown so callous as to place your hope in a lie, and to think that you can be protected by a lie, and to imagine that any story concocted by you will be believed? Who stole your letter of praise from the cell of brother Eusebius at Bethlehem? Through whose schemes and by whose servants was a document found in the hospice of saintly Fabiola and Oceanus, a Christian gentleman and a scholar, who had never seen it before? Or do you suppose that you are absolved of all guilt if you impute to others a guilt that is your own? Will anyone who offends you, however innocent he may be, be considered guilty of slander on the spot? For you have that something that caused Danae[19] to lose her chastity, that Giezi[20] preferred to the sanctity of his master, that caused Judas to betray his Lord.

(5) *He does not approve of a Christian's bringing charges against another Christian. He defends Eusebius of Cremona. The errors of the books of the Periarchon.*

Let us see what it is that my good friend falsified in your scrolls that were not yet corrected, and were not yet put in perfect order, and they were more readily falsified by him because nobody had them in his possession, or a few at the very most. I wrote it before, and I repeat the statement, with God as my witness, that I did not approve of his or of any Christian's bringing charges against another Christian. For why is it

---

17 Croesus and Darius were kings of Lydia and Persia, respectively, and they were notorious for their wealth.
18 Demaratus, the father of Tarquinius Priscus, was a very wealthy immigrant from Corinth. Crassus was the triumvir, surnamed the Rich.
19 Danae was the daughter of Acrisius, king of Argos. Fearing the oracle which said that his daughter would bear a son, whose hand would deprive him of his life, Acrisius shut his daughter up in a subterranean chamber. Jove fell in love with Danae, and under the form of a golden shower he poured through the roof into her bosom, and she bore a son. Acrisius put mother and son in a coffer and cast them into the sea.
20 Giezi was the servant of the prophet, Eliseus. After the prophet had cured the Syrian, Naaman, from leprosy, Giezi was punished with the disease as a penalty for his greed and lying. He had demanded in the prophet's name a talent of silver and two changes of garment for needy friends; (cf. 4 Kings 5.20-27).

necessary for you to make public, for the scandal and ruin of many people, faults which you can either reprove or correct in private? But, inasmuch as each and every individual lives with his own whim, and a friend does not become master on the spot of the will of another person, I do not accept the charge of the falsification of scrolls made against a holy man, even as I reprehend the preferring of charges, even though just. For what changes could a Latin individual make in a Greek translation? Or what cuts or additions could he make in the books of the *Periarchon*, where everything is so perfectly interwoven, and one thing depends on another in such a way that any addition or cut that you would want to make would immediately show up like patches, as it were, on a coat? Therefore, follow the advice yourself that you are giving me; assume a bit of modesty, befitting a gentleman at least, if not a Christian, lest you, who are confronted with the facts, believe in your own contemptible and craven conscience that you have been exonerated by your words. If Eusebius bought your uncorrected scrolls for gold in order to falsify them, produce your own scrolls which have not been falsified; and if you will prove that there is nothing heretical in them, then, he will be considered guilty of the charge of falsification. Change them as much as you like, correct them as you will, you will not prove that they are Catholic. For if it were a matter of an error in words or in a few views, the evil could be cut and replaced with the good. But when the whole argument is the same, that all rational creatures who had fallen of their own will shall be subsequently restored to the one and the same state; and that there will again be other falls from the same beginning, what is there for you to correct, unless you change everything? If you wish to do that, you will no longer be translating the books of someone else, but will be composing your own. But I do not understand the logic of such an argument: 'Because,' he says, 'the scrolls were uncorrected, and had not yet been put in perfect order, they were more readily falsified by Eusebius.' I am either too dull mentally, or the argument seems to me to be very foolish and absurd. If the scrolls had not yet been corrected, and had not yet been put in perfect order, the error in them will not be imputed to Eusebius, but rather to your delay and tardiness, since you were slow to correct them. He will be blamed only for being hasty in circulating in public what you had intended to correct little by little. But if Eusebius falsified them, as you would have it, why do you pretend and allege as an excuse that they appeared in public when they had not as yet been corrected, and had not as yet been put in perfect order? For both the corrected as well as the uncorrected scrolls admit the same falsification. 'Nobody,' you say, 'had these books in his possession, or a few at the very most.' What a glaring discrepancy in one sentence! If nobody had them in his possession, how could they be in the possession of a few? If a few had them in their possession, why do you pretend that nobody had them in his possession? But since you state that they were in the possession of a few, and your very own admission invalidates your assertion that they were not in the possession of anybody, where is the logic to your complaint that your scribe was bought off with gold? Tell me the name of the scribe, tell me how much gold was paid out, tell me where it was paid out, to whom and by whom? Without question, you have discharged from your service a man who has betrayed you, and you have severed relations with a man guilty of such a serious offense? I am afraid that the more likely story is that the copies, which agree and correspond so perfectly that there is not even the slightest difference between one copy and the other, were given to Eusebius and to the others by those few friends of yours. Furthermore, do you call it wise on your part to give others a copy which you had not yet corrected? The composition of the scrolls had not yet been put in perfect order, and others already had in their possession your errors that were to be corrected. Do you not see that the lie is not consistent? And what did it profit you for that brief moment to make public our discussion, in order to avoid the judgment of the bishops, and stand condemned by your own words? It is clear from all this that, in the words of the famous orator,[21] you have the will to tell a lie, but not the skill to invent.

(6) *The difference between procuring and buying.*

I shall follow the order of your letter and append the words themselves exactly as you spoke them: 'I admit that I praised your eloquence, as you say, in my preface; and I would praise it today, if you had not made it odious by your profuse boasting which is not in accord with the views of Tullius.' When did I, who was unwilling to recognize even your praises of my eloquence, boast about my eloquence? Are you saying this because you do not care to be flattered by deceitful praises? You will be openly charged so that you who spurn a praiser will experience an accuser. I was not so foolish as to reprehend your ignorance, which nobody can condemn more effectively than you yourself when you write. But I wanted to show your fellow disciples, who did not study letters with you, what you accomplished in the East during the thirty years, the illiterate writer, who considers impudence, and eloquence, and wholesale reviling of all people to be signs of a good conscience. I am not applying the rod to you, as you say, nor am I trying to teach my old pupil letters with the whip and lashings; but because all of us exegetes cannot bear the irresistible power of your eloquence and of your teaching, and you dazzle our eyes with the brilliance of your genius to such a degree that you think that everybody is your rival, we are really eager to check you; lest, if you once gain preeminence in writing and reach the pinnacle of eloquence, all of us who wish to know anything be denied the opportunity of uttering even a word. I am a philosopher, a rhetorician, a grammarian, a logician, a Hebrew, a Greek, a Latin, a trilinguist. In like fashion, you will also be a bilinguist, whose knowledge of the Greek and Latin languages is such that the Greeks take you for a Latin, and the Latins for a Greek; and Pope Epiphanius will be a pentaglot because he speaks in five languages against you and your Amasius.[22] At

---
21 i.e., Cicero.
22 i.e., Origen.

the same time, I am amazed at the temerity with which you dare to speak against a man of such accomplishments: 'You who keep watch with the eyes of so many disciplines, how are you to be pardoned if you make a mistake and are not to be protected by the shield of perpetual silence of shame.' When I read this, and thought that I had offended somewhere in speech, 'For he who does not offend in word is a perfect man,'[23] and felt that he was going to make public some of my faults, he suddenly said: 'The severe denunciations that you uttered against me got into my hands two days before the departure of the bearer of this letter.'[24] What, then, becomes of your threat, and your words: 'How are you to be pardoned if you make a mistake and are not to be protected by the shield of perpetual shame?' Unless, perchance, you were able to put the scrolls in good order, though hard pressed for time; or you had intended to hire some scholar to search diligently for the ornaments of the gems of your eloquence in my own works. You wrote above: 'Accept with my compliments the copy I sent you which you sought to procure at a great cost.' Now you say with deceptive humility: 'I wanted to imitate you; but, since the individual who was returning to you was in a hurry, I decided to write you a brief note rather than a detailed discourse to others in my behalf against your reviling.' And meanwhile, you enjoy freely your ignorance. For to be sure, on a former occasion, you made the following admission, saying: 'It was useless for you to find fault with a few points, when we admitted openly that you can find fault with all of them.' Nor shall I reprehend you for using the phrase 'procured copy' instead of 'bought copy'; for 'procuring' is indicative of equal opportunity, 'buying,' of a payment of a price; nor for the sentence that 'the individual who was returning to you was in a hurry,' which is a redundancy characteristic of very slovenly speech. I shall reply only

---

23 James 3.2.
24 We have to rely on St. Jerome's word that Rufinus had only two days to reply to his *Apologia*. This is a quotation from Rufinus' private letter to St. Jerome.

to the matter of views, and shall prove, not that you are guilty of solecisms and of barbarisms, but that you are a liar, and deceitful, and impudent.

(7) *Concerning the preface to the books of the Periarchon.*

If your sole purpose in writing the letter to me is to admonish me, and to wish to correct me to avoid giving scandal to the rest of the people, and to silence some individuals while others rage, why do you write books to others against me and distribute them for reading throughout the whole world with the help of your satellites? What becomes of your syllogism with which you try to trap me, and in which you state: 'My excellent master, whom were you trying to correct with this work? If those to whom you are writing, they had committed no wrong; if me whom you are condemning, you had not written to me.' And I shall answer you in your own words: 'My illiterate master, whom were you trying to correct, those who had not sinned, or me, to whom you had not written?' Do you think that the readers are senseless animals, and all of them are ignorant of your cleverness or rather your malice, in which the serpent was also more clever than all the beasts in paradise, that you ask me, whom you attack publicly with accusations, to admonish you in private? Are you not ashamed to call your accusations an *Apology?* You utter complainingly that I am shielding myself against the blows of your fists, and you don the mask of humility, like some pious and religious character, and say: 'If I had made a mistake, why did you write to others instead of refuting me personally?' I shall hurl the very complaint back at you: 'Why, then, did you not do yourself what you allege as your excuse that I did not do? Just as if a man were to strike another individual with his fists and kick him, and were to say to the latter if he tried to resist: "Was it not commanded thee: 'If someone strike thee on the cheek, turn to him the other also'?" '[25] And what was commanded thee, my good man, to beat me and to gouge out my eyes? And if I even

---
25 Matt. 5.39.

as much as move a finger, you will recite to me the precepts of the Gospel. Do you want to know about all the deceits of your cunning, and the snares of little foxes that dwell in the ruins of old walls, of whom Ezechiel says: 'Thy prophets, O Israel, were like foxes in the deserts'?[26] Listen carefully to what you have done. You praised me so highly in your preface[27] that your praises were cast in my teeth, and unless I had declared that I was at variance with such a great praiser, I would have been judged a heretic. After I refuted the charges, that is to say, your praises, and answered the accusations and not the accuser, without disparaging in any way your name, and also inveighed against heretics, in order to prove that I, who had been slandered by you, was Catholic, you became enraged and acted like a mad man, and composed very eloquent books[28] against me; and since you distributed them out to everyone to be read and chanted, the writings, in which you, my former praiser, adorned me with high praises, reached me with great speed from Italy, and Rome, and even from Dalmatia.

(8) *He cleared himself of the suspicion of heresy.*

I admit, I answered the charges promptly; and I sought with all my might to prove that I was not a heretic. And I sent these books of my *Apology* to those whom you had wounded, so that the antidote of my books might follow the poisons of yours. For this fault, you sent both those earlier books and the recent letter, replete with insults and charges. What do you want me to do, my good friend? Shall I hold my peace? It will appear that I am admitting the charge. Shall I speak out? You frighten me with your daggers, and threaten to accuse me, not now before the ecclesiastical, but before the civil courts. What have I done? What sin have I committed? In what way have I hurt you? Was it that I said that I was not a heretic? That I considered myself unworthy of your praises? That I described

---
26 Ezech. 13.4.
27 Rufinus, *Prologus in libros Periarchon Origenis presbyteri* PG 11.111-112.
28 Rufinus, *Apologiae in sanctum Hieronymum libri duo* PL 21.541-624.

openly the frauds and perjury of heretics? How does all this concern you, who keep boasting that you are both Catholic and truthful, and who are more willing to accuse me than to defend yourself? Is the defense of myself an accusation against you? Or will you not be able to be orthodox in any other way except by proving that I am a heretic? Or what does my fellowship profit you? Or where is the logic to your cleverness? You are accused by others, and you accuse someone else. You are assailed by an individual, and you turn your back on him and stir up against yourself another man who is holding his peace.

(9) *Rufinus and Jerome, two old men. He praised the erudition of Origen in his youth.*

I call Jesus, my mediator, to witness that I resort to these words, reluctantly and unwillingly, and that I would have held my tongue forever had you not provoked me. Finally, stop accusing me and I shall stop defending myself. For do you call it edifying for the hearers to see two old men fighting with one another over heretics, especially when both of them wish to appear to be Catholic? Let us stop patronizing heretics and there will be no argument between us. Let us now condemn Origen, who is condemned throughout the whole world, with the same fervor with which we praised him before. Let us join hands; let us unite in spirit; and let us follow with alacrity the two standard bearers of the East and West.[29] We made a mistake in our youth, let us correct our mistake in our old age. If you are a brother, be glad that I have corrected my mistake. If I am a friend, I should rejoice over your conversion. As long as there exists a bitter strife between us, it will appear that we live the right faith out of necessity, not of our own will. Our enmity is bringing to nought for both of us, in turn, the testimony of a true repentance. If our belief is one and the same, if our likes and dislikes are identical (a condition which even Catiline admits gives rise to strong friendships), if we hate heretics in equal measure, and if we condemn our past

---

29 i.e., Theophilus of the East and Anastasius of the West.

error equally, why are we quarreling with each other when we are opposing the same things and defending the same things? Forgive me for praising in my youth Origen's erudition and knowledge of Scripture; and I will pardon you for composing in your old age an *Apology* for his books.

(10) You affirm on oath that my books got into your hands two days before you wrote the letter to me and, for that reason, you did not have the time to answer at your leisure; otherwise, if you had spoken against me after due deliberation and preparation, it would have appeared that you were hurling thunderbolts, not charges. And who will believe you, a very truthful man, that a merchant dealing in oriental merchandises,[30] who had to sell the wares that he had transported from here, and, in turn, to buy goods there which he might, in turn, bring back here, was at Aquileia for only two days, so that you were forced to dictate the letter against me in a hurry and on the spur of the moment? For are your books which you spent three years finishing[31] any more eloquent? Unless, perchance, there was nobody available at the moment to correct your silly production and, for this reason, the whole course of your composition, lacking the art of a Pallas, sinks in the quagmires and gulfs of errors. The lie about time is so manifest that you could not have read my writings in two days, not to mention answer them. It is evident from all this that you either spent many days writing this letter, as the eloquence of the style itself proves; or, if this is a composition done on the spur of the moment, you are, without question, a careless writer; for, while you compose such excellent work on the spur of the moment, you compose a work much worse after proper preparation.

(11) *The custom and rule of commentators.*

But I do not quite understand the meaning of your remark which you offer as an excuse that you translated from the Greek what I had previously translated in Latin; unless, perchance,

---
30 Cf. above, p. 162, n. 1.
31 i.e., the two books of Rufinus' *Apologia* which were begun in the year 399 and completed in the year 401.

you are still finding fault with the *Commentary on the Ephesians*,³² and are assuming a calloused and impudent attitude, as if you had received no reply to this question, and, stopping up your ears, you refuse to listen to the words of the charmer. In this, as well as in other commentaries, we have expounded our own views, as well as those of others, openly acknowledging the views which are heretical and those which are Catholic. For it is the custom of commentators and the rule of exegetes to set forth the various views in their exposition, and to expound the view that is approved either by themselves or by others. And this procedure is adopted, not only by interpretators of Sacred Scripture, but also by the commentators of secular literature, Latin as well as Greek. You cannot claim in your defense that you followed this procedure in the books of the *Periarchon;* for you are condemned by your own preface, in which you declare that you had cut what was evil and what had been added by heretics, and left what was best; so that whatever statement you make in your work, whether good or evil, is now no longer imputed to him whom you are translating, but rather to you, the translator; unless, perchance, you should have corrected the errors of the heretics and brought out into the open the evil of Origen. But because you refer us to the copy, we have replied to you on this point before reading your writings.

(12) *A ridiculous matter and a laughing matter. The Roman faith did not assent to deceits.*

It was not a laughing matter, as you write, but rather ridiculous, that I happened to say at the conclusion of my discussion of the book of Pamphilus, after I had asserted that it was the work of Eusebius³³ and not of Pamphilus, that I also assumed for many years that it was the work of Pamphilus,³⁴ and that I borrowed a copy of this work from you. Notice that your jeer-

---
32 In the second book of his *Apologia,* Rufinus deals at length with St. Jerome's *Commentary on the Epistle to the Ephesians,* pointing out the many errors which are contained therein.
33 Cf. St. Jerome, *De viris illustribus* 81.
34 *Ibid.* 75.

ing laughter frightens me so much that I even now make the same remark. I took from your manuscript what I thought was a copy of Pamphilus. I took the word of a Christian; I believed a monk; I never dreamed that you could contrive such a heinous crime. Later on, however, when the question of the heresy of Origen was raised throughout the whole world, on account of your translation, I made a more thorough examination of the copies, and I found in the library of Caesarea the six volumes of Eusebius' *Apology for Origen*. After reading them, I discovered the first book to be the one which you alone published under the name of the martyr, changing many blasphemies about the Son and the Holy Spirit in good part. And either Didymus or you or someone else was responsible for the changes, even as it has been proven very manifestly that you were responsible for the changes in the books of the *Periarchon*, especially when Eusebius himself writes, as I have already shown in the two books,[35] that Pamphilus published no work of his own. Therefore, you should also tell me the source from whence you received your copy; but do not mention anybody who is dead, for the sake of avoiding the charge, so that when you cannot produce the author you will cite a person who cannot make a reply. But if your own library is the fountain source of this little stream, you are well aware of the consequences, even if I keep silent. But suppose that the title of the book and the name of the author were changed by some chance admirer of Origen. Why did you translate the work into Latin? Obviously, that all might believe the writings of Origen on the testimony of the martyr, the way prepared in advance by the authority of such an illustrious author and witness. The *Apology* of a very learned man is not enough for you, unless you write a volume of your own in his defense;[36] and with these volumes circulated by many of your friends, you now translated safely the books of the *Periarchon* from the Greek, and commended them in your preface, stating that the many things in

---
35 i.e., the *Apologia*.
36 Rufinus, *Liber de adulteratione librorum Origenis* PG 17.615-632.

them which have been falsified by heretics had been corrected after reading the other books of Origen. You also praise me, lest any of my friends contradict you. You hail me as the herald of Origen and praise my eloquence to the skies in order to besmirch my faith. You refer to me as a brother and a colleague, and declare that you are an imitator of my work. You boasted that I had translated seventy of his homilies and a goodly number of his commentaries on the apostle, in which I corrected everything to such a degree that 'the Latin reader would find nothing in them which would be discordant with the Catholic faith';[37] now you condemn those very same books as heretical; you change your view and bring charges against the very person whom you had praised, when you considered him a colleague, and bring charges because you see that he is opposed to your perfidy. Which of us two is the calumniator of the martyr? I, who say that he was not a heretic and was not the author of the book which is reprehended by all; or you, who changed the title of a volume of an Arian and published it under the name of a martyr? You are not content with the scandalizing of Greece, unless you din it also into the ears of the Latins and defame an outstanding martyr to the best of your ability by your translation. You undertook this work, to be sure, with another purpose in mind; it was not your intention to accuse me, but to use me in your defense of the writings of Origen. However, you should know that the Roman faith, praised by the lips of the apostle, is not receptive to such deceits; and that, even if an angel were to preach a Gospel other than that which was once preached, the faith that was sanctioned by the authority of Paul cannot be changed. Therefore, my brother, if the book was falsified either by you, as many believe it was, or by someone else, as you perhaps will try to prove, and if, in your rash judgment, you assumed that it was the composition of the martyr, change its title and deliver the Roman simplicity from so grave a danger. You gain nothing

---

37 Rufinus, *Prologus in libros Periarchon Origenis presbyteri* PG 11.112.

by having the martyr judged a heretic through your own endeavors, and by having him who shed his blood for Christ proven an enemy of the faith of Christ. Say instead: 'I found the book, I thought it was the work of the martyr.' Do not be afraid to do penance. I shall no longer ply you with questions; I shall not ask you the source from whence you got it. Either mention some person who is dead, or say that you bought it from some stranger on the street. It is not your condemnation that I am seeking to achieve, but rather your conversion. It is better that you made a mistake than that the martyr was a heretic. In the meantime, extricate yourself from your present predicament as best you can. See to it yourself what answer you will give in the future judgment to the complaints which the martyr will register against you.

(13) *The reprehending of the commentaries. Didymus and Apollinaris differed.*

You even raise objections against yourself which nobody has raised, and refute charges which nobody has made. For you say that you read in my letter the following statement: 'Tell me: Who gave you permission to cut some things, to change some things, and to add others in your translation?' And you immediately answer your own question and say against me: 'Behold, I say to you: "I ask you: Who gave you permission to quote some passages in your commentaries taken from Origen, some from Apollinaris, and some from your own works, instead of quoting entirely from Origen, or from your own works, or from the works of someone else?"' In the meantime, while you are concerned with another matter, you have shown yourself guilty of a very serious offense, and you have forgotten the old proverb: 'Liars should have good memories.' For you say that in my commentaries I have quoted some passages from Origen, some from Apollinaris, and some from my own works. Therefore, if the passages that I have quoted under the name of others belong to Apollinaris and Origen, what is your reason, then, for leveling at me the charge in your books that, when I make such statements as: 'Another makes this remark,' 'a certain individual holds this view,' I myself am that 'another' and that 'certain individual'? Apollinaris and Didymus differ sharply in the matter of exposition, and style, and doctrine. When I quote different views in the one and the same section, must it be assumed that I am in agreement with these contrary views?. But I shall discuss this question on another occasion.

(14) *What he condemns in the translation of the volume of the Periarchon. The translators of Origen.*

Now I ask you: Who has ever reproached you for either making some cuts or some additions or some changes in Origen? Or who has ever stretched you on the rack, so to speak, and asked you: 'Are the things that you translated good or evil'? It is a waste of time on your part to feign innocence, just to attenuate the importance of the real question with your foolish inquiries. I did not accuse you for translating Origen of your own volition. I also undertook this enterprise, as did Victorinus, Hilary, and Ambrose before me. But why did you lend support to a heretical translation with the testimony of your preface? You force me to repeat again the same arguments and go over my lines. For you say in the same preface that you cut things which had been added by heretics and replaced them with what was good. If you removed the evils of heretics, then, the things which you left intact or added will be either Origen's or yours; for you set them down, to be sure, as good. But you will not be able to deny that many of these things are evil. 'What has all this to do with me?' you will say. 'Impute them to Origen; for I changed only those things which had been added by the heretics.' Explain the reason why you removed the evils of the heretics and left intact all of Origen? Is it not evident that you condemned some of the evil doctrines of Origen in the name of heretics, and you accepted others because you felt that they were not evil, but good and consistent with your faith? It was in reference to these doctrines that I asked you whether they were evil or good. You praised these doctrines in your preface, and admitted that they were left in as the best things after you cut the worst ones. It was in respect to these things that I stretched you on the rack of a real argument, so that if you say that they were good, you will be proven a heretic; if you say that they were evil, you will hear forthwith: 'Why did you praise in your preface things that are evil?' And I did not add the statement that you cunningly allege that I did: 'Why did you translate things that were evil, in order to bring them to the attention of the Latins?' For the purpose of revealing evils at times is not to teach evils, but to warn against them, so that the reader will avoid instead of following errors, so that he will despise the commonplace which is often regarded as wonderful because it is not understood. And you dare to say after all this that I am the author of such writings; when you, as a translator, overstepped the role of a translator where you could make any corrections, and where you could not, you were merely a translator. What you say would be justified if your books of the *Periarchon* had no preface. Hilary also saw to it in the translation of Origen's homilies that both the good and the evil were imputed, not to the translator, but to their author. If you had not said that you had deleted what was very bad and had left in what was very good, you might have extricated yourself from your predicament in some way or other. This is the situation that brings to nought the tricks of your little scheming, and gives you no chance of extricating yourself, being confronted on every side. You should not abuse the simplicity of the reader in this fashion, nor should you assume that all who will read your writings are so foolish that they will not laugh at you, applying salve to a healthy body while allowing wounds to fester.

(15) *On the resurrection.*

I have already learned your views on the resurrection of the flesh from your *Apology:* 'no member will be cut off, nor any part of the body severed.'[38] This is a frank and open confession of your simplicity, which you claim has been accepted by all of the bishops of Italy. I would believe this statement, if

---

38 Rufinus, *Apologia* PL 21.547 (ch. 8).

that book, which is not the book of Pamphilus, did not make me suspect you. And yet I wonder how Italy could have approved what Rome has looked upon with disfavor; how the bishops could have accepted what the apostolic see has condemned.

(16) *Two letters of Theophilus translated into Latin by Jerome.*

You also write that I stated in a letter that Pope Theophilus published recently an exposition of faith which has not yet come into your hands, and you promise to accept whatever he has written. I have no knowledge of having written such a statement, or of ever having sent such a letter. But the only reason why you accept things which are indefinite, and things which you do not know how they will turn out, is that you may reject things which are definite, and may not be held to any consent that you may have given. Within the past two years or so, I have translated two of his letters,[39] one a Synodal, the other a Paschal letter against Origen and his disciples, and other letters against Apollinaris and that same Origen himself; and I made them available to the men of my native tongue for reading, for the edification of the Church. I am unaware of having translated any other of his works. And yet you, who say that you accept the views of Pope Theophilus in all matters, should be careful lest your masters and your disciples hear of this acceptance of yours, and you offend very many individuals who refer to me as a thief and to you as a martyr; be careful lest you incur the wrath of him who sent you a letter against Pope Epiphanius,[40] urging you to hold fast to the truth of the

---

39 St. Jerome translated two Paschal letters of Theophilus which were sent to the bishop of Egypt in the years 401 and 402. These appear as letters 96 and 98 in the collection of St. Jerome's letters. The Synodal letter against Origenism, which is letter 92 among St. Jerome's letters, was sent out in the year 400 to the bishops of Palestine and Cyprus.

40 Isidore, who was sent by Theophilus as his agent to inquire into the quarrel between St. Jerome and John of Jerusalem, had written a letter to Rufinus and John of Jerusalem, in which he declared himself an Origenist, and assured Rufinus that their cause would prevail. The letter fell into the hands of the priest, Vincent, a friend of St. Jerome. Cf. St. Jerome, *Contra Johannem Hierosolymitanum* PL 23.390 (ch. 37).

faith and let no threats change your views. The original of this letter is in the possession of those to whom it was delivered.[41] And after making such remarks, you say in your customary manner: 'That I may clear myself before you, even though you rage, as I did of the charge which you mentioned above.' Now you say: 'What are you thinking of? Do you have any more targets at which to shoot the bow of your loquacity?' And are you offended if I accuse you of using foul language when you appropriate to yourself, an ecclesiastical writer, the indecent language of comedies and the jesting of courtesans and lovers?

(17) *Concerning Bishop Paul.*

You yourself, to be sure, answer your own question when you ask me when it was that I began to embrace the views of Pope Theophilus, and join with him in a fellowship of faith: 'It was then, I believe, when you defended with all your might and with all your zeal Paul,[42] whom he had condemned, and you urged him to recover through an imperial rescript his bishopric from which he had been removed by decree of the bishops.' Before replying in my own defense, I shall speak of the injuries inflicted on others. Does it deserve the name of humanity, or of mercy, to scoff at the misfortunes of others, and display before the public the wounds of others? Is this the lesson you learned from the good Samaritan, to carry back to the inn the man who was half-dead, to pour oil on his wounds, to promise the innkeeper to pay the expenses? Is this the lesson you learned from the story of the lamb which was carried back, of the drachma which was found, of the prodigal son who was welcomed back? Granted, that I had wounded you and had driven you, as you say, by certain provocative acts to this mad impulse of uttering reproaches. What sin did a man who was living in a cloister commit that you should lay bare the scar of his wounds, and tear open the closed skin with an unex-

---
41 i.e., Vincent, to whom the letter had been sent through an error.
42 After Paul had been removed from his bishopric, he was welcomed by St. Jerome at Bethlehem.

pected wound? Should you not have refrained from such an action, even if he were worthy of calumny? I am either mistaken, or it is true what so many people are saying, that you are persecuting the enemies of the Origenists in the person of this one man, and are using the misfortune of one man as an opportunity to vent your rage against both. If you are in accord with the views of Pope Theophilus, and you believe that it is a crime to overthrow the decrees of the pontiffs, what do you say of the others whom he has condemned? What do you say of Pope Anastasius, of whom, as you say, nobody believes it true that the bishop of so great a city could have wronged you, either in your innocence or in your absence? I do not say this because I am passing judgment on the decisions of the pontiffs, or because I have any desire to rescind their decrees; but because each and every individual performs at his own risk any action that seems right to him, and knows himself the judgment that is to be passed over his own judgment. Hospitality is dear to our hearts in our monastery, and we take in with a pleasant smile of tenderness all who come to us. For we are afraid that Mary and Joseph may not find room in the inn, and that Jesus, being turned away, may say to us: 'I was a stranger and you did not take me in.'[43] Heretics are the only persons whom we do not take in; they are the only ones whom you welcome. It is, to be sure, a rule with us to wash the feet of those who come to us, not to discuss their merits. Recall, my brother, his confession and his heart lashed with whips. Remember the prison, the dungeons, the exile, the mines, and you will not be angry that we took him in as he was passing by. Do you think that we are rebellious because we extend a cup of cold water in the name of Christ to those who are thirsty?

(18) *The faction of the heretics was banished. Theophilus is praised.*

Do you want to know the reason why we should love him more dearly, and why you should hate him more intensely? The

---

43 Matt. 25.43.

faction of the heretics was recently banished from Egypt and Alexandria, and they went to Jerusalem, and wanted to join forces with him so that, as they shared the one and the same grievance, they might also have the one and the same charge leveled at them. He repelled them, scorned them, and cast them aside, saying that he was not an enemy of the faith, nor was he declaring war against the Church; that his earlier undertaking was a matter of grievance, not of perfidy; that he had not assailed the innocence of others, but had wanted to prove his own. Do you consider an imperial rescript supplanting the decrees of the bishops as impious? Let him who got it see to its consequences. What do you think of those who, when condemned, storm the palace, and, forming a wedge, persecute the faith of Christ in the person of one man? I shall cite as witness to my fellowship with Pope Theophilus, none other than the very man[44] who you pretend was wounded by me; who, as you full well know, always sent me letters, even at the time when you kept them from being delivered to me, and you kept mentioning the fact in letters, dispatched daily, that his enemy was our friend and a very intimate associate, and you concocted those very lies which you are now penning with brazen impudence, so that you might stir up his hatred against me, and the grief of his wound might become an occasion for an attack on my faith. But this man of prudence and apostolic wisdom came in time and through circumstances to prove my love for him and your scheming plots against us. If my disciples, as you write, were the instigators of the scheming plots against you at Rome, and they stole your uncorrected scrolls while you slept, who stirred up Pope Theophilus against the rebellious in Egypt? Who stirred up the decrees of the kings? Who stirred up a general agreement in this part of the world? You also boast that you were a pupil and a disciple of Theophilus from your youth, although he never taught, on account of his innate modesty, before he was made bishop, and you were not

---

44 i.e., Theophilus himself.

in Alexandria after he became a bishop. And you have the courage to say in order to revile me: 'I neither accuse nor change my masters.' If this is true, it makes your conversion suspect to me. For I am not condemning my teachers, as you charge; but I am apprehensive of the words of Isaia: 'Woe to those who call evil good and good evil; who put darkness for light and light for darkness; who call bitter sweet and sweet bitter.'[45] But you, while drinking the wine of your masters sweetened with honey, have also drunk their poisons in equal measure, and have forsaken your master, the apostle, who teaches that we are not to agree even with an angel or with himself if they err in matters of faith.

(19) *The calumny of Vigilantius.*

I do not understand the wild dream that you have invented in the name of Vigilantius.[46] For when did I write that he was defiled by his communion with heretics at Alexandria? Name the book, produce the letter; nowhere will you find any such reference. With that same license or, should I say, impudence of yours of telling lies, by which you assume that everybody will believe your words, you add: 'When you quoted such a shameful testimony from Scripture against him that I do not dare to repeat it with my own lips.' You, who make the charge more serious by holding your tongue, do not dare to repeat it; and because you have no charges to make against me, you feign modesty, so that the reader will feel that you, who have not spared even your own soul from lies, are sparing me. What is that testimony from Scripture that will not pass those very chaste lips of yours? Or what shameful passage can be mentioned in the Sacred Books? If you are shamed to mention it, at least write it down so that the particular passage may prove

---
45 Isa. 5.20.
46 Vigilantius, a priest from Italy, had come to visit St. Jerome at Bethlehem, carrying a letter of introduction from Paulinus of Nola. On his return to Italy, Vigilantius reported to Paulinus that St. Jerome was an Origenist. In defense of these charges, St. Jerome wrote his *Contra Vigilantium*. Earlier, he had written Vigilantius a sharp letter of rebuke. Cf. St. Jerome, *Epistola* 61, *ad Vigilantium*.

me guilty of impudence. To pass over the rest in silence, I shall prove from this one passage that you possess a calloused disposition for telling lies. Notice how much I fear your charges. If you produce the evidence as you threaten to do, all the charges that are imputed to you will be imputed to me. I have answered you in Vigilantius. For he condemned the same things which you subsequently praised as a friend and condemned as an enemy. I know full well who it was that stirred up his wrath against me; I am well acquainted with your cunnings. I know too well the simplicity that is praised by everybody. Your anger found an opportunity in his foolishness to vent itself against me; and if I refuted it in my letter, lest it appear that you alone possess the staff of a letter, you should not invent the story about obscene language which you have read nowhere at all; but should realize and admit that it was his ignorance that occasioned this reply to your calumnies.

(20) *The letter of Pope Anastasius to John of Jerusalem regarding Rufinus.*

As far as the letter of saintly Pope Anastasius[47] is concerned, you appeared shifty, and in your confusion you find no ground on which to take a firm stand. For, at one moment, you say that the letter was composed by me; now, you say that it should have been delivered to you by the person to whom it was sent. Again, you condemn the injustice of the writer, declaring on oath that, even if he wrote it or not, it does not concern you in the least, since you have the testimony of his predecessor,[48] and because of your love for your own little town, turned down the request of Rome to honor her with your presence. If you suspect that the letter was forged by me, why do you not look for it in the archives of the Roman Church, so that when you

---

47 In the year 401, Pope Anastasius received a letter from John of Jerusalem consulting him about Rufinus and apparently coming to his defense. In making answer, the Pope confirmed the condemnation of Origen and desired to know nothing of Rufinus. The Pope expressed his dissatisfaction with Rufinus' intention to spread the work of Origen. Cf. *Epistola* 1, *Anastasii I Romanae urbis episcopi ad Joannem episcopum Hierosolymorum super nomine Rufini* PL 20.68-73.
48 i.e., Siricius, who was Pope from 384-399.

discover that it was not written by the Bishop, you will catch me guilty of a very manifest crime, and you will not bind me in vain with little spider webs, but will hold me fast with a very sturdy, strong rope. But if it is the letter of the Roman Pontiff, it is foolish on your part to demand a copy of the letter from him to whom it was not sent, instead of waiting for testimony to come from the East from him who sent the letter, when you have the author and the witness of the letter so close at hand. Go instead to Rome, and remonstrate with him in person why he has heaped calumny on your head in your innocence and in your absence. In the first place, for not accepting the exposition of your faith, which, as you write, was approved by all of Italy; and for refusing to use the staff of your letter[49] against your dogs. In the second place, for sending letters against you to the East, and branding you with heresy without your knowledge, and saying that the only reason why you translated the books of the *Periarchon* and made them available to the simple Roman Church was that through your endeavors it might lose the truth of the faith which it had learned from the apostle; and for daring to condemn those very books, which had been fortified by the testimony of your preface, in order to render you more odious. It is no trifling charge that the pontiff of so great a city is clapping on you or has rashly accepted what has been brought against you by someone else. Cry out with a loud voice and exclaim in the streets and in the market places: 'It is not my book; and if it is mine, Eusebius stole the uncorrected scrolls. I published them in a different form, nay more, I did not publish them. I gave them to nobody, or, to be sure, to just a few. And my enemy was so wicked and my friends so negligent that the

---

49 Under the new Pope Anastasius, who was more amenable to the anti-Origen forces, the friends of St. Jerome renewed their agitation against Rufinus. In view of these circumstances, Rufinus felt it necessary to defend himself before the Pope himself. Towards the end of the year 400, he composed his *Apologia ad Anastasium*. He speaks in this work of his confession of faith as a stick placed in the hand of Anastasius to drive away any envious persons who may be barking against him like dogs. Cf. Rufinus, *Apologia ad Anastasium* PL 21.624 (ch. 1).

copies of all of them were falsified by him in the same manner.' This, my very dear brother, is what you should have done instead of turning your back on him, and sending the arrows of your calumnies across the sea against me. For what good does it do your own wounds if I am wounded? Is it a comfort to one who has been struck to see his friend dying alongside of him?

(21) You produce the letter of Pope Siricius who is already asleep in the Lord, and you care nought for the words of Anastasius who is still alive. For how can it harm you in any way, as you say, whether he wrote the letter without your knowledge, or whether, perchance, he did not write it? And if he wrote it, you are content with the testimony of the whole world, that it does not seem possible to anybody that the bishop of so great a city could have wronged you either in your innocence or in your absence. You, whose translation caused Rome to tremble, refer to yourself as 'innocent'; you, who do not dare to answer your accusation, refer to yourself as 'absent.' You are avoiding the judgment of the city of Rome to such an extent that you would rather withstand the attack of the barbarians[50] than the sentence of a peaceful city. Suppose that I forged last year's letter. Who sent the recent letters to the East, in which Pope Anastasius adorns you with such flowery epithets, that, when you read them, you will begin the more to defend yourself than accuse me. And at the same time, consider your matchless wisdom, and your Attic wit, and the charm of your holy eloquence. You are being assailed by others, you are being condemned by charges preferred by others; and, in your rage, you rant against me and say: 'Could I also not describe your manner of departure from the city, the judgment that was passed over you at the time, the things which were subsequently written, the oath which you took, the place where you boarded ship, the pious manner in which you avoided perjury? I could have revealed this information, but I decided

---

50 The Goths under Alaric passed through Aquileia in the year 401 on their way to invade Italy.

to hold back more information than I reveal.' Such remarks are furtherances of your eloquence. And, if I say anything harsh against you after such remarks, you immediately threaten me with proscription and with daggers. And in the meantime, you sport most eloquently in rhetoric, and pretend to pass over in silence the things which you reveal, so that you make crimes out of the charges which you could not prove by passing them over. This is your whole concept of simplicity, and you spare your friend and wait for the tribunal of the judges in such a manner that, while you show me mercy, you lay at my feet a mass of charges.

(22) *The order of Jerome's departure from the city.*

Do you wish to know the order of my departure from the city? I shall describe it to you briefly. In the month of August, when the trade winds were blowing, I boarded ship free from care in the Roman port, accompanied by the saintly priest, Vincent, and my young brother, and other monks who are now residing in Jerusalem. A very large crowd of holy people saw me off. I went to Phegium; I stood for a while on the shores of Scylla, where I learned the ancient stories and the perilous journey of crafty Ulysses, and the songs of the Sirens, and the insatiable whirlpool of Charybdis. And, after the inhabitants of that locality told me many tales and advised me to sail, not by way of the columns of Proteus, but rather by way of the harbor of Jona; for the one was the route for fugitives and the troubled, the other, for the peaceful, I decided to go to Cyprus by way of Malea and the Cyclades. There I was welcomed by the venerable Bishop Epiphanius, about whose testimony you brag. From there, I went to Antioch where I enjoyed the fellowship of Paulinus, bishop and confessor; and set on my way by him, I entered Jerusalem in the middle of a very bitter winter. I saw many marvels; and the wonders that I had previously heard about through reports, I verified with the judgment of my very own eyes. From there, I proceeded to Egypt. I visited the monasteries of Nitria, and I found that poisonous asps were dwelling among the choirs of monks. Straightway, I hurried to return to my Bethlehem where I poured perfume upon the manger and the crib of the Savior. I also saw that well-known lake; nor did I spend my time in lazy idleness, but I learned many things that I knew nothing about before. But please do not keep quiet about the judgment that was passed over me at Rome, and what was written afterwards, especially since you have the testimony of the letters, and I am to be condemned, not by your words which you can feign and utter with impunity and deceitfulness, but rather by ecclesiastical letters. Notice how much I fear you. If you produce either a brief scroll of the Bishop of Rome against me, or of some other Church, I will acknowledge as mine all of the charges that have been written against you. Could I also not have described your departure, your age at the time, the place and the time of your sailing, your place of residence, your associations? But far be it from me to pursue a course of action that I reprehend in you, and to concoct in an ecclesiastical disputation idle stories of old womanish squabbles. It should suffice to have warned your wisdom not to make remarks against another which can be hurled right back at you.

(23) *The calumnies of Rufinus against Epiphanius. The letter of Epiphanius to John.*

It is a strange manner of evading the question on your part in your mentioning of Epiphanius to say that he could not have written against you after the kiss and prayer of reconciliation; as if you were to argue that an individual who but a moment ago was alive could not have died, or as if your reprehension were more credible than your excommunication after the kiss of peace. 'They have gone forth from us,' he says, 'but they were not of us; for if they had been of us, they would surely have continued with us.'[51] The apostle cautions us[52] to avoid a heretic after one or two warnings, who surely was a member of the ecclesiastical fold before he was avoided and condemned. And, at the same time, I cannot keep from laughing, because

---
51 1 John 2.19.
52 Cf. Titus 3.10.

you proclaim loudly in praise of Epiphanius on the advice of some clever individual: 'He is that well-known "silly old man"; he is the "anthropomorphite";[53] he is the one who sang about the six thousand books of Origen in your presence; he is the one who supposes that he has been commanded to preach against Origen in the tongues of all nations; he is the one who prohibits the reading of Origen's books, lest others recognize what had been stolen from him.' Read your letter and his letter, or rather, I should say, his letters, from which I shall quote one testimony regarding your faith, so that it will not appear that he was praised unworthily by you at the present time. 'But may God deliver you, my brother, and the holy people of Christ who have been entrusted to your care, and all of the brothers who are with you, and in particular the priest, Rufinus, from the heresy of Origen and from other heresies and their destruction. For if many heresies have been condemned by the Church, on account of one or two words, which are at variance with the faith, how much more will he be considered among heretics, who has concocted such perversities and such evil doctrines against the faith, and who has risen up as the enemy of the Church of God!'[54] This is the testimony of a saintly man concerning you; you walk with an air of dignity after being honored and praised by him in such language. This is the letter which you have procured with gold from the cell of brother Eusebius, so that you might calumniate the translator and prove me guilty of a very manifest crime, because I had translated the term as 'dearest' instead of 'honorable.' But what has all this to do with you who manage all your affairs with clever design, and walk in public with such an air of

---

53 During the early phase of the Origenist quarrel, John of Jerusalem had preached a sermon on a condemnation of anthropomorphism directed, apparently, against Epiphanius. The Anthropomorphites considered God as having arms and legs, since He is so spoken of in the Scriptures.

54 This is a quotation from the letter of Epiphanius to John of Jerusalem, written in the first half of the year 394. Cf. in the collection of St. Jerome's letters, *Epistola 51, S. Epiphanii ad Joannem episcopum Hierosolymorum* PL 22.523-524.

dignity that you say, if you find people who will believe you, that neither Anastasius nor Epiphanius wrote against you; and had not the letters themselves contradicted and confuted that bold presumption of yours, you would readily spurn the judgment of both of them and say that it is of no concern to you whether they wrote a letter or not, because they could not have written about someone in his innocence or absence. Such evil charges should not be imputed to a saintly man, 'to prove, to be sure, that he made peace with his lips, but kept evil and deceit locked in his heart.' This, to be sure, is the tenor of your argument, and these are the words that you employ in your defense. The whole world acknowledges that this is his letter written against you, and we are proving that the original reached your hands. I am amazed at the measure of shame, or should I say of impudence, with which you deny a fact, the truth of which you do not doubt. Therefore, Epiphanius who made peace with you and kept guile locked in his heart will be disgraced. Would it not be more correct to say that he first warned you; that he wished to correct you and bring you back to the right path; that he did not refuse the kiss of a Judas so that he might overcome the traitor to the faith with his patience; and that after he realized that his efforts and labors were in vain, and that the leopard did not change his spots, nor an Ethiopian his skin, he made known in a letter the thoughts which he had revolved in his mind?

(24) *The calumny of the fictive peace. The friends of Jerome sent to the West.*

You also argue in like fashion against Pope Anastasius, that he could not have written against you because you have in your possession the letter of Bishop Siricius. I am afraid you suspect that you have been wronged in some way. I cannot understand how a man of your ingenuity and wisdom can fall into such an embarrassing situation as to prove yourself foolish, while assuming all along that your readers are foolish. After presenting this eloquent argumentation, you add in conclusion: 'Far be it from saintly men to act in this manner. Such action is wont to proceed from your own school. You made peace with us as we set out and you shot at our backs arrows dipped in poison.' And you intended to impress with your eloquence, with this same kind of cleverness, or, should I say, declamation. We made peace with you, but we did not accept your heresy. We joined hands; we saw you off as you set out so that you might be Catholic, not that we might be heretics. But I would like to know what you mean by those 'arrows dipped in poison,' which you complain I shot at your back. There were the priests, Vincent, Paulinian, Eusebius, Rufinus. Of these, Vincent went to Rome long before you did; Paulinian and Eusebius set out a year after you set sail; Rufinus was sent two years later in the interest of Claudius; all of them were sent for private reasons, or in behalf of another whose life was in danger. Could I have known that some nobleman[55] would see in his dream a ship laden with merchandise entering the harbor at full sails just at the time when you were entering Rome; that an explanation that would not be fatuous would solve all the questions against fate; that you would translate the book of Eusebius as the book of Pamphilus; that you would clap your own work[56] as a sort of cover upon a poisoned dish; and that you would translate that very notorious work of the *Periarchon* in the brilliant style of your eloquence? It is a strange kind of reviling that we dispatched accusers before you could commit an act worthy of being reviled. It was not due, I repeat, it was not due to any carefully laid plan on our part, but rather to the providence of God that those men, who were sent to carry out another mission, should fight against a rising heresy; and, in the manner of Joseph, should avert the threat of a famine by the ardor of their faith.

(25) *Concerning the fictive letter to the Africans. Rufinus had corrected Latin works from the Greek.*

O the limits to which impudence will not go, once it has been given free rein! He has laid to his own charge a crime of some-

---
55 i.e., Macarius.
56 A reference to Rufinus' *Liber de adulteratione librorum Origenis.*

one else so that it would appear that we had invented it. He construes an anonymous charge as spoken against himself; and clearing himself of the sins of another man, he is secure only in his own innocence. For he swears on oath that he did not write the letter to the Africans under my name, in which I confess that I was forced by the Jews to translate lies; and he sends books which contain the very same information of which he swears he is ignorant. It is amazing to me how there could be so much agreement between his cleverness and the wickedness of another man, that he would accept the lies which the other has uttered in Africa and call them true here; and how some ignorant person could have imitated the elegance of his style. You alone have the right to translate the poisons of heretics, and let all the nations drink from the cup of Babylon. You may correct the Latin Scriptures from the Greek, and give to the churches to read something different from what they once received from the apostles. Shall I not have the right to translate after the Septuagint edition which I had corrected very carefully many years ago, and made available to men of my own tongue, for the refutation of the Jews, even those very copies which they themselves admit are very faithful, so that, if they are ever in an argument with Christians, they may not have an avenue of escape, but may be struck down in the main with their own weapon? I recall having written at some length on this subject in many other places, and at the end of the second book,[57] where I answered your accusation; and I curbed in evident fashion your popularity which you use to stir up hatred against me among the simple and the ignorant. I suppose the reader should be referred to that section.

(26) *Rufinus called a martyr and an apostle by his followers.*

I shall not let the following observation pass without comment, lest you complain that he who falsified your scrolls enjoys the glory of a confessor in my estimation, especially since you yourself who are guilty of the same crime are called a

---

57 St. Jerome, *Apologia* 2.34-35.

martyr and an apostle by all the followers of Origen after suffering exile and dark imprisonments at Alexandria. I have already replied to your excuse of ignorance. But because you continue to repeat the same story, and are again reminding me, as if you have forgotten your earlier *Apology*, to keep in mind the fact that you are unacquainted with the Latin, on account of your voracious reading of the Greek volumes for thirty years, attend my words for a moment: I am not finding fault with a few words in your work; otherwise, I would have to delete your entire work; but I wanted to bring to the attention of your disciples, whom you have taught with great zeal to know nothing, your great modesty in teaching what you do not know and writing of what you are ignorant, so that they might look for the same wisdom even in the matter of the views of their master. And when you add the remark that 'sins, not words, are offensive, such as lies, calumny, detraction, false testimony, and general reviling,' and that 'the mouth that belieth, killeth the soul,'[58] and issue the warning that 'such a foul smell should not penetrate my nostrils,' I might believe your words, if I did not see that the facts were contradictory; just as if the fuller and the tanner were to advise the paint dealer to stop up his nose when he passed their shops. Therefore, I shall follow your advice; I shall stop up my nostrils, lest they be irritated by the very sweet odor of your truth and benedictions.

(27) *We praise and condemn different things in the same individual.*

Because of your apparent inconsistency in heaping both praise and condemnation on me, you raised the very novel and ingenious argument that you had the same right to speak both well and ill of me that I had to reprehend Origen and Didymus, whom I had praised on an earlier occasion. Listen, then, my very wise man and the chief of Roman dialecticians. It is not wrong to praise the same individual for one thing,

---

58 Wisd. 1.11.

and to condemn him for another thing; but it is wrong to approve and condemn the same thing. I shall quote an example, so that the wise reader may understand with me what you do not understand. In the case of Tertullian, we praise his genius, but we condemn his heresy. In the case of Origen, we admire his knowledge of Scripture, and yet we do not accept the falsity of his doctrines. In the case of Didymus, we praise, to be sure, both his memory and the purity of his faith regarding the Trinity, but in other matters in which he relied on Origen unwisely we disagree with him. For it is not the vices of masters that are to be imitated, but their virtues. A certain individual at Rome had an African teacher of grammar, a very learned person; and he assumed that he was a rival of his teacher if he merely imitated his lisping and the defects of his speech. In the preface to the *Periarchon,* you refer to me as a brother; you speak of me as a very eloquent colleague and praise the truth of my faith. You will not be able to speak disparagingly of these three testimonies; in other matters, reprehend me to suit yourself, lest it appear that you are contradicting your testimony concerning me. When you refer to me as a brother and colleague, you admit that I am worthy of your friendship. When you extol my eloquence, you no longer accuse me of ignorance. When you confess that I am Catholic in every respect, you will not be able to impute to me the charge of heresy. If you reprehend in me anything else besides these three things, you will not appear to be contradictory. The final conclusion that follows from these considerations is that you are wrong in reprehending in me what you had praised before; and that I am not at fault if I praise in the same individuals what deserves to be praised, and reprehend in them what deserves to be reprehended.

(28) *On the question of souls. The book of Didymus to Rufinus and the Commentary on Osee to Jerome.*

You pass on to the status of souls and reprove my 'smoke screens' at great length, that you may be free to plead ignorance in matters of which you purposely pretend to be ignorant. You ask me, first of all, questions about the celestial matters: How do angels, how do archangels exist? What is the nature of their habitation? What is the difference, if any, between them? What is the reason for the sun? What is the cause of the waxings and the wanings of the moon? What is the nature of the course of the stars? I marvel that you forgot to quote those well-known verses: 'Whence come tremblings of the earth, the force to make deep seas swell, and burst their barriers, then sink back upon themselves; the sun's many lapses, the moon's many labors; whence sprang human kind and the brutes; whence rain and fire; of Arcturus, the rainy Hyades, and the twin Bears; why wintry suns make such haste to dip themselves in Ocean or what delay stays the slowly passing nights.'[59] And, then, quitting matters of the heavens, you take up questions relating to the earth and philosophize on points of lesser importance. For you ask me the following questions: 'What is the cause of fountains? What is the cause of winds? Why are there hailstorms? Why are there rainstorms? Why is there the briny deep? Why are there fresh waters? Why are there clouds, or rains, or lightning, or thunder, or thunderbolts?' So that, after I have replied that I do not know the answers to these questions, you may be safe to plead ignorance about souls, and you may equate the knowledge of one question with the ignorance of so many. Are you, who keep stirring up my 'smoke screen' on every page, not aware that I see through your 'mists and wind storms'? For in order to be thought a sciolist, and to win acclaim of the disciples of Calpurnius[60] for the reputation of your teaching, you confront me with the whole field of the physical world, so that Socrates spoke these words in vain, when taking up for consideration the subject of ethics: 'Things that are beyond us are of no concern to us.' Therefore, unless I give you the

---

59 Vergil, *Georgics* 2.478-480; *Aeneid* 1.743-746.
60 Calpurnius was a Latin rhetorician of the time of Hadrian and Antoninus Pius. Rufinus is often referred to as Calpurnius by St. Jerome.

reason why the ant, which is a tiny insect and whose body is a little speck, so to speak, has six feet, while the elephant with its ponderous weight walks on four; why snakes and serpents crawl on their bellies and chests; why the little worm, which is commonly referred to as a millepede, abounds with a very large battery of feet, will it be impossible for me to have any knowledge of the status of souls? The only reason why you are asking me for my own personal views on the matter of souls is that, once I have expressed it, you may immediately assail me. And if I quote the view of the Church, that God creates souls daily and infuses them in bodies of individuals as they are born, you would immediately produce the sophistical interpretations of the master: 'And where is the justice of God, that He should give souls to persons who are born of adultery and incest? Therefore, is He a cooperator with evil men; and does He personally create souls for adulteresses who engender the bodies?' as if the fault of the sowing lay in the wheat which it is said to have been stolen, and not in him who stole the grain; and the earth is not to nurture seeds in her bosom because the sower sowed them with unclean hand. This is also the source of that mysterious question of yours as to why infants should die when they have received bodies through sins? There is extant Didymus' book addressed to you, in which he says in reply to your question, that they did not commit many sins, and, therefore, it is enough for them merely to have touched the prisons of the bodies. My master and yours dictated for me at my request three books of commentaries on the Prophet Osee at the time when you asked him these questions. All of this makes it clear what he taught me and what he taught you.

(29) *Natural questions.*

You ask me to answer questions on the nature of things. If there were space, I could quote for you either the views of Lucretius according to Epicurus, or those of Aristotle according to the Peripatetics, or of Plato and Zeno according to the Academicians and the Stoics. And to come to the Church where we have the rule of truth, the books of Genesis and the Prophets and Ecclesiastes furnish us much information on such questions. Or, if we are ignorant of such matters, you should have confessed your ignorance of all matters in your *Apology*, as also about the status of souls, and should have asked your calumniators why they were so bold as to question you on one matter, when they themselves were ignorant of such matters. O the richly laden trireme which had come to enrich the poverty of Rome with Oriental and Egyptian merchandise! 'Thou art he, the mightiest Marcellus, who singly, by writing, restorest our state.'[61] Therefore, if you had not come from the East, that very learned gentleman would still be confused amidst the astrologers, and all of the Christians would have been ignorant of their views against fate. It is with good reason that you, who have brought in a ship laden with such merchandise, ask me questions about astrology and the course of the heavens and the stars. I acknowledge my poverty; I have not amassed the wealth that you have in the East. After such a long period of time, Pharao has taught you what Rome did not know; Egypt has imparted you some information which Italy did not possess until now.

(30) *Various views on the soul.*

You write that there are three views regarding the soul among the ecclesiastical exegetes.[62] The first is that which is held by Origen, the second view, held by Tertullian and Lactantius (although it is clear that your statement about Lactantius is a very manifest lie), and the third view, held by us simple and foolish men who do not realize that, if our view is true, God would be condemned by us as being unjust. And, after making this statement, you swear on oath that you do not know what is the truth. Tell me, I ask you: Is there,

---

61 This verse is a parody on the famous line of Vergil, which is a close reproduction of the one in the *Annals* of Ennius, referring to Q. Fabius Maximus, the opponent of Hannibal, who by his tactics was surnamed Cunctator. St. Jerome substitutes the surname Scriptor for Cunctator. Cf. Vergil, *Aeneid* 6.845-846.
62 Rufinus, *Apologia ad Anastasium* PL 21.626 (ch. 6).

in your opinion, some other view besides these three in which there is truth? And is there deceit in these three? Or is there one view among these three that is the truth? If there is some other view, why do you place such strict limits on the freedom of disputants, and why do you keep silent about the truth while you bring forth lies? But if one of these three views is true and the other two false, why are you as ignorant of the false as you are of the true view? Or are you pretending not to know the true view so that you may be free to defend the false views when you so desire? These, to be sure, are the 'smoke screens,' these are the mists with which you are seeking to blind the eyes of the people. As the Aristippus[63] of our times, you are bringing into the harbor of Rome a ship laden with merchandise of all kinds, and, setting up your chair in public, you are playing the role in our midst of a Hermagoras and a Gorgias of Leontine,[64] and you have forgotten, in your great hurry to set sail, and left the merchandise of one little question in the East. And you again shout and boast that you learned at Aquileia and at Alexandria that God is the creator of both the souls and the bodies. And it is, to be sure, this statement that is causing people to ask whether God or the devil created the souls, and not whether the souls existed before the bodies, which is the view held by Origen, and were joined to crass bodies for some act that they committed; or whether they slept torpid and dormant like dormice. You keep silent about this question which everybody is asking, and you reply to one which nobody raises.

(31) You also keep ridiculing frequently my 'smoke screens,'

---

63 Aristippus, a Greek philosopher and native of Cyrene, was a disciple of Socrates. After the death of Socrates, he was the first to travel about the Greek cities, imparting knowledge for money. He had a genuine talent, improvising to make things suit place, time, and person. He was the founder of the Cyrenaic sect, and the precursor of the Epicureans.
64 Hermagoras was a famous rhetorician of Rhodes. Gorgias was a famous statesman and Sophist, who came to Athens on a mission in the year 327 B.C. and settled there. The story is told of Gorgias that he would assemble a crowd and ask each one to suggest a topic he would like to have him discuss. He promised to speak eloquently on any controversial or disputed subject.

because, as you say, I pretend to know what I do not know, and insult the ignorant people by reciting the names of learned men. You, to be sure, who cannot hold back when you speak the flames and thunderbolts conceived in your mouth, are a man of flame, or rather of lightning; and just as that famed Bar-Chochabas,[65] the instigator of the Jewish uprising, kept fanning a lighted blade of straw in his mouth with puffs of breath so as to give the impression that he was spewing out flames, so you, in like manner, another Salmoneus,[66] also light up the place wherever you go and accuse me of 'smoke screens,' of whom it might, perchance, be said: 'You touch the mountains and they smoke.'[67] You do not understand the meaning of the phrase 'smoke of locusts' in the prophet;[68] and all this because the beauty of your eyes cannot bear the pungency of our 'smoke screens.'

(32) *Concerning the oath made in his sleep.*

But as far as the charge of perjury is concerned, since you refer me to your copy, I have also given my reply to you and to Calpurnius[69] at great length in other books.[70] For the present time, it should suffice to say briefly that you demand that of me in my sleep what you have never kept when awake. I am considered guilty of a serious crime if I told young girls and maidens of Christ not to read secular books, and if I promised, when reprimanded in a dream, that I would not read secular books. Your ship, which was promised to the city of Rome in a vision, promises one thing and fulfills another. It had come to solve the question of the astrologers, and it

---

65 Bar-Chochabas was the leader of the Jewish revolt against Hadrian in 132-135 A.D.
66 The story of Salmoneus is told in the *Aeneid* of Vergil (6.585-594). In his arrogance, Salmoneus deemed himself equal to Jove and imitated his thunder and lightning. He rode through the Greek peoples and his own city in Elis, claiming as his own the homage of deity. In the end, he was killed by a thunderbolt of Jove.
67 Ps. 103.32.
68 Cf. Apoc. 9.7, 17.
69 The title of Calpurnius in this instance seems to refer to some friend of Rufinus, not to Rufinus himself.
70 Cf. St. Jerome, *Apologia* 1.30.

dissolves the faith of Christians. The ship which had sailed with full sails over the Ionian and the Aegean, the Adriatic and the Tyrrhenian seas, suffered shipwreck in the port of Rome. Are you not ashamed to rake together such nonsense, and impose on me the necessity of taunting you in like manner? Granted, that somebody had dreamed a glorious dream about you. It would have been modest and wise on your part to have disregarded what you had heard, instead of boasting of the dream of another as if it were some wonderful tribute to you. Notice the vast difference between your dream and mine. I relate humbly that I was reprehended; you keep repeating boastfully that you were praised. You cannot say: 'The dream that somebody else dreamed about me is of no concern to me,' since you state in those very eloquent books of yours that this was the reason that compelled you to translate them, lest that nobleman waste his dream of you. You bend every effort to this end: if you prove that I perjured myself, you will not be a heretic.

(33) *The calumny of infidelity.*

I come to that very serious charge in which you accuse me of infidelity after we reconciled our friendship. I admit that, of all the railing accusations that you either lay to my charge or threaten to do so, there is nothing that I must refute as much as that of fraud, deceit, and infidelity. To err is human, but to lay snares is diabolical. Therefore, did I join hands with you in the Church of the Resurrection[71] after the sacrifice of the Lamb, so that I might steal your scrolls at Rome, so that the dogs might be set loose and devour the uncorrected sheets while you were asleep? And is it credible that we prepared accusers before you committed your crime? We knew, of course, the thoughts that you were revolving in your mind, the dream that someone else was going to dream of you,

---

71 The reconciliation between Rufinus and St. Jerome, and possibly John of Jerusalem, took place, through the efforts of Theophilus of Alexandria, in the early part of the year 397, in the Church of the Resurrection in Jerusalem.

so the Greek proverb would be fulfilled in you, and the fool would be teaching the wise man? If I had sent Eusebius to bark against you, who stirred up the anger of Atarbius[72] and the others against you? Was he not the very person who also judged me a heretic because of your friendship? And after I had cleared myself with him by a condemnation of the teachings of Origen, you locked your doors at home and never dared to see him, lest you either condemn what you were unwilling to condemn, or incur the odium of heresy by openly resisting. Will he not be able to stand as a witness against you because he is your accuser? Before saintly Epiphanius came to Jerusalem and made peace with you with his lips, to be sure, and with a kiss, but kept evil and guile locked in his heart; before I translated for him that letter of rebuke[73] against you, so that he branded as a heretic him whom he approved as orthodox with a kiss, Atarbius was barking against you in Jerusalem, and if he had not promptly retreated, he would have felt the staff, not only of your letter, but also of your right hand, with which you usually drove off the dogs.

(34) *Concerning the uncorrected scrolls.*

'Why,' he says, 'did you accept my scrolls that had been falsified? Why were you so bold as to apply your pen to the books of the *Periarchon* after my translation? If I had erred as a human being, should you not have proceeded against me with a personal letter, and flattered me in your letter even as I am also flattering you at present in my own letter?' My fault lies solely in the fact that I sought to clear myself of your deceitful praises for which I was accused; and I accomplished this without, in any way, defaming your character, so that I

---

72 In the year 393, Atarbius had approached both Rufinus and St. Jerome, demanding of them a formal rejection of Origenism. St. Jerome complied with his demands, but Rufinus refused to talk to him and threatened to drive him off with violence. Atarbius, thereupon, linked Rufinus with the supporters of Origenism, and spread accusations against him in and about Jerusalem. Cf. Murphy, *op. cit.*, 68.
73 This letter appears as letter 51 among the letters of St. Jerome. Cf. *Epistola* 51, *S. Epiphanii ad Joannem episcopum Hierosolymorum* PL 22.517-527.

imputed to many the charges which you alone had brought against me. I did not accuse you of heresy, but rather cleared myself of heresy. Did I know you would be angered if I wrote against heretics? You had said that you had removed what was heretical from the books of Origen; I assumed that you were now no longer a defender of heretics; and, therefore, I inveighed not against you, but against heretics. If I was too severe in this respect, forgive me. I thought that I would also please you. You say that your scrolls, which were lying hid in your cell, or were in the possession of that one individual who had requested you to do the work for him, were stolen and brought out in public by the deceitful schemings and plottings of my servants. And what is your reason for stating above that nobody had them in his possession, or a few at most? If they were lying hid in your own cell, how could they be in the possession of the individual who had requested the work to be done for him? But if one individual for whom they were written had assumed the task of concealing them, then, they were not lying hid just in your own cell, nor were they in the possession of a few who, as you declared, had them in their possession. You contend that they were stolen; and you charge, on the other hand, that they were bought for a great price and an undetermined amount of goods. What a great variation and inconsistency in the telling of a lie about a single matter, and in a short letter! You have the right to make accusations; will I not have the right to defend myself? When you make accusations, you show no respect for a friend. When I answer the accusations, then you recall the rights of friendship. Tell me, I ask you: Did you write the scrolls to be concealed or to be published? If to conceal them, why did you write them? If to publish them, why did you conceal them?

(35) *He avoids the suspicion of heresy.*

But I was reprehended because I did not restrain my friends who accused you. Do you wish me to produce for you their letter, in which they accuse me of hypocrisy because I held my tongue when I knew that you were a heretic; and because I started an internal war within the Church when I indiscreetly offered you peace? You refer to those who suspect that I am your fellow companion as disciples. And because I was too sparing in refuting your praises, they assume that I am a fellow priest of yours. With your preface, you succeeded in doing me more harm as a friend than if you were my enemy. They had been convinced, once and for all, that you were a heretic (whether they were right or wrong is something for them to decide themselves). If I choose to defend you, the only end that I would achieve would be that they would accuse me equally with you. Finally, they taunt me with the compliments you paid me, and they feel that you were not lying when you wrote these praises, but speaking sincerely; and they are severe in denouncing what you had always praised formerly in me. What do you want me to do? Shall I judge my disciples accusers in order to protect you? Shall I intercept with my own heart the darts which have been hurled against my friend?

(36) But as far as the books of the *Periarchon* are concerned, you even owe me a debt of gratitude. For, according to your own words, you cut everything that was harmful and left intact what was better. I translated the exact original of the Greek. Consequently, both your faith as well as the heresy of him whom you translated are made evident. Two outstanding individuals in Christ wrote to me as follows from the City: 'Reply to the charges, lest it appear that you assent to them, if you hold your peace.'[74] With one voice, they all requested me to bring to light the deceits of Origen, and to point out the poisons of the heretics that are to be avoided by the Roman ears. How does all this redound to your discredit? Were you the sole translator of these books? Is there no other person who engaged in this work besides you? Are you, then, also one of the Septuagint translators, so that no one else has the right to translate after your edition? I have

---

74 *Epistola* 83, *Pammachii et Oceani ad Hieronymum* PL 22.743.

also translated many books, as you say, from Greek into Latin. You also have the privilege of translating them, in turn, at your pleasure; and both the good and the bad, to be sure, are imputed to their author. This would also be true in your case, if you had not stated that you had cut what was heretical and had translated what was best. This, to be sure, is your problem which cannot be solved. But if you made a mistake as a human being, condemn your earlier views.

(37) *Rufinus translated Latin books into Greek.*

But what are you going to do about your *Apology* which you wrote in defense of the works of Origen? What are you going to do about the volume of Eusebius? Although you made many changes in this work and translated the writings of a heretic under the name of a martyr, nevertheless, you left in more things which do not agree with the faith of the Church. You even translate Latin books into Greek for us; will you forbid me to make foreign books available to my own people? If I had replied to you regarding some other work in which you had not wounded me, it could have appeared that I translated what you had translated simply to hurt you, so that I might prove that you were either ignorant or deceitful. But as matters stand now, it is a strange kind of complaint that you raise, saying that I replied to you regarding a work in which you brought charges against me. Rome was said to have been thrown into confusion by your translation; everybody begged me to rectify the situation. Not because I was a man of any consequence, but because those who asked me felt that I exerted some influence. You, who translated those volumes, were a friend of mine. What do you want me to do? Should I obey God rather than man?[75] Should I protect the possessions of the Lord or keep the theft of a fellow servant a secret? Shall I not please you in any other way except by also participating with you in the commission of an act worthy of condemnation? If you had not mentioned my name, if you

---

75 Cf. Acts 5.29.

had not adorned me with singular praises, I could have found some avenue of escape, and could have offered various excuses for not translating, in turn, what had been translated. It was you, my friend, who forced me to spend many days on this work, and to bring out into the open what should have been swallowed up by Charybdis; and, although I was wounded, I still respected the rights of friendship towards you, and I defended myself to the best of my ability, and in such a way that I did not accuse you or bring any charges against you. You who consider remarks made against heretics as a rebuke to your own person are too suspicious and querulous. But if I cannot be your friend in any other way except by being also a friend of heretics, it will be easier for me to bear your enmity than their friendship.

(38) *Concerning the letter to Rufinus.*

You also imagine that I concocted a new kind of deceit, that of composing a letter[76] to you in my name, as if written a long time ago, which you never received, to make it appear that I was good and decent. The truth of the matter can be very readily proven. There are many individuals at Rome who have copies of this letter written about three years ago. They refused to send it to you because they were aware of the remarks that you had made against my name, and knew how unspeakable and unbecoming a Christian way of life were the stories that were invented by you. In my ignorance, I wrote the letter presumably to a friend; they did not deliver it to him whom they knew to be an enemy, showing consideration for my error and your conscience. And, at the same time, you contend that, if I had written such a letter to you, I should not have written many evil things against you in another treatise. Your mistake and your just complaints stem entirely

---

76 In the year 399, St. Jerome had sent, along with his translation of the *Periarchon* of Origen, to his friends two letters, one intended for Rufinus, and the other for Oceanus and Pammachius. St. Jerome's friends took it upon themselves to withhold the explanatory letter to Rufinus. For the contents of this letter, cf. St. Jerome, *Epistola* 81, *ad Rufinum*.

from the fact that you imagine everything we say against heretics to be said against you; and, unless I spare them, you feel that you have been wronged. Am I not offering you bread simply because I am dashing out the brains of heretics with a stone? And in order that you may not have to accept the genuineness of my letter, you say that the genuineness of the letter of Pope Anastasius rests also on a similar fraud. I have replied to you before regarding this letter. If you suspect that this is not his letter, you have a golden opportunity of accusing me of falsification in his presence. But if it is his letter, as the letters of this year also prove against you, your efforts to prove that our letter is forged are both in vain and deceitful, since we are producing the evidence from his genuine letter that ours is genuine.

(39) *The disciples of Pythagoras. The Pythagorean precepts and ideas. The principle that Pythagoras was first among the Greeks to discover.*

How eloquent you tried to sound in justifying your lie! And in order that you may not have to produce the six thousand books of Origen, you ask me to produce the records of Pythagoras. Where is that self-assurance of yours, with which you boasted so often with distented cheeks that what you had read in the other books of Origen you had corrected in the books of the *Periarchon;* and that you had put into his own works, not the words of others, but his own? You cannot produce one single twig and branch from that vast forest of books. These are the real 'smoke screens'; this is the mist which you realize I have scattered and dissipated in your own works while you taunt me with them in my own; and, although you have been refuted, you do not submit, but say with impudence greater than your ignorance that I am denying the obvious, so that you, while promising mountains of gold, may not have to produce even a single leathern penny from your treasures. I realize the justice of your hatred against me, and that you are raging against me with genuine fury. But if I did not have the courage to ask you to produce what does not exist, you would have given the impression of possessing what you do not have. You are asking me to produce the books of Pythagoras. But who said that his volumes were extant? Are these not the words that I used in my letter that you are condemning: 'But granted that I made a mistake in my youth and, having been trained in the studies of the philosophers, that is to say, the pagan philosophers, I was ignorant of the Christian doctrines in the beginning of my faith, and I assumed that what I had read in Pythagoras and Plato and Empedocles was also contained in the Apostles'?[77] I spoke not of their books, but of their doctrines, a knowledge of which I could derive from Cicero, Brutus, and Seneca. Read the oration *Pro Vatinio* and the others where mention is made of the brotherhoods. Read the dialogues of Cicero. Investigate the whole coastline of Italy, which was formerly called Magna Graecia, and you will find the Pythagorean teachings inscribed in bronze on public monuments. But to whom are the *Golden Verses* ascribed? Are they not ascribed to Pythagoras? All of his teachings are expressed in concise form in these verses. The philosopher, Jamblichus,[78] composed a very extensive volume of commentaries on these verses, imitating, in part measure, Moderatus, a very eloquent man, and Archippus and Lysides, students of Pythagoras. Of these, Archippus and Lysides conducted schools in Greece, that is to say, in Thebes. They memorized the precepts of their master, and they relied on their ingenuity instead of books. The following is an example of these precepts: '*Phugadeutéon pásēi mechanêi, kaì perikoptéon purì kaì sidérōi kaì mechanaîs pantoíais, apò mèn sṓmatos nóson, apò dè psuchês amathían, koilías dè polutéleian póleōs dè stásin, oíkou dè dichophrosúnēn, homoû dè pántōn ametrían,*' which we can translate into Latin as follows: '*Fuganda sunt omnibus modis et abscindenda,*

---

77 St. Jerome, *Epistola* 84.6, *ad Pammachium et Oceanum* PL 22.748.
78 Jamblichus was the chief representative of neoplatonism in Syria in the early fourth century A.D. His extant works relate to Pythagoras and his doctrines.

languor a corpore, imperitia ab animo, luxuria a ventre, a civitate seditio, a domo discordia, et in commune a cunctis rebus intemperantia.[79] The following are also Pythagorean precepts: 'All goods of friends are common property.' 'A friend is a second self.' 'We must pay special attention to two periods of time, to morning and evening, that is to say, to things which we intend to perform, and to those which we have performed.' 'Next to God, we must cherish truth, which alone makes man most like God.' And those paradoxes which Aristotle discusses with careful attention in his own books: 'Do not overstep the steelyard,' that is to say, 'Do not overstep justice; do not poke the fire with a sword.' Do not irritate with reproachful words a soul that is angered, to be sure, and enraged. 'Do not reprove the crown,' that is to say, 'Cast out grief from your soul.' 'Once you have left,' he says, 'do not return,' that is to say, 'After death do not long for this life.' 'Do not travel the common road,' that is to say, 'Do not follow the errors of the many.' 'Do not take a swallow into the house,' that is to say, 'Do not harbor garrulous and loquacious men under the same roof.' 'Place a load on the shoulders of those who are laden; do not share it with those who are shirkers,' that is to say, 'Increase the precepts for those who are striving for virtue; part with those who are victims of indolence.' And because I had said that I had read the Pythagorean doctrines, listen to the principle that Pythagoras was first among the Greeks to discover: 'Souls are immortal and they pass from one body to another.' Vergil also adopts, to be sure, this view, and says in the sixth book of the *Aeneid:* "All these, when they have rolled time's wheel through a thousand years, the god summons in vast throng to the river

---

79 The English translation is as follows: 'We must banish and cut out by all possible means disease from the body, ignorance from the soul, luxury from the stomach, sedition from the state, discord from the home, and, in general, every type of intemperance.' The Greek version differs somewhat from the Latin, which I have here translated. It begins as follows: 'We must banish by all possible means and cut out by fire and sword and by all possible means disease from the body,' and the rest.

of Lethe, in sooth that, reft of memory, they may revisit the vault above and conceive desire to return again to the body.'[80]

(40) *Other teachings of Pythagoras. Origen incorporated Plato into his own books.*

Pythagoras taught that he was first Euphorbus, then Callides, third Hermotimus, fourth Pyrrhus, and finally Pythagoras; and that after definite cycles of time, things which had once existed will again come into being; and that nothing in the world was thought to be new; that philosophy was a meditation on death, seeking daily to effect the freedom of the soul from the prison of the body: that *'mathĕseis anamnĕseis,'* that is to say, learning was recollection;[81] and many other doctrines that Plato discusses fully in his own books, and especially in the *Phaedo* and *Timaeus*. However, Plato, after establishing the Academy with its countless disciples and realizing the many shortcomings of his own system of teaching, went to Magna Graecia and there he studied the teachings of Pythagoras under Achytas of Tarentum and Timaeus of Locri. And he blended the elegance and charm of Socrates with Pythagoras' teachings. All of this Origen is clearly proven to have incorporated into his own books of the *Periarchon*, merely changing the name. Therefore, wherein did I do wrong if I stated that, in my youth, I assumed that the things which I had read in Pythagoras and Plato and Empedocles were in the apostles? I did not say, as you charge and falsely state, 'in the books' of Pythagoras and Plato and Empedocles, but what I had read in them and what the writings of others informed was in them. And this manner of speaking is very common, as if I were to say: 'I consider the teachings which I read in Socrates as true'; not because Socrates wrote any books, but the views which I read he held in the works of Plato and the other Socratics. And furthermore, I had the desire to imitate the deeds which I had read about in Alexander and Scipio; not because they had related their own adventures, but be-

---
80 Vergil, *Aeneid* 6.748-751.
81 The Latin reads as follows: *'discentias reminiscentias.'*

cause I read about their deeds in the works of others and I admired them for such deeds. Therefore, even if I could not prove that the records of Pythagoras himself are extant, or convince you that they were proven authentic by his son and daughter and his other disciples, you would not prove me guilty of a falsification, because I did not say that I had read his books but rather his teachings. And you prattle in vain that I intended this as a protection for your falsification, so that you might forget those six thousand books of Origen unless I produced one book of Pythagoras.

(41) *Rufinus threatened Jerome with death.*

I shall come to your epilogues, that is to say, your railing accusations, in which you urge me to repent, and threaten me with death unless I have a change of heart, that is to say, unless I hold my tongue against your accusations. And you declare that this scandal will fall upon my own head, because by my reply I drove you, who are very gentle and as meek as Moses, to this madness of writing. For you boast that you know the crimes which I confessed to you alone, my very dear friend, and that you will bring them out in the open; that I should be portrayed in my true colors; and that I should remember that I fell at your feet, begging you not to cut off my head with the sword of your tongue. And after much ranting and raving like a madman, you collect yourself and say that you desire to make peace, but on the condition that I hold my peace hereafter, that is to say, that I do not write against heretics or dare to reply to your accusations. If I comply, I shall be a brother and a colleague, and a very eloquent man, and a friend and a companion; and, what is more important than any of these considerations, you shall declare openly that everything that I have translated from Origen is Catholic. But if I utter even a word and take any action, I shall become, on the spot, a bad fellow and a heretic and unworthy of your fellowship. These are the public notices that you give me; this is your way of urging me to make peace. You do not even allow my grief an opportunity to give way to sighs and tears.

(42) *He reprehends the license to slander. Fulvia and Herodias.*

I could also portray you in your true colors, and rant and rave against you who are ranting and raving against me, and make any remark knowingly or unknowingly; and with equal license or, should I say, with equal frenzy and madness, lay at your feet charges whether true or false, so that it would bring a blush to my cheeks to utter them and a blush to your cheeks to hear them; and taunt you with charges which would condemn either the accuser or the accused, in such a way that I would convince the reader with such a show of seriousness that he would believe that I had written in earnest what I had written in contempt. But far be it from the good conduct of Christians to offer their own blood while seeking the blood of others, and to become murderers by desire without wielding the sword. Such behavior befits your goodness and your meekness and simplicity, who bring forth from the one and the same dunghill of your heart both the perfume of roses and the stench of cadavers; and, the judgment of the prophet notwithstanding, you call bitter what you have praised as sweet.[82] Nor is it necessary for us to stir up a grievance in ecclesiastical treatises which is a matter for the courts of the judges. You shall hear nothing more on this subject except a proverb borrowed from the streets: 'When you say what you want to say, you shall hear what you do not want to hear.' Or if this common proverb sounds vulgar to you, and one who is very learned derives greater pleasure from the sententious remarks of philosophers and poets, read that famous verse of Homer: 'What word you speak, the like you shall hear.'[83] Your excellent holiness and censorship (whose purity is so extraordinary that the devils roar like lions at your napkins and apron), I ask you just this one question: Whose example are you following as your model in writing? What Catholic individual ever taunted his opponent in a debate of factions with

---
82 Cf. Isa. 5.20.
83 Homer, *Iliad* 20.250.

moral turpitude? Is this what your masters taught you to do? Were you trained and instructed in their school to decapitate him whom you could not answer, and sever the tongue that cannot be still? You should not indulge in excessive boasting if you can accomplish what scorpions and poisonous beetles can accomplish. Fulvia[84] did the same thing to Cicero and Herodias[85] to John, because they could not bear to hear the truth; and they pierced with a slitting needle the tongue that spoke the truth. Dogs bark in defense of their masters; and do you not want me to bark in defense of Christ? Many individuals have written against Marcion, Valentinus, Arius, and Eunomius. Who ever taunted them with moral turpitude? Did they not devote all their attention to the refuting of their heresy? These are the tricks of the heretics, that is to say, of your masters, to resort to reviling when convicted of perfidy. It was through such an invention that Eustathius,[86] bishop of Antioch, found out about the sons of whom he had no knowledge. It was through such a trick that Athanasius, bishop of Alexandria, cut off the third hand of Arsenius; for the latter, who was falsely reported as dead earlier, was shown to have two hands when he subsequently turned up alive. It is such stories as these that both your disciples and your masters are concocting about a priest of the same Church; and they are attacking the truth of the faith by gold, that is to say, by your

---

84 Fulvia was the wife of Antony who took an active part in the proscription of her husband. She is said to have sacrificed to her own vengeance several individuals who had given her offense. After the head of Cicero was brought to Antony, she took it on her knees and, with fiendish malice, pierced the tongue with a golden needle.
85 Herodias was the wife of the brother of the sister-in-law of Herod Antipas, king of the Jews, and the wife of his brother, Philip. Antipas divorced his wife and married Herodias. St. John the Baptist exclaimed against this union. As a consequence, he was seized and beheaded at the request of Herodias.
86 Eusebius of Nicomedia had come to Antioch along with other satellites of the Arian impiety. There he hired some woman to say that she had an affair with Bishop Eustathius and had conceived a son with him, whom she clutched to her bosom. Eusebius succeeded in obtaining the banishment of Eustathius through the emperor. Cf. Theodoretus, *Ecclesiasticae historiae libri quinque* PG 82.966-967.

efforts and those of your friends. What shall I say of heretics who, though they are outside the Church, still call themselves Christians? How many of our brothers have written against those very impious men, Celsus and Porphyry? Which one of them was interested in hurling superfluous and taunting charges after the case was closed? Such charges should be registered, not in ecclesiastical treatises, but rather in the complaint books of the judges. Or what does it profit you if you lose the case and prevail in slandering? You do not have to make charges at the risk of your own life. You can gratify your desire by hiring some assassin. And you, who are prepared to kill the man who was formerly your brother, who now stands accused by you, and who was always your enemy, pretend that you are apprehensive of scandal. And yet it is strange how such a wise man like you, who are overcome with anger, should wish to bestow on me the kindness of releasing my soul from its prison, and should not allow it to live with you in the darkness of this world.

(43) *He could not spare heretics.*

Therefore, do you want me to hold my tongue? Stop accusing me. Lay down your sword and I shall discard my shield. I shall not be able to agree with you on one point, that is, to spare heretics and not prove myself a Catholic. If this point is the cause of our discord, I can die, but I cannot keep silent. To be sure, I should have replied to your madness from the whole of Scripture, and should have soothed the fury of your heart with divine words, in the manner of David playing the harp;[87] but I shall be content with the testimonies of a single book[88] and set wisdom against folly, so that, if you despise the words of men, you may not spurn at least the words of God. Listen, then, to what Solomon in his wisdom says of you and all those who are invidious, and reproachful, and contumelious: 'The foolish while they are disposed to malicious railings hate the thought of a wicked deed. Practice

---

87 Cf. 1 Kings 16.23.
88 i.e., the book of Proverbs.

not evil against thy friend.[89] Do not act in a hostile manner against a man without cause.[90] The wicked rejoice in contumely.[91] Remove from thee a froward tongue, and let detracting lips be far from thee;[92] haughty eyes, a lying tongue, hands that shed innocent blood, a heart that deviseth wicked plots, feet that are swift to run into mischief.[93] He that trusted to lies feedeth the winds; and the same runneth after birds that fly away.[94] For he has abandoned the ways of his vineyard, he has caused the wheels of his cultivation to stray from their path. He walks through a dry and desert field and collects barrenness with his hands. The mouth of a fool is next to confusion;[95] and he that uttereth reproach is very foolish.[96] The simple man is a soul which blesseth; the passionate man is an abomination.[97] By the sin of his lips the sinner falls into snares.[98] The ways of a fool are right in his own eyes.[99] A fool on the same day showeth his anger.[100] Lying lips are an abomination to the Lord.[101] He that keepeth his mouth keepeth his soul.[102] And he that is rash in speech shall frighten himself.[103] An evil man doth evil with contumely, and he that is a fool layeth open his folly.[104] You will seek wisdom among the wicked and you shall not find it.[105] He who is rash shall be filled with his own ways.[106] A wise man feareth and declineth

---

89 Prov. 3.29. This and the following quotations are from the Septuagint version.
90 Prov. 3.30.
91 Prov. 3.31.
92 Prov. 4.24.
93 Prov. 6.17, 18.
94 Prov. 10.4.
95 Prov. 10.14.
96 Prov. 10.18.
97 Prov. 11.25.
98 Prov. 12.13.
99 Prov. 12.15.
100 Prov. 12.16.
101 Prov. 12.22.
102 Prov. 13.3.
103 *Ibid.*
104 Prov. 13.16.
105 Prov. 14.6.
106 Prov. 14.14.

from evil; the fool is confident and joins in evil.[107] He that is patient is governed with much wisdom; but he that is impatient exalteth his folly.[108] He that oppresseth the poor, upraideth his Maker.[109] The tongue of the wise knoweth good; but the mouth of fools babbleth out evil.[110] A passionate man stirreth up strifes,[111] and unclean is every man in the eyes of God who exalts his heart.[112] Though hand should be joined to hand unjustly, he will not go unpunished.[113] He that loveth his life spareth his mouth.[114] Contumely goeth before contrition; and evil thought before a fall.[115] He who fixes his eyes devises wicked things and marks out all evils with his lips.[116] The lips of a fool bring him to evil and a bold mouth brings on death.[117] A maligning man will suffer many a loss.[118] Better is the poor man that is just than the rich man who is a liar.[119] It is an honor for a man to separate himself from quarrels; but he who is a fool meddles with such reproaches.[120] Do not love to detract lest you be destroyed. The bread of lying is sweet to a man, but afterwards his mouth shall be filled with gravel.[121] He that gathereth treasures by a lying tongue pursues vanities and shall stumble upon the snares of death.[122] Speak not in the ears of fools, lest perchance the wise despise your words.[123] A dart and a sword and a sharp arrow are dangerous: such also the man who bears false witness against his

---

107 Prov. 14.16.
108 Prov. 14.29.
109 Prov. 14.31.
110 Prov. 15.2.
111 Prov. 15.18.
112 Prov. 16.5.
113 *Ibid.*
114 Prov. 16.17.
115 Prov. 16.18.
116 Prov. 16.30.
117 Prov.18.6, 7.
118 Prov. 18.7.
119 Prov. 19.1.
120 Prov. 20.3.
121 Prov. 20.17.
122 Prov. 21.6.
123 Prov. 23.9.

friend.[124] Like birds and sparrows that fly, so a curse uttered without cause shall come upon him.[125] Answer not a fool according to his folly, lest thou be made like him;[126] but answer a fool according to his folly, lest he imagine himself to be wise.[127] The man that deceives his friends, when he is taken, saith: "I did it in jest."[128] Coals are for burning coals, as wood for fire, and a reproachful man for hot strife.[129] If thine enemy ask you, speaking in a low voice, trust him not; for there are seven mischiefs in his heart.[130] A stone is heavy and sand hard to carry; but the anger of a fool is heavier than them both,[131] and wrath is merciless and anger destructive and jealousy unbearable.[132] The wicked reproaches the poor: and he that trusteth in the conceit of his own heart is very foolish.[133] The fool uttereth all his wrath, but the wise man restrains it in part.[134] An evil son for teeth hath swords and grindeth with his jaw teeth, to devour the needy from off the earth and the poor from among men.'[135] Therefore, taught by these examples, I did not want to bite back at him who bites back at me, or to retaliate in kind; and I chose rather to charm out the fury of a madman by incantation, and to pour the antidote of a single book into a poisoned heart. But I am afraid that my efforts are in vain, and that I shall be forced to sing the well-known song of David and console myself with these words: 'The sinners are alienated from the womb, they have gone astray from the womb: they have spoken false things. Their madness is according to the likeness of a serpent, like the deaf asp that stoppeth her ears, which will not hear

---

124 Prov. 25.18.
125 Prov. 26.2.
126 Prov. 26.4.
127 Prov. 26.5.
128 Prov. 26.19.
129 Prov. 26.21.
130 Prov. 26.23.
131 Prov. 27.3.
132 Prov. 27.4.
133 Prov. 28.26.
134 Prov. 29.11.
135 Prov. 30.14.

the voice of the charmers: nor of the wizard that charmeth wisely. God shall break in pieces their teeth in their mouths; the Lord shall break the grinders of the lions. They shall come to nothing, like water running down; he hath bent his bow till they be weakened. Like wax that melteth they shall be taken away: fire hath fallen on them, and they have not seen the sun.'[136] And again: 'The just shall rejoice when he shall see the revenge of the wicked; he shall wash his hands in the blood of the sinner. And man shall say: "If, indeed, there be fruit to the just; there is, indeed, a God that judgeth them on the earth." '[137]

(44) At the end of your letter, you write the following in your own hand: 'I hope that you desire peace.' To these words, I reply in brief: If you desire peace, discard your arms. I can accede to flattery; I am not afraid of threats. Let us have the one and the same faith, and peace will follow promptly.

---

136 Ps. 57.4-9.
137 Ps. 57.11, 12.

THE DIALOGUE AGAINST THE PELAGIANS

INTRODUCTION

HE LAST CONTROVERSY over heretics which was to engage the attention of St. Jerome and sadden the evening of his life at Bethlehem was the Pelagian, in which he seemed to have engaged rather at the instance of others than on his own initiative. His motive in this controversy appeared to have been rather to win than to condemn the Pelagians, and his attitude less hostile than that of St. Augustine. In this struggle, the Church was to have the services of two of the chief opponents of heresies, St. Jerome and St. Augustine,[1] who took an active part in the quarrel from its beginning to its end and against the chief defenders and teachers of Pelagianism, Pelagius himself, Celestius, and Julian, bishop of Eclanum. St. Jerome, on the other hand, participated actively only in the first phase of the struggle with the Pelagians, from the year 411 to his death in the year 420.

Of the many propositions[2] which the Pelagians set down and taught, the following engaged the special attention of St. Jerome in his work written against the Pelagians: first, that the sin of Adam hurt him alone and not the human race; second, that before the coming of Christ, there existed men who

---

1 St. Augustine was the first to refute the theories of Pelagius and Celestius: first, in the series of sermons which he preached at Carthage at the request of Aurelius, the great bishop of Carthage; and, then, in various treatises which he wrote against them. Of the fifteen treatises which St. Augustine composed against the Pelagian system, the following are the most important: *De peccatorum meritis et remissione et de baptismo parvulorum ad Marcellinum* (412), *De spiritu et gratia* (412), *De natura et gratia contra Pelagium ad Timasium et Jacobum* (415), *Liber de perfectione justitiae hominis* (415), and *Liber de gestis Pelagii ad Aurelium episcopum* (417).

2 St. Jerome quotes a work of Pelagius, though giving only the headings or propositions and the number of the chapters up to 100. Many of these headings are discussed in book one, chs. 25-32.

223

were free from sin; third, that newly born infants are in the same condition as Adam was before the fall; fourth, that man can be without sin and can observe all the commandments of God if he wants to; and fifth, that infants have eternal life, even though they are not baptized.[3]

The most important and fundamental principle of Pelagianism, which was evidently based on the Stoic conception of human nature, consisted in the affirmation of the moral strength and self-sufficiency of man's free will. Relying entirely on his own power, man can always will and do good; in reality there have always been men who have never sinned.[4] Man has always been created free; he has the power of choosing between doing and avoiding what is wrong. He is his own master and acts as he chooses. Willing and acting depend on man alone. In proof of his assertions, Pelagius drew up a list of personages from the Old Testament who, according to him, had never sinned.[5] With such premises, it became impossible to admit original sin. It followed, then, that baptism was not absolutely necessary for salvation. It was given, not for the forgiveness of sin, but was necessary for those who would become members of the kingdom of heaven. Sanctifying grace, therefore, which is given in baptism, was not the necessary foundation of supernatural activity, but only a remedy for actual sins.[6] Pelagius acknowledged in a general way that grace was necessary to avoid evil and do good. But he admitted that grace was necessary, not actually for doing good, but for doing it more easily. By grace, the Pelagians meant many things, even free will.[7]

The denial of original sin by the Pelagians involved a change of view regarding the baptism of children. Distinguish-

---

[3] Cf. St. Augustine, *De gestis Pelagii* 11.23 (PL 44.334).
[4] Cf. F Cayré, *Manual of Patrology and History of Theology* 1 (translated by H. Howitt; Belgium 1935) 391-392.
[5] Cf. St. Augustine, *De natura et gratia* 36.42 (PL 44.267).
[6] Cf. Cayré, *op. cit.*, 392.
[7] Cf J. Tixeront, *History of Dogmas* 2 (translated from the fifth French edition by H. L. B.; St. Louis 1923) 442.

ing between eternal life and the kingdom of heaven, they taught that baptism was necessary for infants to obtain the kingdom of heaven.[8]

Such were the views that Pelagius preached at the beginning of the fifth century at Rome. The particulars of his early life are obscure. He was a monk, seemingly, without membership in any definite community, but not a cleric. He chose to be a layman, preaching on his own authority to the people.[9] He worked slowly and quietly at Rome, developing his views, being sure not to stir up any reaction. He gained many disciples at Rome, in particular Celestius, who was to become the most important leader of the party. The success of Pelagianism in Africa and Sicily was the fruit of his labors. For good reason did St. Augustine call the followers of Pelagianism Celestines.[10]

On hearing of the Gothic invasion of Rome under Alaric, Pelagius and Celestius left Rome in the year 409 for Sicily. Their stay in Sicily was brief, but long enough for Pelagius to write his treatise *De natura* and for Celestius to compose his *Definitions*.[11] Leaving Sicily, they went to Africa, but Pelagius again set sail shortly thereafter for Palestine and the East. Celestius remained alone in Africa. It was in Africa that the struggle against Pelagianism was the most intense and the Pelagian system was denounced for the first time and condemned in the person of Celestius. Celestius' preaching of the new teaching soon aroused hostile attention. He was charged with heresy by Paulinus, priest of Milan, and his six

---

8 Cf. Tixeront, *op. cit.*, 439.
9 Francis X. Murphy, C.SS.R., *Rufinus of Aquileia, His Life and Works* (Washington 1945) 212.
10 Cf. St. Augustine, *De haeresibus* 88.
11 Only fragments remain of these books of Pelagius and Celestius. St. Augustine refuted the work of Pelagius with his *De natura et gratia* written in the year 415; and he composed his *Liber de perfectione justitiae hominis* in the year 415 against the work of Celestius. Pelagius maintained in his work the thesis that it was possible for man to be perfect by his own labors, since the faculty of not sinning was inseparable from nature. Celestius listed sixteen reasons in his work to show that it was possible for man to be without sin.

propositions[12] were denounced and condemned in a provincial council assembled at Carthage in the year 411.[13] Celestius refused to disavow his propositions, and he was condemned, and was forced to leave and take refuge in the East. The heresy was now in the open.

Little is heard of Pelagius and his activity in Palestine whither he had fled in the year 411 from Africa. Although St. Jerome was at Bethlehem when Pelagius was preaching his doctrines in Palestine and making converts to his system, he did not take part in the controversy, nor did he act against Pelagius. He did not care to incur the enmity of his friend, Bishop John of Jerusalem, who favored Pelagius. It was only after his friend, Ctesiphon, had written to him for an opinion on two important propositions laid down by Pelagius, impeccability and apathy, that St. Jerome took up his stand officially against Pelagianism in a long letter written to Ctesiphon in 414.[14] In his letter to Ctesiphon, St. Jerome, in refuting the insanity of the Pelagian doctrine of freedom from the disturbances of the soul and freedom from sin, showed that these views emanated partly from heretics and partly from the Stoic philosophers, especially Pythagoras and Zeno. They had taught that the disorders of the soul could be completely eradicated from the soul by meditation and assiduous exercise of virtues. The Peripatetics, who trace themselves to Aristotle, and the new Academics, of whom Cicero was a disciple, refuted not the facts of their opponents, for they have no facts, but the shadows and wishes which do duty for them.[15] He promised in the letter (ch. 13) to discuss the same subjects at length in a special treatise. Circumstances intervened which prompted St. Jerome to compose this work in the following year. St. Augustine, who became concerned about

---

12 Cf. Tixeront, *op. cit.*, 442.
13 A part of the official report of the council held at Carthage has been preserved in St. Augustine's *De gratia Christi et peccato originali* 2.3-4 (PL 44. 386-387).
14 St. Jerome, *Epistola* 133, *ad Ctesiphontem*.
15 Cf. St. Jerome, *Epistola* 133.1, *ad Ctesiphontem*.

the activities of Pelagius in Palestine, sent Paul Orosius in the year 415 to St. Jerome to confer with him on the activities of Pelagius. In a synod[16] which met at Palestine, Orosius related to the bishops what had happened in Africa in connection with Pelagianism. John, bishop of Jerusalem, summoned Pelagius to come in and answer the charges made by Orosius. The bishop agreed it was better to abstain from any declaration until Pope Innocent I, to whom a letter had been sent, should make a decision. This was a moral victory for Pelagius.[17] A short time later, two Gallic bishops, who were then at Bethlehem, reiterated the accusations of Orosius and presented a libellus drawn up in due form to the council of Diospolis which met at the end of the year 415. When Pelagius was brought in before the council, he repudiated all the errors that had been previously condemned by the council of Carthage in the year 411 in the person of Celestius. The explanation satisfied the judges and Pelagius was declared worthy of ecclesiastical communion. This sentence of the bishops of Diospolis was another victory for Pelagius, and afforded him another lease on life to preach his nefarious doctrines.[18] St. Jerome was dissatisfied with the council and its judgment, and later referred to the council as a 'wretched synod.'[19] As a result of the apparent victories of Pelagius before the councils, St. Jerome felt constrained to take up his pen and openly refute Pelagianism. In his last controversial work, the *Dialogus contra Pelagianos*,[20] St. Jerome resorted to the dialogue form,[21]

---

16 For a description of this synod, called by Bishop John of Jerusalem, cf. Orosius, *Liber apologeticus de arbitrii libertate* 3-7. Orosius relates in this work how he had reminded the Fathers assembled in the synod held at Palestine that St. Jerome had condemned the Pelagian system in a letter written to Ctesiphon, and that he himself was waiting for the work which St. Jerome was at the time engaged in writing.
17 Cf. Tixeront, *op. cit.*, 447.
18 For details of this meeting, cf. St. Augustine, *De gestis Pelagii* 16-20 (PL 44. 343-346).
19 St. Jerome, *Epistola* 143.2, *ad Alypium et Augustinum*.
20 St. Jerome, *Dialogus contra Pelagianos* PL 23.495-590.
21 The dialogue form is not maintained throughout the work. In the last five chapters of the first book, Atticus alone speaks, introducing a series of quotations from the Old Testament to enforce his earlier arguments

in order to preserve an air of impartiality. He introduced two characters, Atticus, the Catholic, and Critobulus, the heretic, engaged in debate. In the manner of Socrates, St. Jerome allowed each speaker to express his own views, so that the truth might become more evident once each side had presented its views. By adopting this type of composition, St. Jerome was able to avoid the complaint that he had written specifically against Pelagius; and, at the same time, it enabled him to present the Catholic view on the topics discussed with greater clarity and to refute the heretical view with greater force.

Especially noteworthy in the *Dialogue* is the demonstration of the Catholic doctrine by means of the Scriptures. St. Jerome brought his great knowledge of the Scriptures to bear on the controversy. Although the tone maintained throughout the entire *Dialogue* is less violent than that of his other ascetic works, nevertheless, St. Jerome spared no pains attacking Pelagianism, which he regarded as a survival of Paganism.[22] In establishing the necessity of grace by his references to Scripture, he did not deny a true personal will, but he made it dependent on divine assistance. In answer to St. Jerome's *Dialogue,* Pelagius composed his four books of *De libero arbitrio,* of which only fragments survive.[23]

The *Dialogus contra Pelagianos* made St. Jerome at once the leader of the orthodox party in the East. Although the tone was moderate in its bitterness, it stirred up great animosity against him. The Oriental Pelagians revenged themselves on St. Jerome by pillaging and burning his monasteries at

---

and to prove that opposition to the will of God, though often implicit, is also reckoned as a sin. Book two can hardly be said to form a dialogue. From the fourth chapter onward, book two consists of a chain of scriptural texts, quoted from the New Testament and the Prophets, to show that sin is universal, and to refute the Pelagian thesis that man can be without sin if he wants to. Cf. W. H. Fremantle, 'Against the Pelagians,' in *A Select Library of Nicene and Post-Nicene Fathers of the Christian Church,* second series, vol. 6 (New York 1912) 448,466.

22 Cf. St. Jerome, *Epistola* 133.1, *ad Ctesiphontem.*
23 For the fragments, cf. PL 48.611-615.

Bethlehem.[24] He had, at least, the consolation of seeing this new heresy condemned. Africa had not been satisfied with the acquittal of Pelagius at Diospolis. The Fathers of the two African councils that met in the year 416, the one at Carthage, the other at Milevis, requested Pope Innocent I to condemn Celestius and Pelagius. The Pope replied on January 27, 417, and formally excommunicated Pelagius and Celestius.

SELECT BIBLIOGRAPHY

Text and Translation:

Fremantle, W. H. 'Against the Pelagians,' in *A Select Library of Nicene and Post-Nicene Fathers of the Christian Church*, second series, vol. 6 (New York 1912) 447-483. (Chs. 34-39 of book one and chs. 1-5, 7-23, and 25-30 of book two have been omitted in Fremantle's translation.)

Migne, J. P. *Patrologiae Latinae cursus completus* (Paris 1846) 23.495-590.

Secondary Writings:

Bardenhewer, O. *Patrology* (translated from the second edition by Thomas J. Shahan; St. Louis 1908).

Cayré, F. *Manual of Patrology and History of Theology* 1 (translated by H. Howitt; Belgium 1935).

Muller, Liguori G., O.F.M. *The De Haeresibus of Saint Augustine* (Washington, 1956).

Murphy, Francis X., C.SS.R. *Rufinus of Aquileia, His Life and Works* (Washington 1945).

Tixeront, J. *History of Dogmas* 2 (translated from the fifth French edition by H. L. B.; St. Louis 1923).

---

24 The sufferings which St. Jerome endured at the hands of the heretics are described in the letters written by Pope Innocent I in his behalf. Cf. Letters 135-137 among St. Jerome's collection of letters. Cf. also St. Augustine, *De gestis Pelagii* 35.66 (PL 44.358).

THE DIALOGUE AGAINST THE PELAGIANS

Preface

(1) *He is influenced by the requests of his brothers to write.* Having written a letter to Ctesiphon,[1] in which I answered the questions that he had raised, I have repeatedly been asked by my brothers why I was putting off any longer the work that I had promised to publish in which I declared that I would answer all of the questions raised by those who preach the doctrine of apathy.[2] This is, to be sure, the doctrine that was the bone of contention between the Stoics and the Peripatetics, that is to say, the Old Academy; for the one school asserted that *páthē*, which we read in Latin as *perturbationes*, such as sorrow, joy, hope, and fear, could be completely eradicated and extirpated from the minds of men; while the other school held that these disturbances can be restrained and mastered and controlled and kept within proper bounds and checked like bridled horses with certain curbs. Cicero discusses their views in his *Tusculan Disputations*[3] and Origen seeks to blend these views with ecclesiastical truth in his *Stromata*,[4] not to mention Manichaeus, Priscillian, Evagrius

---

1 St. Jerome, *Epistola* 133, *ad Ctesiphontem*.
2 Apathy is the Stoic doctrine of freedom from passions.
3 In the second book of his *Tusculan Disputations*, Cicero discusses the endurance of pain; in the third book, the alleviations of distress; in the fourth book, the remaining disorders of the soul.
4 Only a few fragments are extant of the *Stromata* of Origen. They seem to have been nothing more than collections of scholia, simple philological and historical notes to throw light on obscure verses or passages. Cf. F. Cayré, *Manual of Patrology and History of Theology* 1 (translated by H. Howitt; Belgium 1935) 196. They were youthful works containing far too much profane learning. It is possible to regard them as a doctrinal work, similar to the *Stromata* of Clement of Alexandria. St. Jerome states in his letter to Magnus that Origen imitated the *Stromata* of Clement when he composed his ten books of *Stromata*, in

of Ibora, Jovinian,[5] and the heretics of practically the whole

---

which he compared the views of the Christians and the philosophers, and drew proofs of the truth of the Christian religion from the philosophical doctrines of Plato, Aristotle, Numenius, and Cornutus (*Epistola* 70.4, *ad Magnum*). According to Clement in his *Stromata*, three elements enter into the nature of perfection: apathy, charity, and Gnosis, i.e., perfect knowledge. The true Gnostic, or perfect Christian, not only brings his body into subjection and masters his passions, but banishes all traces of sensibility. In his second *Miscellany* (book two), Clement gives a description of the true Gnostic, and outlines the way in which man can become like God. The true Christian resembles God (*Stromata* 2.19-22). The majority of the early heresies were forms of Gnosticism, or were heavily tinged with Gnostic thought. Gnosticism is a generic term applicable to the sects and heretical movements in the early Church, which claimed that redemption was to be achieved through knowledge (Gnosis). Once Gnosticism became a Christian heresy, it showed definite forms. One of these forms was the Gnostic system which joined itself to Christianity closely in essential points.

5 St. Augustine devotes the largest section of the *De haeresibus* to the Manichaeans, for theirs was a heresy which played an important part in his own life, and one which was a formidable enemy of the Catholic faith in the third and fourth centuries. The founder of this sect was Mani, a Persian born in Babylonia. The Greeks and Romans translated his name as Manes, Manikhaios, and Manicaeus. The essence of the Manichaean doctrine is dualism. They believed that there were two natures and substances, one good and one evil. There are good souls and bad souls. The bad souls cannot be purged and, therefore, receive eternal damnation. Both God and the good souls are of one and the same nature. Since, in this system, redemption was to be accomplished by knowledge, Manichaeism may be considered a form of Gnosticism. Cf. Liguori G. Muller, O.F.M., *The De Haeresibus of Saint Augustine* (Washington 1956) 159-172. The Priscillianists, founded by Priscillian of Spain, followed, for the most part, a mixture of Gnostic and Manichaean doctrines. They held that souls were of the same nature and substance as God. Cf. Muller, *op. cit.*, 198-202.

Evagrius was born at Ibora in Pontus and is often referred to as Evagrius Ponticus. St. Jerome refers to him as Evagrius, the Iborite. He was an ardent Origenist and a Gnostic. He wrote a book called *Gnostic*, or scientific problems, a kind of dogmatic or moral theology (cf. Cayré. *op. cit.*, 507). St. Jerome reproached Evagrius with Origenistic tendencies and called him the forerunner of Pelagius (*Epistola* 133.4, *ad Ctesiphontem*). St. Jerome also mentioned in his letter that Evagrius wrote a treatise on *De apatheia*, which is no longer extant (*ibid.* 4). The errors of Evagrius were later condemned by the Fifth Ecumenical Council in the year 553, and he was also anathematized, together with Origen and Didymus, at the Sixth and Seventh Councils.

Jovinian maintained, as did the Stoic philosophers, that all sins were equal, and that it was impossible for man to sin any more after baptism. He was, in reality, teaching salvation by faith alone and baptism.

of Syria, who are erroneously referred to in the pagan tongue as *Massaliani*, and in the Greek as *Euchites*.[6] All of them assert that human virtue and human knowledge can achieve a perfection, and I do not mean in the sense of a likeness to, but an equality with God, to such a high degree that they hold that, once they have reached the pinnacle of perfection, they cannot commit even sins of thought and ignorance. And although I did discuss in brief manner, due to the press of time, a few of the points in the earlier letter that I sent to Ctesiphon in refutation of their errors, in the present work that I am in the process of composing, I shall follow the method of the Socratics of presenting all the arguments that can be stated by both parties, so that the truth might become more evident, once each side has presented its views. Moreover, it is Origen's own peculiar view that it is impossible for human nature to pass through life without sinning; and, on the other hand, that it is possible for any man, who has changed his life for the better, to gain such strength that he never sins again.

(2) *Envy was not the motive.*

However, I shall say briefly, in reply to those who say that it was the fury of envy that prompted me to write this work, that I have never spared heretics, and have endeavored in every possible manner to make the enemies of the Church my own enemies. Helvidius[7] wrote a treatise against the perpetual virginity of Holy Mary. Was I motivated by envy to reply to

---

6 The Massalians were called such after a name meaning the 'praying people.' They had no settled system and no recognized leader. According to St. Augustine, they were called in Greek *Euchites* from their habit of continual prayer. According to Epiphanius (*Haereses* 80), they were not guilty of any error of doctrine, and their manner of life was the only thing worthy of criticism.

7 Helvidius had written a treatise in which he upheld, first, that Mary lost her virginity *post partum*, for she had other children after the birth of Jesus; and second, that the marriage state was not inferior in glory and honor to the state of continence. In reply to Helvidius, St. Jerome wrote his famous *Liber adversus Helvidium de perpetua virginitate B. Mariae;* cf. pp. 3-43.

a man whom I have never seen in the flesh? Jovinian,[8] whose heresy is being revived at the present time, shocked the faith of Rome while I was absent from the city, and his language was so inelegant and so abusive that he was more deserving of pity than of envy. I also replied to him to the best of my ability. Rufinus[9] exerted every effort to make available, not only to one city, but to the whole world, the blasphemies of Origen and the books of the *Periarchon*, and went so far as to even publish the first book of Eusebius' *Apology for Origen* under the name of the martyr, Pamphilus,[10] and, as if the former had expressed himself unsatisfactorily, he spewed forth a new book in his defense. Am I envious of him because I answered him, and because the flood of his eloquence was so torrential that I lost all desire for writing and dictating? Palladius,[11] a slave to villany, tried to revive the same heresy and to add fresh insult to my Hebrew translation. Am I envious both of his genius and his nobility? Even now the mystery of evil is at work and everybody expresses freely his personal views; I am the only one to whom the glory of all men is a source of irritation, and my lot is so wretched that I am

---

[8] Jovinian taught many erroneous doctrines, among which was the view that Mary lost her virginity *in partu* in bringing forth Jesus; and that virginity was no more meritorious than matrimony; that those who received baptism with full faith could sin no more. St. Jerome refuted these errors in his *Adversus Jovinianum*.
[9] Rufinus translated into Latin the *Periarchon* of Origen, a translation that precipitated the serious controversy between himself and St. Jerome. The most important work that came out of this controversy was St. Jerome's *Apologia adversus Rufinum;* cf. pp. 47-220.
[10] Rufinus translated the first book of the *Apologia* of the martyr, Pamphilus, for a scholar by the name of Macarius. Quite an argument was stirred up over this translation; for St. Jerome claimed in his *Apologia* that Eusebius of Caesarea was the real author of the *Apologia*, and that Rufinus had attributed the work to the martyr, Pamphilus, rather than to Eusebius, in order to profit by the prestige of having a martyr favor the cause of Origen (St. Jerome, *Apologia* 1.9-10). Rufinus added, by way of supplement, a small treatise of his own, the *Liber de adulteratione librorum Origenis*.
[11] Palladius, a disciple of the Origenist writer, Evagrius Ponticus, produced a number of monastic biographies known as *Historia Lausiaca*. His work was regarded as a translation of an original by Rufinus. Cf. his account of St. Jerome in his *Historia Lausiaca* (ch. 78).

jealous even of those individuals who do not deserve to be envied. Hence, in order to prove to the whole world that it is not persons that I hate, but rather their errors, and that I am not seeking to bring disgrace upon my brothers, but rather am pitying the lot of those who are being tripped up by what is falsely called knowledge, I have proposed the names of Atticus and Critobulus,[12] using them as the mouthpieces for our own views and those of the adversaries. Nay more, it is the hope and prayer of all of us who profess the Catholic faith that heresy be refuted and individuals be converted. Or, if they choose to persist in error, the blame is certainly not to be placed on us who have written the treatise, but rather on those who have preferred falsehood to truth. And we reply briefly to those calumniators, who impute their own reproaches to these individuals, that it is the view of the Manichaeans to revile the nature of man, and to destroy free will, and to rule out the help of God. And again, that it is a sign of very manifest folly for man to say that he is what God is; and that we must travel the royal road in such a way that we turn neither to the left nor to the right; and that we believe that the cravings of our own will are always guided by the help of God. But if anybody cries out loud that false charges are being brought against him, and boasts that he is in agreement with our views, then, and only then, will he prove that he is in agreement with the true faith, when openly and without guile he condemns the opposite views, lest he hear these words of the prophet said to him: 'And after all this, her treacherous sister Juda hath not returned to me with her whole heart, but with falsehood.'[13] It is a less serious sin to pursue evil which you assumed was good than to lack the courage to defend what you know for certain is good. We, who cannot bear threats, injury, and poverty, how shall we overcome the fires of Babylon? Let false peace not destroy what war has spared. I do not want to learn perfidy through fear, when Christ has left the true faith up to my own will.

---

12 Cf. above, Introduction, p. 228.
13 Jer. 3.10.

Book One

(1) *Whether man can be without sin if he wants to.*

ATTICUS. Tell me, Critobulus, is it true what I hear you have written,[1] that man can be without sin if he wants to, and that the precepts of God are easy?

CRITOBULUS. It is true, Atticus, but my rivals do not understand the statement in the same sense in which it was made by me.

ATTICUS. What, then, is the ambiguity in your statement that gives rise to this diversity of understanding? I do not expect you to answer both propositions with one reply. For two theses have been proposed by you: first, that man can be without sin if he wants to; second, that the precepts of God are easy. Therefore, although these propositions were stated in a single sentence, they should, nevertheless, be discussed separately, so that those whose faith appears to be the one and the same may have no occasion for an argument over the diversity of opinions.

CRITOBULUS. I stated, Atticus, that man could be without sin if he wanted to; not, as certain maligning individuals falsely charge, without the grace of God (for even to think such an idea is a sacrilege), but simply that he could be, if he wanted to, so that the notion of 'with God's grace' might be understood.

ATTICUS. Therefore, is God also the author of your evil deeds?

CRITOBULUS. Not in the way in which you assume. But if there is any good in me, it is accomplished by His prompting and His help.

---
[1] These are two of the principal propositions laid down by Pelagius. Cf. St. Augustine, *De gestis Pelagii* 16.39 (PL 44.343).

ATTICUS. I am not inquiring about nature, but about action. For who doubts that God is the creator of all things? I wish you would answer me this question: The good that you do, is that imputed to you or to God?

CRITOBULUS. To me and to God; to me who works it and to God who helps me.

ATTICUS. And what is the reason for this commonly held view that you rule out the grace of God, and assert that what we humans do is imputed to our own will alone?

CRITOBULUS. I marvel, Atticus, that you expect me to account for the cause and reason of the error of someone else, and question me on a statement that I did not make when the statement that I did make is clear and evident. I said that man could be without sin if he wanted to. Did I add the phrase, 'without the grace of God'?

ATTICUS. But the very fact that you did not add the phrase would seem to indicate that you were denying it.

CRITOBULUS. On the contrary, the very fact that I did not deny it should be reason to suppose that I did affirm it. For there is no reason to assume that we deny what we do not affirm.

ATTICUS. Therefore, you admit that man can be without sin if he wants to, with the grace of God?

CRITOBULUS. Not only do I admit it, I even openly declare it.

ATTICUS. Therefore, is he in error who rules out the grace of God?

CRITOBULUS. Yes. Nay more, he should be judged impious, since all things are governed by the will of God, and our very existence and the cravings of our own will are a gift of God. For the very possession of the free will, and the disposition to do good or evil through our own will flow from His grace who created us to His own image and likeness.

(2) *Whether all this should be imputed to the grace of God.*

ATTICUS. No one doubts, Critobulus, that all things depend on the judgment of Him who is the creator of all things, and everything that we have is to be regarded as His gift. But

I want to know whether you regard this very thing that you impute to the grace of God as a gift of creation, or whether you believe that it is part of every single deed that we perform to the extent that we depend, to be sure, on His help in everything that we do; or whether we do everything that we want to do through our own will and power, once we have been created by Him with a free will? For I know that many of our followers apply the grace of God to all things in such a way that they regard the power of the will as applying, not to the parts, but to the whole, that is to say, not to every single action, but rather to creation.

CRITOBULUS. It is not as you assume, but I set down both propositions, namely, that we have been created such as we are by the grace of God, and that we depend on His assistance for every single action.

ATTICUS. Therefore, we agree that, besides our own will, we depend on the help of God in the good that we do, and on the help of the devil in the evil that we do.

CRITOBULUS. We agree, and on this point there is no argument.

ATTICUS. Therefore, they are wrong in their thinking who rule out the help of God in every single action that we perform, and who seek to twist the true meaning to other meanings by putting constructions that are perverted, nay more, worthy of ridicule, on the following passage: 'Except the Lord build the house, they labor in vain that build it. Except the Lord keep the city, he watcheth in vain who keepeth it,'[2] and other passages of this kind.

(3) *There is need of God's assistance in every single action.*

CRITOBULUS. Why is it necessary for me to speak against others when you have my own answer?

ATTICUS. What is your answer? Are they right or wrong in their thinking?

CRITOBULUS. And what necessity forces me to express my views against them?

ATTICUS. The logical order of the discussion and the regard

---

2 Ps. 126.1.

for truth. Do you not know that every statement that we make either is or is not; and that it is to be classified either as good or evil? Therefore, in spite of your reluctance, you must answer the question that I ask you, and admit that their statement is either good or evil.

CRITOBULUS. If we must rely on God's help in every single action that we perform, will it, then, be impossible for us to fashion a pen for writing purposes, and to smooth and polish it after it has been fashioned, and apply our hand to writing, to maintain silence, to talk, to sit, to stand, to walk, to run, to eat, to fast, to cry, to laugh, and perform other similar acts, unless God helps us?

ATTICUS. As I interpret it, it is clearly impossible.

CRITOBULUS. In what respect, then, do we have a free will, and in what respect is the grace of God preserved in us if we cannot perform even these acts without God?

(4) *The meaning of the gift of the free will. The grace of God does not obstruct freedom.*

ATTICUS. The grace of the free will was not bestowed so as to do away with the assistance of God in every single action.

CRITOBULUS. The assistance of God is not ruled out, since creatures are saved by the grace of the free will that has been bestowed on them once and for all. For if I can do nothing without God and unless He helps me in every action that I perform, He will neither crown me with justice for the good deeds that I perform, nor will He punish me for my evil actions, but in both cases He will either receive or condemn His own assistance.

ATTICUS. Therefore, simply state your reason for ruling out the grace of God. For what you deny to the parts, you must necessarily deny to the whole.

CRITOBULUS. I am not denying grace when I assert that I was created by God in such a way that the power was given to my own will, through the grace of God, either to act or not to act.

ATTICUS. Therefore, God remains idle as far as our actions are concerned, once the power of the free will has been bestowed on us; and we do not have to pray to Him to help us in all of our actions, since it is a matter of our own will and choice either to act if we want to, or not to act if we do not want to.

(5) CRITOBULUS. Just as the order of creation is preserved in the case of the other living creatures, so also, in like fashion, all things are left to our own will, once the power of the free will has been bestowed on us.

ATTICUS. Therefore, as I have stated, do I need not ask God for help in every act that I perform, since this help has been placed, once and for all, in my own judgment?

CRITOBULUS. If He is a cooperator in everything that I do, the act is not to be imputed to me, but to Him who helps me, or rather to Him who cooperates with me, especially since I can accomplish nothing without Him.

ATTICUS. I ask you, have you not read: 'There is question not of him who wills nor of him who runs, but of God showing mercy'?[3] It is clear from this passage that ours, to be sure, is the willing and the running, but the accomplishing of our willing and of our running belongs to the mercy of God; and so it comes that, as far as your own willing and our running are concerned, the free will is preserved, and that all things depend on the power of God, as far as the accomplishing of our willing and our running is concerned. I suppose that, at this point, I should quote the testimonies of Scripture to show how the saints begged God to help them in their every single act, and how they had to rely on Him as their helper and protector in every single deed that they performed. Read through the entire Psalter; read all of the utterances of the saints; you will find that they are nothing more or less than prayers to God in all their actions. From all this, it is clearly evident that you are either denying the grace of God, which you take away from the parts; or, if you grant it to the parts, a concession which you obviously do not wish to make, you are concurring in our view, who preserve the free will in man

---
3 Rom. 9.16.

in such a manner that we do not deny the help of God in every single deed.

(6) *He refutes the teaching of the Pelagians.*

CRITOBULUS. This conclusion of yours is captious and based on the art of the dialecticians. Nobody, however, will be able to rule out, as far as I am concerned, the power of the free will, lest, if God exists as my helper in every single act, the reward be imputed not to me, but to Him who worked in me.

ATTICUS. Glory in the power of the free will so that you may arm your tongue against God, and therein prove that you are free if you are at liberty to blaspheme. However, your own personal views on this matter are no mystery to anyone, and the deceits of your confession have become clear as day. But to get back to the proposition with which we opened our discussion. Tell me, if you please, when you made the statement a moment ago that it was possible for man with the help of God not to sin if he wanted to, do you mean forever, or temporarily and for a short time?

CRITOBULUS. This is a superfluous question. For if I say, 'temporarily and for a short time,' it will still be taken to mean 'forever.' For whatever you grant for a short time, you also admit it forever.

ATTICUS. I do not quite understand what you mean.

CRITOBULUS. Are you so dull as not to understand the obvious?

(7) *Whether man can avoid sin temporarily or forever?*

ATTICUS. I am not ashamed to have no knowledge where I have none. And we must both agree on the definition of the proposition that we are going to discuss.

CRITOBULUS. I assert that he who can avoid sin for one day can also avoid it for another day, and he who can avoid it for two days can also avoid it for three days; he who can avoid sin for three days can also avoid it for thirty days; and in like fashion, he can also avoid sin for three hundred days, and three thousand days, and for as long a time as he wants to.

ATTICUS. Therefore, simply say that man can be without sin forever if he wants to. Can we not do everything that we want to?
CRITOBULUS. Not at all. For I cannot do everything that I want to. But I am only saying that man can be without sin if he wants to.
ATTICUS. I ask you to answer this question: Do you consider me a human being or a brute animal?
CRITOBULUS. If I have any doubts as to whether you are a human being or a brute animal, I will admit that I am a brute animal myself.
ATTICUS. Therefore, if, as you say, I am a human being, why is it that I commit a sin when I pray and wish hard enough not to sin?
CRITOBULUS. Because your will is imperfect. For if you really wanted to, you really would not sin.
ATTICUS. Therefore, you, who contend that I do not really want to be without sin, are without sin because you really want to be without sin?
CRITOBULUS. As if I were speaking of myself, who, I confess, am a sinner, and not of those few and rare individuals, if any, who wish not to sin.

(8) *No example of such a case.*
ATTICUS. In the meantime, in your judgment as well as in mine, I, who am asking the question, and you, who are answering it, are sinners.
CRITOBULUS. But it is within our power not to be sinners if we want to.
ATTICUS. I said that it was my wish not to sin, and you, no doubt, also have the same desire. Therefore, why is it that neither of us can do what each of us wants to do?
CRITOBULUS. Because our will is not complete.
ATTICUS. Then, mention some of our ancestors whose will was complete and who were able to be without sin.
CRITOBULUS. To be sure, it is not an easy matter to prove this point. For when I say that man can be without sin if he

wants to, I am not contending that there ever were some individuals who were without sin; but I am only arguing that they can be if they want to. For 'possibility of being,' which in Greek is termed *dunámis* (possibility), is one thing, and 'being,' what they themselves call *energeía* (actuality), is quite another matter. I can be a doctor, but, in the meantime, I am not a doctor. I can be a craftsman, but, as yet, I have not learned to be one. Therefore, whatever I can be, although I am not yet that thing, nevertheless, I shall be if I want to.

(9) *Whether that which will never be is possible or not?*
ATTICUS. The arts are one thing, that which comes into being as the result of the arts is quite another matter. Medical skill, craftsmanship, and the other arts, are found in many individuals; but to be without sin forever is the disposition of divine power alone. Therefore, either cite the example of those who were without sin forever, or, if you cannot do so, confess your ignorance and stop meddling in the affairs of heaven and deceiving the ears of the foolish with this matter of 'being' and 'possibility of being.' For who will grant you that man can do what no man has ever been able to do? Have you not even been instructed in the rudiments of dialectics? For if a thing is possible for man, impossibility is ruled out. But if a thing is not possible for man, possibility is denied. Either grant me that some individual was able to accomplish what you contend is possible, or, if no person was able to accomplish it, you will be obliged to admit, against your will, that no man can accomplish what you boast is possible. This is the argument over the possible that took place between Diodorus and Chrysippus,[4] two very able dialecticians. Diodorus says that only that is possible which either is true or will be true. And whatever will take place in the future is necessarily possible. But whatever will not take place is impossible.

---

4 Diodorus, surnamed Cronus, lived in Alexandria in the reign of Ptolemy Soter. He was the teacher of Philo. For his discussions *On the Possible*, cf. E. Zeller, *Socrates and The Socratic Schools* (London 1885) 273-274. Chrysippus was the first to base the Stoic doctrine on something like systematic reasoning.

Chrysippus, on the other hand, says that those things are also possible that will not take place; as for example, it is possible for this pearl to be broken, even if it never happens. Therefore, they who say that man can be without sin if he wants to will not be able to prove this assertion to be true, unless they prove that it will take place in the future. But since all future things are uncertain, and especially those things that never have been done, it is clear that they are saying what will not take place will take place. Ecclesiastes confirms this view: 'Everything that shall be has already been done in ages that were before.'[5]

(10) *God's commandments are possible.*
CRITOBULUS. I ask you, answer this question: Did God give possible or impossible commandments?
ATTICUS. I see the direction that your assertion is taking. But we ought to consider this point later on in the discussion, lest we create confusion in the minds of our listeners by piling question upon question. Therefore, withhold comment on the statement that I made, that God gave possible commandments, lest He turn out to be Himself the author of injustice if He demands us to do what is impossible. For the present time, go through with the proposition that you laid down, that man can be without sin if he wants to. For you will either name the individuals who were able to be without sin, or, if nobody was able to be without sin, you will readily confess that man cannot avoid sins forever.
CRITOBULUS. Since you insist that I produce evidence that I need not produce, I ask you to consider the statement of the Lord, that it is easier for a camel to pass through the eye of a needle than for a rich man to enter the kingdom of heaven.[6] And yet He said that an act that has never been performed was possible. For a camel has never passed through the eye of a needle.
ATTICUS. I am surprised that an intelligent man like you has

---
5 Eccles. 1.9, 10.
6 Cf. Matt. 19.24; Mark 10.25.

quoted a testimony that is a contradiction. For, in this statement, no reference was made to what was possible, but rather one impossibility was compared with another impossibility. For just as a camel cannot pass through the eye of a needle, so also, a rich man will not enter the kingdom of heaven. Or, if you can prove that a rich man will enter the kingdom of heaven, it follows that a camel will pass through the eye of a needle. Do not cite Abraham and the other rich men we read about in the Old Testament as examples of rich men who entered the kingdom of heaven, for they ceased to be rich men because they used their wealth to do good; in fact, since they were rich men, not for themselves, but for others, they should be referred to as stewards of God rather than as rich men. But we should strive for the perfection of the Gospel, in which it is commanded: 'If thou wilt be perfect, go, sell all that thou hast, and give to the poor, and come, follow me.'[7]

(11) *His answer to the objection based on the utterance of the Lord. His reply to the examples of Job, Zacharia, and Elizabeth.*

CRITOBULUS. You have unwittingly been caught in the web of your own thinking.

ATTICUS. How so?

CRITOBULUS. In quoting the utterances of the Lord, you assert that man can be perfect. For when He says: 'If thou wilt be perfect, go, sell all that thou hast, and give to the poor, and come, follow me,' He shows that man can be perfect if he wants to and if he fulfills the commandments.

ATTICUS. You have, indeed, dealt me such a stunning blow that I begin to see spots before my eyes. However, this very statement that He makes: 'If thou wilt be perfect,' is addressed to him who could not be perfect, or rather, who would not be, and, therefore, could not be perfect. But you show me a man who wanted to be and could not be perfect, as you promised just now to do.

---

7 Matt. 9.21.

CRITOBULUS. But what necessity compels me to name the individuals who were perfect when it is clear that they can be perfect, according to the words of the Savior spoken to one individual, and in the name of one person to all persons: 'If thou wilt be perfect'?

ATTICUS. You are shirking the question; you are stuck in the same mire; for what is possible was either done at some time or other, or, if it was never done, concede that it is impossible.

(12) CRITOBULUS. Why do I delay any longer? You must be convinced by the authority of Scripture. To pass over the rest, will I not make you hold your peace by citing two testimonies in which Job, Zacharia, and Elizabeth are praised? For unless I am mistaken, it is written in Job as follows: 'There was a certain man in the land of Hus, whose name was Job, and that man was upright and without blame, and a true worshipper of God, and avoiding all evil.'[8] And again: 'Who is there who argues that the just is without sin, and speaks his words through ignorance?'[9] Likewise, in the Gospel, according to Luke: 'There was in the days of Herod, King of Judea, a certain priest, named Zacharia, of the course of Abia; and his wife was of the daughters of Aaron, and her name was Elizabeth. Both, however, were just before God, walking blamelessly in all the commandments and ordinances of the Lord.'[10] If he is a true worshiper of God, and unspotted, and blameless; and if they, who walked in all the ordinances of the Lord, are just in His sight, I think that they are free from sin, and stand in need of nothing that pertains to justice.

ATTICUS. You have cited testimonies that have been detached, not from a section of one or the other of the Testaments, but from individual books. For even Job, after suffering many wounds, is shown to have said many things against the will of God, provoking Him to judgment: 'O that man might so be judged with God, as the son of man is judged with his com-

---

8 Job 1.1 (Septuagint).
9 Job 6.25 (Septuagint).
10 Luke 1.5, 6.

panion!'[11] And again: 'Who would grant me a hearer, that the Almighty may hear my desire: and that he himself that judgeth would write a book.'[12] And again: 'If I should be just, my own mouth shall speak wicked things; if I would be blameless, I shall be found wicked; and if I be washed with snow and be clean of hands, you have plunged me sufficiently in filth. My garments have abhorred me.'[13] And of Zacharia it is written that he said to the angel who promised him the birth of a son: 'How shall I know this? For I am an old man and my wife is advanced in years?'[14] For this remark, he is punished on the spot with silence: 'Thou shalt be dumb and unable to speak until the day when these things shall come to pass, because thou hast not believed my words, which will be fulfilled in their proper time.'[15] From all this, it is clear that they are called just, to be sure, and spotless; but if negligence slowly overtakes man, he can fall; that man is always placed in a precarious position, so that he falls down into vices from the pinnacle of virtues, and rises from the depths of vices to sublime heights; that he is never secure, but is ever apprehensive of shipwreck in fair weather; and that, for this reason, man cannot be without sin, as Solomon says: 'For there is no just man upon earth, that doth good, and sinneth not.'[16] And also in the book of Kings: 'For there is no man who sinneth not.'[17] And the blessed David says: 'Who can understand sins? From my secret ones cleanse me, O Lord; and from those of others spare thy servant.'[18] And again: 'Enter not into judgment with thy servant, for in thy sight no man living shall be justified.'[19] And many other examples with which Holy Scripture abounds.

---

11 Job 16.22.
12 Job 31.35.
13 Job 9.20, 30, 31.
14 Luke 1.18.
15 Luke 1.20.
16 Eccles. 7.21.
17 3 Kings 8.46.
18 Ps. 18.13, 14.
19 Ps. 142.2.

(13) *He refutes the argument from the Gospel of John.*

CRITOBULUS. What, then, will be your answer to the example cited by John the Evangelist: 'We know that no one who is born of God commits sin; but the Begotten of God preserveth him and the wicked one does not touch him. We know that we are of God, and the whole world is in the power of the evil one'?[20]

ATTICUS. I shall render like for like, and shall prove that, according to your interpretation, this brief letter of the evangelist is self-contradictory. For, if no one who is born of God commits sin because His seed abides in him, and he cannot sin because he is born of God, by what logical sequence does the same evangelist say in the same place: 'If we say that we have no sin, we deceive ourselves, and the truth is not in us'?[21] You do not know the reason; you are perplexed and confused. Listen to the same evangelist: 'If we acknowledge our sins, he is faithful and just to forgive us our sins and to cleanse us from all iniquity.'[22] Therefore, we are just when we acknowledge that we are sinners, and our justice depends, not on our own personal merit, but rather on the mercy of God, as Holy Scripture says: 'The just is accuser of himself in the beginning of his plea.'[23] And in another place: 'Tell thy sins, that thou mayest be justified.'[24] 'For God has shut all in sin, that he may have mercy upon all.'[25] And this is consummate justice in man, not to impute any virtue that he can attain to himself, but rather to the Lord, the Giver. Therefore, he who is born of God does not sin as long as the seed of God abides in him; and he cannot sin because he is born of God. But because the enemy oversows the field of the Lord with weeds while the householder is asleep, and the sower sows cockle and wild oats among the good grain at night without our knowledge,

---
20 John 5.18, 19.
21 1 John 1.8.
22 1 John 1.9.
23 Prov. 18.17.
24 Isa. 43.26 (Septuagint).
25 Rom. 11.32.

we must, therefore, be apprehensive of the parable of the householder of the Gospel, who sweeps the threshing floor, and, gathering up the wheat into his barns, leaves the chaff to be scattered by the gusts of winds, and to be burned in the fire. Whence, also, we read it written in Jeremia: 'What hath the chaff to do with the wheat, saith the Lord?'[26] The chaff, however, is separated from the wheat at the consummation of the world. All this proves that, while we live in this mortal body, we are mixed with the wheat. But if you bring forth as an objection the words that he spoke: 'And he cannot sin because he is born of God,' you will hear: And where will be the reward of the will? For, if he does not sin because he cannot sin, the free will will be ruled out, and this act will not be imputed to ourselves, but to the goodness of nature which is not capable of sinning.

(14) *Two other testimonies from the Old and New Testament.*

CRITOBULUS. Up to now, I have cited very easy testimonies in order to drill you for the more difficult ones. What can you say to testimonies which you will not be able to refute by any clever scheme, in spite of your genius? I shall first quote testimony from the Old Testament, and then from the New Testament. Moses is the central figure of the Old Testament; the Lord and Savior, of the New Testament. Moses says to the people: 'You shall be perfect in the sight of your God.'[27] And the Savior says to the apostles: 'You are to be perfect even as your heavenly Father is perfect.'[28] For, it is either possible for the listeners to fulfill the commandments that Moses and the Lord imposed, or, if it is impossible, the blame is not to be placed on those who cannot obey them, but on him who imposed impossible commandments.

ATTICUS. At first glance, this testimony would appear to the inexperienced, and those who have not studied Scripture

---

26 Jer. 23.38.
27 Deut. 18.13.
28 Matt. 5.48.

and have no familiarity with and no knowledge of Scripture, to favor your views. But this confusion is readily solved. And, when you compare testimony with testimony, lest it appear that the Holy Spirit is contradictory, depending on the nature of time and place, according to that which is written: 'Deep calleth on deep, at the noise of the flood gates,'[29] then, the truth will reveal itself, that is to say, that Christ imposed possible commandments when He said: 'You are to be perfect even as your heavenly Father is perfect'; and yet the apostles were not perfect.

CRITOBULUS. I am not talking about the actions of the apostles, but rather about the commandments of Christ. For the blame is not placed on him who gave the commandments, but on those who heard the commandments, which are accepted as being possible, in view of the justice of him who gave the commandments.

ATTICUS. Fine! Therefore, I do not want you to tell me that man can be without sin if he wants to; but that man can be what the apostles were not.

CRITOBULUS. Do you think that I am so foolish as to have the courage to make such a statement?

ATTICUS. Although you are not making such a statement in so many words, nevertheless, this is the statement that you will make if you follow the logical sequence and order of the arguments of the proposition that you laid down. For, if man can be without sin and the apostles obviously were not, it is possible for man to be superior to the apostles, not to mention the patriarchs and prophets, whose justice under the law was not perfect, according to the words of the apostle: 'As all have sinned, and have need of the glory of God. They are justified freely by his grace through the redemption which is in Christ Jesus, whom God has set forth as a propitiation.'[30]

(14a) *He cites the testimony of Paul to the Philippians.*
CRITOBULUS. This is tortuous argumentation, to confound

---
29 Ps. 41.8.
30 Rom. 3.23-25.

ecclesiastical simplicity with the subtleties of philosophers. What has all this to do with Aristotle and Paul? With Plato and Peter? Just as the one was the prince of the philosophers, so the other was prince of the apostles, upon whom was laid, as on a firm and solid foundation, the Church of the Lord which is shaken neither by the force of rivers nor by any storm.

ATTICUS. You are playing the rhetorician, and, while you taunt me with playing the philosopher, you avail yourself of the weapons of the orators. But listen to the words of that same orator of yours: 'Drop the commonplaces; these are bred in our households.'[31]

CRITOBULUS. There is no attempt made here to be eloquent, or to speak in the bombastic manner of orators whose object is to speak fittingly so as to persuade. We are simply making an honest attempt to discover the simple truth and express it in simple language. God either did not impose commandments that are impossible, so that the blame is to be put on those who have not fulfilled commandments that were possible; or, if the commandments are impossible, then, it is not those who do not fulfill conmmandments that are impossible who are guilty of an injustice, but rather he who imposed commandments that are impossible. And such a statement would be tantamount to impiety.

ATTICUS. I see that, contrary to your usual good control, you are exceedingly disturbed, and, consequently, I shall put an end to the argument. But I shall ask you for a few brief moments your views on that passage of the apostle which he writes to the Philippians: 'Not that I have already obtained this, or already have been made perfect, but I press on hoping that I may lay hold of that for which Christ Jesus has laid hold of me. Brethren, I do not consider that I have laid hold of it already. But one thing I do: forgetting what is behind me, I strain forward to what is before, I press on towards the goal, to the prize of God's heavenly call in Christ

---

31 Cicero, *Academica* 4.

Jesus. Let us then, as many as are perfect, be of this mind; and if in any point you are minded otherwise, this also God will reveal to you,'[32] and the rest of the passage, with which, I am sure, you are well acquainted, and which we omit in the interest of brevity. He says that he has not yet laid hold of it, and that he has not yet been made perfect; but that like a bowman he is aiming his arrows at the goal and the target, which the Greek refer to in expressive language as *skopós*, lest the arrow, shot to one side or the other, prove him an unskilled bowman. And he asserts that he always forgets what is behind him, and strains forward to what is before him, thereby teaching us that we are to disregard the past and regard the future, so that what he thought today was perfect, in straining forward to what is better and what is before him, the morrow will prove imperfect. And thus he would teach us that at every step that we take, since we never stand still, but are always on the way, what to us human beings seemed perfect was imperfect; and that the sole perfection and true justice is compatible only with the virtues of God. 'I press on towards the goal,' he says, 'to the prize of God's heavenly call in Christ Jesus.' Oh, Apostle Paul, forgive me, who am but a mere mortal, so to speak, confessing my faults, if I make bold to interrogate you. You say that you have not yet obtained it; that you have not yet laid hold of it; that you have not yet been made perfect; that you always forget what is behind and strain forward to what is before, if by any means you may attain to the resurrection of the dead, and obtain the prize of the heavenly call. How are we to understand your statement that follows immediately: 'We, therefore, as many as are perfect, are of this mind,' or, 'let us be of this mind,' for the copies vary? Of what mind are we, or of what mind should we be? That we have been made perfect; that we have laid hold of what we have not laid hold of; that we have obtained what we have not obtained; that we have been made perfect who have not yet been made perfect? There-

---

[32] Phil. 3.12-15.

fore, of what are we minded, or rather of what ought we to be minded, we who have not been made perfect? To confess that we are imperfect; that we have not yet laid hold of it; and that we have not yet obtained it. This is true wisdom in man: to know that he is imperfect; and, if I may so say, the perfection of all the just, living in the flesh, is imperfect. Whence, also, we read in Proverbs: 'To understand true justice.'[33] For unless there were also false justice, the justice of God would never be referred to as true justice. And the apostle continues in the same passage: 'And if in any point you are minded otherwise, this also God will reveal to you.'[34] It is a strange thing that I hear. He who but a moment ago had said: 'Not that I have already obtained it, or have already been made perfect'; he, who was the Chosen Vessel, who dared to say with the confidence of Christ dwelling within him: 'Do you seek a proof of Christ who speaks in me?'[35] and yet frankly confessed that he had not been made perfect, now ascribes to the multitude something that he specifically denied to himself, and he associates himself with the others, and says: 'Let us then, as many as are perfect, be of this mind.' But he explains in the following verses what he meant by this statement. Let us, he says, who wish to be perfect, according to the measure of human frailty, be of this mind, that we have not yet obtained it; that we have not yet laid hold of it; that we have not yet been made perfect. And because we have not yet been made perfect, and, perhaps, are minded otherwise than is demanded by true and perfect perfection, if we are minded of and understand anything that is different from what is consistent with the knowledge of God, this, also, God will reveal to us, so that we may pray with David and say: 'Open thou my eyes; and I will consider the wondrous things of thy law.'[36]

(15) *Twofold perfection and justice.*

---
33 Prov. 1.3 (Septuagint).
34 Phil. 3.15.
35 2 Cor. 13.3.
36 Ps. 118.18.

It is clear from all this that there are two kinds of perfections in Holy Scripture, and two kinds of justices, and two kinds of fears. The first kind of perfection, and its comparable truth, and perfect justice, and fear, which is the beginning of wisdom, are compatible with the virtues of God; but the second kind of perfection which befits not only human beings, but also every living creature, and our weakness, according to what is said in the Psalms: 'In thy sight no man living shall be justified,'[37] is the kind of justice that is called perfect, not in comparison with God, but according to the knowledge of God. Job, and Zacharia, and Elizabeth are called just, according to this latter type of perfection which can change on occasions into injustice, and not according to the former type which can never change, of which it is said: 'I am God, and I change not.'[38] And this is what the apostle writes in another place: 'And yet what was glorified is without glory because of the surpassing glory';[39] for the justice of the law, to be sure, in comparison with the grace of the Gospel would not appear to be justice. 'For if that,' he says, 'which is done away with is glorious, much more will that be glorious which abides.'[40] And again: 'We know in part and we prophesy in part; but when that which is perfect has come, that which is imperfect will be done away with.'[41] And: 'We see now through a mirror in an obscure manner, but then face to face. Now I know in part, but then I shall know even as I have been known.'[42] And in the Psalms: 'Thy knowledge is become wonderful to me: it is high, and I cannot reach to it.'[43] And again: 'I studied that I might know this thing, it is a labor in my sight, until I go into the sanctuary of God: and understand concerning their last ends.'[44] And in the

---

37 Ps. 142.2.
38 Mal. 3.6.
39 2 Cor. 3.10.
40 2 Cor. 3.11.
41 1 Cor. 13.9, 10.
42 1 Cor. 13.12.
43 Ps. 138.6.
44 Ps. 72.16, 17.

same place: 'I am become as a beast before thee: and I am always with thee.'[45] And Jeremia: 'Every man is become foolish by his knowledge.'[46] And the apostle, also, says: 'The foolishness of God is wiser than men.'[47] And many other passages that I omit in the interest of brevity.

(16) *Man is called just in comparison with men, not in comparison with God.*

CRITOBULUS. My dear Atticus, you have spoken skillfully, to be sure, and accurately. But your efforts and these numerous repetitions of testimonies plead my case. For I am not comparing man with God, but with other men, and, in comparison with other men, any man can be perfect who will exert himself. And, consequently, when I say that 'man can be without sin if he wants to,' I mean according to the measure of man, not according to the majesty of God. In comparison with Him, no creature can be perfect.

ATTICUS. When you speak in this fashion, Critobulus, you are pleading my case. For I, also, am of the opinion that no creature can be perfect according to true and consummate justice. Moreover, no one denies that one individual differs from another individual; that there are different measures of justices among men; that one individual is greater or lesser than another individual; and that individuals who are not just in comparison with other individuals, can still be called just according to their own standard and measure. For example, the Apostle Paul, the Chosen Vessel, who labored more abundantly than all of the apostles, was certainly just when he wrote to Timothy: 'I have fought the good fight, I have finished the course, I have kept the faith. For the rest, there is laid up for me a crown of justice, which the Lord, the just judge, will give to me in that day; yet not to me only, but also to those who love his coming.'[48] Timothy, who was his disciple and follower, who was guided by him in the way of life that

---

45 Ps. 72.23.
46 Jer. 10.14.
47 1 Cor. 1.25.
48 2 Tim. 4.7, 8.

he was to follow and the course he was to pursue in the acquisition of virtues, was also a just man. Are we to suppose for a moment that both of them possessed the one and the same measure of justice, and that he who labored more abundantly than all of them does not have greater merit? 'In my Father's house there are many mansions,'[49] because merits are also different. 'Star differs from star in glory.'[50] And the members in the one Church are different. The sun has its own brilliance, and the moon, also, tempers the darkness of the night. And the five other stars that are called the wandering stars traverse the sky, differing both in their courses and in their brilliance. There are other countless stars that we see shining in the firmament. The brilliance of each of these is different, and yet each and every star is perfect, according to its own standard, to the degree that, in comparison with a greater star, it lacks perfection. Also in the body, whose members are different, the eye performs one function, the hand another, the foot a third. Whence, also, the apostle says: 'The eye cannot say to the hand: "I do not need thy help"; nor again the head to the feet: "I have no need of you." '[51] Are all apostles? Are all prophets? Are all teachers? Do all have all virtues? Do all have the gift of healing? Do all speak with tongues? Do all interpret? Yet strive after the greater gifts.'[52] 'But all these things are the work of the one and the same Spirit, who allots to everyone according as he will.'[53] Notice carefully that in this passage he did not say, 'according as each and every member will,' but 'according as the Spirit itself will.' For the vessel cannot say to its potter: Why hast thou made me for this purpose or that? 'Is not the potter master of the same clay, to make one vessel for honorable, and another for ignoble use?'[54] Whence he added the following verse: 'Strive

---
49 John 14.2.
50 1 Cor. 15.41.
51 1 Cor. 12.21.
52 1 Cor. 12.29-31.
53 1 Cor. 12.11.
54 Rom. 9.21.

after the greater gifts,' so that we may merit greater rewards for our faith and industry than the rest of the anointed, and be superior to those who, in comparison with us, are ranked second or third. In a wealthy home, there are different vessels, some of gold, some of silver, some of bronze, some of iron, some of wood. And although the bronze vessel is perfect according to its own measure, yet, in comparison with the silver, it is said to be imperfect, and, again, the silver vessel in comparison with the golden one is inferior. And in like manner, all things are imperfect and perfect when compared with one another in turn. In a field of good ground and from the same seed, a thirty-fold yield, and a sixty-fold yield, and a hundred-fold yield are produced. According to the figures themselves, there is shown to be a disparity of yield; and yet each and every yield is perfect in its own class. Elizabeth and Zacharia can teach us by the testimony that you adduce, as an impenetrable shield, as it were, of the womb, how vastly inferior they are, as regards sanctity, to the blessed Mary, the mother of God, who, conscious that God was dwelling within her, boldly proclaims: 'For, behold, henceforth all generations shall call me blessed; because he who is mighty has done great things for me, and holy is his name; And his mercy is from generation to generation on those who fear him. He has shown might with his arm.'[55] Notice that in this passage she says that she is blessed, not through her own merit and virtue, but through the mercy of God dwelling within her. John himself, than whom no greater son was ever born of woman, was also better than his parents. For according to the testimony of the Lord, he is compared, not only with men, but even with angels. And yet he, who was greater than all men on earth, is said to have been less than the least in the kingdom of heaven.

(17) *Such a distinction is evident even in a comparison of sinners.*

Why is it so strange that in the comparison of holy men

---
55 Luke 1.48-51.

some are found to be better, and others worse, when, on the other hand, such a distinction is evident in the comparison of sinners? It is said to Jerusalem, who had been pierced with the many wounds of sins: 'Sodom is justified because of you';[56] not because Sodom is just of herself, who, falling into eternal fires, hears it said through Ezechiel: 'Sodom shall be restored to her ancient state';[57] but because, in comparison with Jerusalem who was more wicked, she seems just. For the one murdered the Son of God; the other, through an abundance of bread and an excess of luxury, transcended the limits of lust. The Publican in the Gospel who kept striking his breast, the storehouse, as it were, of evil thoughts, and would not so much as dare to lift up his eyes, because of an awareness of his sins, is considered more just by comparison with the boastful Pharisee. And Thamar, in the guise of a harlot, deceives Juda, and she deserves to hear it said in the judgment of the very one who was deceived: 'She is juster than I.'[58] All of this proves that not only are men not perfect, in comparison with the divine majesty, but not even in comparison with angels and other men who have reached the heights of virtues; since even you, who are better in comparison with someone else whom you have proven to be imperfect, will, in turn, be bested by someone else who excels you. And, consequently, you will not have true perfection, which, if perfect, lacks nothing.

(18) *The sense in which we are admonished to be perfect.*
CRITOBULUS. And in what sense, Atticus, are we urged by the Divine Word to attain perfection?
ATTICUS. In the sense in which I mentioned above, that each and every one of us, according to the measure of his strength, shall press forward to the best of his ability that he may in some way obtain and lay hold to the prize of the heavenly call. Moreover, Almighty God, to whom the apostle teaches the

---
56 Lam. 4.6.
57 Ezech. 16.55.
58 Gen. 38.26.

Son must be made subject, according to the dispensation of the assumed flesh, 'that God may be all in all,'[59] clearly shows that all things have not been made subject to Him. Whence, also, the prophet takes for granted his own subjection to the end, saying: 'Shall not my soul be subject to God alone? For from him is my salavtion.'[60] And because in the body of the Church Christ is the head, it appears that the body, also, has not been made subject to the head, while some of the members still resist. For, if one of the members suffers, all of them suffer with it and the entire body is tormented by the pain of one of its members. Thus, the meaning of my remark will become more evident. As long as we possess that treasure in earthen vessels, and are encased in fragile flesh, or rather, in mortal and corruptible flesh, we deem ourselves blessed if we are made subject to God in particular virtues, and in other virtues in part measure. But when this mortality will be clothed in immortality, and this corruptibility will have put on incorruptibility, and death will be swallowed up by the victory of Christ, then God will be all things in all, so that there will not be only wisdom in Solomon, meakness of soul in David, zeal in Elias and Phinees, faith in Abraham, perfect love in Peter, to whom it was said: 'Simon, son of John, dost thou love me?'[61] zeal of preaching in the Chosen Vessel, and two or three virtues each in others; but He will be completely in all, and the number of the saints will be glorified in the whole choir of virtues, and God will be all things to all.

(19) *As long as we live we cannot have all virtues.*
CRITOBULUS. Therefore, none of the saints can have all virtues as long as he exists in this frail body?
ATTICUS. None of them, because now we prophesy in part, and we know in part. For all things cannot be in all men; for the son of man is not immortal.
CRITOBULUS. And in what sense are we to take the words

---
59 1 Cor. 15.26.
60 Ps. 61.2.
61 John 21.16.

that we read: 'Who has one virtue, seems to have all virtues'?
ATTICUS. In the sense of participation, not of propriety. For it must necessarily be that individuals excel in some virtues. And yet I do not know where these words that you say you have read are written down.
CRITOBULUS. Do you not know that this is the view of the philosophers?
ATTICUS. But not of the apostles. For I am not interested in the teachings of Aristotle, but in the teachings of Paul.
CRITOBULUS. I ask you: Does not the Apostle James write that 'he who offends in one point, is guilty of all'?[62]
ATTICUS. The text is self-explanatory. For he did not open the discussion with the proposition that he who holds the rich in higher esteem than the poor man is guilty of adultery or murder (for it is the Stoics who rave on this point, contending that sins are equal), but with this remark: 'He who said: "Thou shalt not commit adultery," said also: "Thou shalt not kill." Now if thou wilt not commit adultery, yet wilt commit murder, thou hast become a transgressor of the law.'[63] Slight offenses are compared with slight offenses and serious ones with serious ones. A fault that deserves the rod should not be punished with the sword; nor should a crime that deserves the sword be punished with the rod.
CRITOBULUS. Granted, that none of the saints has all virtues. You will certainly grant that he is perfect in the thing that he can do, if he does it.
ATTICUS. Are you not concurring in the view that I mentioned above?
CRITOBULUS. What is that?
ATTICUS. That he is perfect in the thing that he has done, and is imperfect in the thing that he could not do.
CRITOBULUS. But just as he is perfect in respect to what he has done because he wanted to do it, by the same token, he could have been perfect, if he had wanted to do a thing in

---

62 James 2.10.
63 James 2.11.

respect to which he is imperfect, because he did not do it.
ATTICUS. But who does not want to do what is perfect? Or who does not wish to flourish in all virtues? If you expect all things from all men, you do away with diversity as far as things are concerned, with distinction as far as graces are concerned, with variety as far as the Creator, the architect, is concerned, whose prophet sings of Him in his sacred song: 'Thou hast made all things in wisdom.'[64] Lucifer would feel offended because it does not have the brilliance of the moon. The moon, in view of its wanings and eclipses, would protest because it completes the yearly circuit of the sun every month. The sun would raise a complaint and ask what sin had it committed that it should be slower in completing its course than the moon. We mere mortal creatures would, also, cry out in protest and ask the reason why we were created as mere mortals and not as angels, although your master, *Ho Archaîos*,[65] who is the fountain source from which these views proceed, asserts that all rational creatures were created with equal opportunity, so that they break out of the starting gates like four horses yoked abreast to chariots, and they either break down in the middle of the course, or speed on and reach the desired goal. The ponderous elephants and griffins would utter a protest, in view of their great size, and ask why they walk on four feet, while the flies and gnats, and other such insects, each have six legs tucked beneath their wings, and there are some tiny worms that abound with so many feet that no eye can detect the countless simultaneous movements. Let Marcion[66] utter such remarks, and

---

64 Ps. 103.24.
65 This may be a reference, perhaps, to Origen and his *Periarchon*, the word *archaîos* being taken from the title of his work. Some take this title to refer to Plato, the inspiration and master of the Pelagians.
66 Marcionism was a form of Gnosticism. Although there existed great differences between the various sects, nevertheless, there were some fundamental tenets common to all. In reference to the creation of the world, the Gnostics fell into two main groups, dualistic and monistic. The former held that the world was the work of the demiurge, the evil spirit. It was to this notion that St. Jerome is here referring. Marcion was the most dangerous of heretics of the second century. As a Gnostic, he conceived the absolute opposition between the Old and

all the heretics who mock the works of the Creator. If men follow your proposition, they will reach a point where they will reproach every single deed of God, and will lay their hands on Him, wanting to know the reason why He alone is God, and why he has envied men to the extent that He did not allow all men to share His glory equally with Him. Although you are not directly saying this (for you are not so insane as to openly oppose God), nevertheless, you are saying this indirectly, by imputing to man the attribute that belongs to God, that of being without sin like God Himself. Whence the apostle, speaking of the diversity of graces, says: 'There are varieties of gifts, but the same Spirit; and there are varieties of ministries, but the same Lord; and there are varieties of workings, but the same God, who works all things in all.'[67]

(20) *The great difference between man and God.*

CRITOBULUS. You are spending altogether too much time on the one and the same question, trying to convince me that man cannot have all things at the same time, as if God were either unwilling or unable to bestow on His image and likeness a resemblance to its Creator in all things.

ATTICUS. Am I the one who is wasting too much time, or you, who are proposing questions that have already been solved and do not know that likeness is one thing, equality quite another matter; that the one is the painting, the other, the reality. A real horse runs through the open fields; the painted horse, yoked to the chariot, hangs on the wall. The Arians[68] do not grant the Son of God what you attribute to

---

New Testament, Judaism and Christianity, law and grace. The God of the Old Testament was a passionate tyrant, full of pride and ambition. He seemed to imply that there were two Gods, one good, one evil. Cf. St. Augustine, *De haeresibus* 22-23; Liguori G. Muller, O.F.M., *The De Haeresibus of Saint Augustine* (Washington 1956) 146-147.

67 1 Cor. 12.4, 5.

68 The Arians claimed that the Son of God was a creature, and that he was not of the same nature with God the Father. Arianism consisted essentially in the denial of the divine nature of the Word, the Son of God, Christ. Cf. F. Cayré, *Manual of Patrology and History of Theology* 1 (translated by H. Howitt; Belgium 1935) 309.

every human being. Others do not dare to acknowledge the perfect man in Christ, lest they be forced to accept the sins of man in Him; as if creation were greater than the Creator, and He is the Son of man only insofar as He is the Son of God. Therefore, either set down other propositions for me to answer, or stop your boasting and give glory to God.

CRITOBULUS. You have forgotten the answer you gave, and, while you keep adding argument upon argument and running rampant through the wide fields of Scripture with the freedom of an unbridled horse, you have remained absolutely quiet about a very important question to which you promised to give an immediate answer, pretending that it slipped your mind in order to avoid the necessity of giving an answer. But it was foolish of me at the time to comply with your request, thinking that you would promptly return the favor received, and would repay your debt without any prompting.

ATTICUS. Unless I am mistaken, we deferred a reply to the question of the possibility of the commandments. State, then, your thesis if you will.

(21) *The sense in which the commandments of God are possible.*

CRITOBULUS. The commandments that God imposed are either possible or impossible. If they are possible, it lies within our power to fulfill them if we want to. If they are impossible, we are not held liable if we do not fulfill what we cannot fulfill. And, consequently, whether the commandments that God imposed are possible or impossible, man can be without sin if he wants to.

ATTICUS. I ask you to listen patiently, for it is not our aim to gain a victory over an adversary, but to establish the truth against falsehood. All the arts that God gave to the human race are possible, and many individuals, to be sure, have learned them,[69] to say nothing of those arts which the Greeks call *Bánausoi,* a term which we can say applies to manual arts. For example, grammar, rhetoric, the three kinds of phi-

---
69 Cf. Plato, *Symposium.*

losophy—physics, ethics, logic—also geometry, and astronomy, astrology, arithmetic, music, which are also parts of philosophy; medicine, too, which is divided into three parts—*dógma, méthodos, empeiría;* also the knowledge of rights and of laws. Who of us, however intelligent he may be, will be able to master all the arts, when Cicero, that very eloquent orator, holding forth on rhetoric and the knowledge of rights, said: 'A few individuals can master one of these arts, but no one can master both of them.' Therefore, you see that God has commanded what is possible, and yet nobody can fulfill by nature what is possible. He also gave different precepts and various virtues, but we cannot possess all of them at the same time. And so it comes that one virtue, that is primarily and wholly cultivated by one individual, is cultivated in part by another individual; and yet, he who does not possess all virtues should not be considered at fault, nor should he be condemned for what he does not possess, but rather should be justified for what he does possess. The apostle, writing to Timothy, defines the qualifications that a bishop should possess: 'A bishop, then, must be blameless, married but once, reserved, prudent, of good conduct, hospitable, a teacher, not a drinker or a brawler, but moderate, not quarrelsome, not avaricious. He should rule well his own household, keeping his children under control and perfectly respectable.'[70] And again: 'He must not be a new convert, lest he be puffed up with pride and incur the condemnation passed on by the devil. Besides this, he must have a good reputation with those who are outside, that he may not fall into disgrace and into a snare of the devil.'[71] He also describes, in a short paragraph in a letter to his disciple, Titus, the kind of bishops he should ordain: 'For this reason, I left thee in Crete, that thou shouldst set right anything that is defective, and shouldst appoint priests in every city, as I myself directed thee to do. They must be blameless, married but once, having believing

---
70 1 Tim. 3.2-4.
71 1 Tim. 3.6, 7.

children who are not accused of impurity or disobedience. For a bishop must be blameless,' (or, 'without charges,' for this is the more precise meaning of *anégklētos*), 'as being the steward of God, not proud, or ill-tempered, or a drinker, or a brawler, or greedy for base gain; but hospitable, gentle, reserved, just, holy, continent; holding fast the faithful word which is in accordance with the teaching, that he may be able both to exhort in sound doctrine and to confute opponents.'[72] To pass over for the time being the various precepts that apply to different individuals, I shall devote my attention to the commandments that apply to a bishop.

(22) *From the example of the virtues that bishops are required to possess.*

God, certainly, wants the kind of bishops that the Chosen Vessel suggests. As for the first virtue that he mentioned, that he be 'blameless,' there is no individual, or just a few, who have this virtue. For what man is there who does not have either a wart or a mole on a handsome body, so to speak? For if the apostle himself says of Peter that he did not walk upright according to the truth of the Gospel, and he was reprehensible to the extent that Barnabas was also led into the same dissimulation,[73] who will feel offended that a virtue which the prince of the apostles did not possess is denied him? Next, he suggests that you should look for a man who is 'married but once, reserved, prudent, of good conduct, hospitable'; and as for the following virtue, that he be *didaktikós,* 'one who can teach,' and not *docilis,* 'one who is teachable,' as it is translated literally in Latin, you would certainly have a difficult time finding it in conjunction with the other virtues. The apostle would reject one who is also 'a drinker and a brawler and greedy for base gain,' and prefers a man who is not quarrelsome, who is not avaricious, so that he will rule his own household well, and, what is more difficult, 'will keep his children under control and perfectly respectable,' either

---

72 Tit. 1.5-9.
73 Cf. Gal. 2.13.

his own children of the flesh, or of the faith. 'Perfectly respectable,' he says It is not enough that he himself be perfectly respectable, unless his respectability be enhanced by that of his own children, and his associates, and his servants, as David says: 'The man that walketh in the perfect way, he will serve me.'[74] Let us also consider the furtherance of respectability: 'Keeping his children under control and perfectly respectable,' so that they will refrain from immodesty, not only in deed, but also in speech as well, and in desires, lest, perchance, the same fate befall him that befell Heli who rebuked, to be sure, his own sons, saying: 'Do not so my sons: for it is not good report that I hear of you.'[75] He rebuked them and was punished; for hé should not have rebuked them, but rather should have cast them out. What might a man do who smiles at faults, who does not have the courage to correct faults, who is afraid of his own conscience, who has no knowledge of the remarks that are being noised abroad by all the people? As far as the next virtue is concerned, that he be 'without charges' so that he will not be accused by even a single person, that he will be held in good repute even by those who are outside the fold, that he will be free even from the rebukes of his opponents, and that he will please in words those whom he displeases in doctrine, you would certainly not have an easy time finding it; and, especially, the next virtue that he be able to withstand his opponents and overthrow and refute perverse doctrines. It is his view that a new convert should not be ordained a bishop; and, yet, we see in our own times that such a choice is made in the name of perfect justice. If baptism could render a person just, immediately on the spot, and fill him with perfect justice, the apostle would not have refused to accept a new convert; but baptism takes away past sins; it does not confer new virtues; it frees a man from bondage, and promises rewards to the man who has been freed if he makes an honest effort. There is no man, I say, or only a few, who

---
74 Ps. 100.6.
75 1 Kings 2.24.

have all of the virtues that are required of a bishop. And yet, if any bishop lacks one or two of the virtues that have been listed, he will not, therefore, be deprived of the title of just; nor will he be condemned for what he does not have, but rather will be crowned for what he does possess. For to possess all things and to stand in need of nothing is a virtue that belongs to Him, 'Who did not sin, neither was deceit found in his mouth, who, when he was reviled, did not revile';[76] who said with confidence, being conscious of His virtues: 'For the prince of this world is coming, and in me He has nothing';[77] 'who, though he was by nature God, did not consider being equal to God a thing to be clung to, but he emptied himself, taking the nature of a slave, becoming obedient to death, even to the death on a cross. Therefore, God has bestowed upon him a name that is above every name, so that at the name of Jesus every knee should bend of those in heaven, on earth, and under the earth.'[78] Therefore, if you will either never or rarely find a few of the precepts in the person of a bishop, what will you do about every man who is obliged to fulfill all of the commandments?

(23) *Even in corporeal matters all men do not have all things.*

Let us consider the spiritual in the light of the corporeal. One man is fleet-footed, but weak-armed. Another man is slow-footed, but firm-footed in battle. One man has a handsome face, but a raucous voice. Another man has a homely face, but a sweet melodious voice. We see that one is intelligent, but forgetful; that another has a good memory, but a dull mind. In those very declamation pieces, in which we once sported as young boys, not everyone employs the same style, either in the introduction, or the statement of the case, or in the digressions, or in the arguments of the case, or in the presentation of proofs, and in the closing appeal of the epilogues;

---

76 1 Peter 2.22, 23.
77 John 14.30.
78 Phil. 2.6-10.

but their styles vary in eloquence from section to section. I shall say more of the church men. There are many who expound well the Gospels, but, when it comes to the matter of interpreting the meaning of the apostle, they are unequal to themselves. There are others who are speechless when it comes to the Psalms and the Old Testament, and yet express their views excellently when it comes to the New Testament. The gist of my remark is this, that 'the power to do all is not for us all,'[79] and among the rich, never or seldom is it the case that any individual has all things in equal measure among all his possessions. God imposed possible commandments, and I admit it. But each and every one of us cannot possess all the things that are possible, not because of the weakness of nature, lest you calumniate God, but rather because of the debility of the soul which cannot possess all virtues at the same time and forever. And, if you condemn God because He so created you that you have failings and weaknesses, I shall say again that the reproach will be more blasphemous if you condemn Him for not having created you a God. But you will say: 'If I cannot do a thing, I have no sin.' You do have a sin, because you did not do what someone else could do. And, in turn, he who, when compared with you, is better will be a sinner when he is either compared with you, in respect to some other virtue, or when compared with someone else. And thus it comes that he who seems to you to be excellent will be inferior to him who is better than he in some other respect.

(24) *God can preserve man without sin.*

CRITOBULUS. If man cannot be without sin, how can the Apostle Jude write: 'Now to him who is able to preserve you without sin and to set you before the presence of his glory, without blemish'?[80] Does he prove by this testimony that it is possible to keep man without sin and without blemish?

ATTICUS. You do not understand the testimony that you have

---
[79] Vergil, *Eclogues* 7.23.
[80] Jude 24.

quoted. For man cannot be without sin, a proposition that you hold; but God, if He wants to, can preserve man without sin and keep him without blemish through His mercy. I also say this, that all things are possible with God, but with man, all things that he wants to do are not possible; and, in particular, to be something that we read no creature ever was.

CRITOBULUS. I do not say that man is without sin, a condition that you perhaps believe possible, but that man can be without sin if he wants to. For 'being' is one thing, 'possibility of being' is quite another matter. 'Being' demands an example; 'possibility of being' proves the truth of the command.

ATTICUS. You are speaking nonsense, and are forgetting the old proverb: 'Do not bottle moonshine,' and you are wallowing in the same mire, nay more, you are washing a blackener white. In answer to all this, you shall hear nothing else but what is evident to all; you are trying to establish as true a condition that is not true, that never was true, and that, perhaps, never will be true. And to use the very same word and reveal the stupidity of your contradictory argumentation, I hold that you are saying that a condition that cannot be true is true. For the thesis that you have laid down, namely, that man can be without sin if he wants to, is either true or false. If it is true, show me the man who was without sin. If it is false, anything that is false can never be possible. These views, however, which have been exploded, as it were, should be hushed up, and should only be whispered in a low tone within the walls of your library, and should avoid the scrutiny of the public eye.

(25) *He refutes the book of Pelagius.*

Let us take up for consideration the other propositions, which are of such a nature that you will have to keep praying continually throughout the discussion, if only you may get an opportunity of refuting any point, or asking any question that you wish.

CRITOBULUS. I shall listen patiently, for I shall have no desire to speak; and I will prefer to sit and admire the genius of a man whose talent for falsifying leaves me speechless.

ATTICUS. You should judge the falsity or truth of the statements I am going to make only after you have heard me out.

CRITOBULUS. Say what you like, for I have decided to hold my tongue, if I cannot answer you, rather than acquiesce to falsehood.

ATTICUS. What difference does it make, if I refute you holding your peace or speaking your piece, and if I take you captive, as in the story of Proteus,[81] awake or asleep?

CRITOBULUS. After you have said what you want, you will hear from me what you will not want to hear at all. For the truth can be hard pressed, but never suppressed.

ATTICUS. I would like to discuss for a few brief moments your views, so that your followers may see how divine is your genius that stirs up their admiration for you. You say: 'Nobody can be without sin except the individual who has a knowledge of the law'; and with this statement, you exclude a great majority of the Christians from justice, and you, who are preaching the gospel of sinlessness, are proclaiming that practically all men are sinners. For how many Christians have a knowledge of the law which you would rarely or seldom find in many Doctors of the Church? Moreover, in order to win the favor of your Amazons, you wrote in another place, with a great display of generosity: 'Women should also have a knowledge of the law'; when the apostle teaches that women should keep silent in Church, and, if they lack knowledge in any matter, they should consult their husbands at home.[82] It is not enough

---

81 Proteus was the old seer who lived in a cave. At midday, he rose from the sea and slept in the shadows of the rocks of the coast. Anyone wishing to learn from him the future was obliged to catch him at that time. As soon as he was seized, he assumed every possible shape in order to escape the necessity of prophesying. But whenever he saw that his endeavors were of no avail, he resumed his usual form and told the truth. Vergil, in his *Georgics* (book 4), tells the story of Aristaeus, the shepherd, having lost his bees through sickness and hunger, who was sent by his goddess mother, Cyrene, to seize Proteus and get him to tell him how to regain the health of his bees. He seized Proteus while he was asleep and had him tell the truth.

82 Cf. 1 Cor. 14.34, 35.

for you to allow your army of women a knowledge of the Scriptures, unless you can enjoy the pleasure of their voices and their singing. For you add and set down the thesis: 'Women should also sing psalms to God.' But who does not know that women should sing psalms in their own cells, and apart from the company of men, and the gathering of crowds? But you give them permission to do what is unlawful, and, thus, they cite the authority of their master in defense of an act which should be done with modesty and not in view of spectators.

(26) *He refutes again the book of Pelagius.*

You add moreover: 'The servant of God should not let fall from his lips anything that is harsh, but always that which is sweet and pleasant,' and, as if the servant of God were one person and the Doctor and priest of the Church another, forgetting your previous thesis, you set up another proposition: 'The priest or the Doctor should observe the actions of all men and reprove sinners fearlessly, lest he be held responsible for their actions and their blood be required at his hands.' Not being satisfied to quote this thesis once, you repeat the very same proposition and admonish: 'The priest or Doctor should flatter no one, but reprove all men bravely, lest he destroy himself and those who hear him.' Can you be so contradictory in the one and the same work that you do not remember what you have previously said? For, if the servant of God should not let anything fall from his lips that is harsh, but always that which is sweet and pleasant, the priest and Doctor, who should reprove sinners fearlessly and flatter no one, but reprove everybody bravely, will either not be servants of God, or, if the priest and Doctor are not only servants of God, but hold the first place among His servants, it was vain on your part to set aside exclusively for the servants of God the employment of flattery and sweet words, since such an employment is the special mark of heretics, and of those who wish to deceive their hearers, as the apostle says: 'For such do not serve Christ our Lord but their own belly, and by smooth words and flattery deceive the hearts of the simple.'⁸³ Flattery is always insidious, deceitful, and bland. And a flatterer is well defined by philosophers as a 'bland enemy.' Truth is harsh, bitter, stern, unpleasant, and offensive to those who are reproved. Whence, also, the apostle says: 'Have I become your enemy, because I tell you the truth?'⁸⁴ And the comic poet says: 'Flattery wins friends, truth, unpopularity.'⁸⁵ Whence, also, we eat the Pasch in bitterness, and the Chosen Vessel teaches that the Pasch must be celebrated in truth and sincerity;⁸⁶ let the truth in us be sincere and bitterness will follow immediately.

(27) *All things are guided by the will of God.*

But what Christian can agree with the proposition which you set down at another place: 'All men are guided by their own will'? For if not one man, nor a few, nor many, but all men are guided by their own will, what will become of the will of God? And what is your explanation of the following passage: 'The steps of man are guided by the Lord';⁸⁷ and: 'The way of man is not his';⁸⁸ and: 'No one can receive anything, were it not given to him from above';⁸⁹ and in another place: 'For what hast thou that thou hast not received? And if thou hast received it, why dost thou boast as if thou hadst not received it?'⁹⁰ As the Lord, the Savior, says: 'I have come down from heaven not to do my own will, but the will of him who sent me, the Father.'⁹¹ And in another place: 'Father, if it is possible, let this cup pass away from me; yet not as I will, but as thou willest.'⁹² And in the Lord's prayer: 'Thy will be done on earth, as it is in heaven.'⁹³ And why

---

83 Rom. 16.18.
84 Gal. 4.16.
85 Terence, *Andria* 1.1.41.
86 Cf. 1 Cor. 5.8.
87 Prov. 20.24.
88 Jer. 10.23.
89 John 19.11.
90 1 Cor. 4.7.
91 John 6.38.
92 Matt. 26.39.
93 Matt. 6.10.

are you so rash in your view as to take away the help of God entirely? It is clearly evident from this section, the construction you wish to put on the phrase 'not without the grace of God,' which you seek to add to no avail in another section, since you ascribe His grace, not to each and every act, but rather to the power of creation, and of the law, and of the free will.

(28) *The difference between the impious and the unjust.*

Moreover, who can agree with the thesis that you set down as your next heading: 'In the day of judgment, no leniency shall be shown to the ungodly and to sinners, but they shall be consumed in eternal fires,' for you prevent God from showing mercy, and you pass judgment on the sentence of the judge before judgment day, so that if He wanted to spare the unjust and the sinner, He could not, in view of your prescription? For you say: 'It is written in the 103rd Psalm: "Let sinners be consumed out of the earth, and the unjust, so that they be no more."[94] And in Isaia: "The unjust and the sinners shall burn together and they who abandon God shall be consumed."'[95] And do you not know that a threat on the part of God at times hints at clemency? For He does not say that they shall be consumed in everlasting fires, but rather that they shall be consumed out of the earth and shall cease to be unjust. For it is one thing for them to avoid sin and injustice, and quite another matter for them to perish forever and be consumed in eternal fires. Moreover, Isaia, from whom you quote your testimony, says: 'The unjust and the sinners shall burn together,' (without adding the phrase 'forever'), 'and those who abandon God shall be consumed.' This judgment refers, specifically, to heretics who have abandoned the right way of faith and will be consumed, if they are unwilling to return to God whom they have abandoned. This judgment is also in store for you, if you refuse to change for the better. Moreover, is it not gross impudence to group the unjust and

---

94 Ps. 103.35.
95 Isa. 1.28.

the sinners with the impious, in the light of the following
distinctions made by us? Everyone who is impious is unjust
and a sinner, but the conversion of this proposition is not
true, so that we can say that everyone who is a sinner and is
unjust is also impious. For impiety applies, in the strict sense,
to those who have no knowledge of God, or who have changed
the knowledge that they once possessed by transgression. But
sin and injustice, depending on the nature of the faults, allow
the recovery of health, following the wounds of sin and injustice. Whence it is written: 'Many are the scourges of the
sinner';[96] and not, 'eternal destruction.' Israel is changed for
the better by all kinds of scourges and punishments. 'For
whom the Lord loves, he chastises; and he scourges every son
whom he receives.'[97] It is one thing to whip a person with
the love of a master or a parent; it is quite another matter
to vent one's rage against an adversary with a heart filled with
fury, whence the psalmist, also, sings in the first Psalm: 'Therefore the wicked shall not rise again in judgment,' (for they
have already been prejudged unto perdition), 'nor sinners in
the council of the just.'[98] For it is one thing to lose the
glory of the resurrection, quite another matter to perish
forever. 'The hour is coming,' he says, 'in which all who
are in the tombs shall hear his voice. And they who have
done good will come forth unto resurrection of life; but
they that have done evil unto resurrection of judgment.'[99]
Whence, also, the apostle speaks the same thought to the
Romans, because he was also of the same spirit: 'For whoever
have sinned without the Law, will perish without the Law;
and whoever have sinned under the Law, shall be judged by
the Law.'[100] It is the impious without the law who shall perish
forever. It is the sinner under the law, believing in God,
who will be judged by the law and shall not perish. If sinners

---

96 Ps. 31.10.
97 Heb. 12.6.
98 Ps. 1.5.
99 John 5.28, 29.
100 Rom. 2.12.

and the unjust are consumed in eternal fires, are you, who call yourself unjust and a sinner, not afraid of your own judgment? And you argue that man is not without sin, but that he can be. Therefore, he alone is to be saved who has never lived, who is not living today, but who will live in the future, or, perhaps, who will not live in the future; and all those who, we read, lived in the past are to perish. How can you yourself, who are puffed up with the arrogance of a Cato in our midst and swell with pride on the shoulders of a Milo,[101] be so rash as to arrogate to yourself, who are a sinner, the title of master? Or, if you are just, and you are pretending to be a sinner, from a sense of humility, we shall deem it as something wonderful, and shall rejoice that you and your followers are the only persons who have and possess something that none of the patriarchs, none of the prophets, none of the apostles ever had. But if Origen says that all rational creatures are not to perish, and allows repentance to the devil, what has all this to do with us who say that the devil and his satellites, and all of the impious and prevaricators will perish forever, and that Christians, if they have been overtaken by sin, are to be saved after their punishments?

(29) *Two contradictory propositions of Pelagius.*

You add, furthermore, two propositions that are self-contradictory, and, should they be true, you will not be able to open your mouth: 'No one can understand the wisdom and meaning of the Scriptures except him who has studied them.' And again: 'He who is uninformed should not assume to himself a knowledge of the Law.' For you will either be forced to produce the master by whom you were taught, so that you may have the right to assume to yourself a knowledge of the law, or, if he is a kind of master who was not taught by anybody, and he taught you what he himself did not know, it remains that you are not doing right by assuming to yourself a knowl-

---

101 A hint here, perhaps, to the great size of Pelagius. Milo was a celebrated athlete of Crotona. Many stories are related of his extraordinary feats of strength, such as his carrying a heifer, four years old, on his shoulder through the stadium at Olympia.

edge of the Scriptures, without having been taught, and by beginning to be a master before having been a disciple. Unless, perhaps, you boast with humility, as is your wont, that the Lord, who teaches all knowledge, is your master, and, together with Moses, you hear the words of God in a cloud and mist face to face, and come down from there into our midst with horned face.[102] You are not satisfied with all this, but you suddenly change into a Stoic, and thunder at us with the arrogance of Zeno: 'A Christian should be so patient that, if anybody would want to take away his possessions, he would give them away gladly.' Are we not fulfilling our obligation in giving up with submissive resignation what we have, unless we thank the madman and thief and send him on his way with every blessing? The Gospel[103] teaches us that we are also to give our cloak to him who would contend with us in judgment and take away our tunic in a lawsuit. It does not command us to thank him and give up our possessions joyfully. I say this, not because there is anything wicked in such a view, but because it is your tendency on every occasion to exaggerate the ordinary in your pursuit of the grandiose. Whence you add the thesis: 'Elegance of vestments and ornaments are repugnant to God.' Why, I ask you, is it repugnant to God if I have an elegant tunic, if the bishop, the priest, and the rest of the ecclesiastical order proceed to the performance of the sacrifices robed in white vestments? Clerics, beware; monks, beware; widows and virgins, you are courting disaster, unless the public see you looking filthy and dressed in rags! I say nothing of the men of the world, on whom war is openly declared, and who are declared repugnant to God if they wear costly and elegant dress.

(30) *Contradictory propositions of Pelagius.*

Let us also listen to other propositions: 'Enemies are to be loved as neighbors.' And, falling into deep lethargy, you immediately set down this proposition and say: 'An enemy is

---
[102] Cf. Exod. 34.5, 35.
[103] Cf. Matt. 5.40.

never to be trusted,' a proposition that is clearly contradictory, even if I say nothing about it. But you will say that both of these propositions are expressed in the words of Scripture, without taking into account the sense in which they were spoken in their proper context. I have been commanded to love my enemies and to pray for those who persecute me. Was I commanded to love them as my neighbors, and as relatives, and as friends to such a degree as to make no distinction between a rival and a friend? If I love my enemies as my neighbors, what greater love can I have for my friends? Or, if you had once laid down this proposition, you should not have stated the other proposition: 'An enemy is never to be trusted,' lest you be thought to have stated self-contradictory propositions in the same passage. But the law teaches the manner in which we are to love our enemy: 'If the ass of an enemy has fallen down, it is to be lifted up';[104] and the apostle: 'If thy enemy is hungry, give him food; if he is thirsty, give him drink; for by so doing thou wilt heap coals of fire upon his head.'[105] We are not to revile and condemn him, as the world judges, but rather we are to correct him and lead him to penance, so that, being won over by our good deeds, he may be softened by the fire of charity and may cease to be an enemy.

(31) *Whether the kingdom of heaven was promised in the Old Testament or not.*

You add furthermore: 'There is a promise of the kingdom of heaven even in the Old Testament,' and you quote testimonies from the Apocrypha, when it is clear that the gospel of the kingdom of heaven is first preached in the Gospel by John the Baptist, and by the Lord, our Savior, and by the apostles. Read the Gospels. John the Baptist cries out in the desert: 'Repent for the kingdom of heaven is at hand.'[106] And it is written of the Savior: 'From that time he began to preach,

---
104 Deut. 22.4.
105 Rom. 12.20.
106 Matt. 3.2.

and to say: "Repent, for the kingdom of heaven is at hand." [107] And again: 'And Jesus was going about all the towns and villages, teaching in their synagogues, and preaching the gospel of the kingdom of God.'[108] And He commands the apostles: 'And as you go, preach the message: "The kingdom of heaven is near at hand." '[109] But you call us Manichaeans because we prefer the Gospel to the law, and say that there is but the shadow of the truth under the law, and the truth itself in the Gospel; and you do not realize that there is added to your ignorance a degree of impudence. It is one thing to condemn the law, as Manichaeus does; it is quite another matter to prefer the Gospel to the law, which is according to the apostolic teaching. For under the law, we have the words of His servants; in the Gospel, we have the words of the Lord Himself; under the law, there is but the promise; in the Gospel, there is the fulfillment of the promise; under the former, there is but a beginning; in the latter, there is the fulfillment; under the law, there is the laying of the foundations of the work; in the Gospel, there is the erection of the tower of faith and grace. Our reason for making these remarks is to reveal to you the teaching of the perfect master.

(32) *He attacks the principal view of the Pelagians.*

The 100th proposition reads as follows: 'Man can be without sin and can easily keep the commandments of God if he wants to.' We have said enough about this proposition already. And, although he admits that he is the imitator, in fact, that he has completed the work of the blessed martyr, Cyprian, addressed to Quirinus,[110] he does not realize that he has

---

107 Matt. 4.17.
108 Matt. 9.35.
109 Matt. 10.7.
110 When his friend, Quirinus, asked for some writing to complete his education, St. Cyprian composed for him a work entitled *Testimonia ad Quirinum*. In this work, he grouped together a number of biblical quotations in the form of books and chapters, the title of each chapter containing a summary of the theses according to a well thought out plan. Book one treats of the provisional character of the Jewish Law; book two, the fulfillment of the prophecies in Jesus Christ; and book three, Christian faith, duties, and virtues. Cf. Cayré, *op. cit.*, 257.

made contradictory statements in the one and the same book. Cyprian states, in the fifty-fourth proposition of the third book, that no man is without blemish and sin, and he immediately adds the testimonies, in which it is written in Job: 'For who is clean of blemishes? Not even if his life were but one day on earth.'[111] And in the fiftieth Psalm: 'For behold I was conceived in iniquities: and in sins did my mother conceive me.'[112] And in the Epistle of John: 'If we say that we have no sin, we deceive ourselves, and the truth is not in us.'[113] You, on the contrary, assert that 'man can be without sin,' and to impress with the truth of this statement, you immediately add the words, 'and he can keep the commandments of God easily if he wants to,' which no one, or just some rare individual, has ever fulfilled. For, if they are easy, they should be observed by many. But, if it is some rare individual who can fulfill them, to concede this point to you, it is obvious that what is rare is difficult to fulfill. And, to exaggerate this proposition and show the excellence of your own virtue, because it will appear to be spewed forth from the good storehouse of your conscience, you set down the proposition: 'We are not to sin even in slight matters.' And lest, perchance, someone assume that the phrase 'slight matters' refers to deeds, you add the words, 'nor think evil thoughts.' You are unmindful of the old saying: 'Who can understand sins? From my secret ones, cleanse me, O Lord: and from those of others spare thy servant';[114] since the Church acknowledges as sins, even those faults that we have committed through ignorance and the sins that we have committed in thought alone; so much so, that she bids victims be offered for error, and bids the high priest, who prays for all the people, to offer victims, first, for himself.[115] He, certainly, would never have been required to offer sacrifices for others unless he himself were

---

111 Job 14.4.
112 Ps. 50.7.
113 1 John 1.8.
114 Ps. 18.13, 14.
115 Cf. Heb. 7.26.

just, nor, again, would he have offered sacrifices for himself if he were free from the sin of ignorance. At this point, I suppose I should roam at large through the wide fields of the Scripture to prove that error and ignorance are considered a sin.

(33) *There are sins of ignorance.*

CRITOBULUS. I ask you, have you not read: 'Who so much as looks with lust at a woman has already committed adultery with her in his heart'?[116] Therefore, not only are glances and the incentives to sins regarded as sins, but the objects as well, to which we give assent. For we can either avoid an evil thought, and, consequently, we can be free from sin; or, if we cannot avoid it, that which cannot be avoided is not regarded as a sin.

ATTICUS. You are, indeed, presenting a clever bit of argumentation, but you do not realize that your argument is contradicting Sacred Scripture. For the very words of Scripture indicate that even ignorance is a sin. Whence, also, Job offers holocausts for his sons, lest, perchance, they may have sinned unwittingly in thought.[117] And, if a man is killed by the iron of an axe that flies off the handle when a man is hewing wood, the wood hewer is ordered to flee to a city of refuge,[118] and remain in that place until the death of the high priest,[119] that is to say, until he is redeemed by the blood of the Savior, either in the house of baptism, or by repentance, which supplies the efficacy of the grace of baptism through the ineffable mercy of the Savior who does not wish anybody to perish, nor does He find His delight in the death of sinners, but rather that they be converted from their way and live.[120]

CRITOBULUS. I ask you: Is it any kind of justice for me to be held guilty of the sin of error when I am not conscious of such a sin? I am not conscious of having sinned; and do

---
116 Matt. 5.28.
117 Cf. Job 1.5.
118 Cf. Deut. 19.4, 5.
119 Cf. Jos. 20.6.
120 Cf. Ezech. 18.23.

I pay the penalty for an act of which I am not conscious? What more would I suffer if I sinned of my own accord? ATTICUS. Are you asking me to account for God's judgment and disposition? The book of Wisdom (Sirach) gives the answer to your foolish question: 'Seek not the things that are too high for thee, and search not into things above thy ability.'[121] And in another place: 'Be not overwise, do not argue more than is necessary.'[122] And in the same place: 'Seek God in wisdom, and in simplicity of heart.'[123] And lest, perchance, you gainsay this volume, listen to the apostle, the clarion voice of the Gospels, as he sings out: 'Oh, the depth of the riches of the wisdom and of the knowledge of God! How incomprehensible are his judgments and how unsearchable his ways! For "Who has known the mind of the Lord, or who has been his counselor?"'[124] These are the controversies of which he writes, also, in another place: 'Avoid also foolish and ignorant controversies, knowing that they breed quarrels.'[125] And Ecclesiastes (a book about which there is certainly no doubt) says: 'I have said: "I will be wise"; and it departed farther from me. It is a great depth, who shall find it out?'[126] You ask me to give you the reason why the potter has made one vessel for honorable, and another for ignoble use; and you will not acquiesce with Paul, who gives the answer in the name of his Lord: 'O Man, who art thou to reply to God?' [127]

(34) *He cites the testimonies of Scripture as proofs.*

Therefore, listen, for a brief moment, to the testimonies of Scripture, so that your foolish, rather your impious, inquiry may be silenced forever. God says in Genesis: 'I will no more curse the earth for the sake of man's deeds: for the mind of

---

121 Sir. (Ecclus.) 3.22.
122 Eccles. 7.16.
123 Wisd. 1.1.
124 Rom. 11.33, 34.
125 2 Tim. 2.23.
126 Eccles. 7.24, 25.
127 Rom. 9.20.

man is diligently prone to evil from his youth.'[128] Abraham and Sara, when they heard the promise made of a son, Isaac, laugh in their heart, and their secret thoughts do not elude the knowledge of God. They are reproved for their laughing, and their very thoughts are reprehended as bordering, as it were, on infidelity. And, yet, they are not condemned for their diffidence because they laughed, but rather they received the crown of justice because they subsequently believed. In copulating with his daughters, Lot is ignorant of his actions, and, because he was made drunk by them, he is not conscious of any crime, and, yet, his error is considered a fault. Reprove Jacob, a holy man, for falling in love with the beautiful Rachel, for whom he even served a long period of time in servitude, and for being saddened by first copulating with Lia; and accept at length as inevitable the condition of human frailty which also loves beautiful bodies and detests the ugly. Jacob mourns the death of his son and, for a long time, he cannot be consoled by his sons, and he replies to them: 'I will go down to hell, mourning and weeping.'[129] And he proves that he is human, since he does not know, although he is a just man, what has happened to his just son, Joseph. In Exodus, it is written: 'If someone strikes some man and the same shall die, dying let him die. But if it was not voluntary on his part, but God delivereth him into his hands: I will appoint thee a place to which he who killed the man must flee.'[130] It is to be noted in this passage that God delivered the man into his hands, and that he who killed the man through ignorance is condemned to exile. In Leviticus, the following law is laid down: 'If a soul shall sin through ignorance in the sight of the Lord which he commanded not to be done, whether it be the high-priest or the whole synagogue and the rest of the people, and afterwards it shall know its sin that it committed through ignorance, it shall

---

128 Gen. 8.21.
129 Gen. 37.35.
130 Exod. 21.12, 13; Lev. 24.17.

offer a gift, a buck-goat of the flocks without blemish; and he shall put his hand upon the head thereof and immolate it in the place where the holocausts are slain before the Lord, because it is for sin.'[131] And it is stated immediately in the following chapter: 'If he shall touch anything unclean, that he should not touch, and shall do this through ignorance and shall afterwards know it, or if he shall make a promise and shall forget it, he shall proclaim his sin, in which, he sees, he has sinned, and shall offer the Lord for the sins that he has committed, an ewe lamb or a she-goat for the sin that he has committed, and the priest shall pray for him and for his sin and his sin shall be forgiven him. But if his hand be not able to offer a beast for the sins that he committed, let him offer two turtles or two young pigeons to the Lord, one for sin, and the other for a holocaust. And he shall carry them to the priest and the priest shall offer first the one that is for sin and with this he shall be reconciled for the sin that he has committed and it shall be forgiven him';[132] and other similar passages which I omit in the interest of brevity, lest I vex you and rouse your indignation. In the following chapter, Moses, also, says that, in the consecration of Aaron and his sons, he offered a bull-calf for sin; and that Aaron and his sons put their hands upon it, upon the head to be sure, of the bull-calf which was for sin; and he immolated it, and took some of its blood, and touched the horns of the altar round about with his finger, and purified the altar. He did the same thing with the ram, and touched his ear with the blood thereof, and his right hand, and the great toe of his right foot. And, following an account of many other ceremonies performed throughout the seven-day period, which would take too long to relate, we read the following statement: 'And when the eighth day was come, Moses called Aaron, and his sons, and all the elders of Israel, and he said to Aaron: "Take of the herd a calf for sins, and a ram for a holocaust,

---

[131] Lev. 4.*passim*.
[132] Lev. 5.*passim*.

without blemish, and offer them in the sight of the Lord." And to the elders of Israel, thou shalt say: "Take ye of the herd a he-goat for sin, and a calf of a year old, without blemish, for a holocaust." And Moses said to Aaron: "Approach to the altar and offer sacrifice for thy sins," [133] and the rest. 'And again Aaron raised his hands over the people and blessed them. And he came down after he had made sacrifice for sin and for a holocaust and for salvation.'[134] A woman begets children according to the natural law, and is unclean for forty days if she bears a male child; for eighty days if she bears a female child.[135] Condemn the Lord for calling something that He Himself has created unclean. Not only is she herself unclean, but so is everything else that she shall touch. 'And when the days of her purification,' he says 'are expired, for a son or for a daughter, she shall offer a lamb of one year old, without blemish, and a young pigeon and a turtle for sin at the door of the tabernacle of the testimony to the priest who shall offer them in the sight of the Lord and the priest shall render satisfaction for her.'[136] Also of the leper it is said that, on the day of his purification, a victim shall be offered for him for sin, and two turtles and two young pigeons, one for sin and the other for a holocaust.[137] And he who experiences an issue of seed is delivered by duly observing the same order of sacrifice for sin and for a holocaust.[138] And it is stated in conclusion: 'You shall teach the children of Israel to take heed of uncleanness, and they shall not die for their sin, when they shall have defiled the tabernacle of testimony.'[139] Aaron himself is also commanded not to enter into the holy of holies at any time, lest, perchance, he die. 'And when he wishes to enter,' he says, 'he shall offer a calf for sin and a ram for holocaust; and he shall receive

---

133 Lev. 9.*passim*.
134 Lev. 9.22.
135 Cf. Lev. 12.2-4.
136 Lev. 12.6, 7.
137 Cf. Lev. 14. *passim*.
138 Cf. Lev. 15.13-15.
139 Lev. 15.31.

from all the people two buck-goats; he shall offer one of them for his own sin, and the other for the sin of the people, and the ram for holocaust.'[140] One of the buck-goats takes upon himself all of the sins of the people, as a prefiguration of the Lord Savior, and is let go into the wilderness; and, in this manner, God is appeased for the whole multitude. At the end, it is stated: 'If a man eateth of the sanctified things through ignorance, iniquity and wickedness are laid at his feet, and he shall be bound by a vow.'[141] Whence, also, the apostle teaches us that we are to eat the Eucharist of the Lord with caution, lest we eat to ourselves condemnation and judgment.[142] If ignorance is condemned under the law, how much more will full knowledge be condemned according to the Gospel?

(35) *From the book of Numbers.*

Let us pass to Numbers, and let us quote salient passages to refute the impudence of the contentious. A venerable Nazarite with consecrated hair is defiled by the sudden death of another man in his presence, and all the past days of his consecration are nullified; and two turtles and two young pigeons are subsequently offered for him, one for sin and one for holocaust. Also, on the very day itself of his separation, a he-lamb is offered for a holocaust and an ewe-lamb for sin. And after a lengthy description, it is written: 'Let then the strength of the Lord be magnified as thou hast said: "The Lord is patient and full of mercy, taking away iniquity and wickedness, and leaving no man clear, though cleansing him." '[143] The Septuagint translators interpreted the last phrase as follows: 'And he will not cleanse the guilty one, though he cleanse him'; because he is guilty, to be sure, in his own conscience, even after he has been forgiven. And when the people shall be ignorant, he says, and commit one of the things that they should not, the following statement

---

140 Lev. 16.3, 5, 6.
141 Lev. 22.14, 15.
142 Cf. 1 Cor. 11.28, 29.
143 Num. 14.17, 18.

is made after a long list of ceremonials: 'Offer a he-goat out of the herd for sin and the priest shall placate the Lord for the entire synagogue of the children of Israel and the Lord shall forgive them because it is a fault committed through ignorance; and they themselves shall offer their own burnt-offering as a sacrifice to the Lord for their sin in his sight because they were ignorant.'[144] And the following verse is added: 'If one soul shall sin ignorantly, he shall offer a she-goat of a year old for his sin of ignorance before the Lord and the priest shall pray for him because he was ignorant for his sin of ignorance before the Lord and he shall pray for him and it shall be forgiven him.'[145] On the Kalends of each month, a buck-goat out of the herd is offered to the Lord for sin.[146] Also, during the eight-day period of the Pasch, from the fourteenth day of the month to the twenty-first, there is a sacrifice offered for sin.[147] During Pentecost, a buck-goat is offered for sin, and on the Kalends of the seventh month, when trumpets are sounded, the same religious ceremony of the offering of a buck-goat for sin is observed.[148] Also, on the tenth day of this same seventh month, when fasting is observed till sundown, a buck-goat out of the herd is offered for sin, in addition to the buck-goat which is immolated according to the law for sin before the holocaust.[149] Also, during the days of the Scenopegia, when tabernacles were set up, from the fifteenth day of the same seventh month to the twenty-second day thereof, a buck-goat was always offered for sin, among the other victims, so that the words of blessed David might be fulfilled: 'To thee only have I sinned, and have done evil before thee: that thou mayest be justified in thy words, and mayest overcome when thou art judged.'[150] Six cities are appointed to be cities

---

144 Num. 15.*passim*.
145 Cf. Num. 15.27, 28.
146 Cf. Num. 28.
147 *Ibid*.
148 Cf. Num. 29.
149 *Ibid*.
150 Ps. 50.6.

of refuge for those who have sinned, not of their own accord, but through ignorance, either by hurling a stone at someone or by striking him with their hand, either in jest or by chance-medly, without any intended malice. They have sinned through misfortune rather than through design; and yet they are not considered blameless, since they are sent into perpetual exile, and their return before the allotted time cannot be bought for any price or secured through any petition.

(36) *From Deuteronomy.*

In Deuteronomy, a book that contains a narrative of past events, the evidence is clear that we are saved, not through our own efforts and justice, but rather through the mercy of God, as the Lord says through the lips of Moses: 'Say not in thy heart, when the Lord thy God shall have destroyed them in thy sight: "For my justice hath the Lord brought me in to possess this land, because the Lord will destroy those in thy sight for the wickedness of these nations." For it is not for thy justice and the uprightness of thy heart that thou shalt go in to possess their land; but the Lord thy God shall destroy them in thy sight because of their wickedness, so that he might accomplish the word that he spoke to thy fathers, Abraham, Isaac, and Jacob. And know that the Lord thy God will not give thee this excellent land in possession for thy justice, for thou art a very stiff-necked people.'[151] However, the construction that is to be put on the words: 'Thou shalt be perfect with the Lord,'[152] is made clear from the verses that follow. 'When thou art come,' he says, 'into the land which the Lord thy God shall give thee, do not have a mind to imitate the abominations of those nations, neither let there be found among you anyone that shall make his son or daughter pass through fire. Thou shalt not be slaves to divinations, or to all sorts of auguries and wizardry and incantations, so that you consult diviners and soothsayers and the dead spirits. For everyone who does these things is an

---

151 Deut. 9.4-6.
152 Deut. 18.13.

abomination of the Lord. And for these abominations the Lord thy God will destroy them in thy sight; thou shalt be perfect with the Lord thy God.'[153] Finally, he states: 'These nations, whose land thou shalt possess, hearken to soothsayers and diviners. But thou art otherwise instructed by the Lord thy God.'[154] And he adds immediately the following words: 'The Lord thy God will raise up to thee a prophet of thy nation and of thy brethren like unto me; him thou shalt hear.'[155] It is clear from this passage that it is not the person who possesses all the virtues who is here referred to as perfect, but rather the man who follows the perfect and one God. He also speaks of the lot of the exiles who have sinned through ignorance, and of the place whither they are to flee, and adds the comment: 'When thou buildest a new house, thou shalt make a battlement to the roof round about, lest thou be guilty of blood, if anyone fall down from it.'[156] And again: 'If there be among you any man that is not cleansed of an issue at night, he shall go forth out of the camp, and shall not return into camp, and when evening comes, he shall wash himself with water and after sunset shall return to camp.'[157]

(37) *From the book of Josue.*

I shall quote just two testimonies about Josue, the son of Nun. Achan sinned and the entire nation transgressed. And the Lord said to Josue: 'The children of Israel will not be able to stand before their enemies, but shall flee from their adversaries, because there is a curse in their midst. And I shall no more be with you, unless the anathema is destroyed out of you.'[158] And when they made search for the guilty person, and the lot discovered him hiding, Achan, and his sons, and daughters, and his asses, and sheep are killed;

---

153 Deut. 18.9-12.
154 Deut. 18.14.
155 Deut. 18.15.
156 Deut. 22.8.
157 Deut. 23.11, 12.
158 Jos. 7.12.

his tent and all his possessions are destroyed by fire. Granted, that he himself committed a sin. What sin did his children commit, his oxen, his asses, his sheep? Reprehend God, why one man committed a sin, and a number of people were put to death; why even he is stoned to death, and all his possessions are destroyed by the avenging flame? Let us, also, quote the other testimony: 'There was not a city,' he says, 'that the Lord did not deliver to the children of Israel, except the Hevites who dwelt in Gabaon; they took all by fight, because it was the sentence of the Lord that their hearts should be hardened and they should fight against Israel and be killed, and that they should not deserve any clemency and should be destroyed, as the Lord commanded Moses.'[159] If it was done by the will of God that they should neither make peace with Israel nor obtain peace from Israel, let us say with the apostle: 'Why then does he find fault? For who can resist his will?'[160]

(38) *From the books of Kings. Concerning Samuel and Malachim.*

Jonathan tasted of a honeycomb on a rod, and his eyes were enlightened, and he is in danger of his life because he acted through ignorance. For Scripture testifies to the fact that he did not know that his father had given strict orders that no one was to taste any food until the victory of the Lord was accomplished. However, the Lord was so angered that the lot disclosed him hiding, and he confessed openly, saying: 'I did but taste a little honey with the end of the rod, which was in my hand, and behold I must die.'[161] And he was subsequently delivered through the intercession and prayers of the people, who said to Saul: 'Shall Jonathan die, who hath wrought this great salvation in Israel? This must not be. As the Lord liveth, there shall not one hair of his head fall to the ground, for he hath wrought with God this day.

---

159 Jos. 11.19, 20.
160 Rom. 9.19.
161 1 Kings 14.43.

And the people delivered Jonathan, and he did not die.'[162] Samuel is angry with Saul, and he refuses to go with the king. He is subsequently won over by pleadings to show that man can experience a change of heart. He goes to Bethlehem, and considers every son of Jesse to be the very person that the Lord was looking for. And, seeing Eliab, he said: 'Behold the Lord's anointed is before me. And the Lord said to him: "Look not on his countenance and on the height of his stature, because I have rejected him. For man beholdeth one way, God another. For man beholdeth the face, but God the heart." '[163] He makes the same mistake in each case, and he is reproved in each case, giving evidence of the weakness of the human mind. Isboseth, the son of Saul, is killed through a ruse at the hands of Rechab and Baana, the sons of Remmon, the Berothite. And, when they announced the news to David and showed him the head of his enemy, they were killed by David, who said: 'Wicked men have slain a just man in his own house upon his bed.'[164] Isboseth was certainly not a just man, and yet he is called a just man because he was innocently killed. When the ark of the Lord was being transferred to Jerusalem, and the oxen kicked and made the wagon lean to one side, Oza, the Levite, reached out his hand to support the ark that had been tipped, and there follow immediately these words: 'And the indignation of the Lord was enkindled against Oza, and God struck him there for his ignorance, and he died before the ark of God. And David was grieved because the Lord hath struck Oza, and he was afraid of the Lord that day and said: "How shall the ark of the Lord come to me?" '[165] When David, who was a just man and a prophet, and had been anointed as king, whom the Lord chose according to His own heart that he might do His will in all things, saw ignorance punished by the wrath of the Lord, he was afraid and was grieved; nor did he ask the

---
162 1 Kings 14.45.
163 1 Kings 16.6, 7.
164 2 Kings 4.11.
165 2 Kings 6.7-9.

Lord His reason for striking a man who was ignorant, but he feared a similar judgment happening to him. David ordered Joab, the general of his army, to number the people; and Scripture immediately states: 'And David's heart struck him and he said to the Lord: "I have sinned very much in what I have done." '[166] When he issued the order to have this task done, he certainly did not realize what he was saying, and yet he personally blames himself; and for this fault, seventy thousand men are slain with the sword of an angel. When Solomon had completed the rites of the dedication of the temple, he raised both his hands to the Lord, and said: 'When the people sin against thee; for there is no man who sinneth not.'[167] Ahias, the prophet of the Silenites, did not know that the wife of Jeroboam was coming to him, and the Lord said: 'Behold the wife of Jeroboam will come in to consult you concerning her son that is sick; thus and thus shalt thou speak to her.'[168] Eliseus was sitting on the mount, and a woman, whose son had died, came to him and, embracing his feet, she cried out aloud. But when Giezi tried to remove her, the man of God said to him: 'Let her alone, for her soul is in anguish, and the Lord hid it from me, and hath not told me.'[169]

(39) *From the book of Days and the Prophets.*

In the book of Days, we read: 'Sobal, the father Cariathiarim, had sons; they that saw half of the places of rest.'[170] And again: 'But the sons of Salma, the father, Bethlehem and Netophathi, the crowns of the house of Joab, and they that saw half of the place of rest of Sarai,'[171] and the rest. In the same way, 'they that saw'[172] were certainly saintly men, and yet they were not deemed worthy to receive the gift of perfect

---

166 2 Kings 24.10.
167 3 Kings 8.46.
168 3 Kings 14.5.
169 4 Kings 4.27.
170 1 Par. 2.52.
171 1 Par. 2.54.
172 The Latin interpreter has given us here, instead of the proper names, the meaning of those names in the Hebrew.

prophecy; for they did not prophesy the future in a figurative sense, but rather the present in the literal sense. The Prophet Habacuc gives this title to his Canticle: 'A prayer of Habacuc the Prophet for ignorances.'[173] For he had spoken in a bold manner to the Lord, and had said: 'How long, O Lord, shall I cry, and thou wilt not hear? Shall I cry to thee suffering violence, and thou wilt not save? Why hast thou shown me iniquity and grievance, to see rapine and injustice before me? Judgment is done against me and opposition is more powerful. Therefore, the law is torn to pieces, and judgment cometh not to the end, because the wicked prevaileth against the just; therefore, wrong judgment goeth forth.'[174] As a reproof to himself for having spoken these words through ignorance, he writes the Canticle of Penance. If ignorance were no sin, it was a futile effort on his part to compose a book of penance, and his desire to express sorrow over an act that was not a sin was an empty gesture. The concluding chapters of Ezechiel are devoted to a description of the building of a temple, situated on a high mountain. This description serves as a foreshadowing of the sacraments of the future Church to be established after many centuries have run their course. Victims are offered on the first and seventh day of the first month for the sin that all have committed through error or ignorance. Also, during the seven days of the Pasch, a buck-goat is always immolated for sin. On the fifteenth day of the seventh month, the same rite of sacrifices for sin is observed. And, following a description of very many other details, which would be inappropriate to quote at this time, it is written: 'And there was a place bending to the West. And he said to me: "This is the place where the priests shall boil the victims for sin and for ignorance." '[175] Jeremia says to the Lord: 'I know, O Lord, that the way of man is not his, nor is it in a man to walk and to direct his steps.'[176] And for

---
173 Hab. 3.1.
174 Hab. 1.2-4.
175 Ezech. 46.19, 20.
176 Jer. 10.23.

this reason, the heart of man is perverse and unsearchable, and who will know it?[177] We read in Proverbs: 'There is a way which seemeth just to men, and the ends thereof lead to the depths of Hades.'[178] You see, ignorance is also clearly condemned in this text, since man thinks otherwise, and he falls into Hades, seemingly having the truth. 'There are many thoughts,' he says, 'in the heart of man';[179] but, still, it is not his will, which is uncertain, and doubtful, and changeable, that prevails, but the counsel of God. 'Who will boast,' he says, 'that his heart is clean?'[180] 'And who will be sure that he is pure from sin?'[181] 'The bread of lying is sweet to a man, but afterwards his mouth shall be filled with gravel.'[182] 'The steps of a man are guided by the Lord, but how will a mortal be able to understand his own ways?'[183] 'Every man seemeth just to himself, but God corrects the hearts of all.'[184] 'An evil son considers himself just and does not wash his own filth.'[185] 'An evil son has lofty eyes and his eyelids are lifted up on high.'[186] 'For there is the just man who perisheth in his own justice.'[187] Whence, it is said to him: 'Be not over just, nor seek what is not necessary as if for wisdom's sake, lest thou become stupid.'[188] 'For whatever man shall labor to seek, he shall not find it.'[189] 'If the wise man shall say that he knoweth it, he shall not be able to find it.'[190] 'For the heart of the children of men is filled with evil.'[191]

---

177 Cf. Jer. 17.9.
178 Prov. 14.12.
179 Prov. 19.21.
180 Prov. 20.9.
181 *Ibid.*
182 Prov. 20.17.
183 Prov. 20.24.
184 Prov. 21.2. This and the remaining quotations are taken from the Septuagint version.
185 Prov. 30.12.
186 Prov. 30.13.
187 Eccles. 7.16.
188 Eccles. 7.17.
189 Eccles. 8.17.
190 *Ibid.*
191 Eccles. 9.3.

Book Two

(1) *Sacrifice for ignorance, error, and so on.*
CRITOBULUS. You have, to be sure, quoted many passages from Sacred Scripture in detail and accurately, and have tried to obscure the clear light of truth under a cloud, as it were, of confusion. But what has all this to do with the question at issue? For with all these testimonies, you seem to be reproaching the nature of man, and, consequently, casting aspersions on God, if He has so created men that they cannot avoid forgetfulness of memory and the sin of ignorance. Thus, it is clear from all this that it is possible for man not to sin if he wants to. For he has committed an act that he could not avoid. Moreover, where possibility is taken away, blame is also taken away; for no one is condemned for what he could not do.
ATTICUS. I have often said that you do not understand the point I am trying to make, and you are not concerned with the point of the argument, but rather with the commandments of God. Sacrifices are offered for forgetfulness, for error, and for ignorance, just as for sin, whether you believe this commandment of God to be evil, or whether I believe it to be good. It is my intention to observe what He has commanded; yours, to reprehend the commandments of God.
CRITOBULUS. Since you are doing violence to the obvious truth and imputing blasphemy to me, I shall grant you that this was a commandment that was given under the old law, of which it is written: 'The former things have passed away; behold, they are all made new.'[1] Can you also prove from the Gospel that man shall be punished for something of which he

---
[1] 2 Cor. 5.17.

has no knowledge, and shall pay a penalty before he is guilty in conscience?

ATTICUS. We are ignoring God; Manichaeus suddenly appears before us who says that the law has been abolished and only the books of the New Testament are to be read.

CRITOBULUS. But, what have you heard me say that should prompt you to make such a remark? For the law that was given to the ancients was just and holy for those ancient times, and, with the coming of the perfection of the Gospel, the inferior things gave way.

ATTICUS. Therefore, should we not observe the commandments that have been imposed under the law?

CRITOBULUS. There are some commandments that should be observed and some that should be passed over.

ATTICUS. Since I see that you are so well informed, tell me the commandments that I should observe and those that I should disregard.

CRITOBULUS. We should observe the commandments that pertain to life and good conduct, of which it was said: 'The commandment of the Lord is lightsome, enlightening the eyes.'[2] But those that deal with the ceremonies of the law and with the rites of sacrifices should be disregarded.

ATTICUS. I am sorry, but, in spite of your boasting about your knowledge of the law and all of Scripture, you do not understand what I am trying to say.

CRITOBULUS. I understand it when you say it, but not when you are silent.

ATTICUS. Do you think that I am silent when I have tried to prove to you, by quoting so many testimonies, that man sins through ignorance, and that, just as he had to offer victims for sin under the law, so also according to the Gospel, he must do penance for his sin?

(2) *An example from the New Testament in the person of the apostle.*

CRITOBULUS. Cite the testimony from the New Testament,

---

2 Ps. 18.9.

where error, and ignorance, and the impossibility of fulfilling the commandment are considered a sin.
ATTICUS. I need not quote many testimonies. I shall produce one which you certainly will not be able to contradict. The Chosen Vessel says very plainly: 'For I am delighted with the law of God according to the inner man, but I see another law in my members, warring against the law of my mind and making me prisoner to the law of sin that is in my members. Unhappy man that I am! Who will deliver me from the body of this death? The grace of God through Jesus Christ our Lord.'[3]
CRITOBULUS. You have quoted a testimony that pleads my case. If, therefore, we have been delivered from the body of this death through the grace of our Lord Jesus Christ, we should not sin any more at all.
ATTICUS. We have, indeed, been delivered through the baptism of our Savior. But explain his reason for saying: 'I see another law in my members, warring against the law of my mind, and making me prisoner to the law of sin that is in my members.' What is the law that rules in the members of man and wars against the law of his mind? Give me a simple answer. You are silent? Listen to that same apostle who proclaims very plainly: 'I do not understand what I do, for it is not what I wish that I do, but what I hate that I do. But if I do what I do not wish, I admit that the Law is good. Now therefore it is no longer I who do it, but the sin that dwells in me. For I know that in me, that is, in my flesh, no good dwells, because to wish is within my power, but I do not find the strength to accomplish what is good. For I do not the good that I wish, but the evil that I do not wish, that I perform. Now if I do what I do not wish, it is no longer I who do it, but the sin that dwells in me.'[4]
CRITOBULUS. I am surprised that an intelligent person like you puts such a construction on this passage of the apostle

---
3 Rom. 7.22-25.
4 Rom. 7.15-20.

as to think he is speaking these words in his own person and not in the name of others. Could a man who, being fully conscious of Christ speaking within him, proclaimed freely: 'Do you seek a proof of the Christ who speaks in me?';[5] and in another place: 'I have finished the course, I have kept the faith. For the rest, there is laid up for me a crown of justice,'[6] have said of himself: 'I do not find the strength to accomplish what is good'; and: 'I do not the good that I wish, but the evil that I do not wish, that I perform'? What was the good that he wished to do and could not do? And what was the evil that he did not wish to do and yet could not avoid? Therefore, it is not in his own person that he is saying this, but in the name of the human race which is subject to faults on account of the weakness of the flesh.

(3) *The person in whose name Paul spoke. And another one of his testimonies.*

ATTICUS. You deny me a small part, only to grant me the whole. For I understand the passage to refer to one man, albeit the apostle, who is subject to sin; you assert that it is the whole human race. But if it is true, as far as the genus is concerned, we, also, hold it to be true as far as the species is concerned. For the apostle is also a man, and, if he is a man, he is speaking the following words as a man, either of other men or of himself: 'Unhappy man that I am! Who will deliver me from the body of this death?'[7] And: 'For in me, that is, in my flesh, no good dwells.'[8] For the corruptible body weighs down the soul. 'The earthly habitation weighs down the mind with its cares.'[9]

CRITOBULUS. You speak as if I were interpreting this passage as being spoken in the name of the human race and not in the name of the sinner.

---

5 2 Cor. 13.3.
6 2 Tim. 4.7, 8.
7 Rom. 7.24.
8 Rom. 7.18.
9 Wisd. 9.15.

ATTICUS. And who will grant you that the apostle is saying this in the name of the sinner? For, if you take this passage as spoken in the name of the sinner, he should have said: 'O unhappy sinner that I am,' and not, 'O unhappy man that I am.' To be a man, to be sure, is a matter of nature; to be a sinner, of the will. Unless, perchance, the following words that were written: 'Vanity of Vanities, and all is vanity,'[10] also refer to sinners and not to all men. And again: 'Surely man passeth as an image';[11] and again: 'Man is like to vanity; his days pass away like a shadow.'[12] If you are not convinced by this testimony of Paul, listen to another one of the testimonies of the same man which you cannot contradict: 'I have nothing on my conscience,'[13] and the rest. Nay, I do not even judge my own self; I have nothing on my conscience, yet I am not thereby justified. He who said these words certainly had no sin on his conscience. But because he had read: 'Who can understand sin,'[14] and: 'There are ways that seem just to a man, but the ends thereof lead to the depths of Hades,'[15] and again: 'Every man seemeth right to himself, but the Lord directs the hearts of men,'[16] he, therefore, tempered his view, lest, perchance, he may have sinned through ignorance, especially since Scripture testifies: 'There is a just man, who perisheth in his justice.'[17] And in another place: 'Thou shalt follow justly after that which is just,'[18] lest we turn from justice, by having our own view of truth, recalling the experience of Saul and Agag.[19]

(4) *There are men who are just, but nobody who is without sin.*

CRITOBULUS. Lest I appear to be contentious and unduly con-

10 Eccles. 1.2.
11 Ps. 38.7.
12 Ps. 143.4.
13 1 Cor. 4.4.
14 Ps. 18.13.
15 Prov. 14.12.
16 Prov. 21.2.
17 Eccles. 7.16.
18 Deut. 16.20.
19 Cf. 1 Kings 15.

trary, grant me at least this one point, that there are very many individuals in Scripture who are given the title of just.
ATTICUS. Not only are there very many such individuals, but their number is legion.
CRITOBULUS. If the number of individuals who are just is legion, and this fact cannot be denied, why have I spoken evilly when I said that man could be without sin if he wanted to? In other words, this is tantamount to saying that the just man can be without sin, insofar as he is a just man.
ATTICUS. I grant you that they are just men, but I cannot agree with you at all that they are without sin. For I say that man can be without fault, which in Greek is called *kakía*, but I deny that he is *anamártētos*, that is to say *sine peccato*. For this is a virtue that befits God alone; and every creature is subject to sin and stands in need of the mercy of God, as Scripture says: 'The earth is full of the mercy of the Lord.'[20] And lest I seem to be discussing certain little faults, so to speak, of the saints, into which they slipped through error, I shall produce a few testimonies that refer, not to individuals, but rather to all men in general. In the thirty-first Psalm, it is written: 'I said I will confess against myself my injustice to the Lord, and thou hast forgiven the wickedness of my heart.'[21] And it continues immediately: 'For this,' (that is to say, for this impiety or iniquity, for both words can be understood in this passage) 'shall everyone that is holy pray to thee in a seasonable time.'[22] If he is holy, what is his reason for praying for iniquity? If he has iniquity, in what sense is he called holy? In the sense, to be sure, that it is also written in another place: 'A just man shall fall seven times and shall rise again.'[23] And: 'The just is accuser of himself in the beginning of his speech.'[24] And in another place: 'The wicked are alienated from the womb, they have gone

20 Ps. 32.5.
21 Ps. 31.5.
22 Ps. 31.6.
23 Prov. 24.16.
24 Prov. 18.17.

astray from the womb, they have spoken false things.'[25] They have either become subject to sin, at the very moment that they were born, after the likeness of the transgression of Adam who is the figure of him who is to come, or, to be sure, at the very moment that Christ was born of the virginal womb, of whom it was written: 'Every one who opens the womb shall be called holy to the Lord.'[26] All heretics have gone astray by not understanding the mystery of His nativity. The statement: 'He who opens the womb shall be called holy to the Lord,' is more applicable to the special nativity of the Savior than to that of all men, for Christ alone opened the closed doors of the womb of virginity, which, nevertheless, remained permanently closed. This is the closed east door, through which only the high priest enters and leaves, and, nevertheless, it is always closed. Also, the following words that were written in the book of Job: 'Shall man be pure in the sight of God or blameless in his deeds? If he does not trust his servants and finds in his angels wickedness, how much more in those who dwell in houses of clay?'[27] We, like them, are also of the same clay. But if you assert that these words are spoken in the person of Eliphas, the Themanite, you should know that these words were not spoken by him, but rather by the person who revealed to him the thoughts of God, in the shape of an angel, in a vision in his dream. But, granted that these words, which are clearly spoken by an angel, are spoken by Eliphas, are not the following words spoken specifically in the very own person of Job? 'The life of man upon earth is a warfare';[28] and: 'If I have sinned, what can I do?'[29] And: 'Why hast thou forgotten and hast thou not forgotten my iniquity and cleansed me of my sin?'[30] 'For how can a man be justified on earth compared with God?'[31] And

---
25 Ps. 57.4.
26 Luke 2.23; Exod. 13.2; 34.19.
27 Job 4.17-19.
28 Job 7.1.
29 Job 7.20.
30 Job 7.21.
31 Job 9.2.

again: 'If I should be just, he shall not hear me; but I shall be in need of his judgment.'[32] And again: 'Because I am wicked, why do I labor in vain?'[33] 'If I should be washed with snow, and my hands should be clean, you have plunged me enough in filth.'[34] 'If I have sinned, you will protect me. But you will not make me innocent from my iniquity.'[35] 'If I commit wickedness, woe unto me.'[36] And: 'If I shall be just, I will not be able to breathe. For I am filled with ignominy.'[37] And again: 'For who will be clean of sordidness? Not even a single person, even if his life on earth should be but for one day and its months numbered.'[38] But if you say that the pronoun 'who,' does not refer to what is impossible, but at times to what is difficult, I reply to you: And what becomes of the rash proposition that you set down: 'The commandments of God are easy,' and they can be easily fulfilled? Scripture says: 'Man labors for himself in anguish and drives away his ruin,'[39] so that his flesh being oppressed, and brought under control, and dead, the spirit may live in him. And I pass over without comment that ridiculous interpretation of your Demosthenes,[40] that Job did not say, 'Who will be clean of sin,' but rather, 'Who will be clean of sordidness.' He tries to prove in his exposition that it is the sordidness of swaddling clothes in infancy that is here referred to, and not the faults of sins. Or, if this is not his interpretation, you should certainly tell us what his views are. Job states in conclusion: 'What answer shall I give to all these questions? I will lay my hand upon my mouth. One thing I have spoken, I will not add another.'[41] And as far as our Job is concerned, who is spotless and just and

---
32 Job 9.15, 16.
33 Job 9.29.
34 Job 9.30, 31.
35 Job 10.14.
36 Job 10.15.
37 *Ibid.*
38 Job 14.4, 5; 15.14.
39 Prov. 16.26 (Septuagint).
40 This is a reference to Pelagius.
41 Job 39.34, 35.

blameless and free from all evil, I wonder with what measure of justice is he crowned that he stands in no need of the mercy of God? This is what we read in Proverbs: 'Who shall boast that he has a clean heart? Or who will be sure that he is clean of sin?'[42] Assume that in this passage he also used the pronoun 'who,' not in respect to what is impossible, but rather in respect to what is difficult. Correct, then, your view and delete from your book the proposition that 'the commandments of God are easy.'

(5) *He meets the objection from the Gospel of John.*

But if you offer as an objection the following testimony of the Apostle John: 'His commandments are not burdensome,'[43] and from the Gospel: 'My yoke is easy, and my burden light,'[44] it will be a very easy matter to refute you; for it is certain that they imply that the commandments of the Gospel are light in comparison with the Jewish religious rites, which demanded the observance of various types of ceremonies that nobody could fulfill to the letter of the law, according to the view of the Apostle Peter. Whence, also, it is written in the Acts of the Apostles: 'Why then do you now try to test God, by putting on the necks of the disciples a yoke which neither our fathers nor we have been able to bear? But we believe that we are saved through the grace of the Lord Jesus Christ just as they are.'[45] The Apostle James writes: 'If thou judgest the law, thou art not a doer of the law, but a judge.'[46] He judges the law who says that an unjust command has been imposed, and that ignorance is no sin, that it is useless for him to offer victims for error because he has no sin on his conscience. For the law does not demand reasoned proof, but rather authority. He also states in that same letter: 'The wrath of man does not work the justice of God.'[47] And who

---

42 Prov. 20.9.
43 1 John 5.3.
44 Matt. 11.30.
45 Acts 15.10, 11.
46 James 4.11.
47 James 1.20.

of us can be free from anger, of which it is written: 'Anger destroys even the wise'?[48] It is noteworthy that he did not say 'the wrath of God,' but rather the 'wrath of man.' For the wrath of God is just, but the wrath of man proceeds from a disturbed mind; whence, also, it is said in the Psalm: 'Be ye angry, and sin not.'[49] The apostle teaches us the meaning of this verse: 'Do not let the sun go down upon your anger,'[50] so that it is definitely a sin to be angry, even in a slight degree; but it is justice to mitigate anger by quickly repenting. Whence we shall render an account on judgment day for even an idle word. And in the same Gospel, we read: 'He who is angry with his brother without cause shall be liable to judgment';[51] although in many of the ancient copies, the phrase, 'without cause,' has not been added, so that we should not be angry, to be sure, even with cause. What man will be able to say that he is free forever from the fault of anger, a fault that is without justice? And again: 'Boast not for tomorrow, for thou knowest not what the day to come may bring forth.'[52] Whence it is written: 'Do not call any man blessed before death.'[53] For as long as we live, we are engaged in warfare, and as long as we are engaged in warfare, there is no sure victory, which is laid up in the next world for the apostle, the very valiant fighter. The Lord and Savior speaks the following words in the person of His assumed humanity: 'For I am the most foolish of all men, and the wisdom of man is not with me.'[54] And in the sixty-eighth Psalm: 'O God, thou knowest my foolishness';[55] but 'The foolishness of God is wiser than men.'[56] In Ecclesiastes, also, it is written: 'In much wisdom there is much knowledge; and

---

48 Prov. 15.2.
49 Ps. 4.5.
50 Eph. 4.26.
51 Matt. 5.22.
52 Prov. 27.1.
53 Sir. (Ecclus.) 11.30.
54 Prov. 30.2.
55 Ps. 68.6.
56 1 Cor. 1.25.

he that addeth knowledge, addeth grief';[57] for he knows that he lacks perfection and realizes how much he does not know when he considers what he knows. And I hate my life, he says, because the work that I do upon earth is evil.[58] For all is vanity and vexation of spirit. No man knows what is to come, for who will announce it to him, just as it is? There are just men to whom evil happens, as though they had done the works of the wicked, and there are wicked men to whom goodness happens, as though they had done the works of the just.[59] This is said because the judgment of God alone is certain, and those whom we judge to be just turn out to be sinners, and those, on the other hand, whom we think to be sinners are just, according to the knowledge of God. 'How much soever a man shall labor to seek, he shall not find. And if the wise man shall say that he knoweth, he shall not be able to find.'[60] For the same things happen to all men, and the hearts of the children of men are filled with evil and their conditions uncertain,[61] which in Greek is called *periphéreia*. 'Dying flies,' (or, as it appears in Hebrew, 'dead flies') spoil the sweetness of the ointment.'[62] What mortal is there who is not overtaken by some error? What man is there who is not tainted by the poison of heretical and false doctrines? 'The time has come,' he says, 'for the judgment to begin with the household of God. But if it begins first with us, what will be the end of those who do not believe the Gospel? And if the just man scarcely will be saved, where will the impious and the sinner appear?'[63] To be sure, it is the just man who scarcely is saved on judgment day. But he would easily be saved if he had no fault. Therefore, he is just because he flourishes with many virtues, and he scarcely is saved because he stands in need of the mercy of God in some matters.

---

57 Eccles. 1.18.
58 Cf. Eccles. 2.17.
59 Cf. Eccles. 8.17.
60 *Ibid*.
61 Cf. Eccles. 9.2, 3.
62 Eccles. 10.1.
63 1 Peter 4.17, 18.

(6) *The disorders of the human race.*

There are four disorders by which the human race is disturbed. Two of these disorders have to do with the present, two with the future; two originate in what is good, two in what is evil. There is sorrow which is termed *lúpē* in Greek, and joy which they call *chará,* or *hēdonḗ,* although for *hēdonḗ* many use the term 'pleasure.' The first of these disorders stems from what is evil, the other from what is good. And we exceed the limits of moderation if we rejoice over things that we should not, such as riches, power, honors, the misfortunes of our enemies or their death; or, on the other hand, if we are disturbed by the distress of present evils, such as adversities, exiles, poverty, sickness, and the deaths of relatives. The apostle forbids such disturbances. And again, if we long for things that we consider to be good, such as legacies, honors, prosperities of every description, and soundness of body, and other things in which we find enjoyment and delight for the present; and if we fear things that we think to be evil. It is the view of the Stoics, and Zeno, to be sure, and Chrysippus, that it is possible to avoid to a perfect degree all these disorders; but according to the view of the Peripatetics, they are both difficult and impossible to avoid. This view is confirmed by the authority of the entire volume of Sacred Scripture. Whence, also, Josephus,[64] the historian of the Machabees, said that the disorders of the soul could be controlled and ruled, but not eradicated; and the five books of the *Tusculan Disputations* of Cicero are replete with disputations on these matters. For, according to the view of the apostle, the weakness of the body and the spiritual forces of wickedness war against us.[65] The works of the flesh, in the words of the same apostle, and the works of the spirit are manifest, and these are opposed to each other, so that we do not do what we wish.[66] But, if we do not do what

---

64 Josephus, *Liber de Machabeis* 3.
65 Cf. Eph. 6.12.
66 Cf. Gal. 5.17, 19.

we wish, but do what we do not wish, what is your reason for saying that man can be without sin if he wants to? You see that the apostle and all who believe cannot do what they wish. 'Charity covers a multitude of sins,'[67] not only of our past sins, but also of our present sins, so that we will not sin any more if the charity of God abides in us. For this reason, it is said of the woman who was a sinner: 'Many sins are forgiven her, because she has loved much.'[68] We see from all of this that it depends, not only on our own power to do what we will, but also on the mercy of God, if He will help our will.

(7) *God alone is immortal, wise, and perfect by nature.*

God is called the light, and in Him there is no darkness.[69] When he says that no darkness is found in the light of God, he is proving that all the lights of others are stained by some blemish. Moreover, the apostles are also referred to as the light of the world. But it is not written that there is no darkness in the light of the apostles. Also of John, it is written: 'This man came as a witness, to bear witness concerning the light, that all might believe through him. He was not himself the light, but was to bear witness to the light. It was the true light that enlightens every man who comes into this world.'[70] Whence, also, it is written of Him: 'Who alone has immortality and dwells in light inaccessible.'[71] And we read, to be sure, that angels are immortal, and that Thrones and Dominations are immortal, and the other Virtues. But God, alone, is immortal because He is immortal, not by grace like the others, but by nature. Hence, the same apostle writes that God alone is wise,[72] although both Solomon and many other holy men are called wise, and it is said, according to the Hebrew, to the prince of Tyre: 'Thou art wiser than

---

67 1 Peter 4.8.
68 Luke 7.47.
69 Cf. 1 John 1.5.
70 John 1.7, 8.
71 1 Tim. 6.16.
72 Cf. Rom. 16.27.

Daniel.'[73] Therefore, just as He, alone, is called the light, immortal, and wise, although they are many who are immortal, and who are lights, and who are wise, so, also, the perfection of man that proceeds, not from nature, but from grace, shows that those who seem to be perfect are imperfect. However, the following words that are written: 'And the blood of Jesus, His Son, cleanses us from all sin,'[74] must be taken as referring to the confession of baptism, as well as to the mercy of repentance. But it is one thing to be cleansed by God and quite another matter to be faultless of one's self. For if, according to Job: 'The moon doth not shine, and the stars are not pure in his sight, how much less man that is rottenness, and the son of man who is a worm!'[75] For every mouth is stopped and all the world is made subject to God: 'For by the works of the Law no flesh shall be justified before Him.'[76] There is no distinction of persons: 'For all have sinned and have need of the glory of God. They are justified freely by his grace.'[77] But if he writes: 'We reckon that a man is justified by faith independently of the works of the Law. For there is but one God who justifies the circumcised by the Law, and the uncircumcised through faith,'[78] he shows clearly that justice depends, not on the merit of man, but on the grace of God, who accepts the faith of those who believe without the works of the law. Whence he continues: 'Sin shall not have dominion over you.'[79] Why? 'Because you are not under the Law but under grace.'[80] 'For there is no question of him who wills nor of him who runs, but of God showing mercy.'[81] 'Whence also the Gentiles who were not pursuing justice have secured justice, but a justice that is

---

[73] Ezech. 28.3.
[74] 1 John 1.7.
[75] Job 25.5, 6.
[76] Rom. 3.20.
[77] Rom. 3.23, 24.
[78] Rom. 3.28, 30.
[79] Rom. 6.14.
[80] *Ibid.*
[81] Rom. 9.16.

from faith; but Israel, by pursuing a law of justice, has not attained to the law of justice, because they sought it not from faith, but from works. For they stumbled at the stumblingstone.'[82] 'For Christ is the consummation of the Law unto justice for everyone who believes.'[83]

(8) *From the letters of the apostle.*
Practically all of the letters of the apostle begin in this manner: 'Grace be to you and peace from God our Father and Christ Jesus our Lord,'[84] and they conclude in the same manner. It is also written to the Corinthians: 'That you lack no grace while awaiting the appearance of our Lord Jesus Christ, who will also keep you secure unto the end, unimpeachable in the day of our Lord Jesus Christ.'[85] Therefore, although we lack no grace, nevertheless, we await the appearance of our Lord Jesus Christ, who will then keep us secure in all things, and present us unimpeachable when the day of our Lord Jesus Christ and the end of the world shall arrive, so that no flesh may glory in His sight. Paul planted, Apollo watered, but God has given the growth. Therefore, neither he who plants is anything, nor he who waters, but God who gives growth.[86] We are God's tillage; we are God's building. According to His grace, God lays the foundation like a wise architect. 'Do not deceive yourselves,' he says. 'If any one of you thinks himself wise in this world, let him become a fool, that he may come to be wise. For the wisdom of this world is foolishness with God.'[87] 'The Lord knoweth the thoughts of men, that they are vain.'[88] And again: 'For I have nothing on my conscience, yet I am not thereby justified, because he that judges me is the Lord.'[89] The following words are spoken to you, who say you are without sin. 'What hast thou that

---
82 Rom. 9.30-32.
83 Rom. 10.4.
84 1 Cor. 1.3.
85 1 Cor. 1.7, 8.
86 Cf. 1 Cor. 3.6.
87 1 Cor. 3.18, 19.
88 Ps. 93.11.
89 1 Cor. 4.4.

thou hast not received? But if thou hast received it, why dost thou boast as if thou hast not received it?'[90] 'You are already filled, you are already made rich!'[91] And that we may realize that all things do not depend on us, but on the judgment of God: 'I shall come shortly,' he says, 'if the Lord is willing.'[92] For he who says: 'I shall come to you,' indicates that he is willing, shows that he wants to come, promises that he will come. But to temper his remarks with a bit of caution, he says: 'If the Lord is willing.' For, if anybody thinks that he has knowledge of some event, he does not yet have the kind of knowledge that he should have.

(9) *Again from the apostle.*

The Chosen Vessel, overcome with humility, nay more, with an awareness of his weakness, says: 'I am the least of the apostles, and am not worthy to be called an apostle, because I persecuted the Church of God. But by the grace of God I am what I am, and his grace in me has not been fruitless—in fact I have labored more than any of them, yet not I, but the grace of God with me.'[93] He says that he has labored more than all of the apostles, and immediately attributes his labor to the help of God, saying: 'Not I, but the grace of God with me.'[94] Just as he also says in another place: 'But such is the assurance I have through Jesus Christ towards God, not because we are sufficient to think anything as from ourselves, but our sufficiency is from God, who also has made us fit ministers of the new covenant.'[95] For man is not justified by the works of the law, but by the faith of Jesus Christ. Whence he says: 'We also believe in Jesus Christ, that we may be justified by the faith of Christ, and not by the works of the Law; because by the works of the Law no flesh will be justified.'[96] 'For if justice is from the Law,

---

90 1 Cor. 4.7.
91 1 Cor. 4.8.
92 1 Cor. 4.9.
93 1 Cor. 15.9, 10.
94 1 Cor. 15.10.
95 2 Cor. 3.4-6.
96 Gal. 2.16.

then Christ died in vain.'[97] Under the law, there is a curse: 'For it is written: "Cursed is everyone who does not hold to all things that are written in the book of the Law to perform them." '[98] 'Christ redeemed us from the curse of the Law, becoming a curse for us.'[99] 'For if a law had been given that could give life, justice would be truly from the Law. But the Scripture shut up all things under sin, that by the faith of Jesus Christ the promise might be given to those who believe. Therefore the Law has been our tutor unto Christ, that we might be justified by faith.'[100] Whence he adds and sums up the whole question in one verse, saying: 'You who would be justified in the Law are estranged from Christ; you have fallen away from grace.'[101]

(10) *The law has been fulfilled by nobody.*

I mention all these passages in a cursory fashion to prove that the law has been fulfilled by nobody, and that all things that are contained in the law have been commanded by the law. For it is God who works in us both the will and the performance.[102] The apostle labors, and, although he has lived blameless, according to the justice that is from the law, he counts everything as worthless for Christ, that he may be found in Christ, not having his own justice which is from the law, but that which is from the faith of Christ, from God. Whence he writes to the Thessalonians: 'But the Lord is faithful, who will save and guard them from evil.'[103] Therefore, we are saved, not by the power of the free will, but by the mercy of God. And, lest you think that the truth of faith can be subverted by vain argumentations, which raise questions in the minds of the listeners, the same apostle writes to Timothy: 'O Timothy, guard the trust and keep free from profane novelties in speech and the contradictions of so-

---
97 Gal. 2.21.
98 Gal. 3.10.
99 Gal. 3.13.
100 Gal. 3.21, 22, 24.
101 Gal. 5.4.
102 Cf. Phil. 2.13.
103 2 Thess. 3.3.

called knowledge, which some have promised and have fallen away from the faith.'[104] 'For the goodness and mercy of our Savior have saved us, not by reason of good works that we did ourselves, but according to his mercy, in order that, justified by his grace, we may be heirs in the hope of life everlasting.'[105] We have plucked these brief passages from the very wide and very beautiful field, as it were, of the apostolic teachings, in order to put an end to brazen and shameless effrontery.

(11) *From the precepts of the Gospel.*

Let us turn to the Gospels and fill out the light of the apostolic sparks with the very brilliant light of the lamp of Christ. 'Everyone,' he says, 'who is angry with his brother without reason, shall be liable to judgment. But whoever says, "Raca," ' (which means foolish and senseless) 'shall be liable to the council,' (council, no doubt, of the saints and the angelic senate). 'But whoever says, "Thou fool," shall be liable to the fire of Gehenna.'[106] Who of us has it in his power not to be subject to this fault, when we shall render an account on judgment day even for an idle word? If anger, and calumny of speech, and an occasional joke are liable to judgment, and to the council, and to the fires of Gehenna, what punishment will base desire deserve, and avarice, which is the root of all evils? 'If,' he says, 'thou art offering thy gifts at the altar, and there rememberest that thy brother has anything against thee, leave thy gift before the altar and go first to be reconciled to thy brother, and then come and offer thy gift.'[107] It lies within my own power not to have anything against my brother. But that he have anything or not against me, depends on his own will. What shall I do, then, if he is unwilling to be reconciled? Shall I beg him? Shall I bend my knees to him? But he will refuse to listen. If he is unwilling, shall I wrench his neck and force

---
104 1 Tim 6.20, 21.
105 Tit. 3.4, 5, 7.
106 Matt. 5.22.
107 Matt. 5.23, 24.

him to accept the ties of friendship? And is there any enmity worse than friendship made through necessity? For he did not say: 'Ask him to be reconciled to you,' but: 'Be first reconciled to thy brother and then offer thy gift at the altar.' Not because God has commanded what is impossible, but because He has set such heights for patience that it would seem that He has commanded what is well nigh impossible, rather than what is extremely difficult, in refutation of your view in which you state: 'The commandments of God are easy.' We are commanded to cut off a scandalizing hand, eye, and foot. Granted, that this command was spoken in a figurative sense to mean very close friends, relatives, and those who are joined to us by bonds of fraternal and conjugal love. Do we think that it is an easy matter to suddenly sever such close bonds of charity because of certain offenses? And, as far as the following words are concerned: 'Let your speech be, "Yes, yes, no, no," and whatever is beyond these comes from the evil one,'[108] I suppose somebody from your school can be found who has never lied, or who has not heard the following prophetic and apostolic utterance: 'I said in the excess of my heart, "Every man is a liar" ';[109] and who does not know that it is written in another place: 'The mouth that belieth, killeth the soul.'[110] We are commanded to offer the other cheek to him who strikes us on the one cheek. Even our coat is to be handed over to him who takes our tunic. We must submit and go two miles with him who forces us to go one mile. 'To him who asks of thee, give, and from him who would borrow of thee, do not turn away.'[111] If I have two coins and somebody begs me to give them to him, I shall either give them to him and I will have to go begging, or, if I do not give them to him, I shall be found to be a transgressor of the law. However, as far as the following words are concerned: 'Love your enemies, do good to them who hate you,

---
108 Matt. 5.37.
109 Ps. 115.2.
110 Wisd. 1.11.
111 Matt. 5.42.

and pray for those who persecute you and calumniate you,'[112] I suppose there is such a person in your group; in ours, such a person is a *rara avis*. They who make a simple confession of their sins deserve the mercy of the Savior because of their humility; as far as the following words are concerned: 'Take heed not to do your justice,' (that is to say, your alms-deeds), 'before men, in order to be seen by them,'[113] I do not know who can fulfill them. We hire a public crier to dole out crumbs of bread and two coins for each person, and, as we extend a helping hand, we glance in this direction and that, and, if no one is watching us, we draw in our extended hand. Granted, that there may be found one person in a thousand who would not carry on in this manner.

(12) *He presses his point from the same precepts.*

Answer me, I ask you: Where are the easy commandments? 'Do not be anxious,' he says, 'about tomorrow; for tomorrow will have anxieties of its own. Sufficient for the day is its own trouble.'[114] Do you not think of tomorrow, and, like birds, are you content with the present, when your letters of papyrus fly across the rivers of Ethiopia, so that new gifts might be sent from among the apes and peacocks, from Ophir to Solomon?[115] Do you wish to hear about the easiness of the commandments of God? Listen to these words: 'How narrow is the gate and close the way that leads to life! And few there are who find it.'[116] He did not say: 'who walk it,' (for this is a very difficult thing to do), but: 'who find it.' For few find it and much fewer still who walk it. 'The Son of man,' he says, 'has no where to lay his head,'[117] who says in Isaia: 'Refresh the weary, and this is my refreshing.'[118] If He has no where to lay His head and no where to find

---
112 Matt. 5.44.
113 Matt. 6.1.
114 Matt. 6.34.
115 This is a reference to Solomon, king of Israel, who sent a fleet to Ophir from whence much gold was brought back. Cf. 3 Kings 9.28.
116 Matt. 7.14.
117 Luke 9.58.
118 Isa. 28.12.

rest, saying in another place: 'On whom shall I rest but on him that is poor and little and troubleth at my words,'[119] where is the easiness of the commandments? Many interpret the statement: 'I am come to call the just, not the sinners to repentance,'[120] simply according to the sense of the following text: 'It is not the healthy who need a physician, but they who are sick.'[121] Others, however, put a more literal construction on the statement: 'I am not come to call the just,' (for nobody is perfectly just, but is a sinner in some respect), 'but sinners,' (with whom the world is replete), as David says: 'Save me, O Lord, for there is no saint';[122] and: 'They are corrupt, and are become abominable in their plans. They are all gone astray, they are become unprofitable together; there is none that doth good, no not one.'[123] 'Do not keep gold,' he says, 'or silver, or money in your girdles, no wallet for your journey, nor bread, nor two tunics, no sandals, nor staff.'[124] 'These,' you will say, 'are apostolic precepts.' But it is related, to be sure, that the Apostle Peter had sandals, for the angel said to him: 'Gird thyself and put on thy sandals.'[125] Moreover, I suppose he had two coats, not to mention the other things that both you and I have, if, indeed, we have nothing else. I say these things, and shall repeat them again and again on every occasion, that you may be ashamed of your view that 'the commandments of God are easy.'

(13) *Again from the Gospel.*

Brother will hand over brother to death, and the father his child, and the children shall rise up against parents and put them to death. 'And you will be hated,' He says, 'by all for my name's sake.'[126] And, because He gave easy commandments, and He knew that they could be easily fulfilled,

---
119 Isa. 66.2.
120 Luke 5.32.
121 Mark 2.17.
122 Ps. 11.2.
123 Ps. 13.1, 3.
124 Matt. 10.9, 10.
125 Acts 12.8.
126 Matt. 10.22

for that reason He added the following words, just to prove the easiness of the whole matter, saying: 'He who has persevered to the end, will be saved.'[127] 'I have not come,' He says, 'to send peace upon earth, but the sword. For I come to set a man at variance with his father, and the daughter with her mother, and the daughter-in-law with her mother-in-law.'[128] And, lest He compose a rather lengthy sentence by running through all of the items, He sums up the whole matter, saying: 'A man's enemies will be those of his own household.'[129] And, after making the statement: 'He who loves father or mother more than me is not worthy of me; and he who loves son or daughter more than me is not worthy of me,'[130] He added the following words because of the easiness of the commandments: 'And he who does not take up his cross and follow me, is not worthy of me.'[131] The cross of Christ is easy; to walk behind the naked Christ is mere child's game. And where are the rewards that we expect to get after we have overcome the difficulties? The cockle weeds are not gathered up in the present world, lest the wheat be also uprooted at the same time. God's winnowing forks are reserved for the future judgment, when the just shall shine like the sun, and the angels shall come forth, and shall separate the wicked from the midst of the just. Peter begins to sink and he deserves to hear it said to him: 'O thou of little faith, why didst thou doubt?'[132] If he has little faith, I do not know what man has great faith. 'Out of the heart,' He says, 'come evil thoughts, murders, adulteries, immortality, thefts, false witnesses, blasphemies. These are the things that defile a man.'[133] Let him come forth who can testify that these things do not exist in his heart, and I shall admit that perfect justice exists in this mortal body. 'He who would

---

127 *Ibid.*
128 Matt. 10.34, 35.
129 Matt. 10.36.
130 Matt. 10.37.
131 Matt. 10.38.
132 Matt. 14.31.
133 Matt. 15.19, 20.

save his life,' He says, 'will lose it; and he who loses his life for my sake will save it.'[184] Again, I say: Are these easy commandments? 'Woe to the world because of scandals! For it must needs be that scandals come.'[185] And, for this reason, it is written in another place: 'In many things we all offend,'[136] (or go astray). He did not say, 'a few sins,' but 'many,' nor the sins of 'a few individuals,' but of 'all.' 'For they all seek their own interests, and not those of God.'[137] God alone is referred to as good, and the Master, as man, refuses the title of goodness. A very learned man says that he has fulfilled everything according to the law, and for this he is even admired by the Lord; and yet he does not have full justice because he was unwilling to distribute his wealth to the poor. Thereupon, one difficulty is compared with another difficulty, or rather, one impossibility is compared with another impossibility, because a camel cannot pass through the eye of a needle, nor can a rich man enter the kingdom of heaven. Who of us does not clean the outside of the cup and dish and leave the inside defiled with uncleanness? Who can avoid the similitude of the outwardly whited sepulchers, lest Jesus say also to us: 'You indeed outwardly appear just to men, but within you are full of hyprocrisy and iniquity'?[138] We may even be free of other faults, but to be free of the taint of hypocrisy is a virtue possessed by a few of us, or none at all.

(14) *From the example of Christ our Lord and the apostles.*

'Father,' He says, 'if it is possible, let this cup pass away from me; yet not as I will, but as thou willest.'[139] The Son of God, 'Who spoke, and they were made, who commanded and all things were created,'[140] tempers His view: 'Father, if it

---
134 Matt. 16.25.
135 Matt. 18.7.
136 James 3.2.
137 Phil. 2.21.
138 Matt. 23.28.
139 Matt. 26.39.
140 Ps. 148.5.

is possible; yet not as I will, but as thou willest,'[141] and my friend, Critobulus, wrinkles his eyebrows and says: 'Man can be without sin if he wants to.' The apostles hear it said to them: 'Could you not, then, watch one hour with me?'[142] He did not say: 'Did you not want to?'; but 'could you not?' The apostles cannot watch one hour, being overcome by sleep and sorrow and the weakness of the flesh; and you can overcome all sins at the same time and for a long time. The Evangelist Mark writes of the Lord: 'And he could not work even one miracle there, beyond curing a few sick people by laying his hands upon them. And he marvelled because of their unbelief.'[143] It is stated that the Lord could not work even one miracle at Nazareth, and He is kept from doing so, because He was amazed at the unbelief of others; and you can do everything that you want to. Finally, it is written further on: 'He departed for the district of Tyre and Sidon. And he entered a house and wanted no man to know it, but he could not keep it a secret.'[144] He certainly wanted to keep it a secret, and why could He not keep the people from knowing of His arrival as He wanted to? Do you want to know the reason why He could not keep it a secret? Consider the reality of His assumed humanity, and you will be relieved of all scandal. If it is stated that the Son of God could not fulfill an act, according to the flesh and because of the flesh, will we, who are completely earthly and who daily war against the works of the spirit, be able to do all things that we want to, contrary to the view held by the apostle? The Apostle Peter wants to set up three tents on the mount, one for the Lord, a second one for Moses, and a third one for Elias, not knowing what he is saying because he was struck with fear; and do we spew out the insolence of the Pythagorean philoso-

---

141 Matt. 26.39.
142 Matt. 26.40.
143 Mark 6.5.
144 Mark 7.24.

phy?[145] He replies that neither the angels of heaven nor the Son has knowledge of the day and the hour of the final consummation,[146] and do we promise full knowledge? The weakness of the flesh rejoiced to have God dwell within itself, and yet it could not exceed the measure of its weakness, so that the Son of God might be believed to be the Son of Man, not in appearance, according to the view of the ancient heretics, but in reality. Leaving the apostles for a little while, He fell flat on the ground and prayed, saying: 'Father, if it is possible.'[147] Why, I ask you, did He utter such an uncertain statement, who had said in another place: 'Things that are impossible with men are possible with God'?[148] But since He is about to suffer as man, He utters the words of a man. He says: 'If it is possible, let this one hour pass away.' You say: 'It is possible to avoid sins for all time.'

(15) *From other accounts in the Gospel.*

In some copies, and, especially, in the Greek codices, it is written, according to Mark, at the end of his Gospel: 'At length Jesus appeared to the Eleven as they were at table; and he upraided them for their lack of faith and hardness of heart, in that they did not believe those who had seen him after he had risen.'[149] 'And they began to apologize, saying: "This world is the substance of iniquity and incredulity, which does not allow the true virtue of God to be understood because of unclean spirits; therefore now reveal your justice." '[150] If you contradict this passage, you certainly will not dare to refute the following: 'The world is in the power of the evil one,'[151] and the fact that Satan dared to tempt his Lord

---

145 According to the Pythagoreans, man can attain perfect justice and perfect knowledge so as to be equal with God and to be of one substance with Him.
146 Cf. Matt. 24.36.
147 Matt. 26.39.
148 Luke 18.27.
149 Mark 16.14.
150 These verses are not considered to be genuine, and they are not found in either the Greek or authentic copies.
151 1 John 5.19.

and he withdrew, defeated and confused, until the time, to be sure, of His Passion. He is tempted and the successor of Jovinian[152] dares to say: 'Those who have received baptism with full faith cannot be tempted,' nay more, to put it in other words: 'The man who has been baptized cannot sin any more if he does not want to.' Zacharia, who was just, hears it said by an angel: 'Because thou hast not believed my words, thou shalt be dumb and unable to speak until the day of his birth.'[153] The father of a lunatic boy says of the apostles: 'I asked your disciples to cast it out, that is to say, the demon, and they could not.'[154] And the disciples themselves ask the Savior: 'Why could we not cast it out?'[155] And they hear it said to them: 'Because of your little faith.'[156] Why, I ask you? Because the power to do all things was reserved for the Lord. The thought entered the mind of the apostles which of them was the greatest, and they are corrected by the teaching of the Savior, since the least is recognized as the greatest, and humility is changed into sublimity. He is not received by a Samaritan city because His face was set for Jerusalem.[157] James and John, who were truly the sons of thunder, and Phinees and Elias, burning with ardent desire, wish to bring fire down from heaven and they are rebuked by the Lord. They certainly would not have been rebuked if there were no error connected with such a desire. A crowd of people was going along with Him, that is to say, with the Lord, who turned and said: 'If anyone comes to me and does not hate his father and mother, and wife and children, and brethren and sisters, yes, and even his own life, he cannot be my

---

152 Jovinian had taught at Rome at the end of the fourth century that anyone who had received baptism with full faith could not sin any more. He was teaching, in effect, salvation by faith alone and the uselessness of good works for salvation. Cf. F. Cayré, *Manual of Patrology and History of Theology* 1 (translated by H. Howitt; Belgium 1935) 244-245.
153 Luke 1.20.
154 Matt. 17.15.
155 Matt. 17.18.
156 Matt. 17.19.
157 Cf. Luke 9.53.

disciple.'[158] 'He who does not carry his cross and follow me, cannot be my disciple.'[159] Shall I be very bold at this point and exclaim: 'Man can avoid all sins if he wants to, for His commandments are easy?' The Pharisees deserve to hear it said to them: 'You are they who call yourselves just before men, but God knows your hearts; for that which is exalted in the sight of men is abominable before God.'[160] 'It is impossible,' He says, 'that scandals should not come.'[161] I suppose that scandal is a sin because sin comes through scandal. Unless I am mistaken, the words *skôlon* and *skándalon* among the Greeks took their meaning from the words *offensio* and *ruina*. Wherefore: 'In many things we all offend.'[162] Granted, that I have not come to ruin, but I have certainly offended, and not in one thing, but in many things. I believe it is a sin to have offended in something. The apostles said to the Lord: 'Increase our faith.' And He replies to them: 'If you have faith even like a mustard seed,'[163] which is certainly the smallest of all seeds; and my friend, Critobulus, is puffed up in our presence with mountains of faith.

(16) *Sinlessness can be granted by God.*

'And he also told them,' he says, 'a parable, that they must always pray and not lose heart.'[164] It is useless for us to pray always, if it depends on our own will to do what we want to. The apostles said: 'Who can be saved?' They hear it said by the Lord: 'Things that are impossible with men are possible with God.'[165] Therefore, some things that are impossible with men are, to be sure, shown to be possible, by the fact that they are possible with God. Therefore, it would also be possible with God to grant sinlessness to man if He wants to, not by reason of the latter's merits, but by

---
158 Luke 14.26.
159 Luke 14.27.
160 Luke 16.15.
161 Luke 17.1.
162 James 3.2.
163 Luke 17.5, 6.
164 Luke 18.1.
165 Luke 18.26, 27.

reason of God's own mercy; and it would be impossible with man to obtain by the power of the free will what he receives through the will of the giver. It was not enough for the apostles to have asked a short time ago which of them was the greatest in rank, but it is written of them that at the very moment of need and of the Passion: 'There arose a dispute among them, which of them was the greatest.'[166] Indeed, the best time to argue about rank is in the shadow of the cross. 'Simon, Simon,' He says, 'behold Satan has desired to have you, that he may sift you as wheat. But I have prayed for thee, that thy faith may not fail.'[167] And, according to your view, it certainly lay in the power of the apostle, if he had wanted to, that his faith should not fail. When faith fails, sin, surely, enters in. In some copies, Greek as well as Latin, the following words are found written by Luke: 'There appeared to him an angel from heaven to strengthen him,'[168] (referring, undoubtedly, to the Lord, Savior). 'And falling into an agony, he prayed the more earnestly. And his sweat became as drops of blood running down upon the ground.'[169] The Savior is strengthened in His agony by an angel, and my good friend, Critobulus, does not need the help of God, for he possesses the power of the free will. And He prayed so earnestly that drops of blood gushed forth, which He was to shed in full measure in His Passion. 'Why do you sleep?' He says. 'Rise and pray that you may not enter into temptation.'[170] According to your view, He should have said: 'Why do you sleep? Rise and resist, for you have a free will, and once this power has been bestowed upon you by the Lord, you need no one else's help. For if you act in this manner, you shall not enter into temptation.'

(17) *Again from the Gospel story.*

'Of myself,' He says, 'I can do nothing, but as I hear, so

---
166 Luke 22.24.
167 Luke 22.31, 32.
168 Luke 22.43.
169 Luke 22.43, 44.
170 Luke 22.46.

I judge.'[171] The Arians[172] charge that this is calumny, but the Church replies that these words are spoken in the person of the assumed man. You, on the contrary, say: 'I can be without sin if I want to.' He can do nothing of Himself, to show the reality of His humanity. You can avoid all sins, to show that you are *antitheos*,[173] while still encased in the body. He says to His brethren and relatives that He is not going up to the Scenopegia, and, furthermore, it is written: 'As soon as his brethren had gone up, then he also went up to the feast, not publicly, but as it were secretly.'[174] He said that He would not go up, and He did what He had previously said He would not do. Porphyry rants and accuses Him of inconstancy and fickleness, not knowing that all scandals must be imputed to the flesh. 'Moses,' He says, 'gave you the Law, and none of you observes the Law,'[175] which, to be sure, was possible, and yet no one had observed what was possible, nor is blame placed for that reason on him who gave the command, but rather on the weakness of him who heard it, so that the whole world may be subject to God. In the Gospel, according to John, there is found in many of both the Greek as well as the Latin copies, the story of the adulteress who was accused before the Lord. Moreover, the Scribes and Pharisees kept accusing her and kept earnestly pressing the case, for they wished to stone her to death,

---

171 John 5.30.
172 The Arians were the most widely recognized adherents of that error which denied that the Father, Son, and Holy Spirit were of the one and the same substance or essence. They claimed that the Son is a creature. After the Council of Nicaea in the year 325, the Arians split into three groups. One of these, the Semi-Arians, expressed the relationship between the Father and the Son as that of similar substance. They were known as the Homoeans. Cf. J. Tixeront, *History of Dogmas* 2 (translated from the fifth French edition by H. L. B.; St. Louis 1923) 48-51.
173 The meaning of the phrase *antitheos* is 'godlike' or 'a match for the gods.' In Homeric usage, this is the usual epithet applied to heroes. Thus Phoenix is called *antitheos*, 'match for god' (*Iliad* 23.360); and Arcesias is described as being *antitheos*, that is, 'godlike.' (*Odyssey* 14.182).
174 John 7.10.
175 John 7.19.

according to the law. 'But Jesus, stooping down, began to write with his finger on the ground,'[176] the sins, to be sure, of those who were making the accusation, and of all mortal beings, according to what is written in the prophet: 'They that depart from thee shall be written in the earth.'[177] Finally, raising His head, He said to them: 'Let him who is without sin among you be the first to cast a stone at her.'[178] The phrase, 'without sin,' is written in Greek as *anamártētos*. He, therefore, who says that 'without sin' is one thing, and *anamártētos* quite another thing, should either translate the Greek phrase with a new word, or, if it has been translated by the Latins, as the truth of the translation demands, it is clear that *anamártētos* is nothing more or less than 'without sin.' And, because all of the accusers fled (for the very merciful judge had given them an opportunity to retreat in their shame), He again stooped down and wrote on the ground; they began to go away gradually, one by one, and to avoid His eyes, and He remained alone with the woman, to whom Jesus said: 'Where are they who accused you? Has no one condemned thee? She said: "No one, Lord." Then Jesus said to her: "Neither will I condemn thee. Go and from now on sin no more." '[179] The Lord commanded her to sin no more, just as He also commanded other things according to the law. But whether she did it or not, Scripture does not say. 'All,' He says, 'who have came before me were thieves and robbers.'[180] If all were, then, no one is excluded. 'Who have come,' He says, not, 'who have been sent,' of whom the prophet says: 'They came of themselves, and I have not sent them.'[181] According to these words, power is reserved for Christ alone, who came into His own and His own received Him not.[182] 'While I was with them in the world,' He says,

---

176 John 8.6.
177 Jer. 17.13.
178 John 8.7.
179 John 8.10, 11.
180 John 10.8.
181 John 14.14.
182 Cf. John 1.11.

'I kept them in thy name. Those whom thou hast given me I guarded; and not one of them perished except one, the son of perdition.'[183] He did not say: 'I gave them the power of the free will that they themselves might save themselves by their own effort'; but: 'I kept them, I guarded them.' And finally He says: 'I do not pray that you take them out of the world, but that thou keep them from evil.'[184] In the Acts of the Apostles,[185] it is written that dissension arose between Paul and Barnabas over John, surnamed Mark, so that they departed one from another; and Barnabas took Mark with him, and Paul took Silas in the ministry of the Gospel. Paul was very stern; the other very gentle, each having his own way. And yet a dissension is a sign, in some respect, of a weakness. In the same volume, we read: 'Passing through Phrygia and the Galatian country, they were forbidden by the Holy Spirit to speak the word in Asia.'[186] And, because of this curse, I suppose that many heretics are found in that very province even to the present time who oppose the Holy Spirit. 'And when they came,' he says, 'to Mysia, they tried to get into Bithynia, but the Spirit of Jesus did not permit them.'[187] Notice that the Spirit of Jesus is the Holy Spirit, who is called in another place the Spirit of the Father, because of the oneness of substance. They want to preach in Asia and they are forbidden by the Holy Spirit. They try to get into Bithynia and the Spirit of Jesus does not permit them. This would be very tyrannical, if He had once bestowed on them the power of the free will of acting or not acting.

(18) He continues: 'The time of ignorance,' he says, 'God has overlooked, but now He has commanded all men everywhere to repent.'[188] Significantly, he has pointed out that the past time under the law was a time of ignorance. Again,

---
183 John 17.12.
184 John 17.15.
185 Cf. Acts 15.39.
186 Acts 16.6.
187 Acts 16.7.
188 Acts 17.30.

he says: 'I shall come to you, if the Lord is willing.'[189] Why did he interject the will of God if he had the power of his own will? The Apostle James says: 'If anyone keeps the whole law, but offends in one point, he has become guilty in all.'[190] Who is there among us who has not sinned sometime in some point? But if he has sinned (and this fact cannot be denied), and is guilty of all sins through one sin, he is saved, not through his own power, but through the mercy of God. 'If anyone has not sinned in word, he is a perfect man.'[191] If you have sinned sometime in speech, where, then, is that perfection that you take for granted, especially, when he continues: 'But the tongue no man can tame, a restless evil, and full of deadly poison'?[192] I ask you to answer me: If the tongue is a restless evil and full of deadly poison, and if no man can tame the tongue, and if you yourself are guilty of this serious offense, where is the possibility of avoiding sins forever?

(19) *The same writer continues.*

'Whence do wars and quarrels come among you? Is it not from the passions which wage war in your members?'[193] You either do not have human members, or, if man cannot exist without members, admit that passions and indulgence wage war in your members. David had said with confidence: 'Prove me, O Lord, and try me; burn my reins and my heart, for thy mercy is before my eyes, and I am well pleased with thy truth';[194] and again: 'But as for me, I have walked in my innocence'; [195] and: 'My foot hath stood in the direct way.'[196] Although the mercy of God mitigated the truth of His judgment, nevertheless, because David was bold enough to make such statements, he is abandoned to his weakness for awhile,

---

189 1 Cor. 4.19.
190 James 2.10.
191 James 3.2.
192 James 3.8.
193 James 4.1.
194 Ps. 25.2, 3.
195 Ps. 25.11.
196 Ps. 25.12.

and, as you say, to the freedom of his will, and, after first committing adultery, and then murder, he subsequently says: 'Have mercy on me, O Lord, according to thy great mercy. And according to the multitude of thy tender mercies, blot out my iniquity.'[197] I do not say this because I would accuse a holy man, of whom it is written that he did all that God desired, but because he compensated for these faults by doing many other good deeds, and was saved by the mercy of God, who judges according to measures and to whom Asaph said: 'Thou wilt feed us with the bread of tears, and give us for our drink tears in measure.'[198] Nor is God so unjust as to condemn sins alone and not remember good deeds. Whence, also, David himself sings in another place: 'In my abundance I said: "I shall never be moved, O Lord; in thy favor thou gavest strength to my beauty. Thou turnest away thy face from me, and I became troubled." '[199] 'For I said I will confess against myself my injustice to the Lord, and thou hast forgiven the wickedness of my sin.'[200] And the command is given to the just man: 'Commit thy way to the Lord, and trust in him, and he will do it. And he will bring forth thy justice as the light, and thy judgment as the noon day.'[201] 'For the salvation of the just is from the Lord,'[202] because there is no health in their flesh in the face of His wrath. And, according to the apostle who had said: 'For in my flesh no good dwells,'[203] they sigh daily, saying: 'My loins are filled with illusions, and there is no health in my flesh.'[204] For He has made our days short, and our substance is as nothing in His sight. 'All things are vanity, every man living,'[205] whether living in the body or living in virtues, and yet all things are

---

197 Ps. 50.3.
198 Ps. 79.6.
199 Ps. 29.7, 8.
200 Ps. 31.5.
201 Ps. 36.5, 6.
202 Ps. 36.39.
203 Rom. 7.18.
204 Ps. 37.8.
205 Ps. 38.6.

vanity. His condition is one of fluctuation and uncertainty, and, while he does not fear, he suffers a storm in fair weather. For, when he was in honor, he did not understand; he hath been compared to senseless beasts, and is made like to them.[206] 'For nothing,' he says, 'shall he save them,'[207] (a reference, undoubtedly, to the just who are saved, not through their own merit, but through the mercy of God), 'and my offenses are not hid from thee.'[208] These words are spoken in the person of Christ. If He, who did not sin nor was guile found in His mouth, suffered for us and bore our sins, how much more ought we to confess our faults? 'My soul,' he says, 'refused to be comforted,'[209] considering the sins that I had committed. 'I remembered God, and was delighted,'[210] knowing that I was to be saved by His mercy. 'I meditated in the night with my own heart, and I swept my soul. And I said: "Now I have begun, this is the change of the right hand of the Most High." '[211] These are the words of a just man who, after meditating in his sleep and feeling pangs of conscience, says in the end: 'Now I have begun,' either to do penance or to enter the threshold of knowledge; and this very change from good to better is a change, not of my own strength, but of the right hand and power of God.

(20) *The power of God is foretold.*

'Mercy shall be built up forever.'[212] For there is no time when mercy shall not be built up in each and every one of the saints, and in those who make the change from sins to virtues. Who is there amongst us who can be delivered from 'the arrow that flieth in the day, of the business that walketh about in the dark'?[213] 'For, lo, the wicked have bent their bows to

---

206 Cf. Ps. 48.21.
207 Ps. 55.8.
208 Ps. 68.6.
209 Ps. 76.3.
210 Ps. 76.4.
211 Ps. 76.7, 11.
212 Ps. 88.3.
213 Ps. 90.5, 6.

shoot in the dark the upright of heart.'[214] They do not want to wound the wicked, but the upright of heart. The arrow flieth in the day in the persons of heretics, in the understanding of Sacred Scripture. The business walketh about in the dark in the persons of the philosophers, who wish to confound the truth with obscurity of language. 'They that are planted in the house of the Lord shall flourish in the courts of the house of our God.'[215] 'They that are planted in the house of the Lord,' are the just, who have been confirmed in the Church. But they shall not flourish in this present world, but in the next, in the courts of the house of the Lord where possession is sure and secure. 'The Lord is compassionate and merciful, long suffering and plenteous in mercy.'[216] 'The Lord is sweet to all and his tender mercies are over all his works.'[217] You hear that His mercies are so great, and do you dare to put your trust in your own virtue? 'Let all thy works, O Lord, confess to thee.'[218] If men are also part of His works, then, all men should confess their sins. We read it said in Samuel about Solomon: 'He shall build a house to my name, and I shall establish the throne of his kingdom forever. I will be to him a father, and he shall be to me a son.'[219] And again: 'If he commit any iniquity, I will correct him with the rod of men, but my mercy I will not take away from him.'[220] After giving thanks to God, David said in conclusion: 'And this is the law of man.'[221] Have recourse, O Lord, always to thy mercy, and sustain the weakness of my flesh by Thy divine assistance. 'What have I to do,' he says, 'with you also, ye sons of Sarvia? Let Semei curse. The Lord hath bid him curse David. And who shall say to

---

214 Ps. 10.2.
215 Ps. 91.14.
216 Ps. 102.8.
217 Ps. 144.9.
218 Ps. 144.10.
219 2 Kings 7.13, 14.
220 2 Kings 7.14, 15.
221 2 Kings 7.19.

him, why hast thou done so?'[222] For the will of God is not to be discussed, but kindly accepted. And in another place: 'The Lord commanded that the profitable counsel of Achitophel be defeated that he might bring evil upon Absalom,'[223] whose counsel was certainly the counsel of God. And for what reason was the power of the free will subverted by a greater power? Jeroboam, who caused Israel to sin, is reproved for having neglected the commandment of the Lord, and it is said to him: 'I gave thee the kingdom of the house of David, and thou hast not been as my servant David, who kept my commandments, and followed me with all his heart, doing that which was well pleasing in my sight.'[224] Therefore, the commandments of God are possible, which we know David had kept; and, yet, we find holy men growing weary in maintaining justice forever.

(21) *Many have been saved through the merit of their fathers.*

Regarding many kings of the line of David, we read that they were saved, not through their own merit, but through the virtues of their father, David, who did that which was pleasing in the sight of God. And we come to Asa, the king of Juda, of whom it is written: 'Asa did that which was right in the sight of the Lord, as did David, his father.'[225] And after a lengthy account of his many virtues, the story is concluded with these words: 'But the high places he did not take away. Nevertheless, the heart of Asa was perfect with God all the days of his life.'[226] You see that he, too, is referred to as just, and his heart, indeed, was perfect with God, and yet he erred in that he did not take away the high places, as, we read, Ezechias and Josias had done. Elias, whom John the Baptist followed in spirit and virtue and who caused fire to fall from heaven and the waters of the Jordan to part by his prayers,

---

[222] 2 Kings 16.10.
[223] 2 Kings 17.14.
[224] 3 Kings 14.8.
[225] 3 Kings 15.11.
[226] 3 Kings 15.14.

was afraid of Jezabel and fled, and, exhausted, he sat down in
the wilderness under a tree and, wearied from walking, he
prayed for death, saying: 'It is enough for me Lord, take away
my soul, for I am no better than my fathers.'[227] Who can deny
that he was a just man? And yet, fear, not to mention of
woman, but of a human being, proceeds from a disturbance of
the soul which cannot be faultless, as David says: 'The Lord
is my helper, I will not fear what man can do unto me.'[228]
Of Josaphat, the king of Juda, it is written: 'And the Lord
was with Josaphat, who walked in the first ways of David, his
father.'[229] From this it is clear that Josaphat possessed the
justice that David first possessed, and that he did not commit
the sins that David later committed. 'He trusted not in
Baalim,' he says, 'but in the God of his father, and walked in
his commandments, and not according to the sins of Israel.
And the Lord established the kingdom in his hand and all
Juda brought presents to Josaphat. And he acquired immense wealth and riches and much glory.'[230] 'And when his
heart had taken courage for the ways of the Lord, he took
away also the high places and the groves out of Juda.'[231] He
was joined by affinity to Achab, a very wicked king. And, when
he returned to Jerusalem after the battle: 'Jehu, the son of
Hanani, the seer, met him and he said to him: "Thou helpest
the ungodly; and thou art joined in friendship with them that
hate the Lord. And therefore thou didst deserve indeed the
wrath of the Lord. But good works are found in thee, because
thou hast taken away the groves out of the land of Juda, and
hast prepared thy heart to seek the Lord." '[232] And, lest we
suppose that the justice he possessed in the past was destroyed
by the fact that he had committed this sin and was reproved
by the prophet, it is written subsequently of Ochozias, his

---

227 3 Kings 19.4.
228 Ps. 117.6.
229 2 Par. 17.3.
230 2 Par. 17.3-5.
231 2 Par. 17.6.
232 2 Par. 19.2, 3.

descendant, that Jehu found him lying in Samaria, and, when he was brought in, he killed him: 'And they buried him,' he says, 'because he was the son of Josaphat, who had sought the Lord with all his heart.'[233] Of Ezechias it is written: 'And he did that which was right in the eyes of the Lord, according to all that David his father had done. He destroyed the high places, and broke the statues in pieces, and burned the groves, and broke the brazen serpent, which Moses had made.'[234] And again: 'He trusted in the Lord the God of Israel, and after him there was none like him among all the kings of Juda who were before him. He stuck to the Lord, and departed not from him, and kept his commandments, which the Lord commanded Moses, and the Lord was with him and in all things to which he went forth, he behaved himself wisely.'[235] And, when Sennacherib, the king of the Assyrians, had taken all of the cities of Juda: 'Ezechias sent messengers to him, to Lachis, saying: "I have sinned, depart from me, and all that thou shalt command of me, I will give." And the king of the Assyrians put a tax upon Ezechias, king of Juda, of three hundred talents of silver, and thirty talents of gold. And Ezechias gave him all the money that was found in the house of the Lord and in the treasure houses of the king. At that time, he broke the doors of the temple of the Lord and the plates of gold and gave them all to the king of the Assyrians.'[236] Although such great demands were placed on him, Ezechias did not hesitate, in the face of stern necessity, to give to the Assyrian king all that he had consecrated to the Lord, and it is said to him: 'I will protect this city for my own sake, and for David my servant's sake.'[237] not for your sake, for you had already performed a noble deed, when 185,000 soldiers of the Assyrian army were laid low and slaughtered by an angel.

---

233 2 Par. 22.9.
234 4 Kings 18.3, 4.
235 4 Kings 18.5-7.
236 4 Kings 18.14-16.
237 4 Kings 20.6.

(22) *The examples of the Kings Ezechias and Josias.*
The following words, related by Scripture, should also be very carefully noted: 'Ezechias was sick unto death. And Isaia the son of Amos came to him, saying: "Give charge concerning thy house, for thou shalt die." And he turned his face to the wall and prayed to the Lord, saying: "I beseech thee, O Lord, remember how I walked in thy sight, in truth and with a perfect heart and had done that which was good in thy sight." And Ezechias wept with much weeping.'[238] Ezechias was certainly a just man and perfect of heart. He was about to go to the Lord; he should not have wept. Do you want to know the reason for his tears? If you consider that he was human, you will not wonder at the reasons for his grief. For no man goes before the judgment of God without trepidation, being conscious of his sins. And after he had wept, the word of the Lord came to the Prophet Isaia, saying: 'Go back, and tell Ezechias the captain of my people.'[239] He, who had received his death notice, is called the captain of God, because he had humbled himself in all humility. 'Thus saith the Lord,' he says, 'the God of David thy father: "I have heard thy prayer, and I have seen thy tears." '[240] His time of life is prolonged and he is delivered out of the hands of the Assyrians; and he still demands a sign that he might believe the truth of God's promise. Such an action is an indication, at any rate, of little faith. The king of Babylon also sent messages and ambassadors to congratulate him on the recovery of his physical health; and he showed them all the storehouses of his aromatical spices, and of his gold and silver, and the storehouses of his vessels. 'There was nothing,' he says, 'that Ezechias did not show them in the house of the Lord and in all his dominions.'[241] From this we see that even the vessels of the temple were shown to the ambassadors of Babylon. Whence, the wrath of God is also enkindled, and it is subse-

---
238 4 Kings 20.1-3.
239 4 Kings 20.5.
240 *Ibid.*
241 Isa. 39.2; 4 Kings 20.13.

quently revealed to him by the prophecy of Isaia: 'Of thy sons, they shall be eunuchs, and all the vessels of the temple shall be carried into Babylon.'[242] Whence, also, it is written in the book of Days: 'Ezechias fell because his heart was lifted up.'[243] Certainly, no one but the ungodly will deny that Ezechias was a just man. You may say: 'He sinned in certain things and, therefore, he ceased to be just.' But Scripture does not say this. For he did not lose the title of just because he committed small sins, but he possessed the title of just because he performed many good deeds. I say all this to prove, with the testimonies of Sacred Scripture, that the just are not sinners, simply because they have sinned on occasions, but they remain just because they flourish in many virtues. Of Josias it is written: 'He did that which was right in the sight of the Lord, and walked in the way of David his father. He declined neither to the right nor to the left';[244] and yet, although he was a just man, in a time of need and dire necessity, he sent Helcias to Olda, the prophetess, the wife of Sellum, the son of Thecuath, the son of Hasra, keeper of the wardrobe. 'And she dwelt,' he says, 'in Jerusalem in the Second part,'[245] (a reference, undoubtedly, to that part of the city which is enclosed by an inner wall). 'And she answered: "Thus saith the Lord the God of Israel: Go and tell the man that sent you to me."'[246] There is contained in these words a secret reproof of the king, and priests, and all men, because never was there any saint found among men who could predict the future. Finally, Josias is killed by Pharao, the king of Egypt, because he would not hearken to the words of the Lord from the mouth of the Prophet Jeremia, or, as it is written in the Paralipomenon: 'Josias would not return, but prepared to fight against him, and hearkened not to the words

---

[242] Isa. 39.6, 7; 4 Kings 20.17, 18.
[243] 2 Par. 32.25.
[244] 2 Par. 34.2.
[245] 2 Par. 34.22.
[246] 2 Par. 34.23.

of Nechao from the mouth of God.'[247] And it is stated: 'And he died and was buried in the monument of his fathers. And all Juda and Jerusalem mourned for him, particularly Jeremias, whose lamentations for Josias all the singing men and singing women repeat unto this day. And it became like a law in Israel: "Behold it is found written in the Lamentations." '[248]

(23) *Other examples of holy men in Scripture.*

I suppose that it is a sin not to hearken to the words of God from the mouth of any person whatsoever. Of Jeremia himself it is written, although there are many who take these words as spoken, in a spiritual sense, of the Lord, Savior: 'The breath of our face Christ the Lord is taken in our sins, to whom we said: "Under thy shadow we shall live among the Gentiles." '[249] Moses, to whom the Lord spoke face to face[250] and his soul was saved, offended at the waters of contradiction, and he did not deserve to enter the promised land with his brother, Aaron. Of them the psalmist also sings: 'Their judges falling upon the rock have been swallowed up. They shall hear my words, for they have pleased.'[251] And this is the meaning: 'Moses and Aaron, the judges of nations of the Jews, have been swallowed up by the sin of the people on the rock, from whence there flowed rivers of waters, and they themselves were certainly just, and hearkened to the words of God which are very sweet of themselves.' Moreover, the passage continues about the cadavers in the solitude of the dead: 'As when the thickness of the earth is broken up upon the ground, our homes are scattered by the side of hell.'[252] In Osee, God says: 'I will betroth thee to me in justice and judgment,'[253] and He immediately adds, 'and in loving kind-

---

247 2 Par. 35.22.
248 2 Par. 35.24, 25.
249 Lam. 4.20.
250 Cf. Exod. 33.11.
251 Ps. 140.6.
252 Ps. 140.7.
253 Osee 2.21.

ness, and in tender mercies,'[254] 'and in faith,'[255] so that Israel may know from the gift of the giver that He is the Lord Himself. In the same book, it is written: 'I am God and not man, the Holy One in the midst of thee, and I will not enter into the city,'[256] into the den, to be sure, of vices. He Himself is the only one who does not enter into the city which Cain built in the name of his son, Enoch. All of this is chanted daily by the lips of the priests: *ho mónos anamártētos,* which in our language is translated as *qui solus est sine peccato.* To impute such praise to God, according to your view, is vain, if it is shared in common with others. For, according to Amos, we have turned judgment into bitterness, and the fruit of justice into wormwood.[257] The sailors and passengers in the book of Jona say: 'We beseech thee, O Lord, do not destroy us on account of this man and lay not upon us innocent blood, for thou, O Lord, hast done as it pleased thee.'[258] They do not know the reasons why the prophet, a fugitive slave, deserved to be punished; and yet they justify God, and acknowledge the blood of him whose deeds they do not know to be innocent. And in conclusion, they say: 'Thou, O Lord, hast done as it pleased thee.' They do not question the justice of the judgment of God, but acknowledge the veracity of the just judge. Michea proclaims tearfully: 'The holy man is perished out of the earth and there is none upright among men. They all lie in wait for blood, every one hunteth his brother to death. The evil of their hands they call good.'[259] And again: 'He that is best among them is as a brier, and he that is righteous as the thorn of the hedge.'[260] This is justice among men, not to trust, according to the words of that same prophet, a friend, or a spouse, or sons, because, 'a man's

---

254 *Ibid.*
255 Osee 2.21, 22.
256 Osee 11.9.
257 Cf. Amos 6.13.
258 Jona 1.14.
259 Mich. 7.2, 3.
260 Mich. 7.4.

enemies are those of his own household.'[261] This view is confirmed even by the word of the Lord.[262] Whence the following counsel is given by the same prophet: 'I will show thee, O man, what is good and what the Lord requireth of thee; verily to do judgment and to love mercy, and to walk carefully with thy God.'[263] Did he say, 'to have equality with God,' and not this, which is most important, 'to walk carefully with thy God,' so that you will never be secure, so that you will guard your heart by being ever watchful, so that you will be careful, since you walk in the midst of snares, and proceed beneath battlements on walls, so that you will reflect daily on these words: 'They have laid for me a stumbling-block by the way side'?[264] 'God resists the proud, but gives grace to the humble.'[265]

(24) *He who is cautious can avoid sins for awhile.*

He who is cautious and wary can avoid sins for awhile, but he who is secure in his own justice opposes God, and, deprived of His help, he is subject to the snares of the enemy. 'Let rottenness,' says Habacuc, 'enter into my bones and swarm under me, that I may rest in the day of tribulation, that I may go up to my people that are girded.'[266] He prays earnestly for tribulations, and trials, and affliction of soul so that, in the next world, he may join the company of those who are already reigning with Christ. It is clear from all this that here, in this life, there is strife and contention, and, in the next world, there is victory. Jesu, the high priest, son of Josedec, which means 'the just of the Lord,' is described as being clothed in filthy garments, who has not committed any sin and yet has borne our sins, on whose right hand stood Satan to be his adversary.[267] After the

---
261 Mich. 7.6.
262 Cf. Matt. 10.36.
263 Mich. 6.8.
264 Ps. 139.6.
265 James 4.6.
266 Hab. 3.16.
267 Cf. Zach. 3.1.

contest has been finished and victory has been won, it is said to him: 'Take away the filthy garments from him';[268] and: 'Behold, I have taken from you your iniquity';[269] and Jovinian's heir says: 'I am completely without sin; I do not have filthy garments; I am guided by my own will; I am greater than the apostle. He does what he does not wish, and what he wishes that he does not do; I do what I wish, and what I do not wish that I do not do; the kingdom of heaven has been prepared for me, nay rather, I myself have prepared it for myself with my own virtues. My group and I are the only ones who are not guilty of the sin of which Adam is guilty, and the others who believe that they are guilty, according to the likeness of the transgression of Adam. Others, who are cloistered in cells and do not see women, because they are miserable and do not hearken to my words, are tormented with desires. Even if I am walled in by armies of women, I do not have desires. For it is said of me: "Holy stones shall be rolled over the land,"[270] and, therefore, I am not afflicted, because I proclaim the victory of Christ through the power of the free will.' Let us hearken to God, as He proclaims through Isaia: 'O my people, they that call thee blessed lead you astray, throw you down headlong.'[271] Who is more guilty of throwing the people of God down headlong? He who relies on the power of the free will, and scorns the help of the Creator, and is secure in his own will, or he who fears the judgment of God at every thought of His precepts? God says to men of this sort: 'Woe to you that are wise in your own eyes and prudent in your own judgment.'[272] According to the Hebrew, Isaia cries out in anguish, and says: 'Woe is me because I have held my peace, because I am a man of unclean lips and I dwell in the midst of a people that hath unclean lips, and I have seen with my eyes the Lord

---

[268] Zach. 3.4.
[269] Zach. 3.5.
[270] Zach. 9.16 (Septuagint).
[271] Isa. 3.12.
[272] Isa. 5.21.

of hosts!'²⁷³ Because of his virtues, he deserved to enjoy the sight of God, and, because of his awareness of his sins, he confessed that his lips were unclean. Not because he had said anything that was contrary to the will of God, but because he had held his peace, deterred either by fear or modesty, and because he had not exercised the prerogative of a prophet, of condemning a sinful nation. When we, who flatter the rich and accept persons of sins, rebuke sinners, is it for the sake of base gain? Unless, perhaps, we speak with complete frankness to those whose wealth we stand in need of. We may act otherwise; we may refrain from every type of sin, but, if we keep silent about the truth, we are certainly committing a sin. Although in the Septuagint version it is not written, 'because I have held my peace,' but 'because I have been undone,' by the awareness, to be sure, of sins, so that the words of the prophet might be fulfilled: 'I am turned in my anguish, whilst the thorn is fastened.'²⁷⁴ He is pierced by the thorn of sin; you are decked with the flowers of virtues. 'The moon shall blush,' he says, 'and the sun shall be ashamed, when the Lord shall visit upon the host of heaven on high,'²⁷⁵ as it is written in another place: 'Even the stars are not pure in his sight';²⁷⁶ and: 'In his angels he found wickedness.'²⁷⁷ The moon blushes; the sun is ashamed; heaven is covered with coarse goat's hair; and we shall face the majesty of the judge without trepidation, and cheerfully as if we were free of all fault, when mountains shall melt away, those, to be sure, that stood erect and proud, as well as the whole host of the heavens, whether stars or angelic dignities; and the heavens shall be folded together as a book, and all their host shall fall down like leaves.²⁷⁸

---

273 Isa. 6.5.
274 Ps. 31.4.
275 Isa. 24.23, 21.
276 Job 25.5.
277 Job 4.18.
278 Cf. Isa. 34.3, 4

(25) *The justice of God.*

'For my sword,' he says, 'is inebriated in heaven, and it shall now come upon Edom.'[279] The sword of God is inebriated in heaven; and will your kingdom be secure in its holiness? It shall come upon Edom, which means either 'relating to blood,' or 'relating to earth,' so that we may know, on the authority of the prophet, that the whole earth stands in need of judgment. Whence the passage continues: 'There is a victim of the Lord in Bosra,' (which means 'flesh'), 'and a great slaughter in the land of Edom,'[280] that is to say, 'in blood,' according to what is stated by the apostle: 'Flesh and blood shall not possess the kingdom of heaven.'[281] 'Woe to him that gainsayeth his potter, woe to him that saith to his father: "Why didst thou beget me?" and to his mother: "Why didst thou bring me forth?"'[282] These words apply to those who say: 'Why was I created such that I could not be free from sin forever? Why was I fashioned such a vessel that I could not endure hard like adamant instead of being fictile and easily broken whenever touched?' 'All we like sheep have gone astray and the Lord hath borne the sins of us all.'[283] For He has looked about, and sought carefully, and found no one who would judge justly, who would do His will in all things. And for that reason, He offered His arm for salvation and saved all things by His justice, that the whole world might be subject to God and preserved by His mercy. For we are become unclean, not a few of us, but all of us. 'All our works according to the law are reckoned as the rag of a menstruous woman.'[284] In Ezechiel, God speaks to Jerusalem: 'Thou wast perfect through my beauty.'[285] And this is the meaning of the text: 'Thou wast perfect not through your own works, not through your own knowledge and the boast-

---
279 Isa. 34.5.
280 Isa. 34.6.
281 1 Cor. 15.50.
282 Isa. 45.9, 10.
283 Isa. 53.6.
284 Isa. 64.5.
285 Ezech. 16.14.

ing of your heart, but through my beauty which I had put on
you freely through my mercy.' Finally, He says to her later
on, when she is saved, not through her own merit, but
through His mercy: 'I will remember my covenant with thee
in the days of thy youth, and I will establish with thee an
everlasting covenant, and thou shalt remember thy ways and
be ashamed.'[286] And again: 'I will re-establish my covenant
with thee and thou shalt know that I am the Lord, that thou
mayest remember and be confounded and mayest no more
open thy mouth because of thy confusion, when I shall be
pacified toward thee for all that thou hast done, saith the
Lord God.'[287] Thus, it is clearly indicated by these divine
words what was meant in another place by the statement:
'And though cleansing you he shall not make thee innocent';[288]
because even the just, being restored to their former state
after committing sin, do not dare to open their mouth, but
say with the apostle: 'I am not worthy to be called an apostle,
because I persecuted the Church of God.'[289] Finally, in another place, God also says through the same prophet to those
who have received His mercy: 'And you shall remember your
ways and all your wicked doings, with which you have been
defiled; and you shall be displeased with yourselves in your
sight for all your wicked deeds which you committed. And
you shall know that I am the Lord when I shall have done
well by you, for my own name's sake, and not according to
your evil ways, nor according to your very wicked deeds.'[290]
Let us blush and say what those say who have already obtained
their rewards; let us, who are sinners on earth and encased
in this fragile and mortal body, say what we know the saints
are saying in heaven, even though they have been endowed
with incorruptibility and immortality. 'And you say,' he says,
'The way of the Lord is not right, whereas your own ways

---
286 Ezech. 16.60, 61.
287 Ezech. 16.62, 63.
288 Nah. 1.3.
289 1 Cor. 15.9.
290 Ezech. 20.43, 44.

are perverse.'[291] It is arrogance, characteristic of the Pharisees, to calumniate His mercy. The sons of Sadoc, priests of the mystical temple, which means the Church, do not go forth among the people in the garments wherein they ministered,[292] lest they, who are sanctified, be defiled by human intercourse. And do you think that you, who mingle with the common people and are one of the crowd, are clean?

(26) *From Jeremia.*

Let us run briefly through Jeremia, the prophet, and quote the sense of his words, rather than his words. 'Go about the streets of Jerusalem,' he says, 'and seek in the broad streets thereof, if you can find a man that liveth according to justice and faith, and I will be merciful for his sake. Although they say: "The Lord liveth," they swear falsely, and this too is a lie.'[293] He condemns the sacrifices for sins; he decries the eating of the sacrificial victims by those who offer the sacrifices, saying that, when He led their fathers out of the land of Egypt, He did not command them to offer such sacrifices. For He did not give this command willingly, but only as a counterpart to the sacrifices offered to idols, for He would rather have them offer victims to Him than to demons. They have all abandoned Him; there is no one who speaks well, and who does penance for his sins.[294] They follow their own wills like a horse ready for battle.[295] They bend their tongue as a bow;[296] they invent everything and there is no truth in them. He also commands them to avoid the snares of friends and not trust any of the neighbors. For everyone lies in wait for his friends and brother is deceived by brother; and they do these things, not through the evil of nature, but their own will, because they have taught their tongue to lie, and they are carried headlong unto injustice.[297] 'If the Ethiopian,'

---

291 Ezech. 18.25; 33.17.
292 Cf. Ezech. 44.19.
293 Jer. 5.1, 2.
294 Cf. Jer. 8.6.
295 *Ibid.*
296 Cf. Jer. 9.2.
297 Cf. Jer. 9.4, 5.

he says, 'will change his skin, or the leopard his spots, you also will be able to do well, when you have learned what is evil.'[298] Therefore, the Ethiopian skin and the spots of the leopards are matters of learning, not of nature, and are teachable and learnable; but the inborn vice of evil cannot be erased, except by Him with whom all things are possible.

(27) Whence he says to Him who alone is the true physician: 'Heal me, O Lord, and I shall be healed; save me and I shall be saved; thou art my praise and my hope.'[299] For if I consider my condition and my unhappiness, there is nothing else that I can say except this: 'Cursed be the man that brought the tidings to my father, saying: "Behold a man-child is born to thee!" Let that man be as the cities which the Lord hath overthrown. For why did I not die forthwith in the womb, and my mother might have been my grave and her womb an everlasting conception? Why came I out of the womb to see labor and sorrow, and that my days should be spent in misery?'[300] He is so secure in his condition, and he places so much trust in his strength that he prefers death to life. For he was fully conscious of his own wound, and the power of Him, from whom nothing can be hidden, who says through the prophet: 'I am a God at hand and not a God far off.'[301] For nobody can escape the notice of Him who fills heaven and earth, and nobody can conceal from Him the secrets of his heart. He who examines the reins sees within. And that we may know that every good deed that we do is imputed to God: 'I will plant them,' He says, 'that they may not be plucked up, and I will give them knowledge and understanding, that they may know me.'[302] If knowledge and understanding are given by God, and the knowledge of God springs radically from Him who is the object of knowledge, where is that very haughty boasting of yours about the free will?

---
298 Jer. 13.23.
299 Jer. 17.14.
300 Jer. 20.15-18.
301 Jer. 23.23.
302 Jer. 24.6, 7.

We want to know our condition; let us listen to history. When Joachim, the king of Juda, and all his associates and his princes heard the words of Uria, they wanted to kill him.[303] When Uria found this out, he was afraid and fled to Egypt.[304] Why was he, who interpreted the judgment of the Lord and who knew full well that he was proclaiming the will of the Lord, afraid of death? Do we spurn the help of God in every single deed that we do, and have no regard for His will in all that we do, when we read that holy men stood in need of help, even at the hands of human beings? Jeremia is in danger of his life; and it is clearly stated that it was the hand of Ahicam, the son of Saphan, that saved him from being delivered into the power of the people and being stoned to death.[305]

(28) *The grace of the Gospel.*

There is promise of the grace of the Gospel, when the rites of the law and the heavy burden of the ancient precepts have been abolished; and God gives promise of a law, so that all may know him, from the least of them even to the greatest, saying: 'I will forgive their sins and I will remember their iniquities no more.'[306] However, He indicates, in the following text, the kind of justice that was possessed by holy men under the old law: 'The children of Israel and the children of Juda have continually done evil in my sight, from their youth even till the present day, and the city of Jerusalem hath provoked me to wrath from the beginning of its foundation even till the day of its overthrow.'[307] Examine this passage carefully. If you join the beginning and the end, you see that every moment of the intervening time is deserving of blame. Jeremia, who was sanctified in the womb before he was born,[308] who was a virgin, a prophet of the Old Testament,

---

303 Cf. Jer. 26.21.
304 *Ibid.*
305 Cf. Jer. 26.24.
306 Jer. 31.34.
307 Jer. 32.30-32.
308 Cf. Jer. 1.5.

is very much afraid of Sedecia, and he tearfully pleads with him, saying: 'Now, therefore, my lord king, hear my supplication and let my petition prevail in thy sight; do not send me back into the house of Jonathan the scribe, lest I die there.'[309] O prophet, why are you frightened by a godless king? Why are you afraid of a man who, you know, shall die forthwith? Do you, whom Paradise awaits, stand in awe of prison walls? He will reply to me: 'I am human, encased in a mortal and corruptible flesh; I feel pain; I recoil from tortures, which even my Lord shall feel for my salvation. God has pity on the human race, and He does not wish to destroy what he has created.' 'Fear thou not, Jacob,' saith the Lord, 'for I am with thee, and I will utterly consume all the nations, among which I have scattered thee; but I will not utterly consume thee, but I shall chastise thee in judgment, and I shall have pity on thee, so that I shall not leave thee innocent.'[310]

(29) *We are to be saved by the mercy of God.*

Whence, also, we say that the holy men are just, and that they are made pleasing to God after their sins, not only through their own merits, but through the mercy of Him to whom every creature is subject and stands in need of His mercy. Let heretics hearken, who are lifted up by pride, and say: 'We have taken unto us horns by our own strength.'[311] Let them hearken to what Moab heard said to him: 'We heard the pride of Moab, he is exceedingly proud. "His haughtiness and his arrogance and his pride and the loftiness of his heart I know," saith the Lord, "because his strength is not according to the loftiness thereof." '[312] And it is said to men of this kind: 'But their enemies,' (referring, undoubtedly, to the flock of the Lord), 'proclaim, saying: "We have not sinned, because they have sinned against the beauty of justice, and against the hope of their fathers." '[313] Do you

---
309 Jer. 37.20.
310 Jer. 30.10, 11.
311 Amos 6.14.
312 Jer. 48.29, 30.
313 Jer. 50.7.

want to know when all sins shall cease? Hearken to the same prophet: 'At that time,' saith the Lord, 'the iniquity of Israel shall be sought for and there shall be none, and the sin of Juda and there shall none be found.'[314] Why, I ask you? He continues: 'For I shall be merciful to them.'[315] But where there is mercy, sin preceded it. Delete, therefore, the word, 'possibility,' and I shall concede that all things subsist through the grace of God. 'It is good to wait with silence for the salvation of the Lord.'[316] It is good for a man to put his mouth in the dust, to present his cheek to him that striketh him, to be filled with reproaches, to hope in the Lord.[317] For if He hath cast off, He will also have mercy, according to the multitude of His mercies; for He hath not willingly humiliated nor cast off the children of men.[318] It is futile for man to murmur because of his sins. Let us search our ways, and seek and return to the Lord. Let us lift up our hearts with our hands to the Lord in heaven and say to Him: 'We have done wickedly, and provoked thee to wrath; therefore thou art inexorable.'[319]

(30) *We do not know the reasons of the Divine Will.*

Daniel, the prophet, says to Nabuchodonosor, that the Most High rules in the kingdom of men, and He will give it to whomsoever it shall please Him, and He will appoint the lowest and the basest man over it.[320] Ask Him the reason why he appoints the lowest and the basest man as king, and does what He wills; question the justice of the will of Him, of whom it is written: 'He raiseth up the needy from the earth, and lifts up the poor out of the dung-hills, that he may place him with the princes, with the princes of his people.'[321] Is He, perhaps, according to your view, seeking glory and

---

314 Jer. 50.20.
315 *Ibid.*
316 Lam. 3.26.
317 Cf. Lam. 3.25, 29, 30.
318 Cf. Lam. 3.32, 33.
319 Lam. 3.42.
320 Cf. Dan. 4.14.
321 Ps. 112.7, 8.

popular acclaim without judgment and justice, so that he raises the lowly to royal power and humiliates the powerful in exchange? Hearken to the prophet, who says: 'All the inhabitants of the earth are reputed as nothing before him.'[322] For He has done whatsoever He wished in heaven and on earth, and there is no one who will resist His will, or who can say to Him: 'Why hast thou done this?' His works are all true, and His ways justice, and He can humiliate the proud. Antiochus Epiphanius, a very cruel king, overturned the altar and caused justice itself to be trampled underfoot, because it was permitted by the Lord; the reason given is: 'because of many sins.'[323] Therefore, he did not do simply what he himself wanted to do, but what God permitted, because of the sins of the people. Moreover, the passage continues, stating that he did not do this by his own strength, but at the command of Him who ordered it to be done. Moreover, as far as the words are concerned that David uses in his prayers, such as: 'We have sinned, we have done wickedly, we have acted unjustly, we have departed from your commandments and your justices,'[324] and others like them, you are wont to say that he,[325] as well as Daniel, and all the prophets, spoke them, not in reference to themselves who were holy men, but rather in the name of the people. Daniel himself will reply to this view of yours, and will say: 'While I was yet praying and confessing my sins and the sins of the people of Israel.'[326] Therefore, you see that he prayed to God and poured out his supplications in the sight of the Lord, his God, as much for his own sins as for the sins of the people. Do you want to know again when sin and iniquity will have an end? Although the construction put on these words by authors vary, hearken to the same prophet: 'Seventy weeks are shortened

---

322 Dan. 4.32.
323 2 Mach. 5.17.
324 Dan. 3.29.
325 All the MSS lack David, but the editor believes that David probably should be inserted here.
326 Dan. 9.20.

upon thy people and thy holy city, that transgression may be finished and sin may have an end and iniquity may be abolished and everlasting justice may be brought.'[327] Therefore, until that end shall be reached, and this corruptibility and mortality shall be changed to incorruptibility and immortality, it needs must be that we be subject to sin, not because of any fault of nature and creation, as you falsely charge, but because of the weakness and changeableness of the human will, that changes from moment to moment; because God alone is immutable. You ask: 'Wherein did Abel, Enoch, Josue, and the son of Nun, Eliseus, and the other holy man sin?' There is no need to look for a knot in a bulrush. Would that I could keep secret even the manifest sins! If you wish to hear the truth from me, I do not know. 'I have nothing,' he says, 'on my conscience, yet I am not thereby justified.'[328] 'Man seeth the face, but God beholdeth the heart.'[329] In His knowledge and in His sight, no man is justified. Whence, also, Paul boldly says: 'All have sinned and have need of the glory of God';[330] and: 'God has shut up all in sin, that he may have mercy upon all,'[331] and the other passages that we have often quoted.

---

327 Dan. 9.24.
328 1 Cor. 4.4.
329 1 Kings 16.7.
330 Rom. 3.23.
331 Rom. 11.32.

Book Three

(1) *Baptism forgives past sins only.*
CRITOBULUS. I found delight in the flood of words poured out by you, of which it is written: 'In the multitude of words you shall not want sin.'[1] But what has all this to do with the point at issue? You will certainly admit that those who have received the baptism of Christ have no sin. And if they are without sin, they are just. And once they are just, they can preserve their justice forever, if they act cautiously; and, consequently, they can avoid all sin.
ATTICUS. Are you not ashamed to adopt the view of Jovinian[2] that has been refuted and condemned? And he also relies on these testimonies and these arguments of yours, or should I say, you are following views that he has concocted, desiring to teach in the East views that have been condemned sometime ago at Rome, and more recently in Africa.[3] Therefore, read the

---

1 Prov. 10.19.
2 Jovinian had spread at Rome the heretical views that all those who have received baptism with full faith could not sin any more; that all those who have kept the grace of baptism would receive the same reward in heaven; and that all sins were equally grave. These views did much harm among the faithful, for Jovinian was, in effect, teaching salvation by faith alone. The whole Christian system of morality was at stake. The danger was realized and the errors were denounced to Pope Siricius by Pammachius. In a Roman synod held in the year 390, the Pope condemned Jovinian, and this decision was confirmed in a small council held at Milan in the same year. Cf. J. Tixeront, *History of Dogmas* 2 (translated from the fifth French edition by H. L. B.; St. Louis 1923) 244-245. Pammachius sent the treatise of Jovinian to St. Jerome who answered it in the year 393 in his work *Contra Jovinianum*. In book two of this work, St. Jerome answered the proposition of Jovinian that all those who have been baptized with full faith could not sin any more.
3 St. Jerome is here referring to the African synod held in the year 411, in which Celestius and Pelagius were condemned and excommunicated. Cf. above, Introduction, pp. 223-229.

answer that was given to him and consider it as an answer given to you. For in discussing doctrines and questions, we must consider not the person, but the point at issue. And yet you should know this, that baptism forgives past sins and does not safeguard future justice, which is preserved through labor, and industry, and diligence, and, above all, in every instance by the mercy of God, so that it is ours to ask and His to grant what we ask for; ours to make the beginning, His to accomplish it; ours to offer what we can, His to complete what is beyond our power. 'For unless the Lord build the house, they labor in vain that build it. Unless the Lord keep the city, he watcheth in vain that keepeth it.'[4] Whence, also, the apostle commands: 'So run as to obtain it. All indeed run, but one receives the crown.'[5] And, in the Psalm, it is written: 'O Lord, thou hast crowned us as with a shield of thy good will.'[6] For our victory and the crown of our victory are prepared for us by His protection and shield; and we so run in this world as to obtain it in the next; and, there, he will receive the crown who has emerged victor in this world; and it is said to us after baptism: 'Behold, thou art cured. Sin no more, lest something worse befall thee.'[7] And: 'Do you not know that you are the temple of God and that the Spirit of God dwells in you? If anyone destroys the temple of God, him will God destroy.'[8] And in another place: 'The Lord is with you as long as you are with him. If you abandon him, he also will abandon you.'[9] Is there anyone, in your opinion, who can preserve the purity of Christ in the sanctuary of his temple and keep the serenity of his temple from being clouded over with gloom and sadness? We cannot keep constantly the same expression on our face, as philosophers falsely boast Socrates was able to do; how much less the same spirit? As the faces of men are many, so

---

4 Ps. 126.1.
5 1 Cor. 9.24, 25.
6 Ps. 5.13.
7 John 5.14.
8 1 Cor. 3.16, 17.
9 2 Par. 12.5.

also are their hearts different. If it were possible for the waters of baptism to keep us continually submerged, the sins that hover over us would never touch us; the Holy Spirit would protect us. But the enemy wars against us and never retreats, even in defeat, but always lies in ambush, ready to shoot his arrows at the upright of heart from his secret hiding place.

(2) *From the Gospel according to the Hebrews.*

In the Gospel according to the Hebrews,[10] which was written, to be sure, in Chaldaic-Syriac, but transliterated in Hebrew which the Nazarenes use even to the present day (the Gospel according to the Apostles or, as many suppose, according to Matthew, which exists also in the library of Caesarea), the following account is told: 'Behold the mother of the Lord and His brethren said to Him: "John the Baptist baptizes unto the remission of sins. Let us go and be baptized by him." But He said to them: "What sin have I committed that I should go and be baptized by him? Unless perchance this very statement that I made is ignorance."' And in the same volume: 'If thy brother has sinned in word,' He says, 'and he clears himself before thee, forgive him seven times in the day. Simon, His disciple, said to Him: "Seven times in the day?" The Lord answered and said to him: "I even say to you, seventy times seven."' For the word of sin was found even among the prophets after they were anointed by the Holy Spirit. Ignatius,

---

10 The Gospel according to the Hebrews is known to us only through stray references in ancient ecclesiastical writers, such as St. Irenaeus, Clement of Alexandria, Origen, Eusebius, St. Epiphanius, St. Jerome, and others. About the year 390, St. Jerome translated this Gospel from Aramaic into Greek and Latin (*De viris illustribus* 2). Both versions, together with the original, have fallen prey to the ravages of time. As to its contents, we may gather from St. Jerome and the other witnesses that it was closely related to the canonical Gospel of Matthew, though not identical with it. They were alike in their general disposition, and in many other more or less characteristic details. It was the unanimous opinion of the entire ancient Church that the Gospel of Matthew had been composed in Aramaic. Hence, it is not easy to avoid the hypothesis that the Gospel according to the Hebrews was merely a revision and enlargement of the Gospel of Matthew. Cf. O. Bardenhewer, *Patrology* (translated from the second edition by Thomas J. Shahan; St. Louis 1908) 90-91.

an apostolic man and a martyr, writes boldly: 'The Lord chose the Apostles who were sinners above all men.' The psalmist sings of their speedy conversion: 'Their infirmities were multiplied, afterwards they made haste.'[11] If you do not accept the authority of these testimonies, as least accept their antiquity as referring to the views held by all the churchmen. Assume that a man who has been baptized has been carried off by death, either immediately, or within the day itself, and I shall concede to you, a concession that I need not make, that he has not thought or said anything, in which he might have sinned, through error or ignorance. Will he be without sin because he appears, not to have overcome, but rather to have avoided sin, and not rather because he was freed from the prison of sins through the mercy of God and he went to the Lord? We also say that God can do what He will, and that man cannot be without sin of himself and of his own will, as you assert. But, if he can be, it is pointless on your part to add at this point, even the word, 'grace,' which he does not need if he has the power. But if he cannot be without sin, without the grace of God, it was foolish on your part to have said that he could be what he cannot be. For any act that depends on the will of someone else cannot be imputed to him who, you contend, can accomplish it, but rather to him without whom it is clear that he cannot accomplish it.

(3) *The great difference between being and possibility.*
CRITOBULUS. I ask you: What is the meaning of this perversity, or should I say, this irrational argumentation of yours? Do you not even grant that he, who has emerged from the waters of baptism, is without sin?
ATTICUS. Either I cannot express clearly in words my views, or you are too slow to understand my explanation.
CRITOBULUS. How so?
ATTICUS. Recall the statement that you made and the statement that I am making. You laid down the proposition that

---

11 Ps. 15.4.

man could be without sin if wanted to. My reply is that this is impossible with man, not because he is free from sin immediately after baptism, but because that period of time during which he is without sin is imputed, not to human power, but to the grace of God. Therefore, delete the word 'possibility,' and I shall concede that he is without sin. For how can he be without sin who cannot be so of himself? Or what kind of sinlessness is it that comes to an end at the very moment of the death of this body? Or, to be sure, if his life is prolonged, he is subject to the danger of sin and ignorance.

CRITOBULUS. You are confronting me with the art of the dialectician, instead of speaking with Christian simplicity, creating many problems for me with your distinctions between the notion of being and the possibility of being.

ATTICUS. Am I the one who is sporting with the tricks of language, when this whole problem originated in your own workshop? For you say, not that man is without sin, but that he can be without sin; whereas I, on the contrary, grant what you have denied, namely, that man is without sin by the grace of God, and yet he cannot be without sin of himself.

CRITOBULUS. It is futile, then, to give us commandments if we cannot fulfill them.

ATTICUS. No one doubts that God imposed commandments that are possible. But because men do not fulfill what is possible, for that reason, the whole world is subject to God and stands in need of His mercy. Or, to be sure, if you can show me an individual who has fulfilled all things, then, you will be able to prove that there is a man who does not stand in need of His mercy. For everything that is possible takes place in three periods of time, either in the past, or in the present, or in the future. When you made the assertion that man could be without sin if he wanted to, you should prove that this has taken place in the past, or, to be sure, that it is taking place at the present time; as for the future, we shall see about that subsequently. But if you cannot produce any individual who is either completely without sin or who was without all sin, it remains that our disputation is concerned only with the future. In the meantime, as far as the two periods of time, the past and the present, are concerned, you are forced to yield. If there will be some individual subsequently who is greater than the patriarchs, the prophets, and the apostles, and is free of sin, then, you should convince the people of the future, in the future, if you can.

(4) *It is in the power of man not to sin for a time.*
CRITOBULUS. Make any statement you want, offer any arguments you like, you shall never wrest from me the free will which God has granted to me, once and for all, nor will you be able to take away from me the power to act, if I want to, that God has bestowed on me.

ATTICUS. As an example, we shall use just one testimony: 'I have found David, the son of Jesse, a man after my own heart, who will do all that I desire.'[12] There is no doubt that David is a holy man; and yet he, who was chosen to do all that God desired, is reproved for some of his actions. It was surely possible for him, who was chosen for the purpose to do all that God desired. It is not God who is at fault, who foretold that he would fulfill all the desires of His commandments, but he who did not do what was foretold he would do. For he did not say that He had found a man who would continually do all the wishes of His command, but one who would simply do all that He desired. We also say that it is possible for man not to sin for a while, depending on the circumstances and the weakness of the body, so long as his spirit is attentive, so long as the strings of the lyre are not slackened by any defect. But, if he relaxes for even a moment, even as a man rowing his boat upstream immediately slips back if he relaxes his hands and is carried by the current of the river in a direction he does not want to go, so also the state of man, if it relaxes for even a moment, gets to know its weakness and realizes that it cannot do much of itself. Do you suppose that at the time that the

---

12 Acts 13.22; Ps. 88.21.

Apostle Paul wrote these words: 'When thou comest, bring with thee the overcoat' (or cloak), 'that I left at Troas with Carpus, and the books, especially the parchments,'[13] he was thinking about the heavenly mysteries instead of the usual necessities of life and of the body? Show me a man who is never hungry, who is never thirsty, who is never cold, who is never sick, who never has a fever, who is never tormented by the discomforts and difficulties of strangury, and I shall grant you that it is possible for man to think of nothing but virtues. The Apostle Paul is struck by an attendant, and he pronounces this judgment against the High Priest who had given the order to strike him: 'God will strike thee, thou whitewashed wall.'[14] Where is the well-known patience of the Savior who, when He was led as a sheep to the slaughter, opened not His mouth,[15] but addressed kindly the one who struck Him: 'If I have spoken ill, convince me of evil; but if well, why dost thou strike me?'[16] We are not disparaging the apostle, but rather praising the glory of the Lord who, though He suffered in accordance to the flesh, overcame the harm wrought in the flesh and its weakness; to say nothing of the following words uttered by the apostle: 'Alexander, the coppersmith, has done me much harm; the Lord, the just judge, will render to him in that day.'[17]

(5) *The creation of the Creator is not to be blamed.*
CRITOBULUS. You are forcing me to say something that I have long been wanting to say, and yet did not utter the words that were on the tip of my tongue.
ATTICUS. Now, who is stopping you from giving expression to your thoughts? For what you will say is either good, and you should not deprive us of something that is good; or it is evil, and, therefore, it was not for our sake that you held your peace, but rather for modesty's sake.

---

13 2 Tim. 4.13.
14 Acts 23.3.
15 Cf. Isa. 53.7.
16 John 18.23.
17 2 Tim. 4.8, 14.

CRITOBULUS. I shall at length give expression to my thoughts. Your whole disputation is becoming gradually a condemnation of nature, and a direct charge against God who created such a human being.
ATTICUS. Was this the statement that you wanted to make and were unwilling to make it? Say it, I ask you, so that all men may enjoy your wisdom. Are you reproving God because He created man as man? Let the angels also reprove Him because they are angels. Let every creature complain and ask why it is what it was created, and not what it could have been created. Perhaps, at this point, I should sport in boyish declamations, and proceed from the gnat and the ant all the way to the Cherubim and Seraphim, complaining and asking why each and every one of them was not created on a higher plane. And, when I come to the High Powers, I shall complain and ask why it is that God alone is God, and why He did not create all things as gods. For, according to your view, He will be guilty either of impotence or of malice. Reprehend Him for permitting even the devil to exist in this world, and remove the crown, once you have taken away strife.
CRITOBULUS. I am not so foolish as to complain about the existence of the devil, through whose malice death came into the world. What grieves me is that churchmen and those who assume to themselves the title of masters, rule out the free will, the denial of which is the basis of the Manichaean sect.
ATTICUS. Am I ruling out the free will, when my sole concern in my whole disputation was to preserve the omnipotence of God as well as the free will?
CRITOBULUS. How do you mean that you are preserving free will when you state that man can do nothing if God does not help him?
ATTICUS. If he who associates God's help with the free will is deserving of blame, then he who rules out God's help should be deserving of praise.
CRITOBULUS. I am not ruling out the assistance of God, since it is by His grace, to be sure, that we can do everything that

we can do; but I am keeping both notions distinct and in their own proper bounds, so that it is through His grace that God gave us the power of the free will, and it lies within our own will to do or not to do anything; and a reward is in store for those who do, and a punishment for those who do not.

(6) *What God shall crown in us.*

ATTICUS. You seem to me to be very forgetful, and to be repeating the very same lines of the disputation as if nothing were said previously. This, to be sure, was the conclusion that we reached after a lengthy discussion, that the Lord helps and sustains us in all our actions by His grace, by which He granted us a free will.

CRITOBULUS. Why, then, does He crown in us, and why praise what He Himself has worked in us?

ATTICUS. He crowns our will which offered all that it could, and our effort that strove to do all that it could do, and our humility that always had recourse to God's help.

CRITOBULUS. Therefore, if we did not fulfill His commandment, God was either willing to help or He was unwilling. If He was willing to help and did help us, and we did not do what we wanted to do, we are not the ones who failed, but He. On the other hand, if He was unwilling to help, the blame is not put on him who wanted to fulfill the commandments, but on Him who could have helped him, but was unwilling to do so.

ATTICUS. You do not realize that this dilemma that you propose has sunk to the lowest depths of blasphemies, so that in either case, God is either impotent or invidious, and it is not so much praise that He deserves because He is the author and helper of all that is good, as it is blame because He did not prevent what was evil. Therefore, He should be reproved for having allowed the devil to exist, for having permitted in the past, and for permitting, even to the present day, any evil to be done daily in the world. These are questions that are raised by Marcion, and all the dogs of the heretics who tear apart the Old Testament and are wont to construct this sort of a syllogism. God either knew that man, who was placed in Paradise, would transgress His commandment, or He did not know. If He knew, he is not at fault who could not avoid the foreknowledge of God, but He who created him such that he could not elude the knowledge of God. If He did not know it, you also deny His divinity when you deny His foreknowledge. For, according to this kind of logic, He will be blamed for having chosen Saul who was to become subsequently a very impious king. And the Savior will be judged guilty either of ignorance or of injustice for having said in the Gospel: 'Have I not chosen you, the Twelve, as apostles, and one of you is a devil?'[18] Ask him why He chose Judas, the betrayer? Why He entrusted his jewel box to him who, He knew very well, was a thief? Do you want to know the reason why? God judges the present, not the future. Nor does He condemn, by virtue of His foreknowledge, the man who, He knows, will turn out to be the kind of a person who will subsequently displease Him. But His goodness is so bountiful and His mercy so ineffable that He chooses a man who, He sees, is good in the meantime, and who, He knows, will turn out bad, giving him the opportunity of experiencing a change of heart and of repenting for his sins, according to the view expressed by the apostle: 'Dost thou not know that the goodness of God is meant to lead thee to repentance? But according to thy hardness and unrepentant heart, thou dost treasure up to thyself wrath on the day of wrath and of the revelation of the just judgment of God, who will render to everyone according to his works.'[19] For Adam did not sin, because God knew that this would be the case; but God knew in advance, as God, that he would do this of his own will. Therefore, accuse God of lying because He said through Jona: 'Yet forty days and Ninive shall be destroyed.'[20] But He will reply to you through Jeremia: 'In

---

18 John 6.71.
19 Rom. 2.4, 6.
20 Cf. Jona 3.4. In St. Jerome, the phrase is 'three days,' a reference to the time that it would take to preach throughout the city. The city was about fifty miles round. Thus, to go through all the chief streets and public places would take about three days.

short, I shall speak against a nation and against a kingdom, to root out, and to pull down, and to destroy it. If that nation against which I have spoken shall repent of its evil, I also shall repent of the evil that I have thought to do to them. In short, I shall speak of a nation and of a kingdom, to build up and plant it. If it shall do evil in my sight, that it obey not my voice, I shall repent of the good that I have spoken to do unto it.'[21] On a certain occasion, Jona was also sorely grieved for having lied at the bidding of God; but he is convicted of an unjust grief, in preferring to speak the truth and bring destruction on countless peoples, than to tell a lie and secure their salvation. An example is cited to him: 'Thou are grieved for the ivy,' (or 'gourd') 'for which thou hast not labored nor made it to grow, which in one night came up, and in one night perished, and shall not I spare Ninive, that great city, in which there are more than a hundred and twenty thousand persons that know not how to distinguish between their right hand and their left?'[22] If there was such a large number of individuals in the age bracket of little children and simple people, whom you certainly will not be able to prove to be sinners, what shall we say of the various age brackets of both sexes, which, according to Philo and that wisest of philosophers,[23] run their course in seven stages, from infancy to decrepit old age, while the addition of years in the age brackets succeed each other, in turn, in such a way that we can hardly perceive the passage from one age bracket to another?

(7) *God is by no means the author of sin.*
CRITOBULUS. Your whole argumentation is turning out to be an admission on your part, in theory, and a denial, in fact, of the doctrine that the Greeks refer to as *autexoúsion,* and what we call 'free will.' For you make God the author of sins, since you assert that man can do nothing of himself, but by the help

---
21 Jer. 18.7.
22 Jona 4.10, 11.
23 Cf. Plato in his *Timaeus.*

of God, to whom is to be imputed everything that we do. We, on the contrary, say that what man has done, whether it be good or evil, through the power of the free will is imputed to him who did what he wanted to do, and is not imputed to Him who has once granted him a free will.

ATTICUS. Although you are evading the question, you are caught in the web of truth; for in the light of such logic, even if He does not lend any assistance Himself, He will, still, be the author of evils, according to your view, because He could have prevented evils and did not. For it is an ancient saying that he who could have saved a man from death and was unwilling is a murderer.

CRITOBULUS. I am ready to raise my hand in utter astonishment; I submit; you have won, if winning, to be sure, means wishing to subvert the truth, not by facts, but by words, that is to say, not by truth, but by falsehood. I could, indeed, reply to you in the words of the apostle: 'Even though I be rude in speech, yet I am not so in knowledge.'[24] For, while you speak, I seem to agree with your views, being swayed by the deceits of your argumentations; but, when you have finished, it, again, becomes plainly evident to my mind that the source from which your disputation emanates is not the fountainhead of truth and Christian simplicity, but rather the minutiae and the subtle distinctions of the philosophers.

ATTICUS. Do you want me, then, to quote again the testimonies of Scripture? And where is the logic of the boast of your disciples that no one can answer your argumentation and questions?

CRITOBULUS. Not only do I want you to do this, but I even demand that you do so. Show me from Sacred Scripture where a man accomplished something that he was either unwilling or unable to accomplish of himself when the power of the free will has been ruled out.

---

24 2 Cor. 11.6.

(8) *The testimonies of Scripture.*

ATTICUS. We should quote the words of Scripture not as you propose, but as truth and reason demand. Jacob says in his prayer: 'If the Lord, my God, shall be with me, and shall keep me in the way by which I walk, and shall give me bread to eat and raiment to put on, and shall bring me back safely to my father's house, the Lord shall be my God, and this stone, which I have set up for a title, shall be the house of God, and of all things that thou shalt give me, I will offer tithes to thee.'[25] He did not say, did he: 'If you will preserve my free will, I shall seek food and raiment through my own labor, and I shall return to my father's house'? He leaves everything to the will of God, so that he may deserve to receive what he is praying for. An army of angels meets Jacob, as he is returning from Mesopotamia, and they are referred to as the camps of God.[26] He subsequently wrestles with an angel, in the form of a man, and he is strengthened by the Lord. He received the name, 'the most righteous of God,' from the man who wrestled with him.[27] He did not dare to return to his very cruel brother until he was strengthened by the help of the Lord. It is written further on: 'The sun shone upon him, after he was past Phanuel,'[28] which means 'the face of God.' Whence, also, Moses says: 'I have seen the Lord face to face, and my soul has been saved,'[29] not through any inherent quality of nature, but through the condescension of His mercy. Therefore, the sun of justice rises upon us then, and only then, when we are strengthened by the face of God. Joseph is imprisoned in Egypt; and the account tells us at that point that the guard of the prison placed everything in his power and trust. And the reason is given: 'because the Lord was with him and whatever he did was made to prosper by the Lord in his hands.'[30] Whence, also,

---
25 Gen. 28.20-22.
26 Cf. Gen. 32.2, 3.
27 Cf. Gen. 32.29.
28 Gen. 32.32.
29 Gen. 32.31.
30 Gen. 39.23.

the eunuchs have dreams, and Pharao has a dream that cannot be solved, so that, under the circumstances, Joseph is freed, his father and brothers are fed, and Egypt is saved in a time of famine. The account continues: 'But God said to Israel in a vision in the night: "I am the God of thy fathers, fear not to go down in Egypt, for I will make a great nation of thee there and I will go down with thee into Egypt, and I will bring thee back again thence; and Joseph also shall put his hands upon thy eyes." '[31] Where is there any mention made in this text of the power of the free will? Is not this very fact that he dares to go to his son and entrust himself to a nation that does not know the Lord, wholly a matter of the help of the God of his fathers? The nation is freed from Egypt on the strength of the hand and the power of the arm, not of Moses and of Aaron, but rather of Him, who liberated the nation through the miracles of His signs, and who, in the end, struck down every firstborn of Egypt, so that those who earlier held them back by force were compelled to let them go gladly.[32] Solomon says: 'Trust in the Lord with all thy heart, but do not glory in thine own wisdom. In all thy ways acknowledge him, that he may make straight thy ways.'[33] Observe, carefully, what he says: 'We must not trust in our own wisdom, or in any virtues, but in the Lord alone, who directs the steps of men.' Finally, we are commanded to show Him our ways and make known our ways to Him, which are made straight, not by our own efforts, but by His help and mercy. Whence it is written: 'Make straight thy way in my sight,'[34] (or as other copies have it, 'make straight my way in thy sight'), so that what is straight to Him may also appear straight to me. Solomon also says: 'Lay open thy works to the Lord and thy thoughts shall be directed.'[35] For our thoughts are directed then, and only then, when we lay open to the Lord, as to a firm and very

---

31 Gen. 46.2-4.
32 Cf. Exod. 11 and 12.
33 Prov. 3.5, 6.
34 Ps. 5.9.
35 Prov. 16.3.

stable rock, everything that we do and impute everything to Him.

(9) *From the New Testament.*

The Apostle Paul, after describing in a few words the benefits of God, states in conclusion: 'And for such offices, who is sufficient?'[36] Whence, also, he says in another place: 'Such is the assurance we have through Christ towards God. Not that we are sufficient of ourselves to think anything, as from ourselves, but our sufficiency is from God. He also it is who has made us fit ministers of the new covenant, not of the letter but of the spirit; for the letter kills, but the spirit gives life.'[37] Do we still dare to boast about the free will and treat with insult the benefits of God, the Giver, when the Chosen Vessel also writes very clearly: 'But we carry this treasure in vessels of clay, to show that the abundance of our power is God's and not ours'?[38] Whence, also, in another place, he refutes the impudence of heretics and says: 'He who boasts, let him boast in the Lord. For he is not approved who commends himself, but he whom the Lord commends.'[39] And again: 'For in no way have I fallen short of the most eminent apostles, even though I am nothing.'[40] Peter, bewildered by the magnitude of the signs of the Lord, says to Him: 'Depart from me, for I am a sinful man.'[41] And the Lord says to the disciples: 'I am the vine, you are the branches. He who abides in me, and I in him, he bears much fruit; for without me you can do nothing.'[42] Just as the branches and the young shoots of vines wither forthwith if they are cut off from the parent stock, so also the power of man grows weak and is completely lost if it is deprived of the help of God. 'No one,' He says, 'can come to me unless the Father who sent me draw him.'[43] When He says: 'No one can

---

36 2 Cor. 2.16.
37 2 Cor. 3.4-6.
38 2 Cor. 4.7.
39 2 Cor. 10.17, 18.
40 2 Cor. 12.11.
41 Luke 5.8.
42 John 15.5.
43 John 6.44.

come to me,' He is destroying the haughty freedom of the will; for even if a man were to wish to go to Christ, his wish would be in vain and his efforts useless, unless the following requirement were met: 'Unless my heavenly Father draw him.' It should also be noted, at the same time, that he who is drawn does not run of his own will, but is dragged either reluctantly and slowly, or unwillingly.

(10) *He argues from cited passages.*

He who cannot go to Jesus through his own power and efforts, how can he avoid all sins at the same time, and avoid them forever, and assume to himself the title of the power of God? For, if He is *anamártētos* and I am also *anamártētos,* what will be the difference between God and me? I shall quote just one more testimony, lest I make myself obnoxious to you and to the hearers. Sleep is banished from the eyes of Assuerus, whom the Septuagint translators call Artaxerxes, so that, in reading the chronicles of the servants who were faithful to him, he comes upon Mardochal, who disclosed the plots against him and saved his life, so that both Esther found greater favor in his eyes, and the whole people of the Jews were saved from their impending doom. Certainly, a very powerful king who ruled over the entire eastern world, from India to the north and to Ethiopia, wanted to go to bed and sleep and exercise his free will to sleep, after partaking of a very sumptuous banquet and of foods brought in from all parts of the world; and he would have done so had not the Lord, the provider of all that is good, checked the course of nature, so that the cruelty of the tyrant against nature might be overcome. It would take too long if I were to produce all of the examples of Sacred Scripture. Every word uttered by the saints is a prayer to God; every prayer and supplication elicit the mercy of the Creator, so that we, who cannot be saved through our own strength and endeavors, may be saved by His mercy. But where mercy and grace exist, there the will ceases to be free to a certain degree, because it is free only insofar as we wish, and desire, and assent to what is pleasing. Thereupon, it rests on the power of the Lord to enable us to accomplish by His assistance and help what we wish, what we are striving and endeavoring to accomplish.

(11) *The health of the body compared with the health of the soul.*

CRITOBULUS. I had simply stated that the help of God was perceived, not in every act that we perform, but rather in the grace of creation and of the law, lest the free will be destroyed. But there are many of our brothers who say that everything that we do is accomplished by the help of God.

ATTICUS. Anyone who holds such a view will cease to be one of your brothers. Therefore, you, too, will either hold this view so that you may become one of our brothers, or, if you do not hold this view, you will be opposed to us along with those who do not hold our view.

CRITOBULUS. I will be your brother if you affirm my view, or rather, you will be my brother if you do not affirm the opposite view. You admit that there are healthy bodies, and deny the health of the soul which is the stronger of the two. For just as there is disease and injury in respect to the body, so, also, in like manner, there is sin in respect to the soul. Therefore, you who admit that man is healthy at times with respect to the part that is flesh, why would you deny he is healthy with respect to the part that is spirit?

ATTICUS. I shall follow up your proposition: 'You shall never escape today, I shall go wherever you call.'

CRITOBULUS. I am ready to listen.

ATTICUS. And I am ready to speak to deaf ears. Therefore, I shall reply to your proposition. Being composed of body and soul, we follow the nature of each substance. Just as the body is said to be healthy if it is not afflicted with any sickness, so, also, in like manner, the soul is said to be without fault if it is not disturbed by any disorder. And yet, although the body may be healthy, and hale, and hearty, and perfectly sound in all its senses, it is distressed severely either by frequent or occasional maladies, and suffers the discomforts of rheum at times, though it be very strong; so, also, in like manner, the soul sustains the attacks of thoughts, and disorders, and, even though it may survive shipwrecks, it does not sail without danger, and, considering its weakness, it is ever solicitous of death, according to what is written: 'What man is there who shall live and not see death?'[44] —death, which is in store for all mortals, not in the dissolution of nature, but in the death of sin, according to the words of the prophet: 'The soul that sinneth, the same shall die.'[45] Moreover, we know that Enoch and Elias have not yet seen that common death by which even brute animals are released. Show me a body that has never been sick, or one that is sure of enjoying good health forever after sickness, and I will show you a soul that has never sinned, nor will ever sin in the future after it has attained virtues, especially since vices neighbor so closely on virtues, and, if you turn to one side just a bit, you must either go astray or fall down headlong to destruction. How much difference is there between pertinacity and perseverance, between parsimony and frugality, between liberality and prodigality, between prudence and cunning, between fortitude and temerity, between caution and timidity? Some of these qualities pertain to what is good, others to what is evil. This, to be sure, is found to be the case also with respect to bodies. If you take precautions to moderate the flow of bile, the flow of phlegm increases. If you make haste to dry up the humors of the body, the temperature of the blood rises; it becomes poisoned by the flow of the bile and a yellowish color spreads over the face. Although we avail ourselves of the best care of physicians and live on restricted diets, and avoid incentives of diseases and indigestion, we either shiver with the chill or burn with a fever for some unknown reasons, known only to God, or we scream in pain and implore the help of

---

44 Ps. 88.49.
45 Ezech. 18.4.

the Savior, the true physician, and say with the apostles: 'Master, save us, we are perishing.'[46]

(12) *He replies to some objections from Scripture.*
CRITOBULUS. Granted, that no one has been able to avoid all sin as a boy, as a youth, and as a young man. You cannot deny, can you, that very many just and holy men devoted themselves wholeheartedly to virtues after their faults, and that through these virtues they were free from sin?

ATTICUS. This is what I had said to you in the beginning, that it lay in our own power either to sin or not to sin, and to raise a finger to do what is good or what is evil in order to preserve the free will. But we can do this in a limited degree, and for a while, and according to the circumstances of human weakness; but to continue forever in the state of sinlessness is a virtue reserved for God alone, and for Him who, though He was the Word made flesh, was not made subject to the injury done to the flesh and to sins. Nor will you convince me that I can perform an act continually because I can do it for a short while. Can I fast, watch, stay awake, walk, read, sing psalms, sit, and sleep forever?

CRITOBULUS. And why are we encouraged in Sacred Scripture to attain perfect justice, as in the following passages: 'Blessed are the clean of heart, for they shall see God';[47] and: 'Blessed are the undefiled in the way, who walk in the law of the Lord';[48] and in the words of God, speaking to Abraham: 'I am thy God, be pleasing in my sight and spotless,' (or 'blameless'), 'and I will make my covenant between me and thee and I will multiply thee exceedingly'?[49] For, if the commandment that Scripture bears witness to is impossible, it was useless to command us to fulfill it.

ATTICUS. With the various testimonies that you quote from Scripture, you are wearing out the same question and reducing

---
46 Matt. 8.25.
47 Matt. 5.8.
48 Ps. 118.1.
49 Gen. 17.1, 2.

it to a sort of stage device, which enables the one and the same person to appear on stage as Mars or Venus by a change in his assortment of masks; so that he who had entered the stage in an earlier scene as a rough and bloodthirsty male character is made up in a later scene as a dainty female character. However, the texts that you now present as new objections, as it were: 'Blessed are the clean of heart,' and 'Blessed are the undefiled in the way,' and 'Be spotless,' and others of this kind, have been refuted by the answer of the apostle: 'We know in part and we prophesy in part';[50] and: 'We see now through a mirror in an obscure manner. But when that which is perfect has come, that which is imperfect will be done away with.'[51] And, therefore, the clean heart that is subsequently to see God, and that blessedness of an undefiled life, and that spotless existence with Abraham, we possess in an obscure and shadowy manner. Although an individual may be a patriarch, a prophet, an apostle, the following words are addressed to all of them in the name of the Lord Savior: 'If you, evil as you are, know how to give good things to your children, how much more will your Father in heaven give good things to those who ask him?'[52] Finally, even Abraham, to whom it was said: 'Be blameless and spotless,' fell flat to the ground, conscious of his own weakness. And after God had said to him: 'Sarai, thy wife, shall no longer be called Sarai, but Sara shall be her name, and of her I shall give thee a son, and I shall bless him and he shall become nations, and kings of people shall spring from him,'[53] it is immediately stated: 'Abraham fell upon his face, and laughed and said in his heart: "Shall a son be born to him that is a hundred years old? And shall Sara who is ninety years old bring forth?" And Abraham said to God: "O that Ismael may live in thy sight." And God said to him: "Verily. Behold Sara thy wife shall bear thee a son, and thou

---

50 1 Cor. 13.9.
51 1 Cor. 13.12, 10
52 Matt. 7.11.
53 Gen. 17.15, 16.

shalt call his name Isaac,"[54] and the rest. He had certainly heard it said by God: 'I am thy God, be pleasing in my sight and be spotless.'[55] Why did he not believe the promise that God made to him, instead of laughing in his heart, thinking that he was deceiving God and not daring to laugh openly? Finally, he sets forth the reasons for his incredulity, and says in his heart: 'How can a man who is hundred years old beget a son from a wife who is ninety years old?' He says: 'O that Ismael may live in thy sight,'[56] whom thou hast once given to me. I am not asking for something that is difficult; I am satisfied with the favor that I have received. God reproves him for this secret reply, and says: 'Verily.' And this is the meaning of the expression: 'What you think shall not come to pass, shall come to pass. Sara, thy wife, shall bear thee a son, and I shall give him a name, before she conceives, and before he is born. For your mistake of laughing secretly, your son shall receive the name of Isaac, that is, "laughter."' But if you think God is seen in this world by those who are clean of heart, why is it that Moses, who previously had said: 'I have seen God face to face, and my soul has been saved,'[57] prays subsequently that he might see Him and know Him? And, because he had said that he had seen Him, he hears it said by the Lord: 'Thou canst not see my face. For man shall not see my face and live.'[58] Whence, also, the apostle calls him the invisible, the only God,[59] 'who dwells in light inaccessible, whom no man has seen or can see.'[60] And John the Evangelist, reverently proclaims, saying: 'No one has at any time seen God. The only-begotten Son, who is in the bosom of the Father, he has revealed him.'[61] He sees Him, and does not declare the grandeur of Him who

---

54 Gen. 17.17-19.
55 Gen. 17.1.
56 Gen. 17.18.
57 Gen. 32.31.
58 Exod. 33.20.
59 Cf. 1 Tim. 1.17.
60 1 Tim. 6.16.
61 John 1.18.

is seen, nor as much as He who reveals Him knows, but only as much as the human understanding can comprehend.

(13) *True perfection is reserved for heaven.*

However, since it is your view that he who is undefiled in the way and who walks in His law is blessed, let me make clear to you the meaning of the above text from the following interpretation. You have seen from the many testimonies cited above that no one could fulfill the law. But if the apostle has reckoned as dung the things that he previously considered as gains under the law, in comparison with the grace of Christ, that he might gain Christ, how much more ought we to know that the grace of Christ and of the Gospel took the place of the law because no man could be justified under the law? But if no man is justified under the law, how is he undefiled unto perfection in the way who is still walking and striving to reach the goal? He who is in the course and walking in the way is certainly less perfect than he who has reached the end. Therefore, if he is undefiled and perfect who is still walking in the way and still walking in the law, what greater perfection will he have who has reached the end of the road and of the law? Whence, also, the apostle says of the Lord that He will present to Himself at the end of the world and at the consummation of virtues, the church holy, and spotless, and without blemish,[62] which, according to your view, is already perfect in this mortal and corruptible flesh; and you deserve to hear it said to you, together with the Corinthians: 'You are already perfect! You are already made rich! Without us you reign! And would that you did reign, that we too might reign with you,'[63] since perfection, that is true and free of all sordidness, is reserved for heaven, when the lover shall say to his beloved: 'Thou art all fair, O my love, and there is not a spot in thee.'[64] The following text: 'so as to be blameless and guileless, chil-

---

62 Cf. Eph. 5.27.
63 1 Cor. 4.8.
64 Cant. 4.7.

dren of God without blemish,'[65] is also interpreted in the same sense, since he did not say 'you are,' but rather 'so as to be,' reserving perfection for the future, instead of contending that it exists here and now, so that, in the present life, there is labor and strife, and, in the next, rewards for our labor and virtue. Finally, John writes: 'Beloved, we are the children of God, and it has not yet appeared what we shall be. We know that, when he appears, we shall be like to him, for we shall see him just as he is.'[66] Therefore, although we are the children of God, nevertheless, likeness to God and true contemplation of God are promised us then, and only then, when He appears in His glory.

(14) *The arrogance of Pelagius in his letter to Juliana.*

This bombastic arrogance of yours is also the source, from which has burst forth that unbridled impudence of yours regarding prayer, with which you declare to a virgin[67] in a letter written to her, how holy men ought to pray. 'He, indeed,' you say, 'lifts up his hands to God in justice; he pours out his prayers with a good conscience who can say: "For you know, O Lord, how holy, how innocent, how clean of all fraud, wrongdoing, and rapine are the hands that I stretch out to you; how just, how undefiled, and free of all deceit are the lips, with which I pour out my prayers and supplications to you, to have pity on me." ' Is this the prayer of a Christian, or of a boastful Pharisee who also said in the Gospel: 'O God, I thank thee that I am not as the rest of men, robbers, dishonest, adulterers, and like this publican. I fast twice a week; I pay tithes of all that I possess.'[68] He thanks God that through His mercy he is not like the rest of men, expressing his hatred for sins, not assuming to himself justice. You say: 'O Lord, you know how holy,

---

65 Phil. 2.15.
66 1 John 3.2.
67 Cf. St. Augustine, *De gestis Pelagii* 6.16 (PL 44.329), for the story of this letter. The widow referred to here is Juliana, the mother of Demetrias, to whom St. Jerome addressed a letter on the keeping of virginity. Cf. St. Jerome, *Epistola* 130, *ad Demetriadem*.
68 Luke 18.11, 12.

how innocent, how clean of all fraud, wrong-doing, and rapine are the hands that I stretch out to you.' He says that he fasts twice a week, in order to discipline the flesh that revels in vices, and he pays tithes of all that he possesses. 'For the ransom of a man's soul are his riches.'[69] You brag with the devil who says: 'I will ascend above the stars, I will place my throne in heaven, I will be like the Most High.'[70] David says: 'My loins are filled with illusions';[71] and: 'My sores are putrified and corrupted because of my foolishness';[72] and: 'Enter not into judgment with thy servant';[73] and: 'In thy sight no one living shall be justified.'[74] You boast that you are holy, innocent, and pure, and you stretch out to God, hands that are clean. Nor are you satisfied to glory in all your deeds, unless you say that you are clean of all sins of word and tongue, stating how just, how undefiled, and free of all deceit your lips are. David sings: 'Every man is a liar';[75] and this very same view is confirmed by the testimony of the apostle, that God is true and every man is a liar.[76] And you have lips that are unblemished, and just, and free of all deceit. Isaia cries out in anguish: 'Woe is me because I am undone, because although I am a man and have unclean lips, I also dwell in the midst of a people that hath unclean lips';[77] and a Seraphim subsequently takes a living coal with tongs and touches the lips of the prophet to cleanse them, who does not speak in boastful manner like you, but confesses his faults openly, according to what is said in the Psalms: 'What shall be given to thee, or what shall be added to thee, to a deceitful tongue? The sharp arrows of the mighty, with coals that lay waste.'[78] And, after

---

69 Prov. 13.8.
70 Isa. 14.13, 14.
71 Ps. 37.8.
72 Ps. 37.6.
73 Ps. 142.2.
74 *Ibid.*
75 Ps. 115.2.
76 Cf. Rom. 3.4.
77 Isa. 6.5.
78 Ps. 119.3, 4.

uttering such boastful arrogance, and impudent pride in prayer, and confidence in your holiness, like a fool trying to convince the foolish, you say in conclusion: 'lips, with which I pour out my supplications to you, to have pity on me.' If you are holy, if you are innocent, if you are cleansed of all sordidness, if you have sinned neither in word nor in deed, as James says: 'He who does not offend in word, he is a perfect man,'[79] and: 'The tongue no man can tame,'[80] what is your reason for begging for mercy, so that you cry out in anguish, to be sure, and pour out your supplications, inasmuch as you are holy, clean, and innocent, and undefiled of lips, and free of all deceit, and equal to the power of God? Christ prayed, thus, on the cross: 'O God, my God, why hast thou forsaken me? Far from my salvation are the words of my sins';[81] and again: 'Father, into thy hands I commend my spirit';[82] and: 'Father, forgive them, for they do not know what they are doing';[83] He who had thanked God for us and had said: 'I confess to thee, Father, Lord of heaven and earth.'[84]

(15) *From the Lord's Prayer.*

Thus, did He teach His apostles that they who believe should make bold to say daily, at the sacrifice of His body: 'Our Father who art in heaven, hallowed be thy name.'[85] They pray that the very name of God, which is holy of itself, be hallowed. You say: 'You know, O Lord, how holy, how innocent, and how clean are my hands.' They say: 'Thy kingdom come,'[86] expressing a hope for the kingdom in the future, so that, with Christ reigning therein, sin may not reign in their mortal body, and they add: 'Thy will be done on earth, as it is in heaven';[87] so that human weakness may seek to resemble the

---

79 James 3.2.
80 James 3.8.
81 Matt. 27.46; Ps. 21.2.
82 Luke 23.46; Ps. 30.6.
83 Luke 23.34.
84 Matt. 11.25.
85 Matt. 6.9.
86 Matt. 6.10.
87 *Ibid.*

angels, and the will of God may be fulfilled on earth. You say: 'Man can be free of all sin if he wants to.' The apostles pray that their 'daily bread,'[88] or their 'supersubstantial bread' may come, so that they may be worthy to partake of the body of Christ. And you, in consequence of your extraordinary holiness and secure justice, are bold enough to assume to yourself the heavenly gifts. The prayer continues: 'Forgive us our debts, as we also forgive our debtors.'[89] They who emerge from the baptismal fount and have been reborn in the Lord Savior, having fulfilled what was written of them: 'Blessed are they whose iniquities are forgiven, and whose sins are covered,'[90] say at the very moment of their first communion of the body of Christ: 'And forgive us our debts,' debts that had been forgiven them in the confession of Christ. And you, in your arrogance and boastful pride, glory in the purity of your holy hands and the cleanness of your speech. Even though the conversion of man may be as perfect as possible, and his possession of virtues be as complete as possible after faults and sins, can he be as free of fault as they who emerge immediately from the font of Christ? And yet they are commanded to say: 'Forgive us our debts, as we also forgive our debtors,' not under false pretense of humility, as you interpret it, but rather as a sign of fear of human weakness which dreads its own conscience. They say: 'Lead us not into temptation';[91] you say with Jovinian that they who have received baptism with full faith cannot be tempted and cannot sin any more. They say at the end: 'But deliver us from evil!'[92] Why do they ask of God what lies in the power of the free will? O mortal man, you have now been cleansed in baptism, and it is said of you: 'Who is she, that cometh up, cleansed and leaning upon her beloved?;[93] so that she, indeed, is cleansed, but she is not able to

---
88 Matt. 6.11.
89 Matt. 6.12.
90 Ps. 31.1.
91 Matt. 6.13.
92 *Ibid.*
93 Cant. 8.5.

guard her purity, unless she is sustained by the Lord God. You, who but a moment ago were freed from your sins, how is it that you desire to be delivered by the mercy of God, if not in the way I stated, that, when we have done everything, we confess that we of ourselves are insufficient?

(16) *The Pelagian arrogance.*

Therefore, your prayer surpasses in arrogance the arrogance of the Pharisee, and is condemned, in comparison with the publican who, standing afar off, did not so much as dare lift up his eyes to God, but kept striking his breast, saying: 'O God, be merciful to me a sinner.'[94] Whence the Lord pronounces the following judgment: 'I tell you, this man went back to his home justified rather than the other; for everyone who exalts himself shall be humbled, and he who humbles himself shall be exalted.'[95] The apostles humble themselves so that they may be exalted. Your disciples exalt themselves so that they may be cast down. You are not ashamed to say to that same widow, in flattering her, that piety, which is found nowhere in the world, and truth, which is a stranger everywhere, dwell in her in a very special way; nor are you mindful of the saying: 'O my people, they that call thee blessed, deceive thee, and destroy the way of thy steps';[96] and you praise her in these words and say: 'O thou exceedingly fortunate, O thou happy woman, if justice, which is believed to exist nowhere nowadays except in heaven, is found in you, alone, on earth.' Are you teaching her with such flattery or destroying her? Are you raising her up from earth or casting her down headlong from heaven by attributing to a mere frail woman virtues that angels do not dare to assume to themselves? But if piety, truth, and justice are found nowhere on earth, but in one woman, what will become of those just men of yours, who, you boasted, were without sin on earth? You and your disciples are wont to affirm on oath that these

---
94 Luke 18.13.
95 Luke 18.14.
96 Isa. 3.12.

two chapters on prayer and flattery are not yours, when the eloquence of your style is clearly evident in them, and the charm of the Ciceronian phraseology is so wonderful that, while you proceed at a tortoise pace, you dare not publicly profess views that you teach in private and offer for sale. O fortunate art thou, whose books nobody writes but your disciples, so that you can claim and maintain that any view that you feel is offensive is not your own but someone else's! And who is that 'someone else' who will be so talented that he can imitate the charm of your language?

(17) *The way in which infants are without sin.*
CRITOBULUS. I cannot hold off any longer. I have lost all patience, due to the malice of your words. I ask you: What sins have infants committed? Neither knowledge of sin nor ignorance can be imputed to those who, according to the Prophet Jona, do not know how to distinguish between their right hand and their left.[97] They cannot sin and they must perish; their knees wobble, their wailings do not form words, their babbling tongue excites laughter; and yet the torments of eternal misery are in store for those wretched souls.

ATTICUS. Alas, you have begun to be persuasive, not to say eloquent, after your disciples have turned out to be masters. Antony,[98] that excellent orator whose praises Cicero loudly proclaims, says that he has seen many a man who was persuasive, but none so far who was eloquent. Therefore, please do not sport in embellishments that are characteristic of the style of orators, but not of yours. Such embellishments are ordinarily employed to deceive the ears of boys and the inexperienced. But tell me your views in simple language.

CRITOBULUS. I say that you should grant me that those individuals, at least, are without sin who cannot sin.

ATTICUS. I will grant it, provided they have been baptized in Christ, nor will this concession prove forthwith that I am concurring in your view, in which you stated that man could

---
97 Cf. Jona 4.11.
98 Cf. Cicero, *Orator* 5.18.

be without sin if he wanted to; for the former have neither the power nor the will to be without sin, but are without sin through the grace of God which they have received in baptism.
CRITOBULUS. You are forcing me to raise the odious question, and ask you: 'But what sins have they committed?', so that you may forthwith hurl at me the stones of the people, and kill by desire him whom you cannot kill by your own powers.
ATTICUS. He kills a heretic who allows him to be a heretic. However, our reproving gives you life, so that being dead to heresy, you may live for the Catholic faith.
CRITOBULUS. If you know that we are heretics, why do you not bring charges against us?
ATTICUS. Because the apostle teaches me to avoid a heretic after a first and second admonition, and not to bring charges against him, knowing that such a one is perverted and self-condemned by his own judgment.[99] Besides, it is a very foolish effort on my part to judge my own faith according to the judgment of someone else. For if someone else were to say that you are Catholic, why should I lend assent forthwith? Whoever defends you and says that your view is right, when you believe perverse doctrines, does not, thereby, succeed in acquitting you of infamy, but rather in bringing upon himself the charge of perfidy. A multitude of associates will not prove that you are Catholic, but that you are a heretic. Indeed, this whole matter should be trampled under the foot of the Church, lest a spectacle more lamentable than weeping infants, so to speak, present itself. The fear of God should make us despise all other fears. Therefore, either defend your views or discard a view that you cannot defend. Whomsoever you shall hire in your defense will not be called a patron, but an associate.

(18) *Why infants are baptized; and the testimony of Cyprian.*

CRITOBULUS. Tell me, I ask you, and deliver me from all further questioning: Why are infants baptized?

---

99 Cf. Tit. 3.10, 11.

ATTICUS. That their sins may be forgiven them in baptism.
CRITOBULUS. But what sins have they committed? Is anyone released from bonds who has not been bound?
ATTICUS. Are you asking me? The clarion voice of the Gospel, the Doctor of the Gentiles, the Vessel of gold, resplendent throughout the whole world, will give you the answer: 'Death reigned from Adam until Moses even over those who did not sin after the likeness of the transgression of Adam, who is a figure of him who was to come.'[100] But if you raise the objection that it is stated that there are some individuals who did not sin, you should know that these individuals did not commit the sin that Adam did by transgressing God's commandment in the Garden of Eden. However, all men are considered guilty either of the sin of their ancient forefather, Adam, or of their own. He who is an infant is released in baptism from the bond of his parent. He who reaches the age of reason is freed from both the bond of another and from his own by the blood of Christ. And, lest you suppose that my interpretation of this doctrine is heretical, the blessed martyr, Cyprian,[101] whose rival you boast to be in the exposition of the testimonies of Scripture, makes the following statement in a letter, addressed to Bishop Fidus, on the baptism of infants: 'But again, if even to those who are very grave sinners and to those who sinned much against God, when they have subsequently believed, forgiveness of sins is granted, and nobody is prevented from baptism and from grace, how much more should an infant not be prevented who, being newly born, has not sinned except in that, being born according to the flesh according to Adam, he has contracted the contagion of the ancient death at the very first moment of his birth, who approaches the more easily on this very account to the reception of the forgiveness of sins, because to him are forgiven, not his own sins, but the

---

100 Rom. 5,14.
101 St. Cyprian. *Epistola* 64. This was a synodal letter written by a Carthaginian provincial synod in the year 253 to a certain Bishop Fidus, and it treated mostly of the baptism of children.

sins of another? And therefore, dearest brother, this was our opinion in council, that by us no one ought to be prevented from baptism and from the grace of God, who is merciful and kind and loving to all. And since this is to be observed and maintained in respect to all persons, consider that it should be even more observed and maintained in respect to infants themselves and newly-born persons, who, on this very account, deserve more from our help to obtain divine mercy, that at the very beginning of their birth, lamenting and weeping, they do nothing else but entreat.'

(19) *He praises St. Augustine.*

Augustine, a holy man and an eloquent bishop, wrote recently to Marcellinus,[102] who was subsequently killed in his innocence by the heretics through the jealousy of the tyrant, Heraclian, two books on the baptism of infants against your heresy, in which you seek to prove that infants are baptized, not for the forgiveness of sins, but rather for the kingdom of heaven, according to that which is written in the Gospel: 'Unless a man be born again of water and the Holy Spirit, he cannot enter the kingdom of heaven.'[103] He also wrote a third book[104] to this same Marcellinus against those who hold the same view as you do, namely, that man can be without sin if he wants to without the grace of God. And he wrote a fourth

---

102 After the condemnation of Pelagianism for the first time in the person of Celestius in Africa in the year 411, St. Augustine immediately set himself to refute the theories of Pelagius and his disciples. In the year 412, in answer to a letter sent to him by the tribune, Marcellinus, who was puzzled by the Pelagian theories, St. Augustine wrote his *De peccatorum meritis et remissione et de baptismo parvulorum.* In this work, St. Augustine rejected the Pelagian impeccability, and proved the existence of original sin, arguing notably from the traditional custom of child baptism. Marcellinus had been appointed imperial commissioner to superintend the discussion between the Catholics and the Donatists at the Council of Carthage in the year 411. In the year 413, Heraclian, governor of Africa, revolted against Honorius, the emperor, and invaded Italy. The enterprise failed. The Donatists accused Marcellinus of taking part in the rebellion. He was executed in the year 414. Cf. F. Cayré, *Manual of Patrology and History of Theology* 1 (translated by H. Howitt; Belgium 1935) 630.

103 John 3.5.

book recently to Hilary[105] against your doctrine in which you concoct many perverse views. He is said to be also composing other books especially for you which have not yet come into my hand. I believe I should bring this work to a close, lest I hear the well-known dictum of Horace quoted to me: 'Do not carry coals to New Castle.'[106] For we would either be repeating the same views superfluously, or, if we wished to express something new, better positions have already been anticipated by a very brilliant genius. I shall say one more thing, in order to bring this discourse finally to a close, that you should either teach a new creed, that after the Father and the Son and the Holy Spirit, you baptize infants for the kingdom of heaven; or, if you have one baptism for both infants and adults, you should teach that infants should also be baptized for the forgiveness of sins after the likeness of the transgression of Adam. But, if the forgiveness of the sins of another, of which he who could not sin does not stand in need, seems unjust to you, you should align yourself on the side of your favorite,[107] who says that ancient sins are forgiven in heaven and past sins in baptism, so that you, who are influenced by his authority in other matters, may also follow his error in this respect.

---

104 The *De spiritu et littera* of St. Augustine. Marcellinus was puzzled by St. Augustine's statement that man, aided by grace, may be without sin, but that in fact no man is without sin. St. Augustine, therefore, set out to prove the necessity of interior grace in order that man should keep God's laws; and, on the other hand, the necessary defection of the human will in some circumstances. Cf. Cayré, *op. cit.*, 630.
105 This is, apparently, a reference to St. Augustine's *De natura et gratia* on the Pelagian impeccability.
106 Horace, *Satires* 1.10.34.
107 i.e., Origen.

INDICES

GENERAL INDEX

AALMA, 15n.
Aaron, brother of Moses, 282, 333, 360.
Abel, 346.
Abraham, 244, 258, 281, 366, 367.
abscondita virgo, 15n.
Academicians, 226.
Achab, king of Israel, 329.
Achan, 287.
Achytas of Tarentum, 212.
Adam, 299, 336, 376, 378.
adulescentia, 15, 15n.
Aeschines, 79.
Agag, 297.
Ahias, prophet of the Silenites, 290.
Africani de historia Susannae epistola ad Origenem, 158n.
Africa, 5n., 7, 13, 117n., 215n., 225, 226, 227, 229, 347, 377n.
Alaric, the Goth, 189n., 225.
Alexander, the coppersmith, 353.
Alexander, the expounder of Aristotle, 86, 86n.
Alexander, the Great, 212.
Alexandria, ix, xiii, 49, 54, 71n., 75, 80n., 82n., 106, 108, 109, 132, 133, 140n., 150, 185, 186, 196, 201, 242.
Amasius, cognomen of Origen, 170.
Ambrose, St., 5n., 55, 61, 125.
Amos, the prophet, 334.
Anabasioi, 166, 166n.
anamártētos, 298, 322, 362.
Anastasius, Pope, xiv, 54, 56n., 70n., 71, 106, 106n., 125, 140, 140n., 174, 174n., 184, 187, 187n., 188, 188n., 189, 193, 209.
andabatae, 17, 17n., 24, 136, 136n.
anégklētos, 264.
Anna, the prophetess, 21.
ante partum, 4n., 5n., 36n., 232n.

INDEX

Anthropomorphites, 192, 192n.
Antidicomarianites, 5n.
Antigenides, song master, 152n.
Antioch, viii, ix, x, 3, 150, 190.
Antiochus Epiphanius, king of Asia, 345.
Antipater, 79.
antitheos, 321, 321n.
Antony, 79.
apathy, doctrine of, xvi, 226, 230, 230n.
Apocrypha, 23, 23n., 47, 28n., 147, 151, 158, 276.
Aphrodisias, 86n.
Apollinaris of Laodicea, 76, 76n., 79, 87, 87n., 91, 93, 153n., 158, 159, 159n., 179, 182.
Apollinarists, 138, 138n.
Apollo, friend of St. Paul, 307.
Apostles, the Gospel according to the, *see* the Gospel according to the Hebrews.
Apronianus, friend of Rufinus, 55.
Aquila, translator of the Old Testament, 85, 146n., 150n., 153, 154, 155, 157, 158, 159.
Aquileia, viii, 3, 48, 52, 54, 56, 101n., 107, 108, 140n., 162n., 201.
Aquitaine, xv.
Arcesias, hero in Homer, 321n.
Arcesilaus, Greek philosopher, 117, 117n.
archaîos, 260.
Archippus, 210.

Argos, 167n.
Arians, viii, ix, x, 3, 129, 129n., 131, 136n., 138, 261, 261n., 321, 321n.
Arian perfidy, 128; repentant Arians, ix, x.
Arius, 109, 109n., 131, 136, 215; a sort of noonday demon, 132.
Aristaeus, shepherd in Vergil's *Georgics*, 269n.
Aristaeus, champion of Ptolemy, 148.
Aristarchus, 80, 80n.
Aristippus, Greek philosopher, 201, 201n.
Aristotle, 12, 82n., 86, 199, 211, 226, 231n., 250, 259.
Arsenius, 215.
Artaxerxes, 362.
Asa, king of Juda, 328.
Asaph, 325.
Asia, 323.
Asia Minor, 101n.
Asinius Pollio, 99, 99n.
Asper, commentator on Vergil and Sallust, 80.
Assos, 101n.
Assuerus, *see* Artaxerxes.
Assyrians, 330, 331.
Atarbius, 49, 204, 204n.
Athanasius, St., 132, 138n., 139, 215.
Athens, 133n., 201n.
Attic elegance, 212.
Atticus, character in the *Dialogus contra Pelagianos*, 227n., 228, 234, 234n.
Augustine, St., vii, 48, 57,

225n., 226-227, 231n., 232n., 377, 377n., 378n.; and the Pelagian controversy, 223; refutes Pelagius and Celestius, 225n.; his works: *De gratia Christi et peccato originali*, 226n.; *De haeresibus*, xiin., 37n.; *De natura et gratia contra Pelagium ad Timasium et Jacobum*, 223n., 224n., 225n., 378n.; *De peccatorum meritis et remissione et de baptismo parvulorum ad Marcellinum*, 223n., 377n.; *De spiritu et gratia*, 223n.; *De spiritu et littera*, 378n.; Letters, 48, 57; *Liber de gestis Pelagii ad Aurelium episcopum*, 223n., 224, 227n., 229n., 235, 369n.; *Liber de perfectione justitiae hominis*, 223n., 225.
Aurelius, bishop of Carthage, 223n.
Auxentius, the heretic, 137n.
Auxentius, Arian bishop, 5n.
Aventine Hill, 122n.
Azarias, 29.
autexoúsion, 357.

Baana, the son of Remmon, 289.
Babylon, 234, 331, 332; the cup of, 195.
Babylonia, 240n.
Balsaneus, 147n.
Banausoi, manual arts, 262.
baptism, 104, 105, 265; and infants, xii, xv, 224, 225, 374-377; and the Pelagians, xv; St. Augustine on baptism of infants, 377, 377n., 378; and sin, 347, 348-351, 372; and temptation, 318.
Bar, various meanings of the word in Hebrew, 85.
Baranina, Hebrew instructor of St. Jerome, 76, 76n.
Bar-Chochabas, 202, 202n.
Barnabas, the Jew, 264, 323.
Basilides, 147n.
'being,' the question of, 242, 243, 268, 351, 352.
Bel and the Dragon, the story of, 158, 158n.
Bessi, traveling actors of Thrace, 82, 82n.
Bessica, 82n.
Bethlehem, xi, xv, xvi, 23n., 28n., 47, 76n., 142n., 144n., 153n., 167, 183n., 186n., 223, 226, 227, 229, 289.
Bethula, 15, 15n.
Bithynia, 323.
'body of death,' meaning of the phrase, 92-94.
'brothers' of the Lord, 5, 7, 8; according to the Hebrews, 8, 17, 25-37, 28n.; by birth, 30; by race, 30, 31; by kinship, 31-33; by affection, 33, 34.
Brutus, 79, 210.
bishops, qualifications of, 263-266.

Caesarea, 68; the library of,

177, 349.
Cain, 334.
Caiphas, 164.
Calpurnius, cognomen of Rufinus, 198, 198n., 202, 202n.
Calpurnius, the Sallustinian, 99, 99n.
Candidus, the Valentinian, 133, 133n.
Canticle of Canticles, 51.
Canticle of Penance, 291.
Caper, writer of commentaries on grammar, 115, 115n.
Capharnaum, 25.
Caria, 86n.
Carbeades, Greek philosopher, 117, 117n.
Carpus, 353.
Carterius, xix, 4, 5; author of book on asceticism, 4n., 5, 35.
Carterius, bishop of Spain, 104, 104n.
Carthage, xvi, 223n., 226, 229.
Catiline, 174.
Cato, 76, 143, 274.
Celestines, 225.
Celestius, chief disciple of Pelagius, xvi, 223, 223n., 225; 227, 347n., 377n.; in Africa, 225, 226; condemned, 226; *Definitions* of 225, 225n.; excommunicated, 229.
Celsus, 216.
Ceres, 166, 166n.
Chalcis, the desert of, viii, ix, 3.
chard, 304.

Charybdis, the whirlpool of, 190, 208.
Christ, the soul of, 109, 110.
Chromatius, bishop of Aquileia, xiv, 57, 140, 140n., 150, 156, 162n., 165.
Chrysippus, Stoic philosopher, 79, 101, 101n., 117n., 242, 243, 304.
Chrysogonus, disciple of Rufinus, 104, 104n.
Cicero, 99n., 101, 148, 210, 215, 215n., 226, 230, 263; commentaries of Victorinus on the dialogues of, 80; commentaries of Vocatius on the orations of, 80; works: *Academica,* 60n., 117n., 250; *Ad Herennium,* 79; *De oratore,* 79; *Epistulae ad familiares,* 17n., 136n.; *Pro Vatinio,* 210; *Rhetorica,* 79; *Tusculan Disputations,* 100n., 230, 230n., 304.
Cisalpine Gaul, 137n.
Cleanthes, Stoic philosopher, 101, 101n.
Clement, priest of Alexandria, 76, 130, 130n., 132, 349n.; the *Stromata* of, 230n.
Clement, St., of Rome, the *Recognitiones* of, 130, 130n.
Cleophas, 29, 29n.
Claudius, the priest, 194.
cognatio, 31n.
Commentarius in apocalypsim Joannis, 37n.
commentators, the role of, 79, 80, 87, 88, 176.

Concordia, pun on the city of, 103n.
Constantinople, 48, 138.
contradiction, the waters of, 333.
Corinth, 167n.
Cornelii, the clan of the, 99, 99n.
Cornutus, Greek philosopher, 82n., 231n.
Coryphaeus, cognomen of Rufinus, 69.
Council or Synod of Alexandria, ix, 54; of Carthage, 226, 227, 229, 347n., 376n., 377n.; of Diospolis, 227; the Fifth Ecumenical, 231n.; of Jerusalem, xvi; of Milan, 347n.; of Milevis, 229; of Nicaea, 321n.; of Palestine, 227; of Rome, x, xii; the Sixth and Seventh Ecumenical, 231n.
Crantor, Greek philosopher, 117n.
Crassus, Agelastus, 100, 100n.
Crassus, the Rich, 167, 167n.
Cremona, xiii.
Critobulus, character in the *Dialogus contra Pelagianos*, x, 228, 234, 234n., 316, 319, 320.
Crotona, 274n.
Ctesiphon, friend of St. Jerome, xvi, 226, 227n., 230, 232.
Cunctator, Q. Fabius Maximus, 200n.
Cyclades, 190.

Cyprian, St., 53, 138, 138n., 139, 277, 277n., 376; works: *Epistola* 64, 376, 376n.; *Testimonia ad Quirinum*, 277n.
Cyprus, 48, 190.
Cyrenaic sect, 201n.
Cyrene, 117n., 201n.
Cyrene, goddess mother of Aristaeus, 269n.
Cypress, 48, 182n.

Dabre Jamin, the book of Times, 150, 152.
Dalmatia, vii, 163, 173.
Damasus, Pope, viii, x, xi, 3, 4, 47, 84n., 105n., 138, 138n.
Danae, 167, 167n.
Darius, 81, 167, 167n.
David, 216, 219, 252, 258, 285, 289, 290, 324, 325, 328, 345, 352, 370.
Demaratus, 167, 167n.
Demetrias, daughter of Juliana, 369n.
Demetrius, bishop of Alexandria, 133.
Demosthenes, and the letter *rho*, 81; his speech in defense of Ctesiphon, 148; the surname of Pelagius, 300, 300n.
deosculamini, 84.
Desierius, friend of St. Jerome, 146.
devil, 95, 109, 127, 237; the cause of sin, 110-112, 123; the punishment of the, 110; views on the, 111-114, 354, 355, 370.

Dexter, friend of St. Jerome, 142, 142n.
Diana, the burning of the temple of, 34.
didaktikós, 264.
Didymus, the Blind, defender of Origen, 66, 66n., 76, 76n., 79, 87, 87n., 121, 121n., 128, 129, 129n., 159, 177, 196, 197, 199, 231n.; his commentary on the *Periarchon* of Origen, 129n.; his commentary on the Prophet Osee, 199; the theologian of the Trinity, 129n.
Diodorus, surnamed Cronus, 242, 242n.; his book *On the Possible*, 242n.
Dionysius, bishop of Alexandria, 130, 130n., 132.
Diospolis, 227, 229.
discentias reminiscentias, 212n.
discord, the seed-plot of divorce, 41.
disorders of the soul, 304, 305.
Docetism, 36n., 38n.
docilis, 264.
dógma, 263.
Dominicus homo, 138, 138n.
Donatus, teacher of St. Jerome, 80; his commentary on Vergil, 80.
Donatists, 377n.
Donnelly, Philip J., S. J., his work on the perpetual virginity of Mary, 4n.
dunámis, 242.

Ebion, 37, 37n.
Ebionites, 37n.
Eden, Garden of, 376.
Edom, 338.
Egypt, 15, 25, 48, 75, 150, 185, 200, 342, 359, 360.
Eleven, the, 317.
Eliab, 289.
Elias, the prophet, 316, 318, 328, 358, 364.
Eliphas, the Themanite, 299.
Elis, 202n.
Eliseus, the prophet, 167n., 290, 346.
Elizabeth, wife of Zacharia, 16, 245, 253, 256.
Empedocles, 210, 212.
empeiría, 263.
energeía, 242.
Ennianus, *see* Ennius.
Ennius, gentle lambs of, 122, 122n.
Enoch, son of Cain, 334, 346, 364.
Epicurean, 102, 201n.
Epicurus, 199; the worlds of, 66, 66n.
Epiphanius, St., bishop of Salamis, xiii, xix, 28n., 37n., 75, 75n., 124, 124n., 139, 170, 182, 190, 191, 192, 193, 204, 232n.; and the Origenistic controversy, 48-50; his *Panarion*, 5n.; his *Haereses*, 232n., 349n.; the 'Hammer of heretics,' 49n.; knew five languages, 140, 141, 170.
Epistola I, Anastasii I Romanae urbis episcopi ad Jo-

annem episcopum Hierosolymorum super nomine Rufini, 187n.
Esdras, 152; reviser of the Pentateuch, 19.
'eternal fires,' the question of, 111-114.
Ethiopia, the rivers of, 312.
Euchites, 232, 232n.
Eunomius of Cappadocia, the Arian, 130, 130n., 131, 138, 215.
Eusebius, bishop of Caesarea, x, 56, 68, 68n., 69, 69n., 70, 70n., 72, 127, 128, 129, 141, 142, 150, 158n., 159, 176, 194, 349n.; his apology for Origen, 72, 233, 233n.; his *Canon of Times,* 72n.; his *Chronicle,* 72, 72n.; his *Ecclesiastical History,* 72, 72n.; his *Topography of the Holy Land,* 72; his *Universal History,* 72n.
Eusebius of Cremona, the monk, xiii, 49, 50n., 52, 63, 71, 71n., 143, 166n., 167, 168, 188n.
Eusebius of Nicomedia, 215n.
Eusebius, the priest, 194.
Eusthatius, bishop of Antioch, 215, 215n.
Eustochium, 84n., 99n., 157n.
Evagrius of Ibora, 230, 231n.; Origenist and Gnostic, 231n.; his *De apathia,* 231n.; his *Gnostic,* 231n.
Evagrius Ponticus, *see* Evagrius of Ibora.

Ezechias, king of Juda, 328, 330-332.
Ezechiel, the prophet, 291.

Fabiola, 167.
familia, 31n.
Festus, Roman governor, 81.
Fidus, Bishop, 376.
'first born,' the question of the, 8, 9, 23-25.
Flaccus Horace, *see* Horace.
flesh, the resurrection of the, 110, 111, 181.
Florus, the letter of Horace to, 61.
free will, the question of the, 112, 224, 238-240, 355, 357, 358, 359, 360, 361, 362, 365; and the Pelagians, xv.
Fulvia, 215, 215n.

Gabaon, 288.
Gabinius, defended by Cicero, 61.
Gabriel, archangel, 15, 16.
Gamaliel, Hebrew teacher of St. Paul, 81.
Gehenna, the fires of, 310.
Gelasius, on the *De sancta Maria et obstrice,* 23n.
Gennadius, priest of Marseilles, on Helvidius, 5n.; his *De viris illustribus,* 5n.
Giezi, 167, 167n., 290.
Gnosis, 231n.
Gnosticism, 37n., 231n., 260n.
Gnostics, 36n., 147n.
Gorgias of Leontine, Sophist, 201, 201n.

Goths, 189n.
Greece, 68, 210.
Gregory of Nazienzen, St., teacher of St. Jerome, x, 75, 76, 76n., 101, 101n.
Gregory of Nyssa, St., x.
grace of God, 224, 235-240, 306, 351, 355, 362; of Christ, 368, 377; of the Gospel, 342, 343; the need of, 228, 307-310.

Habacuc, the prophet, 291, 335.
Hadrian, the emperor, 202n.
Hannibal, 200n.
haereditabant, 11.
haereditate potientur, 112.
Hebrews, the Gospel according to the, 349, 349n.; translated by St. Jerome into Greek and Latin, 349n.
hēdonē, 304.
Hegesippus, on the lineage of Mary of Cleophas, 29n.
Helen, and Stesichorus, 71n.
Heli, the priest, 265.
Heliodorus, Bishop, 156.
Helvidius, vii, xi, xix, 4, 5, 5n., 6, 7, 8, 9, 11, 12n., 13, 23, 28n., 43, 47, 232, 232n.; his pamphlet against Mary, xi, xin., 5, 5n.
Heraclian, governor of Africa, 377, 377n.
Heraclitus, the obscure philosopher, 102, 102n.
Hermagoras, the rhetorician, 201, 201n.

Hermogenes, the Gnostic, 11n.
Herod, 21, 29.
Herod Antipas, king of the Jews, 215n.
Herodias, 215n.
Hesychius, translator of the Septuagint, 150.
hiatus, figure of, 80.
Hilary, St., 61, 137, 137n., 139; his *De synodis*, 137n., 378; translator of Origen, 61, 125, 181.
Himerius of Terragona, 105n.
Hippolytus, St., on the perpetual virginity of Mary, 4n.
Hismenia, 152, 152n.
Ho Archaîos, reference to Origen, 260, 260n.
Homer, 214; his *Iliad*, 244n., 321n.; his *Odyssey*, 321n.
Homoeans, 321n.
ho mónos anamártētos, 324.
homooúsios, 128.
Honorius, the emperor, 377n.
Horace, 61, 80; his *De arte poetica*, 82n.; his *Epistles*, 61n., 80n., 100n.; his *Satires*, 378n.
Huillus the Jew, and Origen, 75, 76, 77.
hyperbaton, the figure of, 80.

Ignatius, St., on the perpetual virginity of Mary, 4, 4n., 37, 37n., 147n.
ignorance, the sins of, 278-292, 293-303.
impeccability, doctrine of, xvi,

226, 377n., 378n.
Innocent I, Pope, on marriage, 227, 229.
in partu, 4n., 9, 36n., 233n.
Irenaeus, St., on the perpetual virginity of Mary, 4n., 37, 37n., 147n., 349n.
Isaac, 281; name of 'laughter,' 367.
Isaia, 156, 336, 337, 370.
Isboseth, son of Saul, 289.
Isidore, 182n.
Isocrates, 79.
Italy, xv, 54, 56, 58, 71n., 165, 173, 181, 182, 186n., 188, 189n., 210.

Jacob, 19, 83, 281, 359.
Jamblichus, philosopher, 210, 210n.
James, the apostle, 259, 318, 371.
James the Less, 27, 30.
James the Greater, 27.
James the obscure Third, 28, 29, 29n.
Jehu, the son of Hanani, 330.
Jeremia, the prophet, 22, 332, 333, 340-343.
Jerobaal, 29.
Jeroboam, 290, 328.
Jerome, St., reputation, vii; importance as doctrinal writer, vii; and tradition, vii; early life and education, vii, viii; witness to the Roman papacy, viii; ascetic studies, viii; involved in heresy of Sabellianism, viii, ix; involved with schismatic Luciferians, ix, x; and biblical exegesis, x; translates Gospel according to the Hebrews into Greek and Latin, xn.; promotes asceticism at Rome, x, 3-5; settles in Bethlehem, xi; literary labors at Bethlehem, xi, xii; defends virginity of Mary, xii; and the Origenistic controversy, xii-xiv; reconciliation between Rufinus, Bishop John and, xiii; his literal translation of the *Periarchon* of Origen, xiii, xiv; attacks Rufinus, xiv; champion of Catholic faith, xvi, xvii; as a satirist, xvii-xix; as a theologian, xix; second visit to Rome, 3; organizes monastery at Aquileia, 3; his biography of Paul, the monk, 3; his *Chronicle*, 3; secretary and chief counselor of Pope Damasus, 3; defends perpetual virginity of Mary, 5-9; ascetic propaganda at Rome, 47; literary labors at Bethlehem, 47; attitude towards Origen, 48, 49; quarrel with Bishop John of Jerusalem, 49, 50; refutes Bishop John, 50; second phase of controversy between Rufinus and, 51, 52; composes his *Apologia* in reply to Rufinus' *Apologia*, 56, 57; and the

Pelagian controversy, 223-229; his letter to Ctesiphon on Pelagian impeccability and apathy, 226, 232; composes last controversial treatise, the *Dialogus contra Pelagianos*, 227, 228; leader of orthodoxy in the East, his monastery burned by Oriental Pelagians, 228; works: *Adversus Jovinianium* xii, 40n., 233n., 347n.; *Altercatio Luciferiani et orthodoxi*, ix; *Apologiae adversus libros Rufini libri duo*, xiv, xvii, xix, 56, 57, 87n., 149n., 162n., 173, 177, 195n., 202n., 233n.; *Biography of Paul, the Monk*, 3; *Chronicle*, 3; *Commentarius in epistulam ad Ephesios*, 31n., 55, 56, 78, 78n., 86, 87, 88, 89, 90, 91, 92, 93, 94, 95, 96, 97, 176, 176n.; *Commentarius in epistolam ad Galatas*, 29n.; *Commentarius in evangelium Matthaei*, 7, 8, 15n., 37n.; *Commentarius in Isaiam prophetam*, 15n., 82n., 147n.; *De viris illustribus*, 37n., 48n., 87n., 142n., 145n., 159n., 176n., 349n.; *Dialogus contra Pelagianos*, ix, xvi xvii, xix, 227, 227n., 228; *Libellus de optimo genere interpretandi*, xiii, 50, 50n.; *Liber adversus Helvidium de perpetua virginitate B. Mariae*, xi, xvii, xix, 5n., 6-9, 9n., 232n.; *Liber hebraicarum quaestionum*, 15n., 147n.; *Liber tertius vel ultima responsio adversus scripta Rufini*, xiv, xvii, 57, 57n.; Letters: 9: 104; 15: viii, x; 22: 4, 40n., 99, 99n.; 45: xi; 48: xvii; 51: xiii, 139, 192, 204; 57: xiii, 50, 151; 58: xv; 61: xv, 186; 63: viii; 69: 104, 105; 70: 82, 99, 159, 231; 80: 51; 81: 52, 53, 75, 208; 83: 73, 166, 206; 84: 53, 73, 75, 76, 210; 90-94: 75; 92: 182n.; 109: xv; 123: x; 125: 57; 127: 53; 130: viii, 369n.; 133: xvi, 226, 228, 230, 231; 135-137: 229n.; 143: 227; *Praefatio in Danielem prophetam*, 158; *Praefatio in Ezram*, 153; *Praefatio in librum Isaiae*, 157; *Praefatio in librum Job*, 154, 155; *Praefatio in librum Paralipomenon*, 152; *Praefatio in librum Psalmorum juxta hebraicam veritatem*, 156; *Praefatio in libros Salomonis*, 156; *Praefatio in libros Samuel et Malachim*, 149, 149n.; *Praefatio in Pentateuchum*, 149; *Prologus in Genesim*, 149n.; *Contra Johannem Hierosolymitanum*, xiii, 50, 182n.
Jerusalem, xiii, xv, xvi, 16, 18, 24, 27, 29, 50, 185, 190, 203n., 204, 257, 289, 315, 329, 332, 333, 338, 342.

INDEX 391

Jesse, 289.
Jesu, son of Josedec, 335.
Jesus, the soul of, 109, 110.
Jethro, 29.
Jezabel, daughter of the king of the Sidonians, 329.
Joab, general of David's army, 290.
Joachim, king of Juda, 329.
Job, 245, 253, 279, 300.
John, Baptist, 215n., 276, 305, 328.
John, bishop of Jerusalem, xiii, xv, 49, 50, 126, 126n., 139, 182n., 192n., 203n., 226, 227, 227n.
John, Evangelist, 24, 26, 247, 256, 318.
John, surnamed Mark, 164, 323.
Jona, the prophet, 357, 374.
Jonathan, the scribe, 288, 343.
Josaphat, king of Juda, 329.
Joseph, father of the Savior, 13, 14, 15, 16, 17, 20, 21, 22, 38, 39.
Joseph, son of Jacob, 281, 359, 360.
Josephus, historian of the Machabees, 148; his *Antiquities*, 148; his *Liber de Machabeis*, 304n.
Josias, king of Juda, 328, 332, 333.
Josue, 287, 346.
Jovian, the consul, 137n.
Jovinian, the heretic, vii, 231, 231n., 233, 233n., 318, 318n., 347, 347n.; heretical propositions of, xii; on the virginity of Mary, xii.
Juda, 22, 29, 257, 329, 330, 333, 342, 344.
Jude, apostle, 267.
Judea, 26.
Julian, bishop of Eclamum, 223.
Juliana, 369n.
Justin, St., writes on the perpetual virginity of Mary, 4n., 37, 37n.
juvencula, 15.

kakia, 298.
klēronomēsousin, 111.
'know,' the meanings of the verb, 17-23.
kuriakòs ánthrōpos, St. Athanasius' use of the phrase, 138n.

Lactantius, his views on the origin of souls, 114, 118, 120.
Lentulus, 139, 139n.
Leontine, 201.
Lethe, the waters of, 101, 212.
Lia, 281.
Lot, 281.
Lucan, 80.
Lucian, the martyr, translator of the Septuagint, 150.
Lucifer, 281.
Lucifer, bishop of Calaris, opponent of Arianism, ix.
Luciferians, ix, 3.
Lucilius, the satirist, 100, 100n.

Lucretius, 80, 199.
lúpē, 304.
Luscius Lavinius, his reference to Terence as *malivolus vetus poeta*, 99, 99n.
Lusitania, 147n.
Lydia, 167n.
Lysias, 70.
Lysides, 210.

Macarius, the scholar, xiii, 51, 125n., 127, 194n., 200, 233n.
Macedonians, and Didymus, 129n.
Magna Graecia, 210, 212.
Magnus, friend of St. Jerome, 99, 99n., 210.
Malea, 190.
Mani, founder of the Manichaean sect, *see* Manichaeus.
Manichaeans, 231n., 234, 277, 354.
Manichaeus, 131, 230, 231n., 277, 294.
Marcella, friend of St. Jerome, xiv, 3, 52, 53, 56, 59n., 70n.
Marcellinus, the tribune, 377, 377n.
Marcion, the Gnostic, 131, 215, 260, 260n., 355; his *Antitheses*, 65, 65n.
Marcionism, 260n.
Mardochal, servant of Artaxerxes, 362.
Mariology, 4n., 9, 15n., 37n.
Marius Mercator, his *Liber subnotationum in verba Juliani*, 139n.

Mary, the perpetual virginity of, vii, xi, xii, 4, 4n., 5n., 6, 7, 8, 12, 12n.
Mary, the wife of Cleophas, 29, 29n. 30.
Mary, the wife of Joseph, 4n., 5, 6, 7, 12, 14, 15, 16, 17.
Mars, 366.
Marseilles, 5n.
Marullus, 139, 139n.
Massaliani, 232, 232n.
mathēseis anamnēseis, 212.
Matthew, the Gospel according to, *see* Gospel according to the Hebrews.
Meletian schism, x.
méthodos, 263.
Methodus, bishop of Olympus, 72, 72n., 158, 158n.
Mesopotamia, 32, 359.
Michael the archangel, 134, 135.
Middle Academy, 117n.
Milan, 5n., 137n., 140n.
Milesian tales, 82.
Milevis, 229.
Milo of Crotona, 274.
ministers of God, the duties of the, 90.
minutiae, 358.
mi-phahrath, 31n.
Miscellanies of Clement of Alexandria, 82n.
Miscellanies of Origen, *see* the *Stromata* of Origen.
Moab, 19, 343.
Modalism, 131n.
Moderatus, 210.
Moses, 15, 15n., 20, 21, 23, 25,

27, 38, 39, 43, 77, 134, 213, 248, 275, 282, 316, 333, 359, 360, 367; the author of the Pentateuch, 19.
Mount Aventine, 3.
Mount Galaad, 32.
Mount Tabor, 29.
mulier, 40n.

Naaman, the Syrian, 167n.
Nabuchodonosor, king of Babylon, 344.
Nazareth, 316.
Nescu Bar, the meaning of, 84.
New Academy, 117n.
New Testament, xi, xii, 3, 9, 21, 39, 65n., 160, 245, 248, 267, 294.
Nitria, the monasteries of, 190.
Novatian, his *De trinitate*, 138, 138n.
Numenius, Greek philosopher, 82n., 231n.

Oceanus, friend of St. Jerome, xiii, 52, 53, 74n., 92n., 104n., 166n., 167, 208n.
Ochozias, king of Jerusalem, 329.
offensio, 319.
Olda, the prophetess, 332.
Old Academy, 230.
Old Testament, xii, 21, 39, 56, 65n., 144n., 145, 150n., 155, 224, 244, 245, 248, 267, 276, 342, 355.
Olympia, 274n.
Olympus, 72n.
Ophir, 312, 312n.
Orbilius, famous pedagogue, 100, 100n.

Origen, x, xiii, xix, 47, 51, 60, 63, 68, 69, 70, 72, 74, 75, 76, 77, 78, 79, 82, 83, 84, 85, 86, 87, 88, 89, 90, 91, 92, 93, 94, 96, 109, 110, 115, 116, 118, 119, 120, 121, 122, 123, 124, 125, 126, 127, 128, 129, 131, 132, 133, 135, 136, 137, 138, 140, 141, 142, 144n., 146, 150, 153, 154, 159, 174, 175, 176, 177, 178, 179, 182, 187n., 192, 196, 197, 200, 201, 204, 205, 206, 209, 212, 213, 230, 230n., 231n., 232, 233, 260n., 349, 378n.; blasphemies of, 121; his commentaries on the Epistle of St. Paul to the Ephesians, 87, 87n., 96, 97, 97n.; errors of, 85; heretical teachings of, 123, 124; the *Hexapla* of, 146n.; impious views of, 66; incorporated Plato into his own books, 212; his dialogue with Candidus, 136, 137; his reply to the letter of Africanus, 158n.; his *Periarchon*, xiii, xiv, 47, 47n., 59, 66n., 67, 69, 71, 71n., 72, 73, 74n., 77, 78, 90, 92n., 119, 121, 125, 126, 129, 143, 166, 168, 176, 177, 181, 188, 194, 197, 204, 206, 208n., 209, 212, 233, 233n., 260n.; the Psalm-scholia of, 84n.; the six thousand books of, 124, 124n., 141, 209, 213; the *Stromata* of, 82, 82n.; the

Tetrapla of, 150n.; his views on 'eternal fires,' 113.
Origenism, xii, xiii, xiv, xv, 49, 53, 71n., 75n., 106n., 125, 149, 182n., 192n., 204n.
Origenistic controversy, xii-xiv.
Origenists, vii, 73, 82, 103, 184, 186n.; banded together by orgies of lies, 82-84.
original sin, 224; Pelagianism and, xv.
Ostia, xin.
Outlines of Clement, 130n.
Oza, the Levite, 289.
Ozian, king of Juda, 29.

Palestine, xi, xvi, 47, 86n., 225, 226, 227.
Palladius, Origenist, 233, 233n.; his *Historia Lausiaca*, 233n.
Pallas, 175.
Pammachius, friend of St. Jerome, xii, xiii, 48, 50, 52, 53, 55, 56, 59n., 65, 74n., 92n., 166n., 208n., 347n.
Pamphilus, the martyr, 51, 56, 68, 68n., 70, 71, 76, 125n., 141, 142, 143, 150, 176, 177, 182, 194; his *Apology* for Origen, 233, 233n.
Pannonia, vii.
Paradise, 343, 356.
Pasch, the Feast of the, 285, 291.
Passover, the Feast of the, 16.
paternitas, 31, 31n.
páthē, 230.

patriá, 31.
Paul, St., the apostle, 7, 93, 107, 164, 178, 250, 251, 254, 259, 297, 307, 323, 353, 361; the clarion voice of the Gospels, 280, 376; the Chosen Vessel, 252, 258, 264, 295, 308, 361.
Paul, the monk, 3.
Paul, Bishop, 183, 183n.
Paula, 84n., 157n.
Paulinian, brother of St. Jerome, 56, 86, 86n., 194.
Paulinus, bishop and confessor, ix, 190.
Paulinus of Nola, xv, 186n.
Paulinus, priest of Milan, 225.
Paul Orosius, 227; his *Liber apologeticus de arbitrii libertate*, 227n.
Pelagians, vii, xvi; basic propositions of the, xv, xvi, 223-225, 228, 235, 260n.; the 100th proposition of the, 277, 278; and original sin, 224.
Pelagius, xvi, xix, 223, 224, 225, 226, 227, 228, 231n., 274n., 347n., 369; his *De natura*, 225; his *De libero arbitrio* against St. Jerome, 228, 228n.; excommunicated by Pope Innocent I, 229; Jovinian's heir, 336; his letter to Juliana, 369, 369n.; and the Lord's Prayer, 371-373, 377n.; the propositions of, 235n., 268-278; work of Pelagius quoted by St.

INDEX 395

Jerome, 223n.
Pelagianism, xv, xvi, 377n.; survival of Paganism, 228.
Pentecost, the Feast of, 285.
Peripatetics, 199, 226, 230, 304.
periphéreia, 303.
Persia, 167n.
Persius, 80; his *Satires*, 82, 128.
perturnationes, 230.
Pettau, 6, 36.
Phanuel, 359.
Peter, St., the apostle, 130, 130n., 250, 258, 264, 300, 313, 316.
Pharao, king of Egypt, 25, 332, 360.
Pharisee, the, 257, 369, 373.
Pharisees, 319, 321, 340.
Phegium, 190.
Philistion, 139, 139n.
Philo, 242, 357.
Photius, on Clement, 130n.
Phinees, 258, 318.
Phoenix, hero in Homer, 321n.
Phrygia, 323.
Pitane, 117n.
Plato, 82n., 83, 147, 199, 210, 212, 231n., 250, 260n., 357; his *Phaedo*, 212; his *Protagoras*, 148; his *Republic*, 83; his *Sumposium*, 262n.; his *Timaeus*, 212, 357n.
Plautus, 76, 80.
Plotinus, Neo-Platonist, 158n.
Polycarp, St., 37.
Prophyry, 132, 159, 216, 321; his *Against the Christians*, 158, 158n.

'possibility of being,' the question of the, 242, 243, 268, 351, 352.
Priscillian, 230, 231n.
Priscillianists, *see* Priscillian.
probability, the doctrine of, 117, 117n.
probolē, 136, 136n.
prolatio, 136, 136n.
pronuntiatum, 101.
Proteus, the columns of, 190.
Proteus, the old seer, 269, 269n.
Protoevangelium Jacobi, 23n., 28n.
Psalterium, 84, 85n., 155.
Psalterium Romanum, 84n.
Ptolemy, king of Egypt, 147, 147n., 148.
Publican, the, 257, 373.
Principia, friend of St. Jerome, 53n.
Pythagoras, 209, 210, 210n., 212, 213, 226; the *Golden Verses* of, 210; the precepts of, 210-212.
Pythagoreans, 317, 317n.
post partum, 4n., 5n., 6, 7, 8, 9, 36n., 232n.

Q. Fabius Maximus, Cunctator, 200n.
Quirinus, friend of St. Cyprian, 277, 277n.
qui solus est sine peccato, 334.

Rachel, 281.
Raguet, son-in-law of Moses, 29.

rara avis, 312.
Rechab, the son of Remmon, 289.
recognitio, 130.
refuge, cities of, 279, 285, 286, 287.
Remmon, the Berothite, 289.
Resurrection, the church of the, 50, 203, 203n.
Rhodes, 201n.
Riparius, priests of Aquitaine, xv.
Rome, vii, x, xi, xii, xvi, 3, 4, 5, 47, 48, 50, 51, 52, 54, 55, 58, 62, 68, 73, 75, 93, 106, 108, 121, 138n., 140n., 155, 165, 173, 182, 187, 188, 189, 191, 194, 200, 201, 203, 207, 208, 225, 233, 318n., 347.
Rufinus, xiii, 47, 92n., 101n., 103n., 104n., 106, 106n., 108, 124n., 125n., 126, 126n., 161, 162n., 166n., 182n., 187n., 188n., 192, 198n., 202n., 203n., 204n., 208n., 233, 233n.; and quarrel with St. Jerome over Origen, xiii, xiv; reconciliation between St. Jerome and, xiii; translated the *Periarchon* of Origen for Macarius, xiii; adds perface to translation, praising St. Jerome, xiii; embittered by letter of St. Jerome regarding his translation of the *Periarchon,* xiv; answers letter of St. Jerome with his *Apology,* xiv; his *Apology* to Pope Anastasius regarding Origen, xiv; replies to St. Jerome's *Apology* with private letter, xiv; origin of controversy between St. Jerome and, 47n., 48-57; fervent disciple of Origen, 48; noblest ties of friendship between St. Jerome and, 49; and Atarbius, 49; translated first book of the *Apologia* of Pamphilus, 51, 68, 68n.; and Macarius 51, 51n.; the preface to the translation of the *Periarchon,* 51, 51n., 52; and Eusebius of Cremona, 52; the apologetic value of the translation of the *Periarchon,* 52; vilified by St. Jerome after his death, 57, 57n., 58; translates homilies of St. Basil and St. Gregory, 101n.; translates the *Recognitiones* of St. Clement, 130n.; and the *De adulteratione vel corruptione librorum suorum ex libro epistolarum Origenis quarto,* 133, 133n.; and the *Epistulae scriptae ad quosdam charos suos Alexandriam,* 133, 133n.; and the letter to the Africans, 195, 233n., works: *Apologia ad Anastasium,* xiv, 54, 55, 56, 63n., 106, 106n., 108, 111, 115, 116, 119, 124, 141, 161, 188n., 200n.; *Apologiae in sanctum Hieronymum libri duo,* xiv, 55, 56,

57, 57n., 63n., 78n., 86n., 161n., 137, 162n., 173, 175, 176n., 181n., 196, 200; *Epilogus in Apologeticum S. Pamphili martyris ad Macarium seu liber de adulteratione librorum Origenis*, 51, 56n., 77, 77n., 125n., 126n., 127, 128, 130, 131, 133, 136, 139, 140, 177n., 194n., 207, 233n., 234n., 235n., 236n., 238n.; *Prologus in libros Periarchon Origenis presbyteri*, 60n., 63n., 126n., 172, 173, 173n.
ruina, 319.

Sabellianism, viii, viiin., 3, 131n.
Sabellus, 131, 131n.
Sadoc, the sons of, 340.
Salamis, xiii, 48.
Sallust, the commentaries of Asper on, 99n.
Salmoneus, 202, 202n.
Samaria, 330.
Samothrace, 80n.
Samuel, 289.
sanctifying grace, xv; and the Pelagians, xv.
Sara, 281.
Sardanapalus, 76.
Sardinia, ix.
Satan, 112, 317, 335.
Saul, 289, 297, 356.
Scenopegia, the Feast of the, 285, 321.
Scepticism, 117, 117n.
Scipio, 212.

Scribes, the, 321.
Scriptures, x, xi, xii, xvi, 3, 6, 7, 8, 9, 12, 14, 17, 18, 22, 27, 28, 29, 30, 32, 33, 34, 70, 76, 79, 134, 140, 142n., 144, 147, 148, 149, 151, 153, 156, 159, 160, 175, 176, 197, 228, 239, 245, 246, 247, 249, 262, 275, 279, 280, 290, 293, 297, 298, 300, 304, 309, 322, 327, 331, 332, 358, 359, 362, 365, 376.
Scylla, the shores of, 190.
Sedecia, 343.
Semi-Arians, 321n.
Sennacherib, king of the Assyrians, 330.
Seneca, 210.
Septuagint translators, 56, 144, 146, 148, 149, 150, 151, 152, 153, 155, 156, 157, 158, 159, 160, 206, 362.
Sichem, 19.
Sicily, 225.
Sidon, district of, 316.
Simeon, 16, 21.
Simplicius, bishop of Milan, 71n.
sine peccato, 298.
sinlessness, granted by God, 319, 320.
Sirens, the songs of the, 190.
Siricius, Pope, xi, xii, 4, 47, 54, 105n., 106n., 187n., 189, 193, 347n.; denounces errors of Jovian, xii.
skándalon, 319.
skôlon, 319.
skopós, 251.
Socrates, 80, 117n., 198, 201n.,

212, 228, 232, 348.
Solomon, 162, 216, 258, 290, 305, 312, 312n., 327.
Sophronius, friend of St. Jerome, 155n.; translate St. Jerome into Greek, 145n.
sorites, the series of, 101, 101n.
souls, the question of the origin of, 114-119, 197-202.
Spain, 7, 13, 147n.
Spanish lullabies, the apocryphal, 147, 147n.
Stesichorus, 71, 71n.
Stoics, 101, 101n., 199, 226, 230, 259, 275, 304.
Stridon, vii.
Suggrapheus, surname of Rufinus, 69.
Sulpicius Severus, xii; his *Dialogus*, xiin.
Susanna, 15, 158, 158n.
suspeiromēnē, 118.
syllogisms, the seven moods, of, 100.
Symmachus, the Ebionite, 85, 146n., 150n., 153, 154, 155, 157, 158, 159.
Symmachus, pagan senator, 5n.
Syria, 210n., 232.

Tarquinius Priscus, 167n.
Terence, 99n.; the commentaries of Victorinus on the comedies of, 79; his *Heaut.*, 99n.; his *Andria*, 99n., 271n.
Terragona, 105n.
Tertullian, 6, 11n., 36n., 53, 102, 114, 114n., 118, 197, 200; his *Adversus Marcionem*, 36n., 102; his *Adversus Hermogenem*, 11n.; his *De anima*, 114n.; *his De monogamia*, 36n.; his *De pudicitia*, 36n.; his *De virginibus velandis*, 36n.; his *De carne Christi*, 36n.
Testament and Last Will of the Pig, 82, 82n.
Thamar, 22, 257.
Thebes, 210.
Theodoretus, his *Ecclesiasticae historiae libri quinque*, 215n.
Theodotion, 146, 146n., 150, 150n., 153, 154, 155, 157, 158, 159.
Theodotions, 37n.
Theodotus of Byzantium, the Gnostic, 37, 37n.
Theophilus, bishop of Alexandria, xiii, xix, 49, 50, 54, 70, 71n., 75, 75n., 77, 78, 140, 140n., 174, 174n., 182, 182n., 183, 184, 185, 203n.
Theophrastus, cognomen of Rufinus, 115.
'They that saw,' the prophets, 290.
Thomas, St., the apostle, 110.
Thrace, 82n.
Three Children, the song of the, 158, 158n.
Timaeus of Locri, 212.
Titus, disciple of St. Paul, 263.
Troas, 353.
Tullius, *see* Cicero.
Twelve Apostles, the, 356.

INDEX 399

Tyrannius, cognomen of Rufinus, 59, 59n.
Tyre, district of, 316.

Ulysses, 190.
'until,' the meaning of the conjunction, 18-23.
Uria, the prophet, 342.

Valens, the consul, 137n.
Valentinian, the consul, 137n.
Valentinian, the emperor, 137n.
Valentinians, 37n., 104, 136.
Valentinus, oriental school of, 37, 37n., 105, 215.
Valerius Maximus, his *Facta et dicta memorabilia*, 34n.
Varronianus, the consul, 137n.
Venerius, bishop of Milan, 140, 140n.
Venus, 366.
Vergil, his *Aeneid*, 65, 198, 200n., 202n., 211, 212n.; his *Eclogues*, 267n.; his *Georgics*, 198, 269n.
Victorinus, his commentaries on the dialogues of Cicero, 80; his commentaries on the comedies of Terence, 80.

Victorinus, bishop of Pettau, 6, 36, 36n.; his commentary on Origen, 61; his *Commentarius in apocalypsim Joannis*, 37n.
Vigilantius, vii, 186, 186n., 187; on the veneration of relics and night vigils, xiv, xv.
Vincent, priest and friend of St. Jerome, 182n., 183n., 190, 194.
virginity, xi, 42, 43; and marriage compared, xii, 4, 5, 9, 37-43.
virgo, meaning of, 15n., 40n.
virgo adulescentia, 16n.
Volcatius, his commentaries on the orations of Cicero, 80.

Wiesen, David S., author of *St. Jerome as a Satirist*, xviin.

Xenophon, his *Oeconomicus*, 148.

Zacharia, 245, 246, 253, 256.
Zeno, 199, 226, 275, 304.

INDEX OF HOLY SCRIPTURE

(BOOKS OF THE OLD TESTAMENT)

Genesis, 19, 22, 26, 31, 32, 33, 34, 39, 41, 92, 145, 257, 281, 359, 360, 365, 366, 367.
Exodus, 9, 25, 31, 39, 275, 281, 299, 333, 360, 367.
Leviticus, 22, 34, 281, 282, 283, 284.
Numbers, 15, 24, 31, 284, 285.
Deuteronomy, 14, 15, 19, 31, 113, 248, 276, 279, 286, 287, 297.
Josue, 151, 279, 287, 288.
1 Kings, 216, 265, 288, 289, 297, 346.
2 Kings, 289, 290, 327, 328.
3 Kings, 246, 290, 312, 328, 329.
4 Kings, 167, 290, 330, 331, 332.
1 Paralipomenon, 290.

2 Paralipomenon, 329, 330, 332, 333, 348.
Judith, 83.
Esther, 83.
Job, 85, 114, 245, 246, 278, 279, 299, 300, 306, 337.
Psalms, 7, 13, 19, 33, 59, 65, 88, 89, 104, 105, 112, 113, 123, 145, 160, 202, 220, 237, 246, 249, 252, 253, 254, 258, 260, 265, 272, 273, 278, 285, 294, 297, 298, 299, 302, 307, 311, 313, 315, 324, 325, 326, 327, 329, 333, 335, 337, 344, 348, 350, 360, 364, 365, 370 371, 372.
Proverbs, 151, 162, 216, 217, 218, 219, 247, 252, 271, 292, 297, 298, 300, 301, 302, 347, 360, 370.

Ecclesiastes, 113, 243, 246, 280, 292, 297.
Canticle of Canticles, 368, 372.
Wisdom, 82, 196, 280, 296, 311.
Sirach (Ecclus.), 280, 302.
Isaia, 4n., 15, 18, 33, 77, 113, 117, 151, 162, 186, 247, 272, 312, 313, 331, 332, 336, 337, 338, 370, 373.
Jeremia, 22, 134, 145, 234, 248, 254, 271, 291, 292, 322, 340, 341, 342, 343, 344, 357.
Lamentations, 257, 333, 344.
Ezechiel, 114, 173, 257, 279, 291, 306, 338, 339, 340, 364.
Daniel, 127, 158, 344, 345, 346.
Osee, 333, 334.
Amos, 334, 343.
Jona, 8, 25, 26, 28, 29, 33, 36, 84, 112, 119, 146, 151, 160, 164, 247, 255, 258, 266, 271, 273, 305, 321, 322, 323, 348, 353, 356, 361, 367, 377.
Michea, 134, 334, 335.
Nahum, 339.
Habacuc, 291, 335.
Zacharia, 134, 151, 335.
Malachia, 253.
2 Machabees, 345.

(BOOKS OF THE NEW TESTAMENT)

Matthew, 6, 7, 8, 11, 12, 13, 14, 17, 18, 20, 22, 26, 27, 28, 35, 42, 96, 98, 107, 112, 143, 145, 146, 151, 160, 163, 172, 184, 243, 244, 248, 271, 275, 276, 277, 279, 301, 302, 310, 311, 312, 313, 315, 316, 317, 318, 335, 365, 366, 371, 372.
Mark, 8, 26, 27, 34, 35, 42, 243, 313, 316, 317.
Luke, 6, 8, 18, 21, 23, 25, 27, 36, 92, 107, 113, 163, 245, 246, 256, 299, 305, 312, 313, 317, 318, 319, 320, 361, 369, 371, 373.
John, 8, 25, 26, 28, 29, 33, 36, 84, 112, 119, 146, 151, 160, 164, 247, 255, 258, 266, 271, 273, 305, 321, 322, 323, 348, 353, 356, 361, 367, 375.
Acts of the Apostles, 8, 26, 29, 59, 81, 164, 301, 313, 323, 352, 353.
Romans, 31, 88, 94, 104, 164, 239, 247, 249, 255, 271, 273, 276, 280, 288, 295, 296, 305, 307, 325, 346, 356, 370, 376.
1 Corinthians, 8, 18, 26, 33, 39, 40, 42, 98, 103, 112, 135, 147, 149, 151, 253, 254, 255, 258, 261, 269, 271, 284, 297, 302, 307, 308, 324, 338, 339, 346, 348, 366, 368.
2 Corinthians, 81, 143, 252, 253, 293, 296, 308, 358, 361.
Galatians, 8, 29, 98, 103, 108, 164, 264, 271, 304, 308, 309.
Ephesians, 83, 87, 90, 91, 93, 94, 96, 302, 303, 304, 368.
2 Thessalonians, 309.

1 Timothy, 105, 112, 263, 305, 310, 367.
2 Timothy, 254, 280, 296, 353.
Titus, 191, 264, 310, 375.
Hebrews, 273, 278.

1 Peter, 266, 303, 305.
1 John, 191, 247, 278, 301, 305, 306, 317, 369.
Apocalypse, 42, 202.

www.ingramcontent.com/pod-product-compliance
Lightning Source LLC
Chambersburg PA
CBHW032023290426

44110CB00012B/645